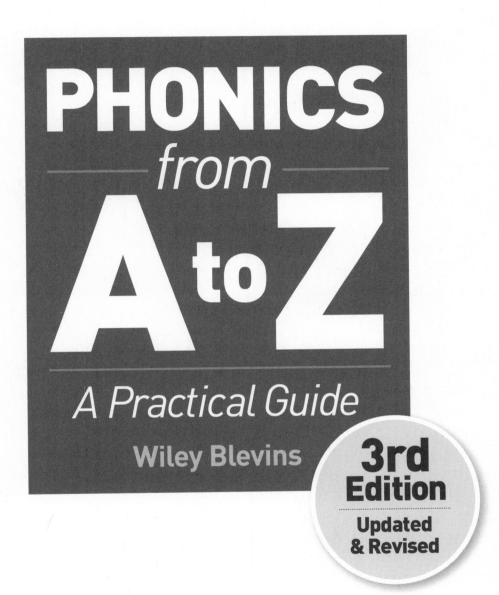

# PHONICS
## from
# A to Z
## A Practical Guide

Wiley Blevins

**3rd Edition**
Updated & Revised

📖 **SCHOLASTIC**

New York • Toronto • London • Auckland • Sydney
Mexico City • New Delhi • Hong Kong

## Dedication

*I would like to dedicate this book to Jeanne Chall, Marilyn Adams, M. E. Curtis, Isabel Beck, Louisa Moats, and the many other professors, colleagues, and classroom teachers who have taught me so much about how children learn to read.*

## Acknowledgments

I would like to thank Terry Cooper, Wendy Murray, and Jeanette Moss for their efforts, support, and extreme patience. I would also like to thank the following teachers, colleagues, and students for their feedback and assistance: Erinn Hudson and her second graders at Ward-Highlands Elementary School in Ocala, Florida, Marissa Noguez, Joan Conway, Beth Ann Sullivan, Kelly Combes, Lou Ann Kleck, Joyce Nafziger, Renee Flory, Carla Hartz, Shelley Stalnaker, Julie Small-Gamby, Emily Teresa, and the staff at Gutman Library at the Harvard Graduate School of Education.

Cover design by Tannaz Fassihi
Interior design by Maria Lilja
Interior illustrations by Maxie Chambliss

Photos ©: cover: choness/iStockphoto; 97: Maria Chang; 101: Hill Street Studios/Getty Images; 107: GMVisuals/iStockphoto; 133: Tashi-Delek/iStockphoto; 150: Liderina/iStockphoto; 180: Steve Debenport/iStockphoto; 208: Tetra Images-Jamie Grill/Getty Images; 268: FatCamera/iStockphoto; 281: Monashee Frantz/Getty Images. All other images courtesy of the author.

ISBN: 978-1-338-11349-5

8 9 10   40   22

# Table of Contents

## SECTION 4: Creating Lessons for Success ......... 132

# What Is Phonics?

*"At one magical instant in your early childhood, the page of a book—that string of confused, alien ciphers—shivered into meaning. Words spoke to you, gave up their secrets; at that moment, whole universes opened. You became, irrevocably, a reader."*

—Alberto Manguel

The sun beat down on me hotter than I had ever felt. I could feel the steam sizzling up from the tarmac as I stepped off the plane. Here I was in Guayaquil, Ecuador. My charge was to teach a class of second graders—many of whom had limited English abilities—to read. It was my first year teaching, and I had journeyed far from Coal City, West Virginia, where I had first learned about the mysteries of books. As I walked toward the airline terminal, the enormity of the challenge and responsibility I had accepted struck me. I suddenly felt even hotter!

Each year millions of teachers enter classrooms across our nation (and the world) with this same challenge. They have to make key decisions as they wrestle with the questions of how best to teach children to read. All children deserve the promise that books hold. Whether they transport us to another world, make us laugh or cry, teach us something new, or introduce us to people we wouldn't otherwise meet, we are thankful for their gifts. In turn, all children deserve the gift of reading. And as educators, we bear the responsibility and honor of delivering that gift.

This book is designed to help you better understand our unique and sometimes complex language and how we can use that knowledge to better teach children to read. Its focus is on phonics—the relationship between sounds and their spellings—and how helping children understand this important piece of the reading "puzzle" can help develop fluent readers who have a passion for books and who understand how books can provide pleasure and information.

The first edition of this book was published more than 20 years ago. Since then I have continued my study and exploration of phonics, how best it's taught, and the common obstacles that stand in the way of teachers delivering the most effective instruction to maximize student learning—especially when they have the basics in place. I have conducted research on topics such as using decodable text and developing fluency, and written numerous phonics instructional programs. I have observed countless teachers offering instruction of the sound-spelling system of our language, worked with district administrators to select and monitor instructional delivery, and analyzed almost every curricular materials produced in the last two decades. I've also delved into advances made through current reading studies, including promising brain research.

This edition is a reflection of that new learning, and it is my goal that it will help you fine-tune your phonics instruction for increased student achievement. Learning how to sound out words is essential for early learners in not only developing early reading skills but also increasing their motivation to read. It is my hope that this resource will provide some of the tools you need in your classrooms. Enjoy!

## Phonics: What and Why

According to a 1992 poll conducted by Peter D. Hart Research Associates, 62% of parents identified reading as one of the most important skills their children needed to learn. In 1994 the same polling firm conducted a survey for the American Federation of Teachers and the Chrysler Corporation and found that almost 70% of teachers identified reading as the most important skill for children to learn.

With such agreement on the importance of reading, how do we best teach children to read? What should be the goals of early reading instruction? The following goals are often cited:

1. Automatic word recognition (fluency)
2. Comprehension of text
3. Development of a love of literature and a desire to read

The first goal—automatic word recognition—is the focus of this book. To become skilled readers, children must be able to identify words quickly and accurately. To do so, they must be proficient at decoding words. **Decoding** words involves converting the printed word into spoken language. A reader decodes a word by sounding it out, using context clues, using structural analysis, or recognizing the word by sight. In order to sound out words, a reader must be able to associate a specific spelling with a specific sound. **Phonics** involves this relationship between sounds and their spellings.

Phonics is not a specific teaching method. In fact, there are many ways to teach it. However, what most types of phonics instruction do have in common is that they focus on the teaching of sound-spelling relationships so that a young reader can come up with an approximate pronunciation of a word and then check it against his or her oral vocabulary.

Approximately 84% of English words are phonetically regular. Therefore, teaching the most common sound-spelling relationships in English is extremely useful for readers. As Anderson et al. (1985) write, "English is an alphabetic language in which there are consistent, though not entirely predictable, relationships between letters and sounds. When children learn these relationships well, most of the words in their spoken language become accessible to them when they see them in print. When this happens, children are said to have 'broken the code.'"

One of the arguments against teaching phonics is that the approximately 16% of so-called irregular English words appear with the greatest frequency in text (about 80% of the time). As you will discover throughout this book, these words are not as "irregular" as they may seem. Although they must be taught as sight words, the reader has to pay attention to their spelling patterns in order to store them in his or her memory. Some detractors of teaching phonics also contend that reading develops in the same way as speaking—naturally. Foorman (1995) responds by saying "humans are biologically specialized to produce language and have done so for nearly 1 million years. Such is not the case with reading and writing. If it were, there would not be illiterate children in the world."

Clearly, then, most children need instruction in learning to read. One of the critical early hurdles in reading instruction is helping children grasp the alphabetic principle. That is, to read, children must understand that this series of symbols we call the alphabet maps onto the sounds of our language in roughly predictable ways. This alphabetic principle is a key insight into early reading. Phonics instruction helps children to understand the alphabetic principle. And it enables children to get off to a quick start in relating sounds to spellings and thereby decoding words.

# The Connection Between Decoding and Comprehension

Phonics instruction helps the reader to map sounds onto spellings. This ability enables readers to decode words. Decoding words aids in the development of and improvement in word recognition. The more words one recognizes, the easier the reading task. Therefore, phonics instruction aids in the development of word recognition by providing children with an important and useful way to figure out unfamiliar words while reading.

When children begin to be able to recognize a large amount of words quickly and accurately, reading fluency improves. Reading fluency refers to the ease with which children can read a text. As more and more words become firmly stored in a child's memory (that is, the child recognizes more and more words on sight), he or she gains fluency and automaticity in word recognition. Having many opportunities to decode words in text is critical to learning words by sight. The more times a child encounters a word in text, the more likely he or she is to recognize it by sight and to avoid making a reading error (Gough, Juel, & Roper-Schneider, 1983).

Reading fluency improves reading comprehension. Since children are no longer struggling with decoding words, they can devote their full attention (mental energies) to making meaning from the text. As the vocabulary and concept demands increase in text, children need to be able to devote more of their attention to making meaning from text, and increasingly less attention to decoding. If children have to devote too much time to decoding words, their reading will be slow and labored. This will result in comprehension difficulties.

But isn't comprehension the most important part of reading? How does this ability to decode words help a reader understand a text? The above flowchart illustrates that strong decoding ability is necessary for reading comprehension. However, it is not the only skill a reader needs in order to make meaning from text. And sounding out words is not the only way to figure out an unfamiliar word while reading.

When they read, children need to be able to use three cueing systems. These systems represent signals in text that interact and overlap to help the reader understand what he or she is reading. The cueing systems are graphophonic, syntactic, and semantic.

1. **Graphophonic cues** involve a reader's knowledge of sound-spelling relationships. Phonics instruction helps children to use these cues.

2. **Syntactic cues** involve a reader's knowledge of the grammar or structure of language. This knowledge helps the reader to predict what type of word might appear in a certain place in a sentence. For example, it might be a naming word (noun),

an action word (verb), or a describing word (adjective). This cueing system also involves an understanding of word order and the use of function words, such as *the* and *an*. For example, read the following sentence and choose a word to fill in the blank:

*We saw the _____ on the road.*

All possible words to fill in the blank must be naming words. You determined this from your knowledge of English syntax.

When children enter school, most of them have an understanding of the basic syntactic structures of English. However, oral language is different from "book language." Written material might pose difficulties for some children because their oral language patterns differ so much from the more formal language patterns of text. Reading many books aloud will help these children gain an understanding of the more formal syntactic structures used for writing.

3. **Semantic cues** involve a reader's knowledge of the world. World knowledge helps the reader use cues in the text to discover the meaning of a word that fits into a specific place in a particular sentence. Readers use their semantic knowledge to determine whether a text makes sense.

# Ten Important Research Findings About Phonics

Countless research studies have been conducted on phonics instruction. Much of this research has focused on the usefulness of phonics instruction and the best ways to teach children about sound-spelling relationships. Below are ten of the top research findings regarding phonics.

## 1 Phonics Instruction Can Help All Children Learn to Read

All children can benefit from instruction in the most common sound-spelling relationships in English. This instruction helps children decode words that follow these predictable relationships.

Phonics instruction is particularly beneficial for children at risk for learning difficulties—those children who come to school with limited exposures to books, have had few opportunities to develop their oral languages, are from low socioeconomic families, have below-average intelligence, are learning English as a second language, or are suspected of having a learning disability. However, even children from language-rich backgrounds benefit from phonics instruction (Chall, 1967). As Chall states, "By learning phonics, students make faster progress in acquiring literary skills—reading and writing. By the age of six, most children already have about 6,000 words in their listening and speaking vocabularies. With phonics they learn to read and write these and more words at a faster rate than they would without phonics."

Phonics instruction is therefore an essential ingredient in early reading instruction. The purpose of this instruction is to teach children how to read with accuracy, comprehension, fluency, and pleasure. The early ability to sound out words successfully is a strong predictor of future growth in decoding (Lundberg, 1984) and comprehension (Lesgold & Resnick, 1982). Weak decoding skills are characteristic of poor readers (Carnine, Carnine, & Gersten, 1984; Lesgold & Curtis, 1981). Readers who are skilled at decoding usually comprehend text better than those who are poor decoders. Why this is so can be gleaned from the work of cognitive psychologists. They contend that we each have a set amount of mental energy to devote to any task. Since decoding requires so much of this mental energy, little is left over for higher-level comprehension. As decoding skills improve and more and more words are recognized by sight, less mental energy is required to decode words and more mental energy can be devoted to making meaning from the text (Freedman & Calfee, 1984; LaBerge & Samuels, 1974).

In addition, successful early decoding ability is related to the number of words a reader encounters. That is, children who are good decoders read many more words than children who are poor decoders (Juel, 1988). This wide reading results in greater reading growth.

Phonics instruction also helps to get across the alphabetic principle (that the letters of the alphabet stand for sounds) by teaching the relationships between letters and the sounds they represent. Beginning readers learn better when their teachers emphasize these relationships (Chall, 1996).

## THREE GOLDEN RULES

*Becoming a Nation of Readers* (Anderson et al., 1985) makes the following three recommendations regarding phonics instruction:

1. Do it early.
2. Keep it simple.
3. Except in cases of diagnosed individual need, complete basic instruction by the end of second grade.

## 2 Explicit Phonics Instruction Is More Beneficial Than Implicit Instruction

According to Chall (1996), "systematic and early instruction in phonics leads to better reading: better accuracy of word recognition, decoding, spelling, and oral and silent reading comprehension." The most effective type of instruction, especially for children at risk for reading difficulties, is **explicit** (direct) instruction (Adams, 1990; Chall, 1996; Honig, 1995; Stahl & Miller, 1989; Anderson et al., 1985; Snow et al., 1998). **Implicit** instruction relies on readers "discovering" clues about sound-spelling relationships. Good readers can do this; poor readers aren't likely to. Good readers can generalize their knowledge of sound-spelling relationships to read new words in which these and other sound-spellings occur. Poor readers must rely on explicit instruction.

Although explicit instruction has proved more effective than implicit instruction, the key element in the success of explicit phonics instruction is the provision of many opportunities to read decodable words (that is, words containing previously taught sound-spellings) in context (Stahl, Osborn, & Pearson, 1992; Juel & Roper-Schneider, 1985; Adams, 1990). In fact, students who receive phonics instruction achieve best in both decoding and comprehension if the text they read contains high percentages of decodable words (Blevins, 2000). In addition, by around second or third grade, children who've been taught with explicit phonics instruction generally surpass the reading abilities of their peers who've been taught with implicit phonics instruction (Chall, 1996).

## 3 Most Poor Readers Have Weak Phonics Skills and a Strategy Imbalance

Most poor readers have a strategy imbalance. They tend to over-rely on one reading strategy, such as the use of context and picture clues, to the exclusion of other strategies that might be more appropriate (Sulzby, 1985). To become skilled, fluent readers, children need to have a repertoire of strategies to figure out unfamiliar words (Cunningham, 1990). These strategies include using a knowledge of sound-spelling relationships, using context clues, and using structural clues. Younger and less skilled readers rely more on context clues than other, often more effective, strategies (Stanovich, 1980). This is partly due to their inability to use sound-spelling relationships to decode words. Stronger readers don't need to rely on context clues because they can quickly and accurately decode words by sounding them out.

Unfortunately, children who get off to a slow start in reading rarely catch up to their peers and seldom develop into strong readers

(Stanovich, 1986; Juel, 1988). Those who experience difficulties decoding early on tend to read less and thereby grow less in terms of word-recognition skills and vocabulary.

A longitudinal study conducted by Juel (1988) revealed a .88 probability that a child who is a poor reader at the end of first grade would still be a poor reader at the end of fourth grade. Stanovich (1986) refers to this as the "Matthew Effect" in which the "rich get richer" (children who are successful decoders early on read more and therefore improve in reading), and the "poor get poorer" (children who have difficulties decoding read less and less and become increasingly distanced from the good decoders in terms of reading ability).

## 4 Phonics Knowledge Has a Powerful Effect on Decoding Ability

Phonics knowledge affects decoding ability positively (Stanovich & West, 1989). Early attainment of decoding skill is important because this accurately predicts later skill in reading comprehension (Beck & Juel, 1995).

One way to help children achieve the ultimate goal of reading instruction—to make meaning of text—is to help them achieve automaticity in decoding words (Gaskins et al., 1988). Skilled readers recognize the majority of words they encounter in text quickly and accurately, independent of context (Cunningham, 1975–76; Stanovich, 1984). The use of graphophonic cues (knowledge of sound-spelling relationships) facilitates word-recognition abilities. In fact, a child's word-recognition speed in first grade has been shown to be a strong predictor of reading comprehension ability in second grade (Lesgold & Resnick, 1982; Beck & Juel, 1995).

However, the inability to automatically recognize frequently encountered words affects reading in the following ways (Royer & Sinatra, 1994):

1. Since words can be stored in working memory for only a limited amount of time (approximately 10–15 seconds), slow decoding can result in some words "decaying" before a meaningful chunk of text can be processed.

2. Devoting large amounts of mental energy to decoding words leaves less mental energy available for higher-level comprehension. This can result in comprehension breakdowns.

## 5 Good Decoders Rely Less on Context Clues Than Poor Decoders

Good readers rely less on context clues than poor readers do because their decoding skills are so strong (Gough & Juel, 1991). It's only when good readers can't use their knowledge of sound-spelling relationships to figure out an unfamiliar word that they rely on context clues. In contrast, poor readers, who often have weak decoding skills, over-rely on context clues to try to make meaning from text (Nicholson, 1992; Stanovich, 1986). Any reader, strong or weak, can use context clues only up to a certain point. It has been estimated that only one out of every four words (25%) can be predicted using context (Gough, Alford, & Holley-Wilcox, 1981). The words that are the easiest to predict are function words, such as *the* and *an*. Content words—the words that carry the bulk of the meaning in a text—are the most difficult to predict. Researchers estimate that content words can be predicted only about 10% of the time (Gough et al., 1983). A reader needs to use his or her knowledge of phonics (sound-spelling relationships) to decode these words.

The above charts show the growth of sight word (word identification) and phonemic decoding (word attack) skills in children who begin first grade above (avg.) or below the 20th percentile in phonological awareness (PA). Those children who had sufficient phonemic-awareness skills understood "how words work." That is, they were better equipped to sound out words while reading and to spell words while writing. The reading development of these children progressed at an

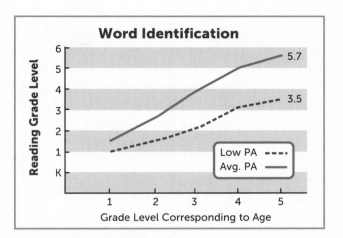

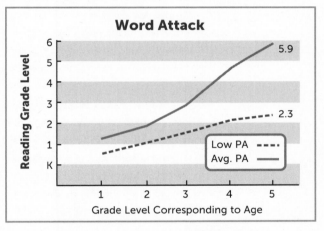

From Torgeson & Mathes, *A Basic Guide to Understanding, Assessing, and Teaching Phonological Awareness*, Pro-Ed, 2000

> **The whole word method (meaning emphasis) may serve a student adequately up to about second grade. But failure to acquire and use efficient decoding skills will begin to take a toll on reading comprehension by grade 3.**
>
> —Jeanne Chall

expected rate. Those children with weak phonemic-awareness skills did not have access to words in the same way. Therefore, they had to rely on memorizing words by sight. As the text became less patterned and repetitious (around Grade 2), the reading skills of these students fell apart, as you can see on the graphs. Look closely at Grade 2 on the graphs. Not only did the reading growth of these students begin to level off, these students began to fall further behind their grade-level peers, and the gap between their reading ability and that needed to handle grade-level reading demands increased dramatically.

## 6 The Reading Process Relies on a Reader's Attention to Each Letter in a Word

Eye-movement studies have revealed that skilled readers attend to almost every word in a sentence and process the letters that compose each word (McConkie & Zola, 1987). Therefore, reading is a "letter-mediated" rather than a "whole-word-mediated" process (Just & Carpenter, 1987). Prior to these findings, it was assumed that readers did not process each letter in a word; rather, they recognized the word based on shape, a few letters, and context.

Research has also revealed that poor readers do not fully analyze words; for example, some poor readers tend to rely on initial consonant cues only (Stanovich, 1992; Vellutino & Scanlon, 1987). Therefore, phonics instruction should help to focus children's attention on all the letters or spellings that make up words and the sounds each represents by emphasizing the full analysis of words. In addition, phonics instruction must teach children strategies to use this information to decode words. This attention to the spelling patterns in words is necessary for the reader to store the words in his or her memory. It also helps the reader to become a better speller because the common spelling patterns of English are attended to to a greater degree and thereby more fully learned (Ehri, 1987; Blevins, 2000).

## 7 Phonemic Awareness Is Necessary for Phonics Instruction to Be Effective

Before children can use a knowledge of sound-spelling relationships to decode words, they must understand that words are made up of sounds (Adams, 1990). Many children come to school thinking of words as whole units—*cat, dog, run*. Before they can learn to read, children must realize that these words can be broken into smaller units—and sounded out. **Phonemic awareness** is the understanding, or insight, that a word is made up of a series of discrete sounds. Without this insight, phonics instruction will not make sense to children.

When a child asks me how to spell a word, I first ask, "What have you tried?" This provides me with information on the child's ability to segment the word, the sound-spellings he or she has learned, and the ways the child approaches spelling. I base my feedback on the child's strategy use. For example, occasionally when a child attempts to spell a word, he or she overarticulates it. This drawing out of each sound can result in misspellings. I bring this to the child's attention and suggest that he or she say the word at a more natural speed to check the spelling. I ask, "Have you added any unnecessary letters?"

## 8 Phonics Instruction Improves Spelling Ability

Reading and writing are interrelated and complementary processes (Pinnell, 1994). Whereas phonics is characterized by putting together sounds to read words that are printed, spelling involves breaking down spoken words into sounds in order to write them. To spell, or encode, a word, a child must match a spelling to each sound heard in the word.

Spelling development lags behind reading development. A word can generally be read before it can be spelled. The visual attention a child needs in order to recognize words is stored in his or her memory. This information—the knowledge of the spelling patterns of English, also known as **orthographic knowledge**—is used to spell. Spelling, however, requires greater visual recall than reading and places higher demands on memory.

Good spellers are generally good readers because spelling and reading share an underlying knowledge base. Poor readers, however, are rarely good spellers. Phonics is a particularly powerful tool in improving spelling because it emphasizes spelling patterns, which become familiar from reading. Studies show that half of all English words can be spelled with phonics rules that relate one letter to one sound. Thirty-seven percent of words can be spelled with phonics rules that relate groups of letters to one sound. The other 13 percent must be learned by memorization. Good spellers have not memorized the dictionary; they apply the phonics rules they know and have a large store of sight words.

Writing, in turn, supports a child's reading development because it slows the process by focusing the child's attention on how print works. Poor spellers experience difficulties in both writing and reading. Poorly developed spelling ability also hinders vocabulary development (Adams, Treiman, & Pressley, 1996; Read, 1986).

Research has revealed two techniques that are particularly powerful in connecting phonics and spelling instruction: **Elkonin boxes** (also known as sound boxes) and the use of dictation during phonics instruction. The Elkonin boxes technique, developed by

Russian researcher D. B. Elkonin (1973), uses a simple grid of empty boxes and counters. Children are asked to segment a word into its constituent sounds. As they segment from one sound to the next, they drag one counter onto each box. This makes the counting of sounds in a word a kinesthetic and highly visual task, which is quite effective for struggling readers. Once the counters are in the boxes, each sound is identified, then the counter is removed and replaced with the letter or spelling that stands for the sound. For example, if the word *sat* is segmented, the child will place three counters, one in each of three boxes. Then the first sound will be identified: /s/. The child will remove the first counter and write the letter s in the box. In this way, children become skilled at taking apart and putting together words. This skill transfers to their free writing when they are using invented spelling to break apart and write words. Children with experience with Elkonin boxes make better choices when using invented spelling.

A 2000 study by Blevins revealed that children who received explicit phonics instruction, followed up by controlled-text reading (decodable text) and guided opportunities to spell words during dictation, outperformed those students in decoding and spelling tasks who did not receive this type of practice. During dictation, a teacher asks children to write letters, words, and simple sentences that are controlled based on what the child has been taught. The teacher guides the child by helping him or her break apart the word, or using some sort of prompt to guide the child to the correct answer. This might involve reminding the child of a mnemonic used to remember the letter-sound connection, directing the child to an alphabet wall frieze, or using Elkonin boxes to break apart a word. The following is a typical dictation exercise.

**Part A:** Write the letter for the sound I say.
/a/    /s/    /t/    /m/    /d/    /p/

**Part B:** Write the following words.
*am*        *at*        *mat*
*Sam*       *sat*

**Part C:** Write the following sentences.
I am Sam.
Pam is sad.

# 9 A Teacher's Knowledge of Phonics Affects His or Her Ability to Teach Phonics

A teacher's knowledge of phonics has a strong effect on his or her ability to teach phonics (Carroll, 1990; Moats, 1995). This knowledge of the English language enables the teacher to choose the best examples for instruction, to provide focused instruction, and to better understand students' reading and writing errors in relation to their developing language skills.

Below are some examples of questions in Moats's Comprehensive Survey of Language Knowledge (2000). She uses this survey to determine the instructional needs of teachers prior to their teaching phonics to their students. How well would you do?

**Question 3:**
A closed syllable is one that _____.
An open syllable is one that _____.

**Question 5:** What is the third speech sound in each of the following words?

joyful ____    should ____    talk ____
tinker ____    rouge ____    shower ____
square ____    start ____
protect ____    patchwork ____

**Question 8:** Underline the consonant digraphs.
spherical  church  numb  shrink  thought  whether

**Question 9:** When is *ck* used in spelling?

**Question 11:** List all the ways to spell long *o*.

**Question 14:** How can you recognize an English word that came from Greek?

---

**Answer Key**

3.  A closed syllable is one that ends in a consonant and has a short-vowel sound.
    An open syllable is one that ends in a vowel and has a long-vowel sound.

5.  What is the third speech sound in each of the following words?
    joyful /f/    should /d/    talk /k/    tinker /ng/    rouge /zh/    shower /r/
    square /w/    start /ä/    protect /ō/    patchwork /ch/

8.  s<u>ph</u>erical  <u>ch</u>ur<u>ch</u>  nu<u>mb</u>  <u>sh</u>rink  <u>th</u>ought  <u>wh</u>e<u>th</u>er

9.  after a short vowel in a one-syllable word

11. o, o_e, oa, oe, ow, ou, ough, ew, au, eau, eo, oh, oo, ot, owe, os, aux

14. It might have *ph* for /f/, *ch* for /k/, or *y* for short or long *i*.

## 10 It Is Possible to Overdo Phonics Instruction

Some teachers may unknowingly overdo phonics instruction (Stanovich, 1993–94; Chall, 1996). Likewise, some teachers may underemphasize phonics instruction to the point that they're doing a disservice to children by not providing them with a valuable decoding strategy.

For many children, a little phonics instruction can go a long way. The awareness these children have that sounds map onto spellings enables them to deduce other sound-spelling relationships from wide reading, especially if the material they read contains a large number of decodable words (Juel, 1991). However, some children (especially children at risk) need teaching that makes these relationships explicit through direct and systematic instruction.

In addition, phonics instruction should focus on applying learned sound-spelling relationships to actual reading, with smaller amounts of time spent on learning phonics rules or generalizations and out-of-context work. Overall instruction must be engaging, thought-provoking, purposeful, and applied.

## WAYS TO GET PARENTS INVOLVED

It's important to involve students' families in the reading development of their children. Here are some tips:

- Communicate what you're doing in your classroom through newsletters, conferences, phone calls, and individual notes. Be specific about the phonics skills you are teaching.
- Provide families with lists of books appropriate for their children to read independently.
- Keep an open-door policy. Encourage family members to volunteer, visit your classroom, or simply offer feedback in writing.
- Send home learning kits filled with books and phonics activities for family members and children to enjoy together.
- Hold a reading workshop on a Saturday or weekday evening to answer questions about phonics and provide family members with strategies to help their children decode words. Videotape the session and post it online for parents who could not attend.

# History of Phonics Instruction in the U.S.

Phonics instruction has developed and changed throughout the history of reading instruction in the United States. At times, there has been an emphasis on teaching children sound-spelling relationships; at other times, phonics instruction has taken a backseat. The following time line highlights some important changes in the way phonics instruction has been treated throughout the history of U.S. reading education.

**Late 1600s:** The *New England Primer* was published in the colonies in the late 1600s. The instruction in this early reading book reflected a strong emphasis on phonics. Students first learned the alphabet, next practiced reading simple syllables, and finally read actual text. The Bible was the primary book students read, and reading was considered a serious matter. The "bottom-up" approach to reading, for which students began with sound-letter relationships, was consistent with the way the early colonists learned to read in other languages. From the time of the ancient Greeks, phonics had been taught to make written language accessible. It's no surprise then that the educated colonists, many of whom were schooled in classics such as Greek and Latin, would advocate phonics instruction. This method of instruction continued unchallenged for over a century and a half.

**Mid-1800s:** During the mid-1800s, things slowly began to change. Instead of only an elite few learning to read, attention began to focus on educating a larger portion of the population. Education of the masses was viewed as a necessity in order for this young democracy called the United States to grow and thrive. In addition, a larger number of published works were becoming available. Comprehension became the focus of educators' attention, and instruction in comprehension was seen as being at odds with phonics instruction. Part of the charge against phonics instruction was led by Horace Mann, the secretary of the Massachusetts Board of Education. He saw phonics as detrimental to creating a nation of eager and skilled readers and advocated a **whole-word method** to reading instruction. Although his influence grew slowly, graded reading books emerged, and the instructional emphasis on comprehension over phonics continued. Although many teachers initially fought this notion, the reading books published began to contain more controlled vocabulary, and the ensuing instruction reflected this. In the late 1920s, this whole-word method, with its accompanying controlled-vocabulary readers, would firmly take root.

**Late 1920s—1940s:** In the late 1920s, the well-respected educator William S. Gray led the criticisms against what he described as the "heartless drudgery" of the existing phonics instruction. He recommended that it be replaced once and for all with the **look-say method** (also known as the sight-word or whole-word method). The Dick and Jane readers, which Gray helped to develop with Scott Foresman and Company, popularized the look-say method. These readers reflected significant changes in reading materials for children.

For example, they contained full-color pictures and stories that appealed to children. The text was carefully controlled so that sight words were used repeatedly to provide children with multiple exposures. This approach followed a "top-down" model in which students began with their prior experiences and knowledge of whole words. Any sound-spelling relationships children learned were learned incidentally. Phonics was seen as a last resort.

**1955:** In 1955, Rudolf Flesch's *Why Johnny Can't Read* took the nation by storm. Flesch attributed decreases in reading abilities among U.S. students to the look-say method and harshly attacked it. He advocated a return to the "sensibility" of phonics. Although Flesch's ideas were certainly not new, his book received considerable attention because of its political tone and severe criticisms. The general public and media embraced the book, and it became an instant best seller. However, the academic community dismissed *Why Johnny Can't Read* because of Flesch's propaganda-style of writing, because his claims couldn't be substantiated by existing research, and because he oversimplified how children learn to read. Undaunted, Flesch continued his attacks, and the public listened with open ears. Here is a passage from *Why Johnny Can't Read*:

> *I say, therefore, that the word method is gradually destroying democracy in this country; it returns to the upper middle class the privileges that public education was supposed to distribute evenly among the people. The American Dream is, essentially, equal opportunity through free education for all. This dream is beginning to vanish in a country where the public schools are falling down on the job.*

Flesch went on to complain that the use of the whole-word method was like animal training; it treated children like dogs. He called it "the most inhuman, mean, stupid way of foisting something on a child's mind." Today, Flesch's book remains popular and is widely quoted. One negative aftermath of this book is the polarization of reading educators. If a teacher advocates phonics, it is assumed that he or she wants to return to the drudgery of the past and is antiliterature, anticomprehension, and antimotivation. If a teacher advocates a whole-language approach, it is assumed that he or she wants to return to the look-say methods of the past and is uninformed about how children learn to read. Neither extreme interpretation is, of course, accurate.

**1967:** The U.S. government was not deaf to the cries being heard throughout the country as a result of Flesch's book and turned to the academic community for answers. One answer came in 1967 with the publication of Jeanne Chall's classic *Learning to Read: The Great*

*Debate.* This book reflected a more scientific and balanced analysis of the reading issue facing our nation. It advocated including early and systematic phonics instruction in the elementary reading curriculum and supported this with a substantial amount of research data. Many follow-up studies by other researchers supported Chall's notion that direct phonics instruction was more beneficial to students than incidental learning. Although Chall's findings were greatly substantiated, phonics instruction received varying degrees of emphasis in the 1970s, '80s, and early '90s, and often took a backseat to an emphasis on quality literature and comprehension.

**1985–1995:** With the publication of *Becoming a Nation of Readers: The Report of the Commission on Reading* (Anderson et al., 1985) and Marilyn Jager Adams's now classic *Beginning to Read: Thinking and Learning About Print*, the spotlight once again highlighted the importance of explicit phonics instruction. These authors described phonics as *"one* of the essential ingredients" in early reading instruction. However, they acknowledged the many other important aspects of early reading and advocated a more balanced, comprehensive approach to reading instruction. They also acknowledged that reading is neither a "bottom-up" nor a "top-down" process. Rather, they and other researchers proposed an "interactive model" of reading in which a reader uses in combination prior knowledge (background experiences) and knowledge of sound-spelling features of words, sentence structure, and word meanings to comprehend text. The instructional focus therefore should not be on one aspect of reading to the exclusion of others.

**1995–2006:** In 2002, President George W. Bush signed into law the No Child Left Behind Act of 2001. This law provided increased funding and emphasis on reading instruction in Grades K–3. With this new law came new accountability. Soon, school districts across the nation began retraining their teachers in five key areas of reading instruction— phonemic awareness, phonics, vocabulary, comprehension, and fluency. To assist schools in making research-based decisions about their reading instruction, many turned to *Preventing Reading Difficulties in Young Children* (Snow et al., 1998) and the 2000 report published by the National Reading Panel. This group of reading authorities reviewed the highest-quality research on reading instruction and presented their findings in *Report of the National Reading Panel: Teaching Children to Read: An Evidence-Based Assessment of the Scientific Literature on Reading and Its Implications for Reading Instruction* (NICHD, 2000). Many states, such as California and Texas, have required an increased emphasis on phonics in the reading basals sold in their states as well as an increase in the training preservice teachers receive on phonics and basic linguistics. Most basals now contain controlled text based on decodability counts.

**2007–Present:** In 2009 (*Visible Learning*) and 2012 (*Visible Learning for Teachers*), John Hattie examined over 1,200 meta-analyses conducted by educational researchers all over the world. These included over 70,000 studies with 300 million students. Hattie used a statistic called *effect size* to determine the impact that a given teacher action had on students' learning. Effect sizes demonstrate the amount of learning expected. From this data set, Hattie determined that an effect size of 0.40 equated to one year of growth for a year of school, which seems to be the minimum we should expect from schools. When he examined phonics instruction, the evidence was compelling, with an effect size of 0.60. Hattie also noted that phonics instruction was more effective for younger students and that the effect sizes decreased as students got older, meaning that we need to be sure students receive this type of instruction as part of their early literacy learning. In 2015, a brain research study out of Stanford revealed that "beginning readers who focus on letter-sound relationships, or phonics, instead of trying to learn whole words, increase activity in the area of their brains best wired for reading" (Wong, 2015). That is, words learned using letter-sounds activate the left side of the brain. This is where the visual and language regions of the brain reside. Words learned using a whole-word method activate the right side of the brain. This is significant because left-brain activation during reading is characteristic of skilled readers and is generally lacking in both children and adults who struggle with reading. The researchers described it as "changing gears" while reading. When you focus your attention on different aspects of a word, you activate, or amplify, different parts of the brain. And it is fascinating that we can now map the brain activity when students read and learn using different teaching methods and practices. Brain research is also suggesting that the learning pathways can be altered with specific methods. This has remarkable potential for teaching and learning and will hopefully be a focus of research in the upcoming decade.

# Stages of Reading Development: Where Phonics Fits In

Before I begin discussing current phonics instruction, I believe it is important for any teacher of reading to get a sense of the big picture. This understanding can help put phonics in its proper perspective and enable you to make instructional decisions based on each student's stage of reading development. I have chosen the stages of reading development proposed by Chall (1983) because it provides a clear and useful framework for how children learn to read. This framework includes six reading levels.

## Stage 0: Prereading

This stage lasts from birth to about age six. The most notable change is the child's growing control over language. By the time a child enters first grade (at around age six), he or she has approximately 6,000 words in his or her listening and speaking vocabularies. During this stage, children also develop some knowledge of print, such as recognizing a few letters, words, and environmental print signs. Many children are able to write their names. It is common to see children "pretend read" a book that has been repeatedly read to them. At this stage, children "bring more to the printed page than they take out."

## Stage 1: Initial Reading or Decoding

This stage generally lasts from kindergarten through Grade 2. During this time children develop an understanding of the alphabetic principle and begin to use their knowledge of sound-spelling relationships to decode words.

## Stage 2: Confirmation, Fluency, and Ungluing From Print

This stage generally lasts from Grade 2 through Grade 3. Children further develop and solidify their decoding skills. They also develop additional strategies to decode words and make meaning from text. As this stage ends, children have developed fluency; that is, they can recognize many words quickly and accurately by sight and are skilled at sounding out words they don't recognize by sight. They are also skilled at using context clues to predict words.

## Stage 3: Learning the New

This stage generally lasts from Grade 4 through Grade 8. During this stage, the reading demands change. Children begin to use reading more as a way to obtain information and learn about the values, attitudes, and insights of others. Texts contain many words not already in a child's speaking and listening vocabularies. These texts, frequently drawn from a wide variety of genres, also extend beyond the background experiences of the children.

## Stage 4: Multiple Viewpoints

This stage generally lasts throughout high school (Grades 9 through 12). Readers encounter more-complex language and vocabulary as they read texts in more advanced content areas. Thus the language and cognitive demands required of the reader increase. Readers are also required to read texts containing varying viewpoints and to analyze them critically.

## Stage 5: Construction and Reconstruction

This stage, which generally lasts through college and beyond, is characterized by a "worldview." Readers use the information in books and articles as needed; that is, a reader knows which books and articles will provide the information he or she needs and can locate that information within a book without having to read it in its entirety. At this stage, reading is considered constructive; that is, readers take in a wide range of information and construct their own understanding for their individual uses based on their analysis and synthesis of the information. Not all readers progress to this stage.

As Chall herself states, the value of this framework is that it "suggests that different aspects of reading be emphasized at different stages of reading development, and that success at the beginning is essential since it influences not only early reading achievement but also reading at subsequent stages of development." This framework highlights the need for beginning-reading programs to provide children with strong instruction in decoding words. It is also a warning that a prolonged stay in any one stage can result in serious reading problems.

As you read the information provided in this book and assess the reading development of your students, keep in mind the stages of reading development framework. Consider how it can be used to modify instruction. For example, what you do instructionally with a third-grade child stuck in Stage 1 is different from what you do with a third-grade child already in Stage 3.

Aside from providing balanced, strong reading instruction that meets the needs of all your children, the greatest gift you can give them is a love of reading. I am constantly reminded of Mrs. Fry, my fourth-grade teacher. Throughout the year she read to us the entire Little House series by Laura Ingalls Wilder. The words seemed to melt off the pages as she read. I can still remember the emotion and excitement in her voice. She made me want to read everything she picked up. Indeed, many of us purchased our own Little House sets of books or checked out of the library every book she recommended. She brought books to life! It is that love of literature we can and must share with our students in order to open the door for them to a world of amazing ideas.

# Opening the Gate

## for Reading Instruction: Alphabet Recognition and Phonemic Awareness

*"The two best predictors of early reading success
are alphabet recognition and phonemic awareness."*

—Marilyn Jager Adams

The birth of my nephew, Trevor, was arguably the most exciting day in my family's history. After Trevor was born, my family and I spent the next five years singing the alphabet song to him; reading to him countless ABC, board, and picture books; praising his efforts to make sense of print ("Yes, Trevor, those golden arches do mean 'yummy burgers.'"); and sitting him in front of the television every time *Sesame Street* came on—all in an attempt to get him "ready" for school. Trevor's development was the topic of many discussions between my sister and me. "Am I reading to him enough?" my sister would ask. "Should I be doing more? Will he really be ready?" We waited to see if the seemingly hundreds of hours we spent getting him "ready" for school would pay off.

While my nephew did seem to benefit from our efforts, too many children enter school each year with limited exposure to books, small speaking and listening vocabularies, varied world knowledge, and only a vague sense of story. Yet it's the task of each kindergarten teacher to get all these children—those from both print-rich and print-poor environments—ready for formal reading instruction.

# Powerful Predictors of Success

How can teachers ensure that all students are "ready" for formal reading instruction? And what are the essential prerequisites for learning to read? Two powerful predictors of early reading success are **alphabet recognition** (knowing the names of the letters and the sounds they represent) and **phonemic awareness** (understanding that a word is made up of sounds and the ability to manipulate sounds in spoken words) (Adams, 1990; Stanovich, 1992; Chall, 1996; Beck & Juel, 1995; Share, Jorm, Maclean, & Matthews, 1984). In essence, these two skills open the gate for early reading. Without a thorough knowledge of letters and an understanding that words are made up of sounds, children cannot learn to read.

In addition to alphabet recognition and phonemic awareness, reading-ready children need to have a sense of story, a basic understanding of the concepts of print, and a firm grasp of the language of instruction.

**The Concepts of Print:** These concepts, also referred to as "print awareness," include making sure children:

- know the difference between words and nonwords.
- know that print is print, no matter what form it appears in (uppercase, lowercase, manuscript, cursive, different fonts, different colors and sizes).
- know that print can appear by itself or with pictures.
- understand that print corresponds to speech, word for word.
- understand the purpose of the empty space between words (word boundaries).
- understand that words are read from left to right on a page.
- understand that lines of text are read from top to bottom on a page.
- can identify the front of a book and a page in it.

**The Language of Instruction:** This includes an understanding of the following terms: *word, letter, beginning, middle, end, base line, sentence, period, comma, question mark, sound,* and *syllable.*

- Tracking print can help children develop the concept of "word."
- Using sentence strips and pocket charts to have children match sentences with a given text can develop the concept of "sentence."

- Activities such as those shown in the Classroom Spotlight below can help children understand the concept of "beginning, middle, and end."

Do these activities in the order they are given.

- Place three books in a row on the board ledge. Point out that the first book is at the beginning of the row, the second book is in the middle of the row, and the third book is at the end of the row. Ask a volunteer to identify the book at the beginning of the row. Continue with other positions and classroom objects.

- Arrange three students at the front of the room. Ask the class which student is at the beginning, middle, or end of the row.

- Write a three-letter word, such as *sat*, on the board. Ask a volunteer to circle the beginning letter in the word. Continue with other words and letter positions.

# Alphabet Recognition:
# What It Is and Why It's Essential

English, like French, Spanish, and many other languages, is an alphabetic language. The invention of the alphabet is often said to be the most important invention in the social history of the world (Adams, 1990). It enabled people to communicate across places and times and to store those communications. However, the alphabet is a series of abstract symbols that by themselves are mere squiggles and lines. Identities and sounds have been attached to these symbols to give them purpose and utility. Together, they create something spectacular—printed words.

To read in any alphabetic language, students have to learn the intricacies of that alphabet and understand the alphabetic principle (that is, that this system of letters stands for a series of sounds). Students have to be able to recognize letters in their many contexts and forms. In fact, a child must memorize four sets of letters: uppercase manuscript, lowercase manuscript, uppercase cursive, and lowercase cursive.

In addition to learning these four forms of each letter, children need to learn to distinguish among similar-looking letters. For example, the letter *E* looks a lot like the letter *F*; the letter *d* looks like a flopped version of the letter *b*. The *d/b* distinction is particularly confusing for children because this is the first time they encounter the orientation of something changing its identity. Up until now, when

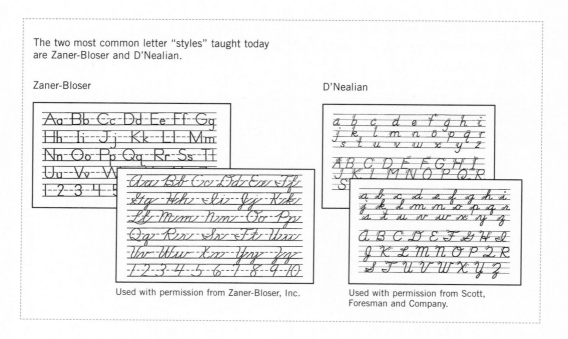

The two most common letter "styles" taught today are Zaner-Bloser and D'Nealian.

Zaner-Bloser

D'Nealian

Used with permission from Zaner-Bloser, Inc.

Used with permission from Scott, Foresman and Company.

children saw a pen it was always a pen, no matter how it was turned, flipped, or moved around. However, if we flop a *b* it is now called a *d*; if we flip an *M* it is now called a *W*. Learning these subtle differences in letters requires time, practice, and careful visual attention.

Letters can be distinguished according to their position on a line; their length; their size; whether they contain horizontal, vertical, diagonal, or curving lines; whether they have descenders (parts of the letter that extend below the base line); and their orientation. It was once believed that children who confused visually similar letters were at serious risk for reading disabilities. However, it is now generally agreed that children who have a problem with letter orientation probably just lack letter knowledge. Training and increased exposure will help them overcome most of these difficulties.

## Beyond "Now I Know My ABC's"

Most children enter school being able to say the alphabet, having acquired the skill by about age four. However, being able to say the names of the letters is not the same as "knowing" the letters. In order to learn to read, children must also be able to rapidly identify the printed forms of the letters in and out of sequence and learn the most frequent sound that is attached to each letter. Instruction during the first two years of school should ensure that children know the alphabet and can use it with ease and efficiency.

Many children enter school already able to identify some of the names of printed letters. In one study, children entering kindergarten could identify on average 14 letters (Hiebert & Sawyer, 1984). The letters the children were most likely to know were those used most frequently or those with the most personal relevance to them (for example, the letters in their name). These children had learned letters by singing the alphabet song, being exposed to alphabet books, and having family members point out and identify letters in environmental print.

However, being able to name and quickly recognize letters is a critical step to learning to read for *all* children. Adams (1990) points out that:

- children who can recognize letters with accuracy and speed have an easier time learning about the sounds associated with letters than those children who are struggling with alphabet recognition. Automatic recognition frees up students' "mental energies" so they can focus on learning sound-spelling relationships.
- accuracy is only one aspect of alphabet recognition. Speed (automaticity) is another critical factor. Both accuracy and speed indicate how well children have learned the letters' identities. Thus, children need to overlearn (memorize) the letters. A child who hasn't memorized the letters of the alphabet may become a "nonalphabetic" reader; that is, he or she will have to rely on sight words to read rather than using a knowledge of letters and the sounds they represent.
- as they learn the letters, children frequently become interested in learning more about them—their sounds and how to use them to write words.

## How to Assess Alphabet Recognition

When assessing students' knowledge of the alphabet, you need to assess both letter names and letter sounds. In addition, you need to assess both accuracy and speed. I've provided two assessments online (see page 320 for details on how to access). One is for monitoring mastery of letter names (both uppercase and lowercase). The other is for mastery of letter sounds. The sequence of the letters for each is based on

The Letter-Name Assessment and the Letter-Sound Assessment can be found online as Resources 2.1 and 2.2; see page 320 for details on how to access.

the typical order in which letters and sounds are acquired (Phillips et al., 2012, Piasta, 2014). I created it this way so that each assessment progresses from simple to complex. In that way, you can use the assessment results to modify your whole-group lessons (e.g., spend less time on letters your students already know and more on those they don't) and form small groups based on specific letter-knowledge needs. Make copies of the assessments and administer individually.

One of the key formal assessments currently being used by school districts to determine a child's speed and accuracy in recognizing letters in relation to grade-level expectations is DIBELS (Dynamic Indicators of Basic Early Literary Skills). For additional information on this assessment, go to http://dibels.uoregon.edu.

## Teaching Alphabet Recognition

Teachers all across the country use a wide range of methods and activities to teach the alphabet. Jill Simpson, teaching in Florida, reads a lot of alphabet books to her students and has them create their own alphabet books as she introduces each new letter. Sadie Connor in Ohio fills her classroom with manipulatives—fuzzy letters, paint, letter cards, and more. She also sings the alphabet song every morning and designates a letter of the day that corresponds to a child's name in her class. Her activities for the day center around that letter and its corresponding sound. Matt Bingham in Maryland has his students write letters in the air, form letters with their bodies, make letters out of clay, and practice writing letters while writing stories. He stresses the sound that each letter stands for by introducing his class to an object (toy, classroom object, and so on) whose name contains the letter/sound being studied. His children then write about that object.

What do all these teachers have in common? They all understand that children learn the alphabet best through the "active exploration of the relationships between letter names, the sounds of the letter names, their visual characteristics, and the motor movement involved in their formation" (Bear et al., 1996). Educators agree that children learn these relationships through a combination of direct instruction and multiple exposures to print. However, there is some disagreement about the sequence in which the alphabet should be taught. Some educators believe that the letters should be taught in order, since the alphabet represents a system with a set sequence that serves a valuable organizational function. And they emphasize the importance of starting with the known when teaching any new skill. Since most children come to school able to sing the alphabet song—with the letters in order—these educators reason that learning the printed forms of the letters in the same order will be easier.

Other educators believe that children should first learn meaningful letters, such as those in their names. Since these letters are of greatest importance, they reason, young learners will internalize them more quickly. In addition, these educators think that the visually confusing letters, such as *b* and *d*, should be taught far enough apart that one can be learned before the other is introduced.

## Sensible Sequencing

Since there is no consensus on a best sequence for teaching the alphabet, you'll have to decide what is best for you and your students. I recommend the following:

**Teach children letter names first.** Most letter names are closely related to their sounds. In fact, 21 letters contain the most common sound assigned to them in their names. For example, *b* (/bē/) and *m* (/em/). The exceptions are *h, q, w, y, g,* and the short vowels. Knowing the names of the letters helps children grasp the alphabetic principle—the notion that each letter stands for a sound. In addition, knowing the names provides you with instructional labels that are familiar to children.

**Put a new spin on a classic song.** Children generally learn the letter names not by seeing the letters but by singing the "Alphabet Song" to the tune of "Twinkle, Twinkle, Little Star." Although a classic, the traditional alphabet song isn't without its shortcomings—most notably the so-called "elemeno" problem. When the song arrives at the letters *L, M, N,* and *O,* they are sung so quickly that they sound like the word "elemeno" instead of the pronunciations of four distinct letters. You can overcome this problem by choosing a different version of the alphabet song, or pointing to the letters on an alphabet chart while singing the song. Alternate versions are available and range from slight modifications of the traditional song (for example, one uses the traditional tune but provides pauses on the letters *N, Q,* and *T*) to an alphabet rap. Also available are alphabet book/audio combinations, such as *Chicka Chicka Boom Boom* (written by Bill Martin, Jr., and John Archambault; performed by Ray Charles, Simon & Schuster).

**Next, teach the shapes and sounds of letters.** When children know the names of the letters, teach their shapes and the most common sound assigned to each. Although many children can say the names of the letters by age four, most need up to two years to learn the corresponding shapes (Adams, 1990). Some children can learn several letters a week; some may need a week to learn one (Ekwall & Shanker, 1993). "Learning the alphabet proceeds in much the same way as learning anything else—by categorizing features that are the same and contrasting those with other features that are different" (Bear et al., 1996).

**Tailor your letter lessons to students' needs.** If you're working with children who have limited alphabet knowledge, don't teach both the uppercase and lowercase forms of the letters simultaneously. If children are in preschool, teach the uppercase letters first since those are easier to distinguish visually. Besides, these are the letter forms preschool children are most likely to have become familiar with outside the classroom because of their exposure to environmental print. If you are working with children in kindergarten and Grade 1, focus on the lowercase letters since these are the letter forms most frequently encountered in text (Adams, 1990).

**Help children to see differences and similarities among letters.** When teaching letter shapes, help children to discriminate small, but important, differences among letters. And remember that children need to be able to recognize letters in isolation and in the context of a word, the latter being more difficult (Clay, 1991). First help children see similarities in letters they know; then progress to pointing out letter differences and introducing other letters. For example, the letters *a* and *b* both contain small circles. Next point out and discuss the subtle differences among similar-looking letters. For example, letters differ in the direction of their extension (*b-p, d-g, q-d*), their left-right orientation (*b-d, q-p, g-p*), their top-bottom orientation (*m-w, n-u, M-W*), and their line-curve features (*u-v, U-V*).

The Confusable Letter Pairs chart (page 35) shows letters that are visually similar and often confusing to children. You need to pay special attention to teaching their differences. Don't teach these letter pairs in close proximity; be sure children have a firm grasp of the first one before you introduce the other. The letters that confuse children the most are those with reversible parts, such as *b-d, p-d, q-b, h-u,* and *i-l* (Popp, 1964).

The following four letter groups are particularly confusing for students and shouldn't be taught at the same time (Manzo & Manzo, 1993).

- *e, a, s, c, o*
- *b, d, p, o, g, h*

- *f, l, t, k, i, h*
- *n, m, u, h, r*

**Provide support for children having difficulty discriminating letters.** The typical four- to four-and-a-half-year-old has the visual-perceptual skill needed to distinguish lowercase letters (Rosner, 1993). However, some children will need extra help. One common letter-reversal problem involves *b* and *d*. Most children who have trouble identifying *b* and *d* can see that the letters are different, but they can't remember which is which (Rosner, 1993). Using memory devices and having an alphabet chart on each child's desk for easy reference helps.

## Confusable Letter Pairs

| Lowercase | | | | Uppercase | |
|---|---|---|---|---|---|
| a-d | c-o | h-n | n-u | C-G | M-N |
| a-o | d-q | h-u | p-q | D-O | M-W |
| b-d | d-g | i-j | u-v | E-F | O-Q |
| b-h | d-p | i-l | v-w | I-J | P-R |
| b-p | f-t | k-y | v-y | I-L | U-V |
| b-q | g-p | m-n | | K-X | V-Y |
| c-e | g-q | m-w | | L-T | |

### CLASSROOM SPOTLIGHT

You can use memory devices to help children distinguish one letter from another. Try these strategies to help children with the visually confusing *b-d*.

- Write the word *bed* on the board and point out that the word visually resembles a bed. Show children that the word begins with the letter *b* and ends with the letter *d* and that the letter *b* comes before the letter *d* in the alphabet and in the word *bed*.

- Write an uppercase *B* on the board. In another color, trace the lowercase *b* that is "hidden" (embedded) in the uppercase *B*. For the letter *d*, teach the letter *c* first. Then point out to children that they need only add a line to the letter *c* to form the next letter in the alphabet—the letter *d*. It's like you have to go through "c" to get to "d."

**Provide letter-writing practice.** To learn and recall the letter shapes, children need plenty of practice writing them as early as possible. Teach letter shapes along with teaching handwriting. If a child hasn't chosen which hand to write with (usually a preference emerges by age four), determine it now. To remember the intricacies of letter orientation, children should keep writing the letters with the same hand.

"Having children write the letters accurately, especially with encouragement to attend to their distinctive features, significantly helps letter recognition" (Clay, 1993). When teaching handwriting, be consistent. Choose only one style of manuscript. The two most common styles currently in use are Zaner-Bloser, which is characterized by straight lines and sharp edges, and D'Nealian, which is characterized by slanted lines and tails resulting in a close resemblance between its manuscript and cursive forms (see page 30). Let children write the letters on unlined paper before they encounter the greater demands of lined

You may need to help children who are having difficulty forming letters by holding the pencil with them and guiding them to form the letter. Think aloud about how you are forming the letter, discussing the unique visual characteristics of the letter. You may want to have children whose manual dexterity is developing more slowly write on unlined paper. For one of my second graders who was having trouble fitting his letters on lined paper, I made a photocopy enlargement. That way, I could both teach him how to use the base line and dashed lines as guides for correctly forming letters and accommodate his inability to write letters in that small a space.

paper. Be sure to spend adequate time helping them develop proper habits in forming the necessary line and curve strokes.

**Use memory devices to help children write letters.** Memory devices can help children learn and remember each letter's distinguishing features. You might even employ clever rhymes. For example:

> **For teaching *E*:**
> Pull straight down, just like me. *(Pull down straight.)*
> Then slide to the right: one, two, three. *(Pull across from left to right three times.)*

> **For teaching *g*:**
> There's a gopher in my garden,
> See him going round. *(Half-circle up and left.)*
> Oops! Now the gopher sees me,
> And he pops down in the ground! *(Pull down straight. Curve up left.)*

**Use copying and tracing appropriately.** Independent writing is the most effective way of teaching children to form the shapes of each letter. But copying and tracing have their place. Having children write the letter while saying its name, and/or the sound associated with it, ensures that they are focusing on the subtle differences in each letter and thinking about it in terms of its name and/or sound. For example, the child says /f/, /f/, /f/ while writing *f f f*. Copying and tracing also help to develop children's fine-motor skills. So emphasize independent writing and use copying and tracing according to each child's needs.

**Use key words and pictures when you introduce sound-spelling relationships.** After you teach the names of the letters (and possibly the shapes) in sequence, teach the most common sound-spelling relationship for each. Use a sequence that will allow you to form simple CVC (consonant-vowel-consonant) words early on and model the principle of blending. Starting in kindergarten, children need to be shown how their letter knowledge applies to the actual reading of words. To help students see this, associate a key word and picture with each letter. For example, when teaching the letter *s*, you might use the word *sun* and a corresponding picture of a sun. Research has shown this letter/key word/key picture combination to be highly effective (Ehri, 1992). You'll find a listing of key words and pictures for each letter in the "Learning About Sounds and Letters" section (page 77) of this book.

**Adjust the pace of instruction according to students' needs.** Children who have a limited alphabet knowledge upon entering school may have trouble gaining the all-important alphabet-recognition skills through the traditional "letter-a-week" method (which isn't as effective as sequences that provide review and repetition of previously taught skills). Without the necessary memorization, early reading instruction becomes cumbersome and difficult. As Adams (1990) writes, "For children who haven't cut their teeth on alphabet letters and picture books, one letter per week is a mere drop in the bucket against the 1,000- to 1,700-hour advantage of their peers." For these children, you'll have to provide lots of extra practice saying the names and identifying the shapes of the uppercase and lowercase letters in and out of sequence as you introduce sound-spelling relationships.

**Include multisensory activities.** On pages 41–47, you'll find tactile (touch), visual, auditory, and kinesthetic (movement) activities for teaching the alphabet. Remember to include letter-recognition activities throughout your daily instruction. For example, point out target letters while reading a Big Book and look for letters in environmental print.

**Read a lot of alphabet books.** Provide opportunities for children to hear, see, say, and write the alphabet in a variety of contexts and for a variety of purposes.

## Alphabet Books Play a Role

Alphabet books, those popular picture books that present the letters of the alphabet in order, fill elementary classrooms everywhere. Many alphabet books center around a common kid-pleasing theme or concept, such as an animal alphabet or a city alphabet. You can use alphabet books to develop alphabet recognition and to build vocabulary. Some of the books, such as *Ashanti to Zulu: African Traditions* by

Margaret Musgrove, promote multicultural awareness. Alphabet books are valuable because:

- they support beginning readers' oral language development.
- they help children learn letter sequence.
- they help children associate a sound with a letter.
- they can help children build vocabulary and world knowledge. Children's knowledge of the world, referred to as "semantic domain" (Lindfors, 1987), grows substantially during the elementary school years. Alphabet books can be extremely beneficial for children with limited world knowledge.
- they can be vocabulary builders for students learning English as a second language.
- they are appealing to at-risk readers who might be intimidated by books containing denser text.

## Tips for Teaching With Alphabet Books

Here are some suggestions for using alphabet books as part of your weekly instruction.

- Read the book the first time in its entirety, without pauses, so that children can enjoy the language and illustrations.
- Reread the book and discuss items of interest, such as finding the objects in the illustration that begin with the sound the letter on that page represents. Keep the discussion playful and gamelike, limiting the letters you focus on to one or two each day.
- Create letter charts, using the words and pictures in the alphabet book. Have children identify words and pictures with a target letter/sound to add to each chart.
- Have children create their own alphabet books using the pattern of the book you just read.

## Alphabet Books A to Z

*26 Letters and 99 Cents* by Tana Hoban (Greenwillow)

*A Is for Angry: An Animal and Adjective Alphabet* by Sandra Boynton (Workman Publishing Group)

*A Is for Autumn* by Robert Maass (Henry Holt and Co.)

*A, My Name Is Alice* by Jane Bayer (Dial)

*ABC for You and Me* by Meg Girnis and Shirley Leamon Green (Albert Whitman & Co.)

*ABC I Like Me!* by Nancy Carlson (Puffin Books)

*ABC Letters in the Library* by Bonnie Farmer (Lobster Press)

*ABC Universe* by American Museum of Natural History

*ABC Yoga* by Christiane Engel (Walter Foster Jr.)

*ABC: Egyptian Art From The Brooklyn Museum* by Florence Cassen Mayers
(Harry N. Abrams)

*ABC: The Alphabet from the Sky* by Benedikt Gross (Price Stern Sloan)

*ABCs in Nature* by Daniel Nunn (Raintree)

*ABeCedarios: Mexican Folk Art ABCs in English and Spanish*
by Cynthia Wells (Scholastic)

*All Aboard ABC* by Doug Magee and Robert Newman (Puffin/Penguin Putnam)

*Alphabeep: A Zipping Zooming ABC* by Debora Pearson
(Holiday House)

*Alphabet City Zoo: Making Pictures with the A-B-C* by Maree Coote
(Melbournestyle Books)

*An Alphabet Salad: Fruits and Vegetables from A to Z* by Sarah L. Shuette (Capstone Press)

*Alphabet Trucks* by Samantha R. Vamos (Charlesbridge)

*Alphabatics* by Suse MacDonald (Bradbury Press)

*AlphaOops!: The Day Z Went First* by Alethea Kontis (Candlewick)

*Animal Action ABC* by Karen Pandell (Dutton)

*Animalia* by Graeme Base (Abrams)

*Anno's Alphabet: An Adventure in Imagination* by Mitsumasa Anno
(HarperCollins)

*Ashanti to Zulu: African Traditions* by Margaret Musgrove (Dial)

*C Is for Curious: An ABC of Feelings* by Woodleigh Hubbard (Chronicle Books)

*Chicka Chicka Boom Boom* by Bill Martin Jr. and J. Archambault
(Simon & Schuster)

*The City ABC Book* by Zoran Milich (Kids Can Press)

*David McPhail's Animals A to Z* by David McPhail (Scholastic)

*Dr. Seuss's ABC: An Amazing Alphabet Book* by Dr. Seuss (Random House Books of Young Readers)

*Eating the Alphabet: Fruits and Vegetables from A to Z* by Lois Ehlert
(Harcourt)

*The Farm Alphabet* by Jane Miller (Scholastic)

*A Gardener's Alphabet* by Mary Azarian (HMH Books for Young Readers)

*I Spy Little Letters* by Jean Marzollo (Scholastic)

*The Icky Bug Alphabet Book* by Jerry Pallotta (Charlesbridge Publishing)

*Into the A, B, Sea: An Ocean Alphabet Book* by Deborah Lee Rose (Scholastic)

*Jambo Means Hello: Swahili Alphabet Book* by Muriel Feelings (Dial)

*LMNO Peas* by Keith Baker (Little Simon)

*Matthew A.B.C.* by Peter Catalanotto (Atheneum Books for Young Readers)

*Miss Spider's ABC* by David Kirk (Scholastic)

*The Monster Book of ABC Sounds* by Allan Snow (Dial)

*Museum ABC* by The New York Metropolitan Museum of Art

*My First Animal ABC* by A. J. Wood (Silver Dolphin Books)

*Olivia's ABCs* by Ian Falcone (Atheneum Books for Young Readers)

*Once Upon an Alphabet* by Oliver Jeffers (Philomel Books)

*Puddle's ABC (Toot & Puddle)* by Hollie Hobbie (Little Brown Books for Young Readers)

*Q Is for Duck: An Alphabet Guessing Game* by Mary Elting (HMH Books for Young Readers)

*Quentin Blake's ABC* by Quentin Blake (Knopf)

*R Is for Rocket: An ABC Book* by Tad Hills (Schwartz & Wade)

*School ABC: An Alphabet Book* by Amanda Doering (Capstone Press)

*So Many Bunnies: A Bedtime ABC and Counting Book* by Rick Walton (Harper Festival)

*The Very Hungry Caterpillar's ABC* by Eric Carle (Puffin)

*The Z Was Zapped* by Chris Van Allsburg (Houghton Mifflin)

See also http://www.themeasuredmom.com/the-50-best-abc-books-for-kids/

# 35 Quick and Easy Activities for Developing Alphabet Recognition

Use these games and activities as warm-ups for the day's formal reading instruction. Many also work well for learning centers. I suggest keeping a learning center chart on which you mark the centers each child has visited. I replace the games the first day of each month so that children have many opportunities to play them all. Display an alphabet chart on a classroom wall for students' reference as they use the games and activities to reinforce their alphabet skills.

1 **Alphabet Corner** Set up an alphabet corner in your classroom. Stock it with letters to trace, plastic letters for word building, alphabet stamps, alphabet puzzles and games, picture cards, alphabet books from your library, materials to make letters (pipe cleaners, glue, stencils), alphabet flash cards, dry-erase boards or mini-chalkboards, alphabet audio files and player, clay, paints, and any other materials you want to include. Allow children time to explore and use the materials in the Alphabet Corner throughout the week.

2 **Alphabet Concentration** This classic game can be played with almost any skill. Limiting the game to 8–12 cards, make a set of letter cards—one letter to a card, two cards for each letter. Place the cards facedown on the desk, table, or floor. Have children turn over two cards at a time. If the cards match, children keep them. The object of the game is to make as many matches as possible. You can have children match uppercase letters only, lowercase letters only, or a mix of upper- and lowercase letters.

3 **Touch It** Provide each letter being studied in a variety of forms (magnetic, foam, and sandpaper letters) for children to trace. To give children a fun way to form their own letters, place hair styling gel (add food coloring to clear gel) in small plastic bags that can be zipped shut. Children will delight in forming the letter they're learning by writing it with their fingers on the outside of the bag. They can then "erase" the letter and continue with other letters.

4 **Name Scramble** Have children use letter cards to spell their names. Then have them scramble the cards and re-form their names. Next have each child ask a classmate to unscramble his or her name. Make sure the student's name card is on the desk for reference. When the name is formed, ask the student to identify each letter in the classmate's name. **Tip:** Some children might need a support clue to help them

remember the correct orientation of each letter. For them, draw a small red dot in the upper right-hand corner of each letter card. Point out that this dot tells where the top of the letter card is.

**5** **Sign Up** To practice writing letters, have children write their names on a large sheet of paper when you take attendance, when they sign out a book from the classroom library, or when they get a restroom pass. Or ask children to write the "letter of the day" on a large sheet of paper for some predetermined purpose, such as lining up for lunch. Provide crayons and markers of many colors. Collect the pages to form an alphabet Big Book.

**6** **Match It** Distribute letter cards, one card per student. Then write a letter on the board. Ask the children whose cards match the letter to step to the front of the classroom. Have a volunteer name the letter and review the sound that the letter represents. Provide feedback such as, "That's right. That's the letter *s* as in *sun*. It stands for the /s/ sound."

**7** **Singled Out** Write on the board a CVC (consonant-vowel-consonant) word that children have recently encountered in a story. Say the name of one letter in the word and invite a volunteer to circle that letter. Review the sound that the letter stands for. Ask children if it is the beginning, middle, or ending sound of the word.

**8** **Let's Go on a Hunt** Write the upper- and lowercase forms of each letter on large note cards. Distribute one note card to each child. Have children find their letter in magazines and newspapers. Suggest that they cut them out and paste them to the back of the card. They might also want to add pictures whose names begin with the sound that the letter represents.

**9** **Round 'em Up** Write a letter on the board in red or some other distinguishing color. Then write a series of letters beside it in yellow or white chalk. Many of the letters should be the same as the one written in red. Ask volunteers to circle the letters that are the same as the one in red. As each letter is circled, have the class state the name of the letter. Finally, have the class count the number of letters circled. Example:

*s   s   t   s   s   s   m   s*

**10** **Word Roundup** Write a series of simple words on the board. Most of the words should begin with the same sound. Read the words aloud. Then have volunteers circle the words that begin with the same letter. Example:

*sat    sun    sad    top    sick    mop*

**11** **Alphabet Walk** Take children on a walk around the school or neighborhood. Have them look for, and identify, learned letters in environmental print.

**12** **Word Pairs** Write a word pair on the board, such as *sat* and *mat*. Read the words aloud. Ask children to identify the letter that is different in each word.

**13** **Hide-and-Seek** Hide letter cards throughout the classroom. Have children search the room for them. When each child has found a card, he or she can return to his or her seat. Then have children share the letter on the card they found as they write it on the board.

**14** **Through-the-Year Alphabet Book** Have children use large sheets of colored construction paper to create a personal alphabet book throughout the year. They should write the upper- and lowercase forms of each letter on one page, then paste or draw pictures of objects whose names begin with the sound the letter stands for and add words that begin with that letter.

**15** **Body Letters** Divide the class into groups of three to five students. Assign each group a letter to form with their bodies. They might form the letter individually (each child forming it), or use the entire group to form it (four children might lie on the floor to form the letter *E*).

**16** **Letter Path** Create a construction paper "stone" path around the classroom with one letter written on each stone. Laminate the stones for durability. Have children "walk the alphabet" each day, saying aloud each letter (or letter and sound) name. **Variation:** As you call letters, have children stand on the appropriate stones.

**17** **Disappearing Letters** Using a small, wet sponge, write a letter on the board. Challenge children to identify the letter before it disappears. Have children sponge on letters for classmates to identify.

**18** **Letter Snacks** As you introduce a letter, choose a snack whose name begins with or contains the sound the letter stands for. This yummy treat will serve as a memory device to help children associate the letter with its sound. Following are snack possibilities for most of the letters. **Note:** Choose whether you will introduce the long- or short-vowel sounds first, and be consistent with your snacks. You might have to choose snacks with names that contain a particular vowel sound in the middle.

| apples/cake | ice cream, dip | raisins |
|---|---|---|
| bananas | Jell-O™/juice | soup/salad |
| carrots/cookies | Kool-aid™ | toast/tacos |
| donuts | lemonade | upside-down cake |
| eggs/green beans | milk | vegetables |
| fish crackers | noodles/nachos | watermelon |
| gum | oatmeal cookies | yogurt |
| hamburgers | pizza/peaches | zucchini bread |

**19** **Alphabet Partner** Divide the number of children in your classroom in half. Use this number to determine the number of letters you will use to make a letter card set. The letter card set should contain two cards for each letter—one uppercase, one lowercase. Then give each child a card. Have children find their upper- or lowercase match.

**20** **Tongue-Depressor Alphabets** On each of a set of tongue depressors write one letter. Have children arrange the tongue depressors in alphabetical order. **Variation:** Write words for children to alphabetize on the tongue depressors.

**21** **Alphabet Caterpillar** Children will have fun creating this letter-perfect creature. Write each letter of the alphabet on a paper circle. Mix the circles and spread them out on the table or floor. Have children work in pairs or small groups to form the caterpillar by placing its body parts (circles) in alphabetical order. Attach antennae to the *A* circle for the caterpillar's head.

**22** **Connect the Dots** Gather pages of connect-the-dot pictures from children's activity books and laminate them. Children can use a wipe-off marker to connect the dots and form the picture. **Variations:** (1) Make multiple copies of each page to keep in a learning center. (2) Create your own connect-the-dot pictures by lightly tracing over pictures in workbooks or coloring books with a pencil and placing dots at intervals along the outline with a pen or marker. Then assign a letter to each dot in the order in which it should be connected. Add any connecting lines, such as curves, necessary to complete the picture, erase your tracing, and photocopy the page.

**23** **Letter Pop-up** Distribute letter cards, one or two per child. Call out a letter. The children holding that letter's cards should pop up from their seats and hold up their cards so you can quickly check for accuracy.

**24** **Moon and Stars** Using construction paper, cut out 26 stars and 26 crescent moons. On each moon, write an uppercase letter. On each star, write a lowercase letter. Have children match the moons and stars. **Variation:** Use other objects that might go together—chicken and egg, dog and doghouse, leaf and tree.

**25** **Special Name Day** Write children's names on note cards and place them in a decorated box or can. Each day, choose one name, which will be the "special name of the day." Spend time having the class identify each letter in the chosen name, write the name on a sheet of paper, group the name with names selected from previous days (for example, by first letter, by boy and girl names, and so on), clap the number of syllables in the name, add the name to a name book organized in alphabetical order, and count the number of letters in the name.

**26** **Play With Names** Have children write their names in various ways. For example, ask them to write their names using only uppercase letters, using pipe cleaners and glue, or using clay.

**27** **ABC Time** Distribute a set of letter cards, one card per student. Say a series of three or four letters. Have the children holding a matching letter card come to the front of the classroom as their letters are called. Then have the group of three or four children holding the cards place themselves in alphabetical order. The rest of the class can offer feedback and determine the group's accuracy.

**28** **Word Wheel** Create a spinning wheel using two cardboard circles of different sizes and a brass fastener. On the outside of one wheel (circle) write the uppercase letters; on the other write the lowercase letters. Then punch a hole in the center of each wheel and attach them using the fastener. Children will spin the top wheel to match upper- and lowercase letters.

**29** **Classroom Labels** As you teach each letter of the alphabet, add labels to objects in your classroom whose names begin with the sound the letter stands for. Invite volunteers to suggest objects to label.

**30** **Alphabet Spin** Write the uppercase letters on a spinner and the lowercase letters on note cards, one to a card. Have small groups of children take turns spinning the spinner, identifying the letter, and finding the letter match in the card pile. Use a timer to make the game more engaging. Decrease the amount of time allowed to find the matching card after each round.

**31** **Alphabet Tic-Tac-Toe** This form of tic-tac-toe is played like the regular game—with one exception. Here, each child is assigned a different letter. Pairs of students play the game using their assigned letters. When most pairs have finished, assign new letters and continue play.

**32** **Alphabet Book Audio** Make an audio recording of an alphabet book to place in a learning center or take-home activity pack. After reading the text for each page (or series of pages), give activity directions ("Find the letter *s* on page 22. Point to it and say *s*. Write the letter with your finger. Next, find the picture of the sun. The word *sun* begins with the letter *s*. The letter *s* stands for the /s/ sound. Say /s/. That's right— sssssssss!")

**33** **Newspaper Search** Distribute a few pages of an old newspaper to each child and assign each a letter. Have the child circle the letter every time it appears on the page. You might want to have children stop after finding five occurrences of the letter.

The blockbuster quality is still there. A huge pile of red silk flowers dominates the stage. When the entire hill is pushed perilously close to the audience in pursuit of a man who escapes up the aisle, the effect is as amazing as when a geyser of flowers becomes the visual equivalent of the fireworks

**34** **Letter Actions** Teach children an action for each letter they learn. As you introduce the letter, model the action and have children perform it. In later weeks, tell children you will hold up a letter card, and they should perform or pantomime the action associated with the letter shown. Here are some possible actions (Cunningham, 1995).

### All the Right Moves

| | | | | |
|--------|--------|--------|--------|------|
| bounce | gallop | laugh  | run    | walk |
| catch  | hop    | march  | sit    | yawn |
| dance  | jump   | nod    | talk   | zip  |
| fall   | kick   | paint  | vacuum |      |

**35** **Alphabet Cereal Sort** Place a pile of alphabet cereal on a napkin on each child's desk. Give children time to sort the cereal letters. Have them count the number of times they found each letter. Use these tallies to create a class chart. Children will enjoy a tasty letter treat when the activity is completed.

---

**TRY IT OUT**

- Select one activity from the "35 Quick and Easy Activities for Developing Alphabet Recognition" to try out with your students.
- Assess your students to determine what stage of reading development each is in. Ask yourself, "How does that compare to the reading demands each child encounters? What can I do to move each child to the next stage of reading development?"
- Assess five students using the Letter-Name Assessment and Letter-Sound Assessment. Compare their speed and accuracy scores with their reading level.

---

# Phonemic Awareness: Playing With Sounds

**Phonemic awareness** is the understanding or insight that a word is made up of a series of discrete (separate) sounds. Each of these sounds is called a *phoneme*. This awareness includes the ability to pick out and manipulate sounds in spoken words. A related term, often confused with phonemic awareness, is *phonological awareness*. **Phonological awareness** is an umbrella term that includes phonemic awareness, or awareness of words at the phoneme level. It also includes an awareness of word units larger than the phoneme. Phonological awareness includes the following (Eldredge, 1995):

- words within sentences
- rhyming units within words
- beginning and ending sounds within words
- syllables within words
- phonemes, or sounds, within words (phonemic awareness)
- features of individual phonemes such as how the mouth, tongue, vocal cords, and teeth are used to produce the sound

Phonemic awareness is not the same thing as phonics. Phonemic awareness deals with sounds in spoken words, whereas phonics involves the relationship between sounds and written symbols. Phonics deals with learning sound-spelling relationships and is associated with print.

Most phonemic-awareness tasks are purely oral. However, recent research shows that the combination of letter work and phonemic awareness is quite powerful.

According to Adams (1990), there are five basic types of phonemic-awareness tasks or abilities. Each task type includes activities that become progressively more complex. Although some of the tasks can be more accurately labeled phonological-awareness tasks, the goal of most of them is awareness at the phoneme level. These task types and sample activities include the following:

## Task 1—Rhyme and Alliteration

1. **Rhyme**
   Example: I once saw a <u>cat</u>, sitting next to a <u>dog</u>. I once saw a <u>bat</u>, sitting next to a <u>frog</u>.
2. **Alliteration**
   Example: <u>S</u>ix <u>s</u>nakes <u>s</u>ell <u>s</u>odas and <u>s</u>nacks.
3. **Assonance**
   Example: The l<u>ea</u>f, the b<u>ea</u>n, the p<u>ea</u>ch—all were within r<u>ea</u>ch.

## Task 2—Oddity Tasks (phoneme categorization)

1. **Rhyme**
   Example: Which word does not rhyme: *cat, sat, pig? (pig)*
2. **Beginning consonants**
   Example: Which two words begin with the same sound:
   *man, sat, sick? (sat, sick)*
3. **Ending consonants**
   Example: Which two words end with the same sound:
   *man, sat, ten? (man, ten)*
4. **Medial sounds (long vowels)**
   Example: Which word does not have the same middle sound:
   *take, late, feet? (feet)*
5. **Medial sounds (short vowels)**
   Example: Which two words have the same middle sound:
   *top, cat, pan? (cat, pan)*
6. **Medial sounds (consonants)**
   Example: Which two words have the same middle sound:
   *kitten, missing, lesson? (missing, lesson)*

## Task 3—Oral Blending

1. **Syllables**
   Example: Listen to these word parts: *ta . . . ble.*
            Say the word as a whole. What's the word? *(table)*
2. **Onset/rime**
   Example: Listen to these word parts: */p/. . . an.*
            Say the word as a whole. What's the word? *(pan)*
3. **Phoneme by phoneme**
   Example: Listen to these word parts:/s/ /a/ /t/.
            Say the word as a whole. What's the word? *(sat)*

## Task 4—Oral Segmentation (including counting sounds)

1. **Syllables**
   Example: Listen to this word: *table.*
            Say it syllable by syllable. *(ta . . . ble)*
2. **Onset/rime**
   Example: Listen to this word: *pan.* Say the first sound
            in the word and then the rest of the word. *(/p/. . . an)*
3. **Phoneme by phoneme (counting sounds)**
   Example: Listen to this word: *sat.* Say the word sound by sound.
            *(/s/ /a/ /t/)* How many sounds do you hear? *(3)*

## Task 5—Phoneme Manipulation*

1. **Initial sound substitution**
   Example: Replace the first sound in *mat* with /s/. *(sat)*
2. **Final sound substitution**
   Example: Replace the last sound in *mat* with /p/. *(map)*
3. **Vowel substitution**
   Example: Replace the middle sound in *map* with /o/. *(mop)*
4. **Syllable deletion**
   Example: Say *baker* without the *ba*. *(ker)*
5. **Initial sound deletion**
   Example: Say *sun* without the /s/. *(un)*
6. **Final sound deletion**
   Example: Say *hit* without the /t/. *(hi)*
7. **Initial phoneme in a blend deletion**
   Example: Say *step* without the /s/. *(tep)*
8. **Final phoneme in a blend deletion**
   Example: Say *best* without the /t/. *(bes)*
9. **Second phoneme in a blend deletion**
   Example: Say *frog* without the /r/. *(fog)*

* These tasks are best done using letter cards.

## Tips on Sequencing Phonemic Awareness Instruction

- The first four phonemic-awareness task types should be a part of the kindergarten curriculum, although not all children will master all the task types.
- Rhyming, alliteration, and oddity task activities (with picture clues) are relatively easy for kindergartners. Most children are able to complete rhyming and alliteration tasks by the age of five; some children can do these tasks as early as age three (Maclean, Bryant, & Bradley, 1987).
- Recent research states that "focusing early phonemic-awareness instruction on blending, segmenting, and manipulating phonemes has been shown to produce greater improvements in phonemic awareness and future reading achievement in young children than time spent on rhyming and alliteration" (Reutzel, 2015; Yeh & Connell, 2008). Although rhyme and alliteration activities and associated books are plentiful and loads of fun, the instructional benefit isn't as strong as devoting the majority of instructional time to working with words at the phoneme, or sound, level.
- Segmenting words sound by sound (phoneme counting) is critical for spelling words, and approximately 70% of children acquire the skill by the end of first grade (age six) (Mann, 1991).
- Phonemic manipulation tasks are more complex. Many of these tasks are difficult even for second graders, though some kindergartners can master some of the easier phoneme-deletion tasks (Task 5: 4 and 5) (Treiman, 1992). However, I recommend focusing on these tasks no earlier than middle first grade.
- Note that it's not essential for students to master each task type before moving on to the next. Rather, a mix of appropriately sequenced activities throughout lessons keeps children engaged and provides ample practice with all types of phonemic-awareness tasks. However, instruction in oral blending (Task 3) should begin before instruction in oral segmentation (Task 4).

In addition to these five task types, phonemic-awareness exercises include phoneme discrimination (speech perception) activities, which also help children to focus on specific sounds in words. For example, you might ask students to listen for vowel sounds. Since vowel sounds are necessary for decoding, and children's early invented spellings often omit vowels, they'll need lots of practice in hearing and distinguishing these sounds in words.

The following chart represents a suggested scope and sequence for 20 weeks of instruction. The scope and sequence is designed for the second semester of kindergarten but can be modified for first grade.

| Skill | Scope and Sequence ● = 1 week | | | | | | | | | | | | | | | | | | | |
| --- | --- | --- | --- | --- | --- | --- | --- | --- | --- | --- | --- | --- | --- | --- | --- | --- | --- | --- | --- | --- |
| | Week 1 | Week 2 | Week 3 | Week 4 | Week 5 | Week 6 | Week 7 | Week 8 | Week 9 | Week 10 | Week 11 | Week 12 | Week 13 | Week 14 | Week 15 | Week 16 | Week 17 | Week 18 | Week 19 | Week 20 |
| Rhyme/Alliteration | ● | ● | ● | ● | ● | ● | ● | ● | ● | ● | ● | | | | | | | | | |
| Oddity Tasks | | | ● | ● | ● | ● | ● | ● | ● | ● | ● | ● | ● | | | | | | | |
| Oral Blending | | | | ● | ● | ● | ● | ● | ● | ● | ● | ● | ● | ● | ● | ● | ● | ● | ● | ● |
| Oral Segmentation | | | | | | | | ● | ● | ● | ● | ● | ● | ● | ● | ● | ● | ● | ● | ● |
| Phonemic Manipulation | | | | | | | | | | | | | | | | | ● | ● | ● | ● |
| Linking Sounds to Spellings | | | | | | | | | | | | | | | | | | | ● | ● |

# Articulation

Articulation exercises help children attend to the differences in mouth formation when making sounds. Research has shown that these exercises assist children in orally segmenting words and in spelling (Castiglioni-Spalten & Ehri, 2003). They are also effective with English-language learners as they help these learners focus on the unique and subtle differences in the sounds of English. See the charts on pages 52 and 53.

# Consonant Sounds Mouth Position Chart

**/t/** t
**/d/** d
**/n/** n
**/l/** l

(tongue pressed against roof of mouth behind top teeth)

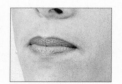

**/p/** p
**/b/** b
**/m/** m

(lips closed)

**/k/** k
**/g/** g

(tongue pressed against bottom of mouth)

**/th/** th

(tongue between teeth)

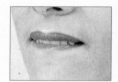

**/f/** f
**/v/** v

(top teeth on bottom lip)

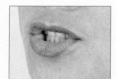

**/ch/** ch
**/j/** j
**/sh/** sh

(lips stuck out)

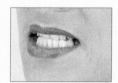

**/s/** s
**/z/** z

(teeth together, lips apart)

The 25 consonant phonemes on the chart below are "closed" sounds in the English language—those that are made with some obstruction of the air stream during speech production. They are grouped by their place and manner of articulation. Phonemes that are produced similarly tend to be more confusable than phonemes that are pronounced differently. Many children need direct instruction to learn to identify of these sounds, the letters that represent them, and a key word that has the sound in it.

|  | Lips | Lips/Teeth | Tongue Between Teeth | Tongue Behind Teeth | Roof of Mouth | Back of Mouth | Throat |
|---|---|---|---|---|---|---|---|
| **stop** | /p/ /b/ | | | /t/ /d/ | | /k/ /g/ | |
| **nasal** | /m/ | | | /n/ | | /ng/ | |
| **fricative** | | /f/ /v/ | /th/ /th/ | /s/ /z/ | /sh/ /zh/ | | |
| **affricative** | | | | | /ch/ /j/ | | |
| **glide** | | | | | /y/ | /hw/ /w/ | /h/ |
| **liquid** | | | | /l/ | /r/ | | |

# Vowel Sounds Mouth Position Chart

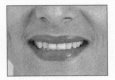

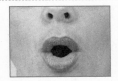

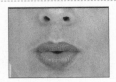

**Smile Sound**

The long-*e* sound is a "smile sound." We look like we are smiling when we say this sound. The lips are close together, but not closed. Ask children to say the sound with you, noticing your mouth position. Have children place their hand under the chin as they say each of the following sounds in sequence: /ē/, /i/, /e/, /a/, /ī/, and /o/. Help them to notice how their mouth opens slightly with each sound.

**Doctor Sound**

The short-*o* sound is an "open sound." The lips form a circle. Ask children to say the sound with you, noticing your mouth position. Remind them that the letter *o* stands for the /o/ sound. When making this sound, your mouth is in the shape of an *o*. The sound you make is the same as when you are at the doctor's office and he is checking your tonsils.

**Surprise Sound**

The /o͞o/ sound is a "surprise sound." This is the sound you make when you see fireworks on the Fourth of July. The lips are close together and oval in shape. Have children practice the sound as they look in a mirror. Help them to notice how their mouth opens a bit as they move from the /o͞o/ sound to the /o/ sound.

Vowels are a class of open speech sounds that are not consonants. Every syllable in English has a vowel sound. The 15 vowels on this chart (excluding the *r*-controlled vowels on the lower right) are arranged by place of articulation, from high, roof of mouth to the front position at the top of the mouth. Say them in order, looking in a mirror, to feel how the mouth position shifts one step at a time. The diphthongs /oi/ and /ou/ are separate because they glide in the middle and do not have one place of articulation. Most linguists also consider the long-*i* sound a diphthong.

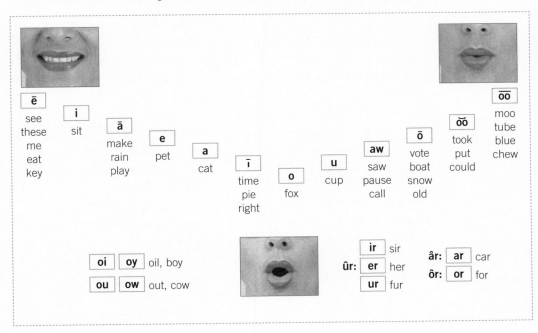

# Why Phonemic Awareness Is Important

Children sometimes come to school unaware that words consist of a series of discrete sounds. Phonemic-awareness activities help them learn to distinguish individual sounds, or phonemes, within words. They need this skill in order to associate sounds with letters and manipulate sounds to blend words (during reading) or segment words (during spelling). "It is unlikely that children lacking phonemic awareness can benefit fully from phonics instruction since they do not understand what letters and spellings are supposed to represent" (Juel, Griffith, & Gough, 1986).

Many children have difficulties with phonics instruction because they haven't developed the prerequisite phonemic-awareness skills that other children gain through years of exposure to rhymes and songs and being read to. Phonemic-awareness training provides the foundation on which phonics instruction is built. "Children who begin school with little phonemic awareness will have trouble acquiring the alphabetic principle, which will, in turn, limit their ability to decode words" (Ball & Blachman, 1991).

Thus, children need solid phonemic-awareness training for phonics instruction to be effective. For example, phonics instruction that begins by asking a child what sound the words *sit, sand,* and *sock* have in common won't make sense to a child who has difficulty discriminating sounds in words, cannot segment sounds within words, or does not understand what is meant by the term *sound*. Children must be able to segment and auditorily discriminate /s/ in the words *sit, sand,* and *sock* before it makes sense to them that the letter *s* stands for this sound in these written words. In addition, children must be able to segment the sounds in a word such as *sit* (/s/ /i/ /t/) in order to spell the word. Once children gain a basic level of phonemic awareness, and formal reading instruction begins, this instruction increases children's awareness of language. "Thus, phonemic awareness is both a prerequisite for and a consequence of learning to read" (Yopp, 1992).

Research indicates that approximately 20% of children lack phonemic awareness (Shankweiler & Liberman, 1989). Without early preventive measures, many of these children end up being labeled learning disabled or dyslexic and continue to fall behind their peers in reading development (Snider, 1995). They'll be forced to rely on memorizing words rather than fully analyzing them, which quickly becomes cumbersome and inefficient. In addition, these struggling readers tend to read less, have less exposure to words, and are less likely to memorize a large number of these words—further complicating their reading difficulties. However, this doesn't have to be the scenario. Promising phonemic-awareness training studies have revealed two important points:

1. Phonemic awareness can be taught.
2. It doesn't take a great deal of time to bring many children's phonemic-awareness abilities up to a level at which phonics instruction begins to make sense to them.

In fact, some studies (Honig, 1995) have shown that as few as 11–15 hours of intensive phonemic-awareness training spread out over an appropriate time period produces results. Overall, a number of studies have shown that training in phonemic awareness has important effects on children's ability to master word-reading skills (Ball & Blachman, 1991; Fox & Routh, 1975; Torgesen, Morgan, & Davis, 1992). Alexander et al. (1991) showed how intensive phonemic-awareness instruction helped a group of children with severe reading disabilities achieve average levels of reading abilities. "The purpose of training is to help children respond to reading instruction more effectively. Specifically, it helps children understand how spoken language is represented by the alphabetic system" (Torgesen & Bryant, 1994). The goal is awareness of how words work. Therefore it is unnecessary to spend a lot of instructional time on phonemic awareness once children have a solid understanding of how to blend and segment words.

\* One special note: When children begin learning letter-sound relationships, combining phonemic awareness and phonics work can accelerate children's progress (Ehri, 2005). One example of this is including word-building exercises in weekly instruction.

# How to Assess Phonemic Awareness

I suggest that phonemic-awareness assessment begin in midyear kindergarten and continue throughout the elementary grades. Use the assessment online (see page 320 for details on how to access) or give one of the following commercially available assessments.

This Phonemic Awareness Assessment can be found online as Resource 2.3. See page 320 for details on how to access.

- Lindamood Auditory Conceptualization Test in Lindamood and Lindamood (3rd Edition, Pro-Ed)

- Test of Auditory Analysis Skills in Rosner (1993)
- Test of Phonological Awareness—Second Edition: Plus (TOPA-2+) (Torgesen & Bryant, 2004)
- Yopp-Singer Test of Phonemic Awareness in Yopp (1995)
- DIBELS (Dynamic Indicators of Basic Early Literacy Skills). Go to http://dibels.uoregon.edu or www.soprisWest.com.

# Phonemic Awareness and Writing

In addition to formal assessments, you can assess students' developing phonemic-awareness abilities through their writings. When children write they practice many of the skills important to reading (Clay, 1985). My students' writings have provided me with some of my most valuable assessment information. Not only do these writings reveal the sound-spelling relationships that the children have learned, they show how, or if, they are segmenting words. I can use this information to tailor my instruction in the areas of phonics and phonemic awareness. Lots of opportunities to write using inventive spellings can benefit children with weak phonemic-awareness skills because when they write, children have to turn spoken language into written language (Griffith & Klesius, 1992). The more children practice writing and receive instruction in mapping sounds to spellings, the better they can become at segmenting sounds in words (Griffith & Olson, 1992).

Researchers Mann, Tobin, and Wilson (1987) developed a system for scoring kindergartners' inventive spellings. They dictated a list of words for children to spell, then gave each word a score from 1 to 4 based on the correctness of the child's attempts. For example, if the word *name* was dictated, the following scores would be given:

**4 points:** The word *name* is spelled in the conventionally correct way. (*name*)
**3 points:** The word *name* is spelled in a way that captures the entire phonological structure of the word. However, the word is not spelled in the conventional manner. (*nam*)
**2 points:** The word *name* is spelled in a way that captures part of the phonological structure of the word. (*na* or *nme*)
**1 point:** The word *name* is spelled in a way in which only the initial sound is shown. (*n*)

Mann, Tobin, and Wilson used the scores on this assessment to predict first-grade reading achievement. You might give a similar assessment to kindergartners in the middle of the year to determine which children need additional phonemic-awareness training. But keep in mind that a child's ability to spell words correctly also involves his or her knowledge of sound-spelling relationships. Therefore, any assessment of a child's early inventive spellings must take into account the sound-spelling relationships previously taught to that child. For example, if a child has not learned that the letter *t* stands for /t/, then a misspelling such as *dp* for the word *top* means more than the child is simply unable to segment the word.

Student samples showing inventive spellings

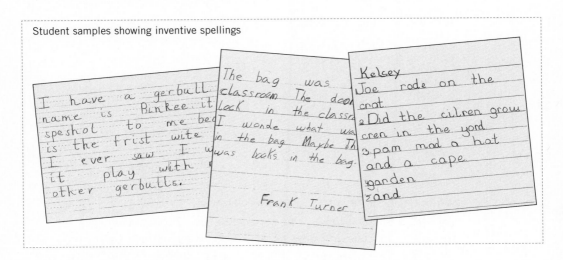

## How Inventive Spelling Fits In

Inventive spelling is a stage of spelling development. Whenever we, as adult skilled readers and writers, attempt to spell unfamiliar words, we rely on our abilities to segment words, sound by sound, and map a spelling onto each sound. This is inventive spelling. When students are writing their first draft of a story or informational paragraph, encourage them to try to spell each word they want to use. You don't want them to feel limited by their word choices because they are unsure of a word's spelling. Nevertheless, the goal is always to move children toward the use of standard spellings. Spelling words correctly is important and should be valued in the classroom. Attention to correct spelling in appropriate situations (such as writing final drafts, letters to people in the community, and so on) and direct instruction are the key to achieving this goal. You'll need to explain to parents the importance, and correct use, of inventive spelling. And make sure that students' work that you display in the classroom (that is, final drafts) reflects the highest standards, including correct spelling.

# Blevins Phonemic Awareness-Phonics Quick Assessment

Administer this quick spelling survey to your students during the first week of Grade 1. Read each word aloud and have students write it on their paper. Collect the papers and compare each child's answers to the rubric provided. The assessment can be used to determine a child's phonemic awareness and phonics needs and better inform you as you group students for small-group instruction.

**Form A**
1. sat
2. big
3. rake
4. coat
5. flower

**Form B**
1. sad
2. bit
3. rope
4. chain
5. grower

| Scoring Rubric | | | | | |
|---|---|---|---|---|---|
| 5 | 4 | 3 | 2 | | 1 |
| A | B | C | D | E | F |
| 1. sad | 1. sad | 1. sd | 1. S | 1. seivne | 1. ephah |
| 2. big | 2. bag | 2. bg | 2. B | 2. bog | 2. pebl |
| 3. rakce | 3. rak | 3. lk | 3. D | 3. rigvet | 3. ehplr |
| 4. cote | 4. kot | 4. kt | 4. F | 4. tetvai | 4. siehgt |
| 5. flowre | 5. flar | 5. fw | 5. F | 5. levneia | 5. cseph |

## Points to Consider

**Student A:** This child's spelling reveals strong phonemic-awareness and phonics skills. The use of the final *e* in the spellings for *rake* and *coat* reveal an advanced level of phonics. Since a child's spelling ability lags behind reading ability, this reveals that Student A can read words with final *e* and beyond. This assessment provided information on the types of reading materials appropriate for Student A and the spelling instruction necessary to move this child to the next level (for example, a focus on long-vowel spellings).

**Student B:** This child's spellings are typical of a child beginning Grade 1. This child has strong phonemic-awareness skills as evidenced by the spelling of *flower*, in which more letters are used to represent the increase in sounds (all the other words have three sounds).

**Student C:** This child's lack of attention to vowel sounds and spellings is also typical of many first graders. The use of Elkonin boxes (see page 60) to segment words by sound using counters along with minimal contrast reading practice, as shown below, will help this child progress.

I have a green _____ .    hot    hat    hit

**Students D–F:** These children have weak phonemic-awareness skills. They show no sense of providing more letters for more sounds in a word or any consistency in relating the sounds to letters. In addition, these children have weak phonics skills. Students D and E show some signs of initial sound knowledge. However, Student F uses primarily the letters in her name (Steph). These students are below level and will require immediate and intensive intervention to get back on track for reading success.

# Teaching Phonemic Awareness

Teaching phonemic awareness to children is one of my favorite classroom activities because the exercises are fun. Children delight in playing with language using rhymes, songs, word games, and puppets. In many ways, these activities are extensions of the language play many children had at home in their preschool years. Although children might think they're just having fun, phonemic-awareness exercises have an important place in your reading instruction and make nice warm-up activities at the beginning of your daily reading period. Research has shown that **explicit phonemic-awareness instruction increases reading and spelling achievement** among preschoolers, primary-grade children, and students with learning disabilities (Ball & Blachman, 1991; Lundberg, Frost, & Petersen, 1988; Yopp, 1992).

Most phonemic-awareness instructional activities are oral and provide an engaging way for children to discriminate the sounds that make up words. The two main types are oral blending and oral segmentation. I call these the "power skills" because they have the most impact on reading and writing growth.

**Oral blending** exercises help children hear how sounds are put together to make words. They prepare children to decode (sound out or blend) words independently. Children who have trouble blending words orally have trouble blending, or sounding out, words while they read. Oral blending exercises begin with blending larger word parts, such as syllables, and progress to blending onsets and rimes, and finally whole words sound by sound. The earliest oral blending exercises should use words that begin with continuous consonants (those that can be sustained without distortion) such as *s, m, l, f, r,* and *z*. This makes it easier for children to hear the distinct sounds and more efficient to model the principle of oral blending, because all the sounds in the words can be "sung" together in a more natural manner. For example, you can stretch out the word *sat* and sing it like this, *sssssssssaaaaaaaaat*. And you can add movements to help children notice when you go from one sound to the next as you say a word. Many children benefit from these visual cues.

**Oral segmentation** activities help children separate words into sounds. These exercises should begin with a focus on syllables, which are easier to distinguish than individual sounds. Segmentation activities prepare children for spelling, for which they begin segmenting words into their component sounds in order to write them. Children who can't orally segment words have difficulty breaking them apart in order to spell them. You can tell if a child is developing the necessary segmentation skills when he or she begins asking questions, such as, "What makes the /a/ sound in *cat*?" or "What makes the /sh/ sound in *shop*?"

Phonemic-awareness training, including oral blending and segmentation instruction, can have a significant impact on reading and writing development. And phonemic awareness continues to develop as phonics instruction begins. In fact, some aspects of phonemic awareness continue to develop through high school. Once a basic level of phonemic awareness is achieved and phonics instruction can be effective, the research shows that phonics and phonemic awareness enjoy a reciprocal relationship, benefiting from each other. Indeed, the combination of blending and segmenting sounds and learning sound-spelling relationships has proved to be very powerful.

Use Elkonin boxes, also known as sound boxes, to help children segment words (Elkonin, 1973). Begin by making sure children can stretch a word. For example, tell children that you want to stretch the word *sat* like a rubber band. Say *ssssaaat* as you move your hands in a stretching motion. Then tell children that you want to mark each sound in the word. To do so, you will stretch the word again. Then you will drag one counter onto each box on the Elkonin boxes as you move from sound to sound. Ask children to repeat using their Elkonin boxes and counters.

Sample Elkonin box for the word *sat*

## Some Ideas to Keep in Mind

**Don't stress written words or letters.** Even though a child can possess some level of phonemic awareness before knowing the alphabet, written words or letters should not be the focus of phonemic-awareness activities until he or she can readily identify the letters. But once children know the alphabet, these visual cues benefit many children. This generally happens in the second half of kindergarten. At this point, **the combination of phonemic awareness and phonics instruction is a powerful union** (Fox, 1996). Before that, using print may distract from the purposes of the activities or cause confusion for children.

**Keep the tone fun and informal.** Although the phonemic-awareness activities give you evaluative information about children's progress, avoid using the activities as assessments. It is important that children be engaged in playing with language, not concerned about being assessed. Respond favorably and enthusiastically to their attempts.

**Monitor each child's progress.** In small groups, all children can participate in and enjoy these language play activities. However, children progress through the phonemic-awareness activities at varying rates. Some catch on quickly; others do not. Continue informally to monitor children throughout the year. Watch for patterns of difficulty over time.

**Model, model, model!** Continually model for children how to accomplish the various phonemic-awareness tasks. And provide corrective feedback. Much of the learning occurs through this feedback. Following are some sample models for rhyming, oral blending, and substituting sounds (phonemic manipulation).

## Sample Phonemic-Awareness Teaching Models

**Rhyme Model:** Explain to students that rhyming words are words that have the same ending sounds, such as *pop* and *mop*. Model how to make a rhyme. For example, you might say, "The words *pop* and *mop* rhyme because they both end with /op/. Listen: /p/ . . . *op, pop*; /m/ . . . *op, mop*. I can make another word that rhymes with *pop* and *mop*. This word begins with /h/ and ends with /op/. It's *hop*. Can you make a word that rhymes with *pop* and *mop*?"

**Oral-Blending Model:** Model how to blend sounds into words. For example, you might say, "I'm going to say a word very slowly, sound by sound. Then I'll say the word a bit faster. Finally I'll say the word the way it is usually said. For example, if I hear the word parts /m/ /a/ /t/, I can blend them together like this: *mmmmmaaaaaat, mmaat, mat*."

Begin blending models with short CVC words (e.g., *sat, sun, map*) that start with continuous consonants, such as *m, s, l, f,* and *r*. To help children visually note when you change from sound to sound as you blend the word, add movements. For example, you might move your hands from right to left as you change from sound to sound. You might also want to point out the mouth position (lips, tongue) and throat vibration (if applicable) when making each sound.

**Phonemic Manipulation Model:** Model how to substitute a sound and make a new word. For example, explain to children that you are going to take a word and make new words using it. You might say, "I can make a new word. I can take the /s/ off *sit*, put on a /p/, and I have a new word—*pit*. Can you take the /s/ off *sat* and put on a /m/ to make a new word? What is the new word?" *(mat)* Note: Model with letter cards.

**Keep assessing phonemic awareness.** Most poor readers—whatever their grade level—have weak phonological sensitivity (phonemic-awareness skills), which may be standing in the way of their becoming good readers and writers. So intermediate-level teachers should be aware of the importance of phonemic awareness, assess the skills of their poor readers, and provide any needed training.

**Provide lots and lots of language experiences.** Nothing can take the place of reading, writing, and listening to stories in an early literacy program. So whatever you do with phonemic awareness, do it within the context of a print-rich environment with multiple language experiences.

### Commercial Training Programs

Children with weak phonemic-awareness skills benefit from a complete phonemic-awareness training program. If your reading program is not as strong as you'd like in phonemic awareness, you might want to integrate one of the handful of commercially available training programs that focus on these skills. These are:

- *Auditory Discrimination in Depth/Lindamood Phonemic Sequencing* developed by C. H. Lindamood and P. C. Lindamood. Allen, TX: DLM/Teaching Resources Corporation, 2007.
- *Phonological Awareness Training for Reading* developed by Joseph K. Torgesen and Brian R. Bryant. Austin, TX: PROD-ED, Inc., 2013.
- *Sound Foundations* developed by B. Byrne and R. Fielding-Barnsley. Artarmon, New South Wales, Australia: Leyden Educational Publishers, 1991.
- *Sound and Letter Time* written by Michal Rosenberg and Wiley Blevins. New York: Scholastic, 2006.

# Using Literature to Develop Phonemic Awareness

One of the easiest and most accessible ways to improve children's sensitivity to the phonemes that make up our language is to use children's books that play with speech sounds through rhyme, alliteration, assonance, and phonemic manipulation (Griffith & Olson, 1992; Yopp, 1995). Use classroom collections of rhymes or any trade books that spotlight these skills. The following books are excellent resources. Read and reread the books so that children can enjoy their playful language. While reading the books, discuss the language. For example, you might comment on words that rhyme or a series of words that begin with the same sound. Many of the books can be extended by having children create additional rhyming verses or writing another version of the story, using rhyme or alliteration.

## Books With Rhyme

*Bears on the Stairs: A Beginner's Book of Rhymes* by Muriel and Lionel Kalish (Scholastic)

*Buzz Said the Bee* by Wendy Cheyette Lewison (Scholastic)

*Carrot/Parrot* by Jerome Martin (Simon & Schuster)

*Chicken Soup with Rice* by Maurice Sendak (Scholastic)

*Each Peach Pear Plum* by Janet and Allan Ahlberg (Puffin Books)

*A Giraffe and a Half* by Shel Silverstein (HarperCollins)

*Giraffes Can't Dance* by Giles Andreae (Cartwheel Books)

*Hop on Pop* by Dr. Seuss (Random House)

*How Big Is a Pig?* by Claire Beaton (Barefoot)

*Hunches in Bunches* by Dr. Seuss (Random House)

*The Hungry Thing* by Jan Slepian and Ann Seidler (Scholastic)

*I Can Fly* by Ruth Krauss (Western Publishing)

*"I Can't" Said the Ant* by Polly Cameron (Scholastic)

*I Saw You in the Bathtub* by Alvin Schwartz (HarperCollins)

*Is Your Mama a Llama?* by Deborah Guarino (Scholastic)

*It Does Not Say Meow and Other Animal Riddle Rhymes* by Beatrice Schenk de Regniers (Houghton Mifflin)

*Jamberry* by Bruce Degen (Harper & Row)

*Llama Llama Red Pajama* by Anna Dewdney (Viking)

*Miss Mary Mack and Other Children's Street Rhymes* by Joanna Cole and Stephanie Calmenson (Morrouno)

*One Duck Stuck* by Phyllis Root (Candlewick)

*101 Jump-Rope Rhymes* by Joanna Cole (Scholastic)

*The Random House Book of Poetry for Children* (Random House)

*Sheep in a Jeep* by Nancy Shaw (Houghton Mifflin)

*Sing a Song of Popcorn* by Beatrice Schenk de Regniers, Eva Moore, Mary Michaels White, and Jan Carr (Scholastic)

*Street Rhymes Around the World* by Jane Yolen (Wordsong)

*Yours Till Banana Splits: 201 Autograph Rhymes* by Joanna Cole and Stephanie Calmenson (Beech Tree)

## Books With Alliteration

*A, My Name Is Alice* by Jane Bayer (Dial)

*All About Arthur (an absolutely absurd ape)* by Eric Carle (Franklin Watts)

*Alphabears* by Kathleen Hague (Henry Holt)

*Aster Aardvark's Alphabet Adventures* by Steven Kellogg (Morrow)

*Busy Buzzing Bumblebees and Other Tongue Twisters* by Alvin Schwartz (Harper & Row)

*Dr. Seuss's ABC* by Dr. Seuss (Random House)

*Faint Frogs Feeling Feverish and Other Terrifically Tantalizing Tongue Twisters* by Lillian Obligade (Viking)

*K Is for Kissing a Cool Kangaroo* by Giles Andreae (Scholastic)

*M Is for Mischief: An A to Z of Naughty Children* by Linda Ashman (Dutton)

*Six Sick Sheep: 101 Tongue Twisters* by Joanna Cole and Stephanie Calmenson (Beech Tree)

*Some Smug Slug* by Pamela Duncan Edwards (Katherine Tegen Books)

## Books With Phonemic Manipulation

*Andy (That's My Name)* by Tomie de Paola (Aladdin)

*The Cow That Went Oink* by Bernard Most (Harcourt)

*Don't Forget the Bacon* by Pat Hutchins (Morrow)

*There's a Wocket in My Pocket* by Dr. Seuss (Random House)

*Zoomerang a Boomerang: Poems to Make Your Belly Laugh* by Caroline Parry (Puffin Books)

For additional books, see "Read-Aloud Books for Developing Phonemic Awareness: An Annotated Bibliography" by Hallie Kay Yopp. *The Reading Teacher* 48, no. 6, March 1995.

# 35 Quick and Easy Activities for Developing Phonemic Awareness

## Activities to Develop Rhyme and Alliteration

**1 Favorite Rhyme** Write a favorite rhyme on chart paper. Read it aloud as you track the print. Reread the rhyme doing one or all of the following:

- Have children point out the rhyming words in the poem. Then frame the rhyming words as you reread the poem. Now have children clap every time you read one of the rhyming words. In later readings, pause before the rhyming words and let children provide them.
- Substitute poem words. For example, using a sticky note, substitute the first word in a rhyming pair. Children then suggest a rhyming word to replace the second word in the pair. Write the word on a sticky note and place it in the appropriate place in the poem. Help children read the "new" poem.
- Have children clap the rhythm of the poem as you read it aloud.
- Have children substitute the syllable *la* for every syllable they hear in the poem.

**2 Do You Know?** Write the song "Do You Know?" (below) on chart paper. Sing it to the tune of "Muffin Man." Track the print as you sing. Sing the song several times, asking children to suggest one-syllable rhyming words to replace the words *king* and *ring*. Write the words on sticky notes and place them in the appropriate places in the song.

### Do You Know?
Do you know two rhyming words,
Two rhyming words,
Two rhyming words?
Oh, do you know two rhyming words?
They sound a lot alike.

King and ring are two rhyming words,
Two rhyming words,
Two rhyming words.
King and ring are two rhyming words.
They sound a lot alike.

**3** **Extend the Rhyme** Explain to children that you're going to say aloud three rhyming words (such as *cat, hat*, and *sat*). Tell them you want them to listen carefully to the words and then suggest other words that rhyme with those words. For example, children might respond with *bat, fat, mat*, and *pat*. Continue with other sets of rhyming words.

**4** **Create a Rhyme** Using the following incomplete poem, have students create rhymes by suggesting words to fill in each blank. Write the words they suggest on sticky notes and place them in the rhyme. Then help the class to read the rhyme they created. You can do the same activity with rhymes from your classroom collection. Write the rhyme on chart paper, replacing the second word in a rhyming pair with a blank.

> **Once I Saw**
> Once I saw a cat,
> And it wore a funny little _____.
> Tra-la-la, la-la-la-la-la-la
> Silly little cat.
>
> Once I saw a goat,
> And it wore a funny little _____.
> Tra-la-la, la-la-la-la-la-la
> Silly little goat.

**5** **Round-Robin Rhyme** Invite children to sit in a circle. Tell them that you're going on an imaginary trip. Explain that you will tell them one item that you want to take on the trip and they are to take turns repeating that item name and then name another item that rhymes. For example, if you say, "I'm going to the park, and I'm taking a *mat*," the next child in the circle might say, "I'm going to the park, and I'm taking a *mat* and a *hat*." Continue around the circle until children run out of items with rhyming names. **Variation:** Have children say aloud items whose names begin with the same sound. For example, "I'm going to the park, and I'm taking a *ball*, a *bat*, a *basket*, a *blanket*, and a *banana*."

**6** **Picture Rhyme** Have children each fold a piece of paper in half. Ask them to draw pictures of two things whose names rhyme. For example, a hat and a bat. Help children label the pictures with the items' names. Gather the drawings and bind them into a rhyme book for the class library. **Tip:** Provide children who are struggling with this activity with the name of one item to draw, such as a *star, pan, pig, pen*, or *coat*. Then have them come up with the second item.

**7** **Rhyme Book** Paste a different picture at the top of enough pages for each child in the class. Pass out the pages and have each child draw (or find in a magazine) a picture of an object whose name rhymes with the picture on his or her page. Then gather the pictures and bind them into a class book.

**8** **Silly Sentences** Help children create silly alliterative sentences. For example, "Six snakes sell sodas." Create an alliteration book using the sentences and have each child illustrate his or her sentence.

## Oddity Task Activities

**9** **Picture Cards** Make a set of picture cards (pictures only, no words) using index cards and drawings or magazine pictures. (Picture cards are particularly helpful for younger children. The visual cues allow them to think about the sounds in words without having to store a lot of information in their memory.) Then display a picture card set such as the following: fan, feet, man, mop, six, soap. Mix the cards and have volunteers pick the two cards whose picture names begin with the same sound. When two cards are selected, say aloud the name of each picture and ask children to tell you what sound each begins with. Then have children suggest other words that begin with the same sound as the two picture names. **Variations:** You can also use picture cards for distinguishing rhymes, ending consonant sounds, and medial vowel sounds. (A list of 500 picturable items can be found on page 255.)

**10** **Picky Puppet** Distribute a set of picture cards evenly among the children. Each child should have at least two cards. Then, using a classroom puppet or a sock puppet, explain to children that this puppet is a "sound puppet" who likes only things whose names begin with a sound it chooses. For example, if the puppet likes licorice, it will also like other things whose names begin with the /l/ sound. Tell children that the sound puppet will name an object it likes. If they have any picture cards whose names also begin with the first sound in the object's name, they should hold up those cards. Have the puppet provide corrective feedback by reiterating the beginning sound of each card to check children's responses. Example:

> **Puppet:** I like marshmallows.
> *One child holds up the* mop *picture card.*

**Puppet:** I see a mop. M-m-mop. *Mop* begins with /m/, just like *mmmmmarshmallows*.

**11** **Find Your Match** Make picture cards using large index cards. Punch holes in the top two corners of each card and string a piece of yarn through them to create a picture-card necklace. Distribute one picture card to each child. Have children find their match by finding the classmate whose picture card begins with the same sound, ends with the same sound, or rhymes (according to the skill you are working on).

**12** **Stand, Sit, and Turn Around** Using children's names, say a sound, such as /s/. Ask all the children whose names begin with /s/ to stand up, sit down, turn around, jump and clap, or some other movement. Continue the activity using picture cards.

## Activities for Oral Blending

**13** **Put It Together** For this activity you say a word in parts. Children should listen carefully and orally blend the parts to say the word as a whole. For example, if you say /m/ /a/ /n/, children are to respond with *man*. **Variation:** Use a classroom puppet to make the activity more playful. Explain to children that the puppet likes to say only whole words. Tell them that you'll say a word in parts and they should guess what the puppet will say. The puppet can then provide corrective feedback and model blending, when necessary.

**14** **Sound It Out** Write the song "Sound It Out" (below) on chart paper. Sing the song to the tune of "If You're Happy and You Know It." At the end of the song, say a word in parts for children to orally blend. For example, /s/...*at*. Then sing the song several times. At the end of each singing, point to a child to provide word parts for the class to blend.

> **Sound It Out**
> If you have a new word, sound it out.
> If you have a new word, sound it out.
> If you have a new word,
> Then slowly say the word.
> If you have a new word, sound it out.

**15** **Old MacDonald Had a Box** Write the song "Old MacDonald Had a Box" on chart paper. Explain to children that this is a different version of the popular song "Old MacDonald Had a Farm." Track the print as you sing. Sing the song several times. During each singing, orally segment a different one-syllable word for children to orally blend. You might segment the word by onset and rime (/k/... an) or phoneme by phoneme (/k/ /a/ /n/), according to children's instructional level. Here are word parts whose words you can substitute for *can* in the song:

- /p/... *en*
- /s/... *ock*
- /m/... *op*
- /h/... *at*
- /r/ /o/ /k/
- /t/ /o/ /p/
- /f/ /a/ /n/
- /b/ /a/ /t/

**Old MacDonald Had a Box**
Old MacDonald had a box, E-I-E-I-O.
And in the box he had a /k/...an, E-I-E-I-O.
With a <u>can</u>, <u>can</u> here
And a <u>can</u>, <u>can</u> there,
Here a <u>can</u>, there a <u>can</u>,
Everywhere a <u>can</u>, <u>can</u>.
Old MacDonald had a box, E-I-E-I-O.

**Variation:** Sing the original version of "Old MacDonald Had a Farm." Then have children change the E-I-E-I-O part by singing a rhyming counterpart, such as SE-SI-SE-SI-SO or ME-MI-ME-MI-MO.

**16** **Guess It!** This game can be played in many ways. In this version, you orally segment the name of an animal. Children guess the animal's identity. For example, you might tell children that you are thinking of the names of farm animals. Children must guess each animal's name. Example:

> **Teacher:** I'm thinking of an animal.
> It's a /p/... *ig*. What am I thinking of?
> **Children:** A pig!

**Extension:** Continue with other categories such as zoo animals, classroom objects, numbers, colors, or household items.
**Variation:** Place picture cards in a bag. Draw out one picture at a time, not showing it to children. Tell children that you see, for example, a /k/... *at*. Ask them to orally blend the word parts to guess the picture name. Then display the card so that children can check their responses. Finally, invite children to be the "teacher" and segment the words for the class to guess. When children become skilled at segmenting and

blending words by onset and rime, repeat the activity, asking them to segment and blend the words phoneme by phoneme.

**17** **Break the Code Game** Divide the class into teams of three to five players. Say a word in parts and ask one of the teams to "break the code." For example, if you say the word parts /s/…*ad*, the team should respond with the word *sad*. If that team gets it wrong, give other teams the opportunity to provide the correct answer, modeling how to string together the word parts to say the word as a whole. Teams get one point for each code they break. Play until one team has ten points.

**18** **Draw It** Have each child fold a sheet of paper into fourths. Then orally segment the name of an easily drawn object, such as a hat. Ask children to orally blend the word parts and then draw a picture of the word in one section of their paper. In the early exercises, segment the words by onset and rime, such as /h/…*at*. In later exercises, segment the words phoneme by phoneme, such as /h/ /a/ /t/. Begin with two- or three-phoneme names (for example, *tie*—/t/ /ī/; *kite*—/k/ /ī/ /t/) and progress to four-phoneme names (for example, *box*—/b/ /o/ /k/ /s/).

**19** **Name Game** When you're lining up children for recess or lunch, practice blending. Say a child's name in parts, such as /s/…*am*. That child can get in line as the class blends the word parts to say the child's name as a whole. (This is a great transition activity.)

**20** **Blend Baseball** Divide the class into two teams. Say aloud a word in parts, such as /s/ /a/ /t/. If the child can blend the word, he or she can go to first base. Play the game just like baseball.

**21** **Team Sound-Off** Divide the class into teams of three or four children. Assign each team a sound, such as /s/. Then call to the front of the classroom three children, for example one child from the /s/ group, one child from the /a/ group, and one child from the /t/ group. Have the three children sequence their sounds to form a word. Then they should say the sounds and ask the rest

of the class to blend together the sounds to form the word. Teams take turns answering, and each team that guesses correctly gets one point.

# Activities for Oral Segmentation

**22** **First Sound First** Ask children to listen to the following set of words: *sat, send, sick.* Point out that all these words start with the same sound. This sound is /s/. Tell children that you want them to listen carefully to each new set of words you say and then tell you what the first sound is. Finally ask them to volunteer other words that begin with that sound. Example:

> "Can you tell me what the first sound is in *fish, foot, fan*? That's right, it's /f/. What other words do you know that begin with /f/?"

**Extension:** Have children listen for the last sound. "Can you tell me what the last sound is in *foot, bat, pet*? That's right, it's /t/. What other words do you know that end with /t/?"

**23** **What's the Sound?** Write the song "What's the Sound?" (below) on chart paper. Sing it to the tune "Old MacDonald Had a Farm." Track the print as you sing. Sing the song several times, encouraging children to join in. During later singings, replace the words *sad* and *silly* with the following:

- *mop* and *money*
- *leaf* and *lucky*
- *ten* and *table*

**What's the Sound?**
What's the sound that these words share?
Listen to these words.
Sad and silly are these two words.
Tell me what you've heard. *(sssssssss)*
With a /s/, /s/ here, and a /s/, /s/ there,
Here a /s/, there a /s/, everywhere a /s/, /s/.
/s/ is the sound that these words share.
We can hear that sound!

**24** **Sound Roll** Place a small group of children in a circle and give each child a picture-card necklace (see activity 11). Roll a ball to one child. That child rolls the ball to another child in the circle whose picture card's name also begins, ends, or rhymes with his or her picture card's name. Limit the picture cards in each group to two or three sounds or rhymes.

**25** **Segmentation Cheer** Write "Segmentation Cheer" on chart paper and teach children the cheer. Each time you say the cheer, change the words in the third line. Have children segment this word, sound by sound. You might want to use these words in subsequent cheers: *soap, read, fish, lime, make, mop, ten, rat, pig, cat, dog, lip.*

**Segmentation Cheer**
Listen to my cheer.
Then shout the sounds you hear.
Sun! Sun! Sun!
Let's take apart the word *sun*!
Give me the beginning sound.
*(Children respond with /s/.)*
Give me the middle sound.
*(Children respond with /u/.)*
Give me the ending sound.
*(Children respond with /n/.)*
That's right!
/s/ /u/ /n/—Sun! Sun! Sun!

### CLASSROOM SPOTLIGHT

Elkonin boxes and counters can be used to help children segment the sounds in words. I always begin by drawing two connected boxes on a sheet of paper, stating aloud a two-sound word such as *see*, and dragging one counter to each box as I say each sound in the word. I am careful to string together the sounds, instead of pausing between each sound. For example, I say *sssseeee* instead of /s/ pause /ē/ pause. Slowly, I allow children to take over the dragging of the counters. Eventually, I progress to using three- and four-sound words.

**26** **Secret Sound** Explain to children that you're going to play a word game. You'll say three words, and you want them to listen closely and tell you what sound they hear that is the same in all the words. For example, if you say *teeth, bean,* and *feet,* children respond with /ē/. Make sure the target sound is in the same position (initial, medial, or final) in all the words.

**27** **Where Is It?** This activity helps children differentiate sound position in words. Distribute one counter to each child. Then have children each draw three connected boxes on a sheet of paper (see sample on page 73). Explain that you're going to say a list of words that all contain /s/. Some words contain /s/ at the beginning, some in the middle, and some at the end. Tell children that if they hear /s/ at the beginning of the word, they should place the counter in the first box. If they hear /s/ in the middle, they should place their counter in the center box. And if they hear /s/ at the end, they should place their counter in the last box. You'll be able to check quickly for accuracy. Use the following word list: *send, missing, sock, bus, less, passing, messy, safe*. On subsequent days, continue with other sounds and word lists such as the following:

/p/ *pack, mop, happy, pocket, hope, open, pudding, trap, pencil, keep*

/m/ *man, moon, ham, summer, room, hammer, made, dream, lemon*

/d/ *dog, duck, pad, pudding, middle, door, toad, read, puddle, dig*

| | | |
|---|---|---|
| | | |

**28** **Count the Sounds** Distribute three counters to each child. Then have children each draw a series of three connected boxes on a sheet of paper. Explain that you're going to read aloud a word. Tell them that they should count how many sounds they hear in the word and place one counter on a box on their paper for each sound they hear. For example, if you say the word *sat*, children should place three counters on their paper, one on each box. You might need to extend the sounds in each word to be sure children hear each discrete sound. For example, you might need to say *sssssaaaaat* for children having difficulty distinguishing the sounds in the word *sat*. And you might want to add movements. For example, move your hands from right to left as you say the word, emphasizing when you change from one sound to another.

Have children segment each of the three related words in each column listed below before moving on to the next column. Help them understand that only one sound is different in each new word in the column. Ask them which sound in each new word is different. Use these and other words:

| | | | | |
|---|---|---|---|---|
| *at* | *mop* | *run* | *in* | *cup* |
| *sat* | *map* | *sun* | *pin* | *cap* |
| *sit* | *tap* | *bun* | *pan* | *cat* |

**Variation to the segmentation boxes:** Have children do one of the following:

- Slap their knee the number of sounds they hear in a word.
- Walk in place or march the number of syllables or sounds they hear in a word.
- Play on a musical instrument one note for each sound they hear. For example, beat on the drum one time for each sound in a word.

**29** **Graph It** Display the following picture cards: *bee, tie, sun, mop, fan, leaf, glass, nest*. Have children sort the cards according to the number of sounds each picture name contains. Then create a graph using the cards.

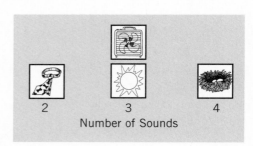

Number of Sounds

## Phonemic Manipulation Activities

**30** **Initial Sound Switch** Explain to children that you're going to play a word game. They're going to make new words by replacing the first sound in each word you say with /s/. For example, if you say the word *hand*, children are to say *sand*. Continue with these and other words: *hit, well, funny, bun, mad, bend, rat, rope*. **Extension:** After children become skilled at substituting initial consonant sounds, have them substitute final consonant sounds (e.g., replace the last sound in *man* with /p/—*map*) and then medial vowel sounds (e.g., replace the middle sound in *ride* with /ō/—*rode*).

**31** **Row Your Boat** Write the song "Row Your Boat" on chart paper. Have children sing the song a few times. Then tell them that you'll sing it again, but this time you'll change the line "Merrily, merrily, merrily, merrily," to "Serrily, serrily, serrily, serrily." To illustrate this, write the word *merrily* on the board, erase the letter *m* and replace it with the letter *s*. Pronounce the nonsense word formed. This will show children that replacing one sound (and letter) in a word creates a new word. Continue singing the song. Each time, change the first letter in the word *merrily* to create a new third line. You might choose to use the nonsense words *werrily, jerrily*, and *berrily*.

**Row Your Boat**

Row, row, row your boat,
Gently down the stream.
Merrily, merrily, merrily, merrily,
Life is but a dream.

You can do this same type of phonemic manipulation with other popular children's songs. For example:

- "I've Been Working on the Railroad": Substitute the initial sounds in "Fe-Fi-Fiddly-I-O" to make "Me-Mi-Middly-I-O" or "Se-Si-Siddly-I-O" and so on.
- "Happy Birthday": Substitute the initial sound throughout with /b/ to create lines such as "Bappy Birthday bo boo." In addition, you might substitute each syllable in the song with *la, lo, pa, bo,* or *ta.*

**32** **Sound Switcheroo** Explain to children that you want them to listen carefully to the sounds in the word you're going to say. Tell them that you'll then play switcheroo (change one sound in the word—the beginning, middle, or ending sound) with one of these sounds. Children should then tell you which sound was switched. For example, if you say *mat* and then *sat*, children should respond that /m/ was switched with /s/. Continue with these and other word pairs:

| | | |
|---|---|---|
| man/pan | fan/fat | run/sun |
| hat/hot | pick/pack | ball/bell |
| leaf/loaf | pig/pin | fish/dish |
| gate/game | tap/tape | van/ran |
| zip/lip | cup/cap | hot/hop |

**33** **Consonant Riddles** Explain to children that they're going to play a consonant riddle game. You'll say a word. Then they think of a word that rhymes with your word and starts with a given sound. Example:

**Teacher:** What rhymes with *pat* and starts with /s/?
**Children:** *Sat*

Continue with these and other riddles:

- What rhymes with *hit* and starts with /s/? *(sit)*
- What rhymes with *land* and starts with /h/? *(hand)*
- What rhymes with *pick* and starts with /s/? *(sick)*
- What rhymes with *fun* and starts with /r/? *(run)*

**34** **Sound of the Day** Select a sound of the day, such as /l/. Throughout the day, say children's names with that sound in place of the first sound. Peter will be called "Leter," Bonnie will be called "Lonnie," and Harry will be called "Larry." You may want to take attendance this way and may want to encourage each child to experiment with saying his or her classmates' names with the sound of the day.

**35** **Picture Search** Display a picture or turn to a favorite page in a trade book. Explain to children that you will say the name of an object, animal, or person in the picture, but that you'll say the name without its first sound. You want them to guess the correct name. For example, if you see a picture of a dog, you'd say *og*.

For additional phonemic-awareness activities, see *Phonemic Awareness Activities for Early Reading Success* (Scholastic, 1997) and *Phonemic Awareness Songs and Rhymes* (Scholastic, 1999), both by Wiley Blevins.

## TRY IT OUT

- Select one activity from the "35 Quick and Easy Activities for Developing Phonemic Awareness" to try out with your students.
- Examine samples of student writing for evidence of phonemic-awareness development. Look at students' invented spellings and assess their ability to segment words and attach accurate spellings to each sound.
- Assess five students using the Phonemic Awareness Assessment. Determine instructional modifications based on student results.

# Learning About Sounds and Letters

*"... knowledge is power. The teacher with some knowledge of linguistics can be a far better kidwatcher, as well as be able to participate more learnedly in conversations and debates about teaching methodology."*

—Sandra Wilde

**W**hy is the most common vowel sound in English the colorless murmur we refer to as the schwa (/ə/) sound? Why do the vowels *e, i, o,* and *u* act as consonants in words such as *azalea, onion, one,* and *quick*; and the consonants *w* and *y* act as vowels in words such as *snow* and *fly*? Why don't the word pairs *five/give, low/how, paid/said,* and *break/speak* rhyme?

These and other questions might cause one to reconsider the teaching of reading and writing because of the seemingly irregular and unpredictable nature of the English language. However, 84% of English words conform to "regular" spelling patterns. Of the remaining 16%, only 3% are highly unpredictable, such as *colonel* and *Ouija* (Bryson, 1990). Given the high degree of regularity of spelling, it's apparent why it's important to teach children the most common sound-spelling relationships in English and help them attend to common spelling patterns in words. As teachers, we need to have a working knowledge of the many sounds in our language and the even greater number of spellings that can represent them.

# Teachers and Linguistics

In 1995, Louisa Moats examined teacher preparation in the areas of reading and learning disabilities and surveyed teachers' background knowledge of language. Five of the fifteen survey items follow (answers provided).

1. How many speech sounds are in the following words?

   | | |
   |---|---|
   | ox (3) | boil (3) |
   | king (3) | thank (4) |
   | straight (5) | shout (3) |
   | though (2) | precious (6) |

2. Underline the consonant blends: doubt, known, fir<u>st</u>, pu<u>mp</u>kin, <u>squ</u>awk, <u>scr</u>atch.
3. What letters signal that a "g" is pronounced /j/? *(e, i, y)*
4. List all the ways you can think of to spell "long a." *(a, ai, a_e, ey, ay, eigh)*
5. Account for the double "m" in *comment* or *commitment*. (*The first* m *closes the syllable to make it short;* com *is a Latin morpheme—the smallest unit of meaning in language—as are* ment *and* mit.)

The results of her survey showed that the majority of teachers could benefit from additional training in linguistics. Only about half of the teachers surveyed could successfully answer most of the questions. Participants' knowledge of phonics was particularly weak. Only about 10–20% of the teachers could identify consonant blends; almost none could consistently identify digraphs; less than half could identify the schwa sound in words; and only 30% knew the conditions in which the letters *ck* were used to stand for the /k/ sound. Moats contends that some of her survey results can be attributed to:

1. a lack of teacher training in phonics and linguistics.
2. the fact that most adult readers think of words in terms of spellings instead of sounds. Therefore, their knowledge of print may stand in the way of attending to individual sounds in words—a skill they no longer need because they have acquired automaticity.
3. the fact that some adults have underdeveloped metalinguistic skills. That is, the skills they have acquired are sufficient for reading but not for explicit (direct) teaching of reading and spelling.

During my years as a teacher, I've improved my ability to assess children's reading and writing skills as I've increased my understanding of the English language. The more I learn about English, the more regular its spelling seems. For example, at one time I thought of words such as *love* and *come* as being "irregular" since they didn't follow the typical o_e spelling for the long-o sound. But when I realized the large number of words that follow a similar spelling pattern (*shove, glove, above, some,* and so on), a regularity began to emerge. The o_e spelling pattern is not random; rather, it can represent either the /ō/ sound or the /u/ sound in words. Now these are the two sounds I try out when confronted with this spelling pattern in an unfamiliar word. In addition, the more I learn about English and its spelling patterns, the more my students' reading and writing errors make sense. This knowledge has helped me target specific difficulties students have had and to design appropriate instruction. If you have a basic knowledge of phonics and linguistics you'll be able to help your students in the following ways (Moats, 1995):

1. **Interpreting and responding to student errors.** You can use student mistakes to modify instruction. For example, when a student substitutes *k* for *g* in a word, knowing that the sounds these two letters represent are formed in almost the same manner helps to explain the student's error. You can instruct students in the major difference between these two sounds (voicing).

2. **Choosing the best examples for teaching decoding and spelling.** You can help children distinguish auditorily confusing sounds such as /e/ and /i/, and use words for instruction that provide the clearest, simplest examples.

3. **Organizing and sequencing information for instruction.** You'll be able to separate the introduction of auditorily confusing sounds such as /e/ and /i/, and teach easier concepts before more complex ones (such as teaching consonants before consonant clusters).

4. **Using your knowledge of morphology to explain spellings.** You can use your knowledge of roots (Latin, Greek) to explain spelling patterns and guide children to figure out word meanings.

5. **Integrating the components of language instruction.** You'll be able to take better advantage of the "teachable moment" and more completely integrate the language arts.

**Linguistics** is the formal study of language and how it works. You don't have to be a linguist to be an effective teacher of reading and writing. However, a deeper understanding of our language can enhance any teacher's abilities. This chapter begins by defining a few basic terms associated with linguistics and another related area of study—**phonetics** (the study of speech sounds). It concludes by providing brief information on each sound in the English language, its most common spellings, and word lists for instruction.

# The Sounds of English

A **phoneme** is a speech sound. It's the smallest unit of sound that distinguishes one word from another. The word *phoneme* is derived from the root *phon* (as in the word *telephone*), which refers to "voice" or "sound." The following pairs of words differ by only one phoneme, the first—*cat/hat, men/pen*.

Since sounds cannot be written, we use letters to represent or stand for the sounds. A **grapheme** is the written representation (a letter or cluster of letters) of one sound. For example, the /b/ sound can be represented by the letter *b*; the /sh/ sound can be represented by the letters *sh*. The word *sat* has three phonemes (/s/ /a/ /t/) and three graphemes *(s, a, t)*. The word *chop* also has three phonemes (/ch/ /o/ /p/) and three graphemes *(ch, o, p)*.

Linguists disagree on the actual number of sounds in the English language. The number varies according to dialect, individual speech patterns, changes in stress, and other variables. However, for the sake of our study, we will deal with the 44 phonemes commonly covered in elementary school reading programs (see chart on page 81).

The 44 English phonemes are represented by the 26 letters of the alphabet individually and in combination. Therefore, a letter can sometimes represent more than one sound. For example, the letter *a* can stand for the different sounds heard in such words as *at, ate, all, any, was,* and *father*. Likewise, a phoneme can sometimes be represented by more than one grapheme. For example, the /f/ sound can be represented by *f (fan), ph (phone),* or *gh (laugh)*.

Adding to the complexity, some letters do not represent any sound in a word. For example, the letter *k* in the word *knot* is silent. In addition, some letters do not represent a unique or distinctive sound. For example, the letter *c* stands for either the /s/ sound (usually represented by the letter *s*), or the /k/ sound (represented by the letter *k*). The letters *q* and *x* also represent no distinctive sound.

## The 44 Sounds of English

### Consonant Sounds

| | | | |
|---|---|---|---|
| **1.** /b/ (bat) | **8.** /l/ (leaf) | **15.** /v/ (vase) | **22.** /th/ (thumb) |
| **2.** /d/ (dog) | **9.** /m/ (mop) | **16.** /w/ (wagon) | **23.** /t͟h/ (the) |
| **3.** /f/ (fan) | **10.** /n/ (nest) | **17.** /y/ (yo-yo) | **24.** /hw/ (wheel) |
| **4.** /g/ (gate) | **11.** /p/ (pig) | **18.** /z/ (zebra) | **25.** /ng/ (ring) |
| **5.** /h/ (hat) | **12.** /r/ (rock) | **19.** /ch/ (cheese) | |
| **6.** /j/ (jump) | **13.** /s/ (sun) | **20.** /sh/ (shark) | |
| **7.** /k/ (kite) | **14.** /t/ (top) | **21.** /zh/ (treasure) | |

### Vowel Sounds

| | | | |
|---|---|---|---|
| **26.** /ā/ (cake) | **31.** /a/ (cat) | **36.** /ə/ (alarm*) | **41.** /oi/ (boy) |
| **27.** /ē/ (feet) | **32.** /e/ (bed) | **37.** /â/ (chair) | **42.** /ou/ (house) |
| **28.** /ī/ (bike) | **33.** /i/ (fish) | **38.** /û/ (bird) | **43.** /o͞o/ (moon) |
| **29.** /ō/ (boat) | **34.** /o/ (lock) | **39.** /ä/ (car) | **44.** /o͝o/ (book) |
| **30.** /yo͞o/ (cube) | **35.** /u/ (duck) | **40.** /ô/ (ball) | |

*The target vowel sound occurs in the first syllable of *alarm*.

To distinguish between a letter and a sound in writing, sounds are placed between *virgules*, or slashes. For example, to indicate the sound that the letter *s* stands for, we write /s/. Other markings aid us in representing sounds in written form. These markings are called *diacritical marks*. The chart on page 82 shows some of the most common diacritical marks. The two most common are the macron and the breve. The macron ( ¯ ) is used to represent long-vowel sounds, such as the /ā/ sound in *gate*. The breve ( ˘ ) is used to represent short-vowel sounds, such as the /ă/ sound in *hat*. Short-vowel sounds can also be written using only the letter between virgules, such as /a/. The International Phonetic Alphabet has conventionalized the symbols for every sound of every language in the world. These differ somewhat from the symbols commonly found in dictionaries. For the sake of consistency, this book deals with only those markings and symbols commonly found in children's dictionaries and taught in elementary reading programs.

## Diacritical Marks

| Markings | Symbol | Example |
| --- | --- | --- |
| macron | — | /ā/ as in *cake* |
| breve | ˘ | /ă/ as in *cat* |
| tilde | ~ | /ñ/ as in *piñon* |
| dieresis | ¨ | /ä/ as in *car* |
| circumflex | ^ | /ô / as in ball |

Phonics instruction involves teaching the relationship between sounds and the spellings used to represent them. There are hundreds of spellings that can be used to represent the 44 English phonemes. Only the most common need to be taught explicitly. Throughout this book I refer to these most common sound-spelling relationships. I choose the term *sound-spelling* instead of the more common *sound-symbol* because it is more accurate. Many sound-spelling relationships are represented by more than one symbol or letter. For example, the /ch/ sound is represented by the letters, or spelling, *ch*; the /ē/ sound can be represented by the spellings *e, ea,* or *ee*. When teaching phonics, we want children to pay attention to these spelling patterns to develop their understanding of English *orthography*, the spelling system of our language.

The 44 English sounds can be divided into two major categories—consonants and vowels. A **consonant** sound is one in which the air flow is cut off either partially or completely when the sound is produced. In contrast, a **vowel** sound is one in which the air flow is unobstructed when the sound is made. The vowel sounds are the music, or movement, of our language.

### CLASSROOM SPOTLIGHT

Try this technique to help students understand how sounds are produced. Have them form a specific sound while looking into small, individual mirrors. Ask them to note the position of the mouth and tongue. For some children this is an "aha moment"—they realize that different sounds are formed in different ways and, further, that words are made up of a series of different, discrete sounds. Some children focus on mouth and tongue positions to determine each sound in a word as they attempt to write it. They then attach a spelling to each sound to write the word. Some commercially available programs that train children to attend to mouth and tongue positions (e.g., Auditory Discrimination in Depth) give sounds kid-friendly labels, such as "lip poppers" and "scrapers," to help children remember specific sounds and their corresponding spellings.

# Consonants

Of the 26 letters in the English alphabet, 21 are generally considered consonants. These include *b, c, d, f, g, h, j, k, l, m, n, p, q, r, s, t, v, w, x, y,* and *z.* The letters *w* and *y* sometimes act as vowels, as in the words *my, happy,* and *show.* Of the 44 English phonemes, 25 are consonant phonemes. (See the chart on page 81.) Eighteen of these phonemes are represented by a single letter, such as /b/ and /m/; seven are identified by a digraph, such as /sh/ and /ch/. A **digraph** is a letter cluster that stands for one sound. The letters *c, q,* and *x* do not have a unique phoneme assigned to them. The sounds they represent are more commonly represented by other letters or spellings.

Consonants can be further categorized according to (1) how they are produced, (2) where they are produced in the mouth, and (3) whether they are voiced. The five major categories of consonants based on their manner of articulation include the following:

1. **Plosives (stops):** formed by closing or blocking off the air flow and then exploding a puff of air (examples: /b/, /p/, /d/, /t/, /g/, /k/). Place your hand in front of your mouth when producing these sounds. Do you feel a burst of air?

2. **Fricatives:** formed by narrowing the air channel and then forcing air through it—this creates friction in the mouth (examples: /f/, /v/, /th/, /th/, /z/, /s/, /zh/, /sh/). A subgroup of this is the **affricative**, which is a sound produced by the sequence of a stop followed by a fricative (examples: /ch/, /j/).

3. **Nasals:** formed when the mouth is closed, forcing the air through the nose (examples: /n/, /m/, /ng/). These sounds are also referred to as nasal stops.

4. **Liquids:** formed by interrupting the airflow slightly, but no friction results (examples: /l/, /r/).

5. **Glides:** sometimes called semivowels because they are formed in similar ways as vowels (examples: /w/, /y/, /h/).

In addition to how sounds are produced, where they are produced in the mouth distinguishes one sound from another. For example, the fricative /v/ is formed using the lips and teeth. Therefore, it is referred to as a **labiodental** (labio = lips; dental = teeth). The fricative /z/ is formed using the front of the mouth. Therefore, it is referred to as an **alveolar**; the alveolar ridge is the front of the mouth where the teeth arise. Similarly, the fricative /sh/ is formed using the roof of the mouth. Therefore, it is referred to as a **palatal**; the hard palate is the roof of the mouth. Other labels you might encounter include **velar** (the velum, or soft palate, is the back of the mouth) and **bilabial** (the lips).

The chart below shows most of the consonant sounds according to where they are articulated. It also divides sounds according to those that are **voiced** and those that are **unvoiced**. When you produce a voiced sound, the vocal cords vibrate. When you produce an unvoiced sound, there's no vibration. To test this, place your hand on your throat. Then make the /b/ sound. You'll feel a vibration because this is a voiced sound. Now make the /p/ sound, the voiceless counterpart of /b/, and you won't feel vibration.

One aspect of consonant sounds that must be addressed is the issue of allophones. An **allophone** is a slightly different version of each phoneme. It generally results from the ease (or lack of ease) in articulating a sound in relation to its surrounding sounds. For example, pronounce the words *late* and *later*. The t in *later* sounds more like /d/. Pronounce the words *like* and *pill*. The l in *like* is pronounced with greater force and clarity than the l in *pill*. Therefore, when sounds are coarticulated, the surrounding sounds and the ease with which the

## Consonant Sounds Mouth Position Chart

 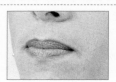 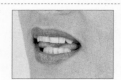 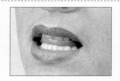

| | | | |
|---|---|---|---|
| **/t/** *t* | **/p/** *p* | **/k/** *k* | **/th/** *th* |
| **/d/** *d* | **/b/** *b* | **/g/** *g* | |
| **/n/** *n* | **/m/** *m* | | |
| **/l/** *l* | | | |
| (tongue pressed against roof of mouth behind top teeth) | (lips closed) | (tongue pressed against bottom of mouth) | (tongue between teeth) |

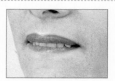 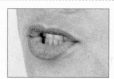 

| | | |
|---|---|---|
| **/f/** *f* | **/ch/** *ch* | **/s/** *s* |
| **/v/** *v* | **/j/** *j* | **/z/** *z* |
| | **/sh/** *sh* | |
| (top teeth on bottom lip) | (lips stuck out) | (teeth together, lips apart) |

| Place of Articulation | Voiced | Unvoiced | Nasal |
|---|---|---|---|
| lips (bilabial) | /b/ (plosive) | /p/ (plosive) | /m/ |
| front of mouth (alveolar) | /d/ (plosive) /z/ (fricative) | /t/ (plosive) /s/ (fricative) | /n/ |
| back of mouth (velar) | /g/ (plosive) | /k/ (plosive) | /ng/ |
| lips and teeth (labiodental) | /v/ (fricative) | /f/ (fricative) | |
| teeth (dental) | /th/ (fricative) | /th/ (fricative) | |
| roof of mouth (palatal) | /zh/ (fricative) /j/ (affricative) | /sh/ (fricative) /ch/ (affricative) | |

mouth must move to form each sound affect the resulting sound. These slight sound variations don't bother us when we read, but children's invented spellings often reflect them.

Most of the consonant phonemes are highly reliable, or dependable. That is, when we see the most common letter or spelling for each consonant sound, it generally stands for that sound. These regularities result in several generalizations that are helpful for the teacher of reading. The list on pages 86–87 shows several of the most reliable consonant generalizations (Groff, 1977; Henderson, 1967; Mazurkiewicz, 1976). It's not necessary to teach these generalizations to children. It's better to point them out at appropriate moments to help students clarify and organize their understanding of English spelling patterns. (On the following pages, you'll find more information on how to use these generalizations with students.)

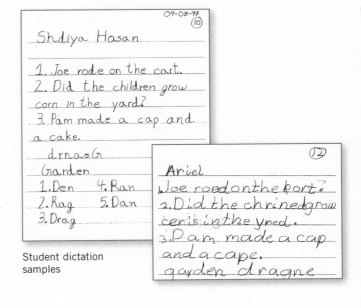

Student dictation samples

# Consonant Generalizations

1. Some letters represent no sound in words.
2. Some sounds are almost always represented by the same spelling, such as *th*, *v*, and *h*.
3. Some spellings appear to be purely arbitrary, such as *igh* in *night* and *eau* in *beau*.
4. The English spelling system often uses doubled letters, especially in the middle of words. However, only one sound is produced unless the sounds cross morpheme boundaries, such as *bookcase* or *unknown*.
5. Certain letters are almost never doubled: *j, k, q, w, x,* and *v*.
6. English spellings have been influenced by other languages, such as *qu* and *th* from Latin-French, *ou* and *ch* from French, and *ps* from Greek.
7. When the letter *c* comes before *e, i,* or *y* in a word, it usually represents the /s/ sound (examples: *cent, city, cycle*).
8. When double *c* comes before *e* or *i* in a word, it usually represents the two sounds /ks/ (example: *success*).
9. When the letter *g* comes before *e, i,* or *y* in a word, it usually represents the /j/ sound.
10. When the letters *c* and *g* are followed by *e* at the end of words, they are usually pronounced /s/ and /j/, respectively (examples: *race, cage*).
11. When the letter *h* appears after *c* in a word, the letter pair can be pronounced /ch/, /k/, or /sh/. Try /ch/ first. Note that *ch* before another consonant is usually pronounced /k/ (example: *chlorine*).
12. The letters *sh* and *ph* almost always represent one sound— /sh/ and /f/, respectively.
13. The letters *gh* represent /g/ at the beginning of words and /f/ at the end of words. However, *gh* is often silent, as in *night*.
14. The digraph *th* has two pronunciations—/th/ and /th̸/.
15. The digraph *wh* is pronounced /hw/. However, when it appears before the letter *o*, only the *h* is pronounced (example: *whole*).
16. The letters *se* indicate that the *s* may be pronounced /s/ or /z/. Try /z/ first, as in *these*.
17. When the letter *s* is followed by *y, i,* or *u* in the middle of words, it may be pronounced /zh/ or /sh/. Try /zh/ first (examples: *measure, fission*).

18. When the letter *i* follows *c, s, ss, sc*, or *t* in the last part of a word, it is usually silent and indicates that these graphemes represent /sh/ (example: *nation*).
19. When the letter *e* follows *v* and *z* at the end of words, it is silent and indicates that *v* and *z* rarely come at the end of words.
20. When the letter *e* follows *ng* at the end of words, it indicates that *ng* stands for /nj/ (example: *strange*).
21. When the letters *le* appear at the end of a word, the *l* is pronounced /ul/ (example: *table*).
22. When a word ends in *dure, ture, sure*, or *zure*, the first letter in each ending is pronounced /j/, /ch/, /sh/, /zh/, respectively.

Consonants can appear by themselves or in combination with other consonants. Two consonants that appear together can be a cluster or a digraph. A **cluster** refers to two or more consonants that appear together in a word, each consonant retaining its own sound. For example, the cluster *sn* in *snail* represents the /sn/ sounds. The combined sound that the cluster stands for is called a **blend**. In contrast, sometimes when two consonants appear together in a word, they stand for one sound that is different from either sound of each individual consonant. This is called a **digraph**. The digraph *sh* stands for the /sh/ sound. This sound is not a combination of the /s/ and /h/ sounds; rather it is a new and unique sound. There are both consonant and vowel digraphs. An example of a vowel digraph is *oa*, which stands for the /ō/ sound.

# Vowels

Nineteen of the 44 English phonemes are vowel phonemes. (See the chart on page 81.) The letters *a, e, i, o*, and *u* are classified as vowels. These five letters are used to represent many different sounds. Therefore, each vowel is used for a variety of purposes. For example, the letter *o* has at least ten distinct sounds assigned to it *(on, old, son, corn, room, look, word, lemon, out, oil)* and is used in more than thirty different ways *(oasis, old, road, though, shoulder, snow, on, gone, thought, soldier, one, son, enough, does, other, look, could, room, through, to, two, buoy, oil, boy, buoyant, out, how, drought, lemon, word, colonel, Ouija, board)*.

In addition, the consonants *w* and *y* often act as vowels, as in the words *show, fly*, and *happy*. The letter *y* acts as a vowel when it appears at the end of a word or syllable. The letter *w* acts as a vowel when it is used in combination with another vowel, as in the words *few, how, slow, thaw,* and *threw*. As vowels, the letters *w* and *y* do not represent distinctive sounds.

The most important distinguishing characteristic of a vowel is its place of articulation. Vowels can be produced in the front, central, or back part of the mouth. This refers to the approximate place in the mouth in which part of the tongue is raised. In addition, the degree to which the tongue is raised distinguishes sounds. The sounds can be produced with the tongue raised to a high, mid, or low degree. The chart on page 89 illustrates this.

Missing from this chart are the diphthongs. A **diphthong** is a sound in which the position of the mouth changes from one place to another as the sound is produced. The sounds /oi/ and /ou/ are commonly classified as diphthongs. In addition, two so-called long-vowel sounds— long *i* (/ī/) and long *u* (/yōō/)—are often classified as diphthongs. The long-*u* sound is actually a combination of a consonant and vowel sound. To note the difference between a diphthong and other vowel sounds, say aloud the /ā/ sound as in *gate*. Notice that the mouth, tongue, and lips remain in same position while the sound is produced. Now try the /oi/ sound as in *boy*. Note how the mouth, especially the lips, change position while the sound is being produced. This is characteristic of a diphthong. Interestingly, Southern dialects generally produce most of their vowels as diphthongs. This helps to explain the singsong, rhythmic nature of Southern speech.

In basal reading programs, vowels are generally grouped in the following categories:

1. **Long-vowel sounds:** The macron ( ⁻ ) is the diacritical mark used to represent long-vowel sounds. The word *macro* means "long" or "great." Long-vowel sounds are also referred to as glided sounds. The long-vowel sounds covered in most basal reading programs include /ā/, /ē/, /ī/, /ō/, and /yōō/, although long *i* and long *u* are generally classified as diphthongs by linguists. Common long-vowel spelling patterns include CVCe *(race)* and VCe *(age)*. Long-vowel sounds are often represented by vowel digraphs such as *ai, ay, ee, ea, oa, ow, ey, igh,* and *ie*. The vowel sound in an open syllable is generally a long-vowel sound *(ti/ger, a/pron)*. An open syllable is a syllable that ends in a vowel.

2. **Short-vowel sounds:** The breve ( ˘ ) is the diacritical mark used to represent short-vowel sounds. Often no mark is used. The short-vowel sounds include /a/, /e/, /i/, /o/ and /u/. Short-

# Vowel Sounds Mouth Position Chart

**ē** — see, these, me, eat, key

**i** — sit

**ā** — make, rain, play

**e** — pet

**a** — cat

**ī** — time, pie, right

**o** — fox

**u** — cup

**aw** — saw, pause, call

**ō** — vote, boat, snow, old

**ŏŏ** — took, put, could

**o̅o̅** — moo, tube, blue, chew

**oi** **oy** — oil, boy

**ou** **ow** — out, cow

**ûr:** **ir** sir | **er** her | **ur** fur

**âr:** **ar** car

**ôr:** **or** for

| Vowel Sounds | | | |
|---|---|---|---|
| | **Front** | **Central** | **Back** |
| **High** | /ē/ /ī/ | | /o̅o̅/ /ŏŏ/ |
| **Mid** | /ā/ /e/ | /ə/ (schwa) /ər/ (schwar) | /ō/ /ô/ |
| **Low** | /a/ | /u/ | /o/ |

vowel sounds are also referred to as unglided sounds. The most common short-vowel spelling pattern is CVC *(cat)*. Short-vowel sounds are usually represented by the single vowels *a, e, i, o,* and *u.* The vowel sound in a closed syllable is often a short-vowel sound *(bas/ket).* A closed syllable is a syllable that ends in a consonant.

3. **Other vowel sounds:** The other vowel sounds include diphthongs (/oi/, /ou/), variant vowels (/o̅o̅/, /ŏŏ/, /ô/, /ä/), schwa (/ə/), and *r*-controlled vowels (/ôr/, /ûr/, /âr/). In addition to the letter *r,* the letters *l* and *w* also affect the vowel sound that precedes or follows.

**Many vowel generalizations are unreliable.** For example, the commonly taught generalization, "When two vowels go walking, the first does the talking" has been found to be only about 45% reliable. However, if you limit the generalization to the vowel digraphs *ai, ay, ee,* and *oa,* it becomes a highly useful generalization. The list that follows shows several of the most reliable vowel generalizations (Groff, 1977; Henderson, 1967; Mazurkiewicz, 1976). It's not necessary to teach these generalizations to children. Point them out at appropriate moments to help students clarify and organize their understanding of English spelling patterns. (You'll find more information on using these generalizations with students on page 226.)

### Vowel Generalizations

1. A single vowel followed by one or two consonants usually stands for a short sound. However, it may be a long sound. Try the short sound first.
2. The letter *e* following a vowel and a consonant (other than *c, g, l, ng, s, th, v, z,* and *ur*) usually indicates that the vowel represents a long sound.
3. The letter *a* before *l* in a word, and in the spellings *au* and *aw,* usually represents the /ô/ sound.
4. When the vowel digraphs *ai, ay, ee,* and *oa* appear together in a word, the first vowel usually represents its long sound.
5. The letter *y* usually represents the long-*i* sound at the end of short words *(fly)*, but the letters *y* and *ey* usually stand for the long-*e* sound in longer words *(happy, monkey)*.
6. Some vowel spellings are used in reading to distinguish word meanings *(meat/meet)* but cause problems in spelling.
7. The final *e* (silent *e*, *e*-marker) accounts for many of the sound distinctions in words.

### All the vowels, except *a*, can also act as consonants.

1. The letter *e* stands for the /y/ sound in the word *azalea*.
2. When the letter *i* follows *c, s, ss, sc, t,* and *x*, it stands for the /sh/ sound *(nation)*. The letter *i* can also stand for the /y/ sound, as in *union, opinion, senior, brilliant, civilian, junior, onion, million, spaniel,* and *stallion*.
3. The letter *o* stands for the /w/ sound in *one* and *once*.
4. The letter *u*, when it follows *s* and *ss*, stands for the /zh/ sound *(measure)*. The letter *u* can also stand for the /w/ sound, as in *liquid, quiet, quick, queen, quill, quilt, suite, suave, language,* and *penguin*.

Pages 93–131 detail each of the 44 English sounds. Information on how each sound is produced, the common spelling patterns used to represent each sound, and **word lists for instruction are included**. The notable exclusions from this section are the consonants *c*, *q*, and *x*, and the digraphs *gh* and *ph*. These consonants and digraphs do not represent distinctive sounds. However, word lists for each can be found under the most common sound it represents. Some additional information on each of these includes the following:

## The letter *c*

The letter *c* can stand for many sounds. It can stand for the /k/ sound, as in *cat*. The letter *c* generally stands for the /k/ sound when it comes before the letter *a*, *o*, or *u* in a word *(cat, cot, cut)*. This is sometimes referred to as the "hard" sound of *c*. The letter *c* can also stand for the /s/ sound, as in *city*. The letter *c* generally stands for the /s/ sound when it comes before the letter *e*, *i*, or *y* in a word *(cent, cinder, cycle)*. This is sometimes referred to as the "soft" sound of *c*. The word *cello* is an exception. In this word, the letter *c* stands for the /ch/ sound. In addition, the letter *c* usually stands for the /k/ sound when it is followed by a consonant, as in *cliff* and *cry*. The consonant digraph *ck* also stands for the /k/ sound. Many consider the *c* silent in this digraph. The most notable exception to this is when the letter *c* is followed by the letter *h*. The letters *ch* can stand for the /k/ sound, as in *chemistry* and *school*, or the /ch/ sound, as in *cheese*. When the letter *c* follows the letter *s*, the two letters combined can stand for the /sk/ sounds, as in *scold* and *scream*; or the *c* can be silent, as in *science* and *scene*. When the letter *c* is doubled in a word, one of the *c*'s is usually silent. When they come before the letters *u* or *o*, the double *c*'s usually stand for the /k/ sound, as in *occupy* and *tobacco*. When they come before the letters *e* or *i*, they usually stand for the /ks/ sounds, as in *success, accident, access*, and *accept*. The *c* before *i* and *e* in these words stands for the /sh/ sound: *conscious, special, ocean, official, social, delicious, racial*. Note that the letter *i* is silent in these words.

## The letter *q*

The letter *q* can be deleted from our alphabet and replaced with the letter *k*. The letter *q* almost always represents the /k/ sound and is usually followed by the letter *u*. In some words the letter *u* is silent *(antique, bouquet, croquet)*. In most words the *u* stands for the /w/ sound *(quack, quail, quake, quart, quarter, queen, question, quick, quiet, quill, quilt, quirk, quit, quite, quiz, require, request, square*, and *squash)*.

## The letter *x*

The letter *x* frequently stands for the /ks/ sounds, as in *ax, box, fix, flax, fox, lox, mix, ox, sax, six, tax,* and *wax*. It also stands for the /gz/ sounds, as in *exact, exit, exist, exam, auxiliary, exhaust,* and *exhibit*. We generally use /gz/ when the letter *x* appears between two vowels. The letter *x* can also stand for the /z/ sound, as in *xylophone, anxiety, xylem,* and *Xerox*. There are words in which we pronounce the name of *x*, as in *x ray* and *x-ograph* (/eks/). Other sounds that the letter *x* represents include: /ksh/ *anxious, anxiously*; /k/ *excite, exceed, excellent, except, excuse*; and /kzh/ *luxury*. The letter *x* is silent in the word *Sioux*.

## The digraphs *gh* and *ph*

The digraphs *gh* and *ph* can stand for the /f/ sound *(tough, phone)*. The digraph *gh* can also be silent, as in *light*. The digraph *ph* almost always stands for the /f/ sound, as in *phone* and *graph*. However, in the word *diphthong*, the *p* stands for the /p/ sound and the letter *h* is silent.

# /b/ as in *bat*

**How formed:** The /b/ sound is a voiced bilabial plosive (stop). Its voiceless counterpart is /p/. To make the /b/ sound, lightly press the lips together. Then exert a steady pressure. This creates a tone that results from the vibration of the vocal cords and the lips. The /b/ sound is not completed until the lips open for a puff of breath.

**Spellings:** The /b/ sound is most frequently represented by the letter *b*, as in *bat* or *cab*. The letter *b* is a very reliable letter for this sound. That is, when you see the letter *b* in a word there is a great probability that it stands for the /b/ sound. Also, the letter *b* has no other sound assigned to it. However, sometimes the letter *b* is silent. For example, one *b* is silent when *b* is doubled in words, such as *lobby* and *rubber*. In addition, the letter *b* is silent when it follows the letter *m*, as in *climb, lamb,* and *bomb*, or comes before the letter *t*, as in *doubt* and *debt*. An exception to this is a word such as *limber*, in which the *m* and the *b* are in different syllables.

Other spellings of the /b/ sound include: *bh* (*Bhutan*), *pb* (*cupboard*).

## Words for Instruction

### Initial Position

| | | | | | | | |
|---|---|---|---|---|---|---|---|
| back | barn | bean | belt | bind | bond | bound | bun |
| bad | base | bear | bench | birch | bone | bow | bunch |
| badge | basket | beast | bend | bird | book | bowl | bunk |
| bag | bass | beat | bent | bit | boom | box | bunt |
| bait | bat | bed | best | bite | boost | boy | burn |
| bake | batch | bee | bet | boar | boot | buck | burst |
| ball | bath | beech | bib | boast | bop | bud | bus |
| balloon | bathe | beef | bid | boat | born | budge | but |
| ban | beach | been | big | bog | boss | bug | butterfly |
| band | bead | beet | bike | boil | botch | bull | button |
| bank | beak | beg | bill | bold | both | bum | buzz |
| bar | beam | bell | bin | bolt | bottle | bump | by |

### Final Position

| | | | | | | |
|---|---|---|---|---|---|---|
| bib | cob | crib | grab | lab | rub | sub |
| Bob | club | cub | job | rib | scrub | tab |
| cab | crab | dab | knob | rob | sob | tub |

---

**CLASSROOM SPOTLIGHT**

### Ways to use word lists

You can use the words (primarily one-syllable) in the word lists throughout this section during phonics and spelling instruction in the following ways:

- to create word lists for blending practice
- to create connected text for reading practice
- to create word lists for word sorts
- to create activity pages
- to create word lists to be sent home for reading practice
- to create words lists to add to a word wall
- to create word lists for dictation (spelling)

## 2 THE 44 SOUNDS OF ENGLISH · /d/ as in *dog*

**How formed:** The /d/ sound is a voiced alveolar plosive (stop). Its voiceless counterpart is /t/. To make the /d/ sound, place the front of the tongue in back of the upper front teeth while slightly opening the jaws.

**Spellings:** The /d/ sound is most frequently represented by the letter *d*, as in *dog* or *bed*. The letter *d* is a pretty reliable letter for this sound. However, one *d* is silent when *d* is doubled in words, such as *ladder* and *sudden*. The letter *d* can also stand for other sounds, such as the /t/ sound in *hoped* and *looked*, or the /j/ sound in *graduate, soldier,* and *badge*.

Other spellings of the /d/ sound include: *dh (dhurrie), ed (called), ld (should)*.

## Words for Instruction

### Initial Position

| | | | | | | | |
|---|---|---|---|---|---|---|---|
| dad | day | den | dill | dirty | dog | dot | dump |
| damp | deaf | dent | dim | dish | doll | down | dune |
| Dan | deal | desk | dime | disk | dollar | doze | dunk |
| dark | debt | dew | dine | dive | dome | duck | dusk |
| dash | deck | did | ding | do | done | due | dust |
| date | deep | die | dip | dock | door | dug | dye |
| dawn | deer | dig | dirt | doe | dose | dull | |

### Final Position

| | | | | | | | |
|---|---|---|---|---|---|---|---|
| bad | cloud | freed | lad | mood | pod | sad | stead |
| bead | cod | glad | laid | mud | pond | said | steed |
| bed | creed | good | lead | need | raid | seed | stood |
| bid | did | greed | led | nod | read | sled | toad |
| bird | fad | hand | lid | pad | red | slid | wed |
| braid | fed | hid | load | paid | rid | sod | weed |
| bread | feed | hood | loud | plead | road | speed | wood |
| bud | food | kid | mad | plod | rod | spud | word |

---

## CLASSROOM SPOTLIGHT

### Ways to use sound formation information

Use the information on how each sound is formed to assess students' writings. For example, knowing that the letters *d* and *t* are so closely related might help you make sense of spelling errors in which students switch these two sounds. Here are some other ways sound formation information can help with assessment:

- As you read a student's writings, keep in mind the student's dialect or accent (how he or she might articulate specific words).
- Be aware that some children overarticulate sounds when trying to segment words to spell them. This will help you understand other spelling errors
- If you are working with mirrors (see page 82) to focus children's attention on mouth position and the vocalization of sounds, use this information to help you explain to students how each sound is formed.

# 3 THE 44 SOUNDS OF ENGLISH

# /f/ as in *fan*

**How formed:** The /f/ sound is a voiceless labiodental fricative. Its voiced counterpart is /v/. To make the /f/ sound, place the lower lip slightly under the upper teeth. The sound is created when breath seeps out between the edge of the teeth and the lower lip.

**Spellings:** The /f/ sound is most frequently represented by the letter *f*, as in *fan* or *if*. The letter *f* is a pretty reliable letter for this sound. However, one *f* is silent when the letter *f* is doubled in words, such as *muffin* and *off*. The letter *f* also stands for the /v/ sound in the word *of*. The other common spellings for the /f/ sound are the digraphs *ph*, as in *phone*, and *gh*, as in *cough*. The digraph *gh* can cause confusion because it can also be silent, as in *knight* or *sigh*, or just the letter *h* can be silent in words such as *ghost*. Generally, the letters *gh* stand for the /f/ sound when they appear in the final position and are preceded by *au* (*laugh*) or *ou* (*enough*).

Other spellings of the /f/ sound include: *pph* (*sapphire*), *lf* (*calf, half*), *pf* (*pfennig*), *ft* (*often*).

## Words for Instruction

### Initial Position

| | | | | | | | |
|---|---|---|---|---|---|---|---|
| fad | false | feast | few | fire | foe | foot | four |
| fade | fame | feather | fib | first | foil | football | fowl |
| fail | fan | fed | fig | fish | fold | for | fox |
| faint | far | feed | fight | fist | folk | force | fun |
| fair | farm | feel | file | fit | fond | fork | fur |
| fake | fast | fell | film | five | food | form | fuse |
| fall | fate | fence | fine | foam | fool | fort | fuzz |

### Final Position

| | | | | | | | |
|---|---|---|---|---|---|---|---|
| beef | deaf | grief | if | life | proof | roof | spoof |
| brief | elf | hoof | knife | loaf | puff | scarf | wife |
| chef | goof | huff | leaf | off | reef | shelf | wolf |
| chief | | | | | | | |

### Other Spellings

| | | | |
|---|---|---|---|
| alphabet | nephew | phonics | cough |
| autograph | orphan | photo | enough |
| digraph | pamphlet | photograph | laugh |
| elephant | pharmacy | phrase | laughter |
| emphasis | pheasant | telegraph | rough |
| graph | phone | triumph | tough |
| hyphen | phoneme | trophy | |

# /g/ as in *gate*

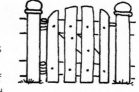

**How formed:** The /g/ sound is a voiced velar plosive (stop). Its voiceless counterpart is /k/. To make the /g/ sound, raise the back part of the tongue and press it against the front part of the soft palate. This rising of the tongue is a sort of bunching backward. The nasal passage is blocked, thus forcing all of the air to emerge through the mouth. The vocal cords are vibrating and the throat muscles exert pressure. You can feel this by placing your hand against your throat.

**Spellings:** The /g/ sound is most frequently represented by the letter *g*, as in *goat* or *bag*. This sound is sometimes referred to as the "hard sound" of *g*. The letter *g* usually represents the /g/ sound when it is at the end of a word *(bag)*, or when it is followed by *a (gate)*, *o (got)*, *u (gum)*, or any consonant *(green)*. The letter *g* is not a very reliable letter. It can stand for several other sounds. It can stand for the /j/ sound, as in *gentle*. This is sometimes referred to as the "soft sound" of *g*. The letter *g* usually represents the /j/ sound when followed by *e (gem)*, *i (giant)*, or *y (gym)*; when it appears in the medial position *(magic, agent)*; or when it appears at the end of a word and is followed by the letter *e (age, page)*. The most notable exceptions include *girl, get, give, gill,* and *gift*. Note that in words such as *guard* and *guilt*, a seemingly unnecessary letter *u* has been inserted to aid in proper pronunciation. The letter *g* can also be silent when doubled in words, such as *giggle* or *egg* (exceptions include *exaggerate* and *suggest*); when it appears before the letter *n*, as in *gnat, sign,* or *foreign*; or when it appears with *h* in words such as *night* and *though*. In addition, the letter *g* is a part of the digraphs *gh (tough)* and *ng (ring)*. In words borrowed from French, the letter *g* can stand for the /zh/ sound, as in *garage* and *rouge*.

Other spellings of the /g/ sound include: *gh (ghost, spaghetti)*, *gue (plague)*, *½x (exact)*.

## Words for Instruction

### Initial Position

| | | | | | | | |
|---|---|---|---|---|---|---|---|
| gain | gasp | geese | girl | goat | gone | guitar | gust |
| game | gate | get | give | goes | good | gum | |
| gap | gave | gift | go | gold | goof | gun | |
| gas | gear | gill | goal | golf | goose | gush | |

### Final Position

| | | | | | | | |
|---|---|---|---|---|---|---|---|
| bag | dig | flag | jug | Meg | rag | smug | wag |
| big | dog | fog | keg | mug | rig | snag | wig |
| bog | drag | frog | lag | nag | rug | snug | zag |
| bug | drug | hog | leg | peg | sag | tag | zig |
| chug | dug | hug | log | pig | shag | tug | |
| clog | fig | jig | lug | plug | shrug | twig | |

# /h/ as in *hat*

**How formed:** The /h/ sound is a voiceless glottal (pharyngeal) fricative. The sound is simply a breath. It is always made with the vowel sound that follows it, as in *hat*, or with the /w/ sound, as in *what* (/hw/). In words containing the digraph *wh*, the /h/ sound is vocalized before the /w/ sound. In many English dialects, the breathy quality of this digraph is disappearing. People speaking these dialects don't distinguish the /hw/ sound in *what* from the /w/ sound in *wet*.

**Spellings:** The /h/ sound is most frequently represented by the letter *h*, as in *hat*. The only other notable spelling of the /h/ sound is *wh*, as in *who, whom*, and *whose*. The letter *o* follows *wh* in all these words. The letter *h* is a pretty reliable letter when it appears at the beginning of a word. However, sometimes it is silent, as in *heir, honor, honest*, and *hour*. The letter *h* is also silent when it appears at the end of a word following a vowel, such as *oh, hallelujah*, and *hurrah*; when it follows the letters *g, k*, and *r*, as in *ghost, rhyme*, and *khaki*; when it appears between a consonant and a following unstressed vowel, as in *shepherd* and *silhouette*; and when it appears after *ex*, as in *exhaust* and *exhibit* (one exception is *exhale*).

The letter *h* is an extremely useful letter. It is used in combination with other consonants to form the following six digraphs: *sh, th, wh, ch, ph*, and *gh*. The digraph *gh* may cause confusion. Sometimes it stands for the /f/ sound, as in *enough* and *laugh*; other times it is silent, as in *night* and *though*.

## Words for Instruction

| Initial Position | | | | | |
|---|---|---|---|---|---|
| hair | has | heart | hip | hoof | hum |
| half | hat | heat | his | hook | hung |
| hall | hate | heel | hit | hop | hunt |
| halt | have | help | hive | hope | hurl |
| ham | hay | hem | hoe | horn | hurt |
| hammer | he | her | hog | horse | husk |
| hand | head | here | hold | hose | hut |
| hang | heal | high | hole | hot | |
| hard | hear | hill | home | house | |
| hare | heard | him | hood | how | |

**Word Walls** are a great way to display learning and a great reference for children during reading and writing. Periodically review the words on the Word Wall. You might have the class chorally read all the words under a specific letter, or have children quiz each other by pointing to words in random order as a partner reads them aloud. Encourage children to add words throughout the year. Use the word lists provided to add words that might be useful to children when they're reading or writing.

## 6 THE 44 SOUNDS OF ENGLISH  /j/ as in *jump*

**How formed:** The /j/ sound is a voiced affricative. It is a combination of the /d/ and /zh/ sounds. Its voiceless counterpart is /ch/. The /j/ sound is made like the /ch/ sound, with the lips slightly rounded and stuck out. The teeth are together and the tongue is pressed against them. The teeth spring apart and the tongue is so unwilling to remove itself to let the vibrating breath emerge that we almost, but not quite, hear a sound of /d/ in conjunction with the /j/ sound.

**Spellings:** The /j/ sound is frequently represented by the letter *j*, as in *jump*. The letter *j* is a very reliable letter; it almost always stands for the /j/ sound. The most notable exception is the word *hallelujah*, in which the letter *j* stands for the /y/ sound. The letter *j* sometimes stands for the /h/ sound in words borrowed from other languages, such as *San Juan, José, junta,* and *Navajo.* The letter *j* is almost never in the final position in words. There are several other spellings that can represent the /j/ sound. The most frequent include *dg (judgment)* or *dge (judge, knowledge, edge)* at the end of a word or syllable, and *g (gentle, huge).* The letter *g* generally stands for the /j/ sound when it comes before the letters *i, e,* or *y.*

Other spellings of the /j/ sound include: *d (graduation, education), di (soldier), ch (Greenwich), gg (exaggerate), jj (Hajji), de (grandeur), dj (adjust).*

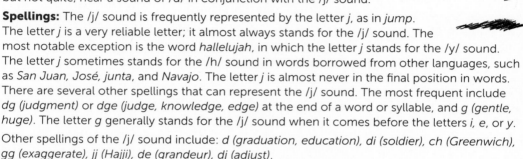

## Words for Instruction

### Initial Position

| jab | jail | jay | jet | join | joy | jump | jury |
|---|---|---|---|---|---|---|---|
| jacket | jam | jeans | jig | joint | jug | jump rope | just |
| jacks | jar | jeep | job | joke | juice | June | |
| jade | jaw | jerk | jog | jolt | July | junk | |

### Medial/Final Position

| badge | budge | edge | fudge | grudge | lodge | ridge | wedge |
|---|---|---|---|---|---|---|---|
| bridge | dodge | fidget | gadget | ledge | nudge | smudge | |

### Other Spellings

| | | | | | |
|---|---|---|---|---|---|
| garage | geography | gym | damage | manager | stingy |
| gee | George | gypsy | danger | message | strange |
| gem | geranium | age | engineer | orange | stranger |
| general | germ | bulge | forge | package | urgent |
| generous | giant | cabbage | fringe | page | village |
| genius | gigantic | cage | hinge | passage | wage |
| gentle | ginger | change | huge | pigeon | |
| gentleman | gingerbread | collage | large | rage | |
| genuine | giraffe | courage | magic | stage | |

# /k/ as in *kite*

**How formed:** The /k/ sound is a voiceless velar plosive (stop). Its voiced counterpart is /g/. The /k/ sound is made very much like the /g/ sound. The back part of the tongue is raised and pressed against the front part of the soft palate. The nasal passage is blocked, thus forcing all of the breath to emerge through the mouth. The difference between the /g/ and /k/ sounds is that the vocal cords are not vibrating when the /k/ sound is made.

**Spellings:** The /k/ sound is sometimes represented by the letter *k*, as in *kite* and *look*. The letter *k* is a very reliable letter. It has no other sound assigned to it. However, sometimes the letter *k* is silent when it comes before the letter *n* in a word or syllable, as in *knee*, *knife*, *knob*, and *unknown*. The other most frequent spellings of the /k/ sound include *ck* at the end of a word or syllable (*sock*, *rocket*); *c* when followed by *a*, *o*, or *u* (*cat*, *cot*, *cut*); or *q* (*queen*, *quick*). The letter *q* is almost always followed by the letter *u*. In words such as *queen* and *quit*, the letter *u* stands for the /w/ sound (a consonant sound); in words such as *opaque*, *mosque*, *antique*, and *plaque*, the letter *u* is silent.

Other spellings of the /k/ sound include: *ch* (*chorus*, *chloroform*, *chemistry*, *school*), *lk* (*talk*, *walk*), *que* (*opaque*), *cc* (*account*), *cch* (*bacchanal*), *cq* (*acquaint*), *cqu* (*lacquer*), *cque* (*sacque*), *cu* (*biscuit*), *gh* (*lough*), *kh* (*Sikh*, *khaki*), *q* (*Iraq*), *qu* (*liquor*), *sc* (*viscount*), *x* (*except*), ½x (*next*), ½xi (*noxious*).

## Words for Instruction

### Initial Position

| | | | | | | | |
|---|---|---|---|---|---|---|---|
| kale | keep | kept | key | kill | kind | kiss | kite |
| kangaroo | kelp | kettle | kid | kilt | king | kit | kitten |
| keen | | | | | | | |

### Medial/Final Position

| | | | | | | | |
|---|---|---|---|---|---|---|---|
| bank | look | think | chick | lack | pick | sick | stuck |
| beak | milk | took | chicken | lick | pocket | slack | suck |
| bike | oak | weak | click | lock | quack | slick | tack |
| bleak | peak | week | clock | locker | quick | snack | tick |
| book | peek | back | crack | locket | rack | sock | tock |
| break | seek | black | deck | luck | racket | socket | track |
| cook | shook | block | dock | muck | rock | speck | trick |
| desk | sink | brick | duck | neck | rocket | stack | truck |
| fork | skunk | buck | jack | nickel | sack | stick | tuck |
| hook | soak | bucket | jacket | pack | shack | stock | wick |
| leak | steak | checkers | kick | package | shock | stockings | wreck |

### Other Spellings

| | | | | | | | |
|---|---|---|---|---|---|---|---|
| cab | cane | cart | coal | coin | cool | cough | cub |
| cage | cap | case | coast | cold | cope | could | cube |
| call | cape | cash | coat | colt | cord | count | curl |
| came | car | cast | cob | comb | corn | court | curve |
| camp | card | cat | cod | come | cost | cove | cut |
| can | care | cave | coil | cone | cot | cow | cute |

# /l/ as in *leaf*

**How formed:** The /l/ sound is a voiced alveolar lateral (resonant). It generally has a "light" sound at the beginning of a word (*look*) and a "dark" sound at the end of a word or syllable (*ball*). To make the /l/ sound, lightly touch the front of the tongue behind the upper front teeth while allowing vibrating breath to emerge.

**Spellings:** The /l/ sound is most frequently represented by the letter *l*, as in *leaf* and *goal*. The letter *l* is a very reliable letter; it has no other sound assigned to it. However, sometimes the letter *l* is silent in words. For example, one *l* is silent when doubled in words, such as *yellow* and *bell*. The letter *l* is also silent when it is followed by the letters *f, m, k,* or *d* in the same syllable, as in *calf, calm, yolk,* and *could*. However, careful speakers pronounce the /l/ sound in words such as *milk* and *bold*.

Other spellings of the /l/ sound include: *tle (castle), ½le (people), lle (faille), sl (lisle, island), cle (muscle), ln (kiln)*.

## Words for Instruction

### Initial Position

| | | | | | |
|---|---|---|---|---|---|
| lab | lane | least | lie | list | loose |
| lace | lap | leaves | life | lit | lose |
| lack | lash | left | lift | live | lot |
| lad | last | leg | light | loaf | love |
| ladder | latch | lemon | like | loan | luck |
| lag | late | lend | limp | loaves | lug |
| laid | leaf | less | line | log | lump |
| lake | leak | lest | link | lone | lunch |
| lamp | lean | let | lion | long | lunchbox |
| land | leap | lick | lip | look | |

### Final Position

| | | | | | |
|---|---|---|---|---|---|
| bail | goal | pail | steal | bill | kill |
| boil | hail | pencil | steel | cell | mill |
| bowl | heal | pool | tail | dill | pill |
| camel | heel | pretzel | tool | doll | sell |
| coal | jail | rail | towel | dull | sill |
| coil | mail | sail | veal | fell | tell |
| cool | meal | school | veil | fill | till |
| fail | nail | seal | wheel | gill | well |
| feel | nickel | shovel | wool | gull | will |
| foil | owl | soil | bell | hill | yell |

# /m/ as in *mop*

**How formed:** The /m/ sound is a voiced bilabial nasal. To make the /m/ sound, press the lips together lightly and vibrate slightly while the breath is emerging through the nasal passage. The /m/ sound is one of three nasal sounds (/m/, /n/, /ng/). These sounds are responsible for resonance in the voice.

**Spellings:** The /m/ sound is most frequently represented by the letter *m*, as in *mop* and *ham*. The letter *m* is a very reliable letter; it has no other sound assigned to it. However, sometimes the first *m* is silent when *m* is doubled in words, such as *hammer* and *common*. The letter *m* is sometimes silent in technical words, such as *mnemonics*.

Other spellings of the /m/ sound include: *mb (lamb), chm (drachm), gm (paradigm), lm (calm), mn (hymn), ½m (criticism)*.

## Words for Instruction

### Initial Position

| | | | | | |
|---|---|---|---|---|---|
| mad | marble | meat | mill | moat | much |
| made | march | men | mind | monkey | muck |
| maid | mash | mend | mine | moon | mud |
| mail | mask | mesh | mirror | mop | mug |
| main | mat | mess | miss | more | mush |
| make | match | met | mist | most | musk |
| man | math | mice | mitt | motorcycle | must |
| mane | may | mild | mitten | mouse | mute |
| many | meal | mile | mix | mouth | mutt |
| map | mean | milk | moan | move | my |

### Final Position

| | | | | | |
|---|---|---|---|---|---|
| beam | drum | gum | mom | scream | team |
| boom | farm | ham | plum | seam | whom |
| broom | firm | him | ram | seem | worm |
| bum | gem | hum | roam | slam | yam |
| clam | gloom | jam | room | steam | yum |
| dream | gram | loom | Sam | sum | zoom |

Computers and tablets can be used to assist children during independent reading. Many stories are available online and as e-books and offer features that allow children to highlight and hear confusing words read aloud. Computers and tablets also offer a motivational factor that is important when working with struggling readers.

## 10 THE 44 SOUNDS OF ENGLISH — /n/ as in *nest*

**How formed:** The /n/ sound is a voiced alveolar nasal. To make the /n/ sound, press the tongue tightly against the upper gum. This prevents the vibrating breath from emerging through the mouth. The /n/ sound is one of three nasal sounds (/m/, /n/, /ng/). These sounds are responsible for resonance in the voice.

**Spellings:** The /n/ sound is most frequently represented by the letter *n*, as in *nest* and *can*. The letter *n* is a very reliable letter and is the only letter that is assigned this sound. However, sometimes the letter *n* can be silent. For example, one *n* can be silent when *n* is doubled in words, such as *runner* and *dinner*. The letter *n* can also be silent when it follows the letter *m*, as in *column* or *hymn*. The letter *n* is also a part of the digraph *ng*, which stands for the /ng/ sound, as in *king* and *sing*. The letter *n* by itself can also stand for the /ng/ sound as in *think* and *sank*. When the letters *n* and *g* appear together in a word but in different syllables, both the /ng/ and /g/ sounds are pronounced instead of the /ng/ sound. Words in which this occurs include *finger* and *kangaroo*. In words such as *ungrateful*, the prefix *un* represents one syllable and the letter *n* is pronounced as /n/, the letter *g* as /g/.

Other spellings of the /n/ sound include: *kn (knife)*, *gn (gnat, sign)*, *mn (mnemonic)*, *pn (pneumatic, pneumonia)*, *½gn (vignette)*, *mp (comptroller)*, *½n (cañon)*, *nd (handsome)*.

## Words for Instruction

### Initial Position

| | | | | | |
|---|---|---|---|---|---|
| nab | near | new | night | noise | now |
| nag | neck | newspaper | nine | noon | nub |
| nail | need | next | nip | north | nurse |
| name | needle | nice | nix | nose | nut |
| nap | nest | nick | no | not | |
| napkin | net | nickel | nod | note | |

### Final Position

| | | | | | |
|---|---|---|---|---|---|
| apron | clown | green | mean | run | train |
| balloon | coin | grin | men | seen | twin |
| ban | corn | hen | mitten | seven | van |
| bean | den | horn | moon | skin | violin |
| been | down | in | pain | spin | wagon |
| bin | drain | jean | pan | spoon | when |
| brain | fan | join | pen | sun | win |
| bun | fin | lawn | pin | tan | |
| button | flown | lemon | plan | ten | |
| can | fun | lion | pumpkin | then | |
| chain | gain | main | rain | thin | |
| clean | gown | man | ran | tin | |

# 11 THE 44 SOUNDS OF ENGLISH  /p/ as in *pig*

**How formed:** The /p/ sound is a voiceless bilabial plosive (stop). Its voiced counterpart is /b/. To make the /p/ sound, close and press the lips together. Then quickly open the lips to emit a puff of breath.

**Spellings:** The /p/ sound is most frequently represented by the letter *p*, as in *pig* or *map*. The letter *p* is a very reliable letter for this sound. However, sometimes the letter *p* is silent. For example, one *p* is silent when *p* is doubled in words, such as *supper, happy*, and *dripped*. In addition, *p* is usually silent when followed by the letters *n, s,* or *t*, as in *pneumonia, psychology*, and *ptomaine*. The letter *p* is also a part of the digraph *ph*, which stands for the /f/ sound, as in *phone* and *photograph*.

Another spelling of the /p/ sound is *ph* (*diphthong, diphtheria*).

## Words for Instruction

### Initial Position

| | | | | | | | |
|---|---|---|---|---|---|---|---|
| pack | pan | pea | pencil | pillow | poke | pour | push |
| pad | pant | peach | penny | pin | pole | puddle | put |
| page | pass | peak | pet | pine | pond | puff | putt |
| pail | past | pear | pickle | pint | pop | pull | puzzle |
| pain | pat | pedal | pie | pipe | pork | pumpkin | |
| paint | patch | peel | pig | pit | port | punt | |
| pal | paw | peg | pike | pod | post | puppet | |
| pale | pay | pen | pill | point | potato | purse | |

### Final Position

| | | | | | | | |
|---|---|---|---|---|---|---|---|
| cap | deep | heap | leap | pop | skip | stop | up |
| cheap | dip | hip | lip | pup | sleep | sweep | weep |
| chip | drip | hop | map | rap | slip | tap | whip |
| chop | drop | jeep | mop | rip | snap | tip | wrap |
| clip | flap | keep | nap | sap | soap | top | zap |
| crop | flip | lamp | peep | sheep | stamp | trap | zip |
| cup | flop | lap | pep | sip | step | trip | |

---

## CLASSROOM SPOTLIGHT

### P is for *Parents*

One critical issue in phonics instruction is communicating to students' families what you are doing. Here are some ways to help parents understand:

- At open house and in family letters, share with students' families why and how you teach phonics.
- At open houses, display phonics charts and other work that reflect phonics instruction.
- In family letters, provide a regular feature that lists the skills you have worked on that week and an activity for families to do at home to reinforce the skill.

Sending home reading material with specific suggestions for involving parents helps them to see their children's growing reading abilities and the importance you place on reading as the ultimate goal and focus of all skills instruction.

# /r/ as in *rock*

**How formed:** The /r/ sound is a voiced, resonant consonant sound in most American pronunciations. To make the /r/ sound, open the jaws enough for the tip of the tongue to rise toward the top of the mouth. Then immediately drop the tongue tip back down as if to get ready for the next sound.

**Spellings:** The /r/ sound is most frequently represented by the letter *r*, as in *rock* or *car*. The letter *r* is a very reliable letter. It has no other sound assigned to it. The other most common spelling for the /r/ sound is *wr*, as in *write* or *wrong*. In this spelling, the letter *w* is silent.

Other spellings of the /r/ sound include: *rhy (rhyme), rrh (myrrh), l (colonel), rps (corps), rt (mortgage)*.

## Words for Instruction

### Initial Position

| | | | | | | | |
|---|---|---|---|---|---|---|---|
| rabbit | rake | rate | rib | rip | rocket | rot | rush |
| race | ram | rattle | rich | ripe | rod | round | rust |
| rack | ramp | rave | ride | rise | roll | row | |
| radio | ranch | raw | rig | road | roof | rub | |
| rag | range | ray | right | roast | room | rude | |
| rail | rank | real | rim | rob | root | rug | |
| rain | rap | red | ring | robe | rope | rule | |
| raise | rat | rent | rink | rock | rose | run | |

### Final Position

| | | | | | | | |
|---|---|---|---|---|---|---|---|
| bear | chair | door | four | hammer | jar | letter | spider |
| car | deer | finger | guitar | her | ladder | pear | zipper |

### Other Spellings

| | | | | |
|---|---|---|---|---|
| wrap | wreck | wring | write | wrote |
| wreath | wrench | wrist | wrong | |

## CLASSROOM SPOTLIGHT

### Non-English Speakers

Children whose primary language is not English may have difficulties pronouncing some of the sounds in English. For example:

- Children speaking Japanese or Mandarin may have difficulty distinguishing between the /l/ and /r/ sounds.
- Children speaking Spanish, Mandarin, Cantonese, and Laotian may substitute the /b/, /w/, or /p/ sounds for the /v/ sound.
- Children who speak the many languages that either do not contain consonant blends or contain only a small number of blends may have trouble learning these sound-spellings in English.

For additional information on challenges children learning English as a second language face, consult *The ESL/ELL Teacher's Book of Lists* by Jacqueline E. Kress (Jossey-Bass).

## 13 THE 44 SOUNDS OF ENGLISH — /s/ as in *sun*

**How formed:** The /s/ sound is a voiceless alveolar fricative. Its voiced counterpart is /z/. To make the /s/ sound, place the blade of the tongue near the alveolar ridge. Then force air through the narrow groove formed by the tongue. The breath stream strikes the teeth to produce a hissing sound.

**Spellings:** The /s/ sound is frequently represented by the letter *s*, as in *sun* or *bus*. The letter *s* is quite unreliable because it can stand for several sounds. In addition to the /s/ sound, the letter *s* can stand for the /z/ sound, as in *rose, is, dogs, dessert*, and *reason*; the /sh/ sound, as in *sure, sugar*, and *pressure*; and the /zh/ sound, as in *measure* and *pleasure*. In addition, the letter *s* is a part of the digraph *sh*, which stands for the /sh/ sound, and it is a part of many consonant clusters, such as *sc, sk, sl, sm, sn, sp, st, sw*, and *str*. When *s* is followed by the letter *c*, the two letters can stand for the /sk/ sounds, as in *scold*, or the *c* can be silent, as in *science* or *scent*. The letter *s* can also be silent when doubled in words, such as *kiss, lesson, dress*, and *kindness*. Another common spelling for the /s/ sound is *c* when followed by *i, e*, or *y*, as in *circle, cent, cycle*, and *face*.

Other spellings of the /s/ sound include: *ps (psychology), sch (schism), st (listen), sth (isthmus), tsw (boatswain), ½x (next), z (waltz)*.

## Words for Instruction

### Initial Position

| | | | | | | | |
|---|---|---|---|---|---|---|---|
| safe | sandwich | seal | sent | sign | size | son | south |
| sag | sang | see | serve | silk | so | song | sow |
| sage | sap | seed | set | sill | soak | soon | sub |
| said | sat | seek | seven | since | soap | soot | such |
| sail | sauce | seem | sew | sing | soar | sore | sue |
| sake | save | seen | sick | sink | sock | sort | suit |
| sale | saw | seep | side | sip | sod | soul | sum |
| salt | sax | self | sieve | sir | soft | sound | sun |
| same | say | sell | sigh | sit | soil | soup | surf |
| sand | sea | send | sight | six | some | sour | |

### Final Position

| | | | | | | | |
|---|---|---|---|---|---|---|---|
| boss | gas | less | mess | moss | pass | this | us |
| bus | kiss | loss | miss | octopus | plus | toss | yes |
| circus | | | | | | | |

### Other Spellings

| | | | | | | | |
|---|---|---|---|---|---|---|---|
| ceiling | cereal | city | chance | force | mice | peace | since |
| celery | cigar | ace | choice | glance | mince | pencil | slice |
| cell | cinch | advice | concert | grace | notice | place | space |
| cellar | cinder | Alice | dance | groceries | office | pounce | spruce |
| cement | circle | bounce | face | ice | officer | prince | trace |
| cent | circus | brace | fancy | lace | ounce | race | truce |
| center | citizen | Bruce | fence | mercy | pace | rice | twice |
| | | | | | | | voice |

# 14 THE 44 SOUNDS OF ENGLISH /t/ as in *top*

**How formed:** The /t/ sound is a voiceless alveolar plosive (stop). Its voiced counterpart is /d/. To make the /t/ sound, separate the teeth and the tongue. Then press lightly against the inside of the upper jaw. The unvocalized breath is briefly held above the tongue. Then quickly drop the tongue and allow the breath to escape with a sharp, explosive sound.

**Spellings:** The /t/ sound is frequently represented by the letter *t*, as in *top* or *cat*. The letter *t* is fairly reliable. However, sometimes the letter *t* is silent. For example, one *t* is silent when *t* is doubled in words, such as *bottom* and *little*. The letter *t* is also silent when it follows the letters *f* or *s*, as in *often* and *listen*. In addition, the letter *t* is silent in words borrowed from French, such as *bouquet, beret, debut,* and *ballet*. The letter *t* also appears in the digraph *th*, which can stand for the /th/ *(thing, with)* or /th̷/ *(that)* sounds, and *tch*, which stands for the /ch/ sound *(watch, pitch)*. In the *tch* digraph, the letter *t* is silent. The letter *t* can stand for other digraph sounds /ch/ and /sh/ when it is followed by the letters *i, e,* or *u*, as in *question, righteous, picture,* and *natural*.

Other spellings of the /t/ sound include: *th (Thomas, thyme), bt (doubt, debt), cht (yacht), ct (ctenophore, indict), ed (talked, asked), ght (bought), phth (phthisic), tw (two), pt (receipt)*.

## Words for Instruction

### Initial Position

| | | | | | |
|---|---|---|---|---|---|
| tab | tap | telephone | tip | toothbrush | town |
| table | tape | tell | tire | top | toy |
| tack | tar | ten | to | torn | tub |
| tag | tea | tent | toad | toss | tube |
| tail | teach | tick | toe | tote | tuck |
| take | team | tide | toll | touch | tug |
| talk | tear | tie | tomato | tough | tune |
| tall | tease | till | ton | tour | turn |
| tame | tee | time | tone | tow | turtle |
| tan | teen | tin | tool | towel | |

### Final Position

| | | | | | |
|---|---|---|---|---|---|
| bat | cot | great | meet | point | sleet |
| beat | cut | greet | met | pot | spot |
| beet | dot | hat | moat | put | sweet |
| bet | eight | heat | neat | quit | tent |
| bit | fat | hit | nest | rat | vote |
| blot | feet | hot | net | rocket | wait |
| boat | fit | hut | not | rot | wet |
| boot | flat | jacket | nut | rut | what |
| but | float | jet | paint | sat | wheat |
| carrot | foot | let | pat | seat | yet |
| cat | get | lot | pet | set | |
| cheat | goat | mat | pit | shut | |
| coat | got | meat | pleat | sit | |

## 15 THE 44 SOUNDS OF ENGLISH — /v/ as in *vase*

**How formed:** The /v/ sound is a voiced labiodental fricative. Its voiceless counterpart is /f/. To make the /v/ sound, place the lower lip slightly under the upper teeth. Then vibrate the vocal cords. You should be able to feel the vibration of the lip against the teeth.

**Spellings:** The /v/ sound is most frequently represented by the letter *v*, as in *vase* or *give*. The letter *v* is a very reliable letter for this sound and has no other sound assigned to it.

Other spellings of the /v/ sound include: *f (of), ph (Stephen), vv (flivver), lv (halve).*

### Words for Instruction

| Initial Position | | | | | |
|---|---|---|---|---|---|
| valentine | vain | vat | vent | view | vote |
| van | van | vault | verse | vine | |
| vase | vane | veal | very | visit | |
| violin | vase | vein | vest | voice | |

| Final Position* | | | | | |
|---|---|---|---|---|---|
| alive | dive | give | leave | rave | wave |
| arrive | dove | glove | live | save | weave |
| brave | drive | grave | love | serve | wove |
| carve | drove | grove | move | shave | |
| cave | five | have | pave | sleeve | |
| cove | gave | hive | prove | stove | |

*Note: Words ending in the /v/ sound are written using the letter *v* followed by an *e*. Point this out to students.

Connect phonics practice to the real world. In addition to reading books, engage children in reading newspapers, magazines, and environmental print. You might have children search the newspaper for words with the sound-spelling relationship they are learning.

## 16 THE 44 SOUNDS OF ENGLISH — /w/ as in *wagon*

**How formed:** The /w/ sound is a voiced semivowel (resonant). To make the /w/ sound, close the lips but do not press them together. Then vibrate the vocal cords. You should be able to feel the vibration of the lips. In words with *w* in which the lips do not meet *(throw, answer)*, there is no vocal cord vibration and therefore no /w/ sound.

**Spellings:** The /w/ sound is frequently represented by the letter *w* at the beginning of a word or syllable, as in *wagon* or *always*. The letter *w* is not a very reliable consonant letter because it can also act as a vowel when it follows another vowel, as in *throw*. In addition, the letter *w* is silent in words that begin with *wr (write)* or *who (whose)*. It is also silent in the word *two*. The letter *w* is a part of the digraph *wh*, as in *which* and *why*. The digraph *wh* stands for the /hw/ sound. In some foreign words, the letter *w* stands for the /v/ sound, as in *Wagner*.

In addition to the consonant *w*, the vowels *o* and *u* can stand for the /w/ sound. The vowel *o* stands for the /w/ sound in words such as *one, once,* and *choir*. The vowel *u* stands for the /w/ sound when it follows the letter *q* in words, such as *quick* and *queen*.

Other spellings of the /w/ sound include: *ju (marijuana), ou (Ouija, bivouac)*.

## Words for Instruction

| Initial Position | | | | | |
| --- | --- | --- | --- | --- | --- |
| wad | war | we | well | wind | wolf |
| wade | ware | weak | went | window | won |
| wag | warm | wealth | west | wing | wood |
| wage | warn | wear | wet | wink | wool |
| wagon | wash | weave | wick | wipe | word |
| waist | wasp | web | wide | wire | work |
| wait | waste | weed | wife | wise | world |
| wake | watch | week | wig | wish | worm |
| walk | water | weep | wild | wishbone | worry |
| wall | wave | weigh | will | wit | worst |
| wand | wax | weird | wilt | with | would |
| want | way | weld | win | woke | |

## 17 THE 44 SOUNDS OF ENGLISH — /y/ as in *yo-yo*

**How formed:** The /y/ sound is a voiced palatal semivowel (resonant). To make the /y/ sound, separate the teeth and press the sides of the tongue against the upper teeth. Raise the middle of the tongue to create an obstruction to the flow of air that passes over the arched tongue. The lips should be stretched from side to side while making the sound.

**Spellings:** The /y/ sound is represented by the letter *y*, as in *yellow* or *beyond*. The /y/ sound can also be represented by the vowels *i (onion)* and *e (azalea)*. The letter *y* is not a reliable letter for the /y/ sound. It represents the consonant sound /y/ about 3% of the time. This occurs when the letter *y* appears at the beginning of a word or syllable. When the letter *y* appears elsewhere in a word, it represents a vowel sound. The letter *y* is used as a vowel 97% of the time and can stand for the /ī/ sound (fly), /i/ sound (lymph), /ē/ sound (baby), or be a part of a long vowel digraph *ay (play)*.

Other spellings of the /y/ sound include: *j (hallelujah)*, *ll (tortilla)*, *½gn (vignette)*.

### Words for Instruction

| Initial Position | | | |
|---|---|---|---|
| yacht | yarn | yes | young |
| yak | yawn | yield | your |
| yam | year | yoke | yowl |
| yank | yeast | yolk | yo-yo |
| yard | yellow | you | yuck |

### CLASSROOM SPOTLIGHT

One activity my students enjoy when working with the /y/ sound is the yarn toss. As we sit in a circle, I say a word that begins with /y/ and toss a ball of yarn to a student in the circle. The student then says another word that begins with /y/ as he or she tosses the yarn ball while holding on to the end piece of the yarn. The activity continues as a yarn web is created connecting all the students. As each student says a word, I write it on the board and we check to see if the /y/ sound is represented by the letter *y*. At the end of the activity, we have a ready-made list for our Word Wall.

# 18 THE 44 SOUNDS OF ENGLISH — /z/ as in *zebra*

**How formed:** The /z/ sound is a voiced alveolar fricative. Its voiceless counterpart is /s/. To make the /z/ sound, let a vocalized breath emerge over the tongue in a steady stream. You should be able to feel the tongue vibration.

**Spellings:** The /z/ sound is sometimes represented by the letter *z*, as in *zebra* and *quiz*. The letter *z* is not a commonly used letter. The letter *s*, as in *does, nose,* and *dogs,* represents the /z/ sound more frequently than the letter *z*. The letter *z* is a moderately reliable letter. Sometimes the letter *z* is silent. For example, one *z* is silent when doubled in words such as *jazz* and *dizzy*. The letter *z* can also stand for the /s/ sound, as in *quartz, pretzel,* or *mezzo*; and the /zh/ sound, as in *azure*. In those words containing *tz*, the /s/ sound is easier to pronounce than the /z/ sound.

Other spellings of the /z/ sound include: *ss (scissors), x (xylophone, Xerxes), sc (discern), cz (czar), si (business), sp (raspberry), sth (asthma), thes (clothes), ½x (exact).*

## Words for Instruction

| Initial Position | | | | |
|---|---|---|---|---|
| zag | zebra | zinc | zipper | zoo |
| zap | zero | zing | zone | zoom |
| zeal | zest | zip | zonk | |

| Medial/Final Position | | | | |
|---|---|---|---|---|
| blizzard | daze | freeze | prize | snooze |
| breeze | doze | froze | quiz | squeeze |
| buzz | dozen | fuzz | size | trapezoid |
| buzzard | fizz | hazy | sneeze | whiz |

| Other Spellings | | | | | |
|---|---|---|---|---|---|
| amuse | cheese | excuse | is | raise | these |
| as | chose | fuse | noise | rise | those |
| because | close | girls | nose | rose | was |
| birds | daisy | has | pause | shoes | wise |
| boys | dogs | his | please | suppose | |
| cars | easy | hose | praise | tease | |

## 19 THE 44 SOUNDS OF ENGLISH — /ch/ as in *cheese*

**How formed:** The /ch/ sound is a voiceless palatal affricative. It is a combination of the /t/ and /sh/ sounds. Its voiced counterpart is /j/. To make the /ch/ sound, slightly round and stick out the lips, close the teeth, and press the tongue against them. The teeth spring slightly apart to let the breath explode.

**Spellings:** The /ch/ sound is frequently represented by the digraph *ch*, as in *cheese* or *lunch. Ch* is not a very reliable digraph. It can also stand for the /k/ sound in words of Greek origin, such as *chemical, character, chorus, orchestra, stomach,* and *school* (the word *ache* is of Anglo-Saxon origin); or the /sh/ sound in words of French origin, as in *Chicago, chiffon,* and *machine.*

Other spellings of the /ch/ sound include: *t (nature, situation),* tch *(match, catch),* c *(cello),* che *(niche),* te *(righteous),* tu *(natural),* th *(posthumous),* ti *(question).*

## Words for Instruction

| Initial Position | | | | | |
|---|---|---|---|---|---|
| chain | chart | cheep | chew | chin | chow |
| chair | chase | cheerful | chick | chip | chuckle |
| chalk | chat | cheese | chicken | chipmunk | chug |
| change | cheap | cheeseburger | child | chirp | chum |
| chap | cheat | cherry | children | chocolate | chunk |
| chapter | check | chess | chilly | choose | churn |
| charge | checker | chest | chime | chop | |
| charm | checkup | chestnut | chimney | chose | |

| Final Position | | | | | |
|---|---|---|---|---|---|
| beach | hunch | quench | trench | itch | stitch |
| bench | inch | ranch | batch | latch | stretch |
| branch | lunch | reach | catch | match | switch |
| bunch | much | rich | clutch | notch | watch |
| church | munch | sandwich | crutch | patch | witch |
| clinch | peach | search | ditch | pitch | |
| couch | perch | such | fetch | scratch | |
| crunch | pinch | teach | hitch | sketch | |
| each | punch | touch | hutch | snatch | |

# /sh/ as in *shark*

**How formed:** The /sh/ sound is a voiceless palatal fricative. Its voiced counterpart is /zh/. To make the /sh/ sound, the lips are slightly rounded and stuck out. The teeth are together and the tongue is relaxed. The air emerges in a steady stream.

**Spellings:** The /sh/ sound is frequently represented by the digraph *sh*, as in *shark* and *fish*. The digraph *sh* is a very reliable spelling for this sound. Whenever we see the letters *sh* together in a word they stand for the /sh/ sound unless they appear in separate syllables, such as in *mishap* or *dishonor*. The /sh/ sound can be represented by many other spellings, such as *s* (*sure, sugar*), *ti* (*nation*), *ch* (*machine*), and *ci* (*special*). The *ch* spelling for the /sh/ sound occurs mostly in words of French origin, such as *chalet, chamois, chef, machine, parachute, sachet, cliché, chic, Chevrolet, Michigan*, and *Chicago*.

Other spellings of the /sh/ sound include: *sch* (*schwa*), *ce* (*ocean*), *c* (*oceanic*), *chs* (*fuchsia*), *psh* (*pshaw*), *sci* (*conscience*), *se* (*nauseous*), *si* (*mansion*), *ss* (*tissue, issue*), *ssi* (*mission*), *sc* (*crescendo*), *t* (*negotiate*), ½*x* (*luxury*), ½*xi* (*noxious*).

## Words for Instruction

### Initial Position

| | | | | | |
|---|---|---|---|---|---|
| shack | shape | shed | shin | shop | shove |
| shade | share | sheep | shine | shore | shovel |
| shadow | shark | sheet | ship | short | show |
| shake | sharp | shelf | shirt | shorts | shower |
| shall | shave | shell | shock | shot | shuck |
| shallow | shawl | sherbet | shoe | should | shut |
| shame | she | shield | shoelace | shoulder | shy |
| shampoo | shear | shift | shoot | shout | |

### Final Position

| | | | | | | |
|---|---|---|---|---|---|---|
| ash | cash | dash | fresh | leash | push | splash |
| blush | clash | dish | gash | mash | rash | trash |
| brush | crash | fish | gush | mesh | rush | wash |
| bush | crush | flash | lash | mush | smash | wish |

### Other Spellings

| | | | | | |
|---|---|---|---|---|---|
| action | attention | nation | vacation | social | delicious |
| addition | fraction | station | patient | suspicion | vicious |

## CLASSROOM SPOTLIGHT

Provide quiet time each day for children to do independent reading. I suggest at least 10–15 minutes. During independent reading time, model good reading habits by reading a book of your choice. Share your excitement about the book and encourage children to share the books they are enjoying. Periodically, you might want to use this time to conduct student conferences or circulate around the room to help any children experiencing decoding difficulties. Question the child about what strategy he or she is using and why. You might want to point out an alternative strategy, explain why it can be used, and model how to use it.

## 21 THE 44 SOUNDS OF ENGLISH — /zh/ as in *treasure*

**How formed:** The /zh/ sound is a voiced palatal fricative. Its voiceless counterpart is /sh/.

**Spellings:** The /zh/ sound is never represented by the letters *zh*. This letter combination doesn't appear in English words. The /zh/ sound is, instead, represented by a wide range of spellings including: *si (vision, occasion), s (pleasure, measure), g (rouge, garage), z (azure), zi (brazier), ssi (scission), ti (equation), ½x (luxurious)*.

### Words for Instruction

| Medial Position | | | | | |
|---|---|---|---|---|---|
| Asia | decision | garage | occasion | sabotage | treasure |
| azure | equation | luxurious | pleasure | seizure | usual |
| bonjour | exposure | measure | rouge | television | vision |
| casual | | | | | |

## 22 THE 44 SOUNDS OF ENGLISH — /th/ as in *thumb* (voiceless)

**How formed:** The /th/ sound is a voiceless dental fricative. To make the /th/ sound, place the tip of the tongue between the teeth. Force the air through the front of the tongue without vibration.

**Spellings:** The /th/ sound is most frequently spelled by the digraph *th*, as in *thin* or *bath*. The digraph *th* represents two sounds—the voiceless /th/ sound, as in *thin*, and the voiced /t͟h/ sound, as in *the*. The letters *th* are fairly reliable for these two sounds. However, sometimes the letters *th* stand for the /t/ sound, as in *Thomas* and *thyme*, and sometimes they are silent as in *isthmus*. When the letters *th* appear together in a word, but are in separate syllables (*boathouse*), the *t* stands for /t/ and the *h* stands for /h/.

Another spelling of the /th/ sound is *chth (chthonian)*.

### Words for Instruction

| Initial Position | | | | | |
|---|---|---|---|---|---|
| thank | thermometer | thin | thirsty | thought | throw |
| Thanksgiving | thermos | thing | thirteen | thousand | thumb |
| thaw | thick | think | thirty | three | thump |
| theater | thief | third | thistle | thread | thunder |
| theme | thimble | thirst | thorn | through | |

| Final Position | | | | | |
|---|---|---|---|---|---|
| bath | broth | growth | north | south | worth |
| Beth | cloth | length | oath | teeth | wreath |
| birth | death | math | path | thief | |
| booth | fifth | moth | Ruth | tooth | |
| both | fourth | mouth | sixth | with | |

**23** THE 44 SOUNDS OF ENGLISH    **/th̸/ as in *the*** (voiced)

**How formed:** The /th̸/ sound is a voiced dental fricative. To make the /th̸/ sound, place the tip of the tongue between the teeth. Force the air through the front of the tongue while the tongue vibrates.

**Spellings:** The /th̸/ sound is most frequently spelled by the digraph *th*, as in *the* or *that*. Most of the words containing the /th̸/ sound are of higher frequency in English than those containing the /th/ sound. The digraph *th* represents two sounds—the voiceless /th/ sound, as in *thin*, and the voiced /th̸/ sound, as in *the*. The letters *th* are fairly reliable for these two sounds. However, sometimes the letters *th* stand for the /t/ sound, as in *Thomas* and *thyme*, and sometimes they are silent, as in *isthmus*. When the letters *th* appear together in a word, but are in separate syllables *(boathouse)*, the *t* stands for /t/ and the *h* stands for /h/.

## Words for Instruction

| Initial Position | | | | | | |
|---|---|---|---|---|---|---|
| than | the | them | there | they | those | thus |
| that | their | then | these | this | though | |

| Medial/Final Position | | | | |
|---|---|---|---|---|
| bathe | gather | smooth | together | whether |

**24** THE 44 SOUNDS OF ENGLISH    **/hw/ as in *wheel***

**How formed:** The /hw/ sound is rapidly disappearing from the English language. Many dialects do not distinguish the /hw/ sound in *whether* from the /w/ sound in *weather*. Listen carefully as you say aloud these words. Do you pronounce the beginning sound differently? When making the /hw/ sound, /h/ (just a puff of air) is vocalized before /w/. The jaws are apart to produce /h/, then close as the lips come closer together to produce /w/. You should be able to feel a slight vibration of the lips.

**Spellings:** The /hw/ sound is represented by the digraph *wh*. This spelling appears only at the beginning of a word or syllable. The digraph *wh* can also represent /h/, as in *who, whom, whose,* and *whole*.

## Words for Instruction

| Initial Position | | | | | |
|---|---|---|---|---|---|
| whack | wheel | wherever | whim | whirl | whittled |
| whale | wheelbarrow | whew | whimper | whisk | whiz |
| wham | wheelchair | whey | whine | whisker | whoops |
| what | when | which | whinny | whisper | whopper |
| whatever | whenever | whiff | whip | whistle | why |
| wheat | where | while | whir | white | |

## 25 THE 44 SOUNDS OF ENGLISH /ng/ as in *ring*

**How formed:** The /ng/ sound is a voiced velar nasal. To make the /ng/ sound, raise the back of the tongue toward the top of the mouth similar to the production of the /g/ and /k/ sounds. However, relax the soft palate to allow the air to flow through the nose. The /ng/ sound is one of three nasal sounds (/m/, /n/, /ng/). These sounds are responsible for resonance in the voice.

**Spellings:** The /ng/ sound is frequently represented by the letters *ng*, as in *ring*. This sound never occurs at the beginning of a word or syllable and always follows a vowel sound. The letters *ng* are only moderately reliable for this sound.

At the end of words, the letters *ng* always stand for the /ng/ sound. However, within words the two letters *n* and *g* can cause confusion. For example, the letter *n* alone may stand for the /ng/ sound and the *g* for /g/, as in *finger*; or the letter *n* may stand for the /n/ sound and the *g* for the /g/ sound, as in *ungrateful, ongoing,* or *engulf*. The letters *ng* can also stand for the /n/ and /j/ sounds as in *angel, change, plunge,* and *ranger*.

The letter *n* alone can represent the /ng/ sound when followed by *k*, as in *pink, rank, think,* and *sink*. In the words *linger* and *mango* you also hear the /g/ sound after /ng/.

Other spellings of the /ng/ sound include: *ngg (mah-jongg), ngue (tongue), nd (handkerchief)*.

### Words for Instruction

| Medial/Final Position | | | | |
|---|---|---|---|---|
| angry | linger | strong | bank | sank |
| bang | long | strength | brink | shrunk |
| clang | longer | thing | drink | sink |
| clung | rang | wing | drunk | sunk |
| finger | ring | wrangler | honk | tank |
| gang | rung | wringer | ink | thank |
| gong | sang | young | junk | wink |
| hang | sing | | link | |
| hung | song | | mink | |
| hunger | sprung | | pink | |
| king | strangler | | rank | |

# /ā/ as in *cake*

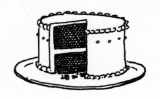

**How formed:** The /ā/ sound is referred to as the long-*a* sound. To make the /ā/ sound, the front part of the tongue is midheight in the mouth. The lips are unrounded and the facial muscles are relatively tense.

**Spellings:** The most common spellings of the /ā/ sound include *a_e (cake)*, *ai (pain)*, and *ay (say)*.

Other spellings of the /ā/ sound include: *a(r) (vary)*, *ai(r) (fair)*, *ey (they, obey)*, *ae (Gael)*, *ag (champagne)*, *aig (campaign)*, *aigh (straight)*, *ao (gaol)*, *au (gauge)*, *é (exposé)*, *e (suede)*, *ea (steak)*, *ee (matinee)*, *eh (eh)*, *ei (veil)*, *eig (feign)*, *eigh (sleigh, eight)*, *eilles (Marseilles)*, *er (dossier)*, *es (demesne)*, *et (beret)*, *hei (heir)*, *ie (lingerie)*, *ué (appliqué)*, *uet (bouquet)*.

## Words for Instruction

| | | | | | |
|---|---|---|---|---|---|
| bake | grade | skate | claim | rain | hay |
| blade | grape | space | drain | rail | jay |
| brace | lake | stage | fail | raise | lay |
| brake | late | take | faint | sail | may |
| brave | made | tale | faith | snail | maybe |
| cage | make | tape | frail | Spain | pay |
| cake | male | trace | grain | stain | play |
| came | maze | trade | jail | strain | player |
| case | name | vase | laid | tail | pray |
| cave | page | wade | maid | trail | ray |
| chase | place | wake | mail | train | say |
| date | plate | wave | main | vain | spray |
| face | race | whale | nail | waist | stay |
| fade | rake | aid | paid | wait | stray |
| flake | sale | aim | pail | bay | sway |
| flame | same | bait | pain | birthday | today |
| game | save | braid | paint | clay | tray |
| gate | shade | Braille | plain | day | way |
| gave | shake | brain | praise | gay | |
| grace | shape | chain | raid | gray | |

# /ē/ as in *feet*

**How formed:** The /ē/ sound is referred to as the long-e sound. To make the /ē/ sound, the front part of the tongue is high in the mouth. The lips are unrounded and the facial muscles are relatively tense.

**Spellings:** The most common spellings of the /ē/ sound include e *(we)*, ee *(feet)*, ea *(heat)*, y *(lazy)*, and ie *(field)*.

Other spelling of the /ē/ sound include: *ey (key), uay (quay pronounced "key"), ae (Caesar), e'e (e'en), e_e (precede), ei (receive), eip (receipt), eo (people), i_e (machine), is (debris), oe (amoeba), ea_ue (league), it (esprit), ui (mosquito), agh (shillelagh), ois (chamois).*

## Words for Instruction

| | | | | | | |
|---|---|---|---|---|---|---|
| be | peek | weep | lean | weak | lady | thirty |
| me | peel | wheel | leap | wheat | lately | tiny |
| we | peep | beach | leash | yeast | lobby | tricky |
| bee | queen | bead | least | zeal | lucky | ugly |
| beech | reef | beak | meal | any | many | windy |
| beef | screech | beam | mean | baby | mommy | babies |
| beep | screen | bean | meat | beauty | muddy | belief |
| beet | see | beat | neat | bunny | navy | believe |
| cheek | seed | bleach | pea | candy | ninety | berries |
| cheep | seek | bleak | peach | carry | only | brief |
| cheese | seem | cheap | peak | chilly | party | brownie |
| creep | seen | cheat | plead | city | penny | Charlie |
| deed | seep | clean | pleat | county | plenty | chief |
| deep | sheep | cream | reach | daddy | pony | cities |
| deer | sheet | deal | read | daisy | pretty | cookies |
| fee | sleep | dear | real | dirty | puppy | field |
| feed | sleet | dream | scream | dizzy | quickly | fierce |
| feel | speech | each | sea | dusty | sandy | grief |
| feet | speed | east | seal | duty | seventy | niece |
| flee | steel | eat | seam | easy | shiny | parties |
| free | steep | feast | seat | eighty | silly | pennies |
| greed | street | flea | sneak | family | sixty | pierce |
| green | sweep | gleam | speak | forty | sleepy | relief |
| greet | sweet | heal | steal | fifty | slowly | shield |
| heed | teen | heap | steam | funny | smoothly | shriek |
| jeep | teeth | heat | stream | fuzzy | sticky | siege |
| keep | three | jeans | tea | gravy | story | thief |
| knee | tree | lead | teach | happy | strawberry | yield |
| meet | weed | leaf | team | jelly | sunny | |
| need | week | leak | treat | kitty | thirsty | |

## 28 THE 44 SOUNDS OF ENGLISH /ī/ as in *bike*

**How formed:** The /ī/ sound is referred to as the long-*i* sound. Most linguists categorize this sound as a diphthong.

**Spellings:** The most common spellings of the /ī/ sound include *i_e (bike), y (my), i (child), ie (tie),* and *igh (high).*

Other spellings of the /ī/ sound include: *ais (aisle), ay (kayak), aye (aye), ei (stein), eigh (height), ey (geyser), eye (eye), is (island), uy (buy), ye (lye), ia (diamond), oy (coyote), ui_e (guide).*

## Words for Instruction

| | | | | | |
|---|---|---|---|---|---|
| bike | like | size | cry | kind | fight |
| bite | lime | slice | dry | mild | flight |
| bride | line | slide | fly | mind | fright |
| chime | live | spice | fry | rind | high |
| chive | mice | spike | my | wild | knight |
| dime | mile | splice | pry | wind | light |
| dine | mine | stride | shy | cries | might |
| dive | nice | strive | sky | die | night |
| drive | nine | tide | sly | died | right |
| fine | pike | time | spy | dries | sigh |
| fire | pine | tire | try | flies | sight |
| five | pipe | twice | why | fries | slight |
| grime | price | twine | bind | lie | thigh |
| hide | rice | whine | blind | pie | tight |
| hike | ride | white | child | skies | |
| hive | ripe | wide | climb | spies | |
| ice | rise | wife | find | tie | |
| kite | shine | wise | grind | tries | |
| life | side | by | hind | bright | |

# 29 THE 44 SOUNDS OF ENGLISH — /ō/ as in *boat*

**How formed:** The /ō/ sound is referred to as the long-*o* sound. To make the /ō/ sound, the back part of the tongue is midheight in the mouth. The lips are rounded and the facial muscles are relatively tense.

**Spellings:** The most common spellings of the /ō/ sound include *o (go), o_e (home), oa (boat), ow (show),* and *oe (toe).*

Other spellings of the /ō/ sound include: *ou/ough (boulder/though), ew (sew), au (mauve), aut (hautboy), aux (faux pas), eau (beau), eaux (Bordeaux), eo (yeoman), oh (oh), ol (yolk), oo (brooch), ot (depot), owe (owe), os (apropos).*

## Words for Instruction

| | | | | | |
|---|---|---|---|---|---|
| bold | alone | lone | yoke | roam | pillow |
| bolt | bone | nose | zone | roast | row |
| cold | broke | note | boat | soak | shadow |
| colt | choke | phone | cloak | soap | show |
| fold | chose | poke | coach | throat | shown |
| go | close | pole | coal | toad | slow |
| gold | clothes | pose | coast | toast | snow |
| hold | clove | robe | coat | whoa | sparrow |
| jolt | code | rode | croak | below | stow |
| mold | cone | rope | float | blow | swallow |
| no | cope | rose | foam | blown | throw |
| old | cove | slope | goal | bow | thrown |
| poll | dome | smoke | goat | bowl | tow |
| pro | dose | spoke | groan | crow | willow |
| roll | doze | stone | Joan | flow | window |
| scold | drove | stove | load | flown | yellow |
| scroll | froze | stroke | loaf | glow | doe |
| so | globe | those | loan | grow | foe |
| sold | grove | throne | moan | grown | goes |
| stroll | hole | tone | moat | know | hoe |
| told | home | vote | oak | known | Joe |
| toll | hope | whole | oats | low | toe |
| troll | hose | woke | roach | mellow | woe |
| volt | joke | wrote | road | mow | |

**/yo͞o/ as in *cube***

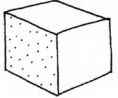

**How formed:** The /yo͞o/ sound is referred to as the long-*u* sound. It is a combination of a consonant and a vowel. Some linguists categorize this sound as a diphthong.

**Spellings:** The most common spellings of the /yo͞o/ sound include *u_e* (*cube*), *u* (*music*), *ew* (*few*), and *ue* (*cue*).

Other spellings of the /yo͞o/ sound include: *eu* (*feud*), *ueue* (*queue* pronounced *"cue"*), *eau* (*beauty*), *hu* (*huge*), *ieu* (*purlieu*), *iew* (*view*), *yew* (*yew*), *you* (*you*), *yu* (*Yule*), *ewe* (*ewe*), *ut* (*debut*).

## Words for Instruction

| | | | | | |
|---|---|---|---|---|---|
| cube | puke | January | unit | mew | fuel |
| cute | use | menu | united | pew | hue |
| fume | bugle | museum | university | preview | rescue |
| fuse | community | music | unusual | review | value |
| huge | future | pupil | usual | view | beautiful |
| mule | human | regular | Utah | argue | beauty |
| muse | humid | uniform | few | continue | |
| mute | humor | union | hew | cue | |

## CLASSROOM SPOTLIGHT

Use the word lists when you're creating sentences for Daily Oral Language practice. Write two sentences on the board, each containing grammar, spelling, and punctuation errors. Have children, as a class, suggest ways to correct the sentences. Though this daily exercise should take no more than five minutes, these small review sessions significantly reinforce basic grammar, spelling, and punctuation skills. **Tip:** During student writing conferences, remind children of what they have reviewed in Daily Oral Language as you focus their attention on specific sentences with errors. Then give them an opportunity to correct their writing errors before you correct them.

## 31 THE 44 SOUNDS OF ENGLISH — /a/ as in *cat*

**How formed:** The /a/ sound is referred to as the short-*a* sound. To make the /a/ sound, the front part of the tongue is low in the mouth. The lips are unrounded.

**Spellings:** The most common spelling of the /a/ sound is *a* (*cat*).

Other spellings of the /a/ sound include: *a_e* (*have*), *ai* (*plaid*), *al* (*half*), *au* (*laugh*), *aa* (*baa*), *a'a* (*ma'am*), *ach* (*drachm*), *ag* (*diaphragm*), *ui* (*guimpe*), *ah* (*dahlia*), *i* (*meringue*), *ua* (*guarantee*).

## Words for Instruction

| | | | | | |
|---|---|---|---|---|---|
| act | cat | flap | lamp | past | slam |
| add | catch | flash | land | pat | slant |
| am | champ | flat | lap | patch | snap |
| as | chat | gap | lash | path | span |
| at | clam | gas | last | plan | splash |
| back | clamp | gasp | latch | plant | stack |
| bad | clan | glad | mad | quack | stamp |
| bag | clap | glass | man | rack | stand |
| ban | clash | grab | map | rag | strand |
| band | class | grand | mash | ram | tab |
| basket | crack | grant | mask | ramp | tack |
| bat | craft | graph | mass | ran | tag |
| batch | cramp | grass | mast | rant | tan |
| bath | crash | had | mat | rap | tap |
| black | dab | ham | match | rash | task |
| blast | dad | hand | math | rat | than |
| bran | damp | has | nag | sack | that |
| branch | dash | hat | nap | sad | track |
| brand | drag | hatch | pack | sag | trap |
| brass | fact | jack | pad | sand | van |
| cab | fad | jam | pal | sap | vat |
| camp | fan | jazz | Pam | sat | wag |
| can | fast | lack | pant | scratch | yam |
| cap | fat | lad | pants | slab | |
| cast | flag | lag | pass | slack | |

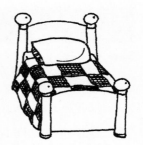

# 32 THE 44 SOUNDS OF ENGLISH /e/ as in *bed*

**How formed:** The /e/ sound is referred to as the short-*e* sound. To make the /e/ sound, the front part of the tongue is midheight in the mouth. The lips are unrounded and the facial muscles are lax.

**Spellings:** The most common spellings of the /e/ sound include *e (bed), ea (head), e_e (ledge)*.

Other spellings of the /e/ sound include: *ai (said), a_e (care), a (any), ae (aesthete), ay (says), eg (phlegm), ei (heifer), eo (leopard), ie (friend), u (bury), ue (guess)*.

## Words for Instruction

| | | | | | |
|---|---|---|---|---|---|
| bed | chest | help | met | shed | them |
| beg | crest | hem | neck | shelf | then |
| bell | deck | hen | nest | shell | vest |
| belt | den | jet | net | sled | vet |
| bench | desk | kept | peck | slept | web |
| bend | dress | led | peg | smell | well |
| bent | egg | left | pen | spell | went |
| best | elf | leg | pest | spend | wept |
| bet | elm | lend | pet | spent | west |
| bled | end | less | press | stem | wet |
| blend | fed | lest | red | step | when |
| bless | fell | let | rest | stress | wreck |
| cell | fled | men | sell | tell | yell |
| cent | fresh | mend | send | ten | yes |
| check | gem | mesh | sent | tent | yet |
| chess | get | mess | set | test | |

### Other Words for Instruction

| | | | | | |
|---|---|---|---|---|---|
| ahead | feather | instead | ready | wealthy | ledge |
| bread | head | lead | spread | weather | pledge |
| breakfast | health | leather | sweater | dense | sense |
| dead | heaven | meant | thread | fence | tense |
| dread | heavy | read | wealth | hedge | wedge |

## 33 THE 44 SOUNDS OF ENGLISH — /i/ as in *fish*

**How formed:** The /i/ sound is referred to as the short-*i* sound. To make the /i/ sound, the front part of the tongue is high in the mouth. The lips are unrounded and the facial muscles are lax.

**Spellings:** The most common spelling of the /i/ sound is *i (fish)*.

Other spellings of the /i/ sound include: *y (gym), i_e (give), a_e (damage), e (pretty), ee (been), ei (counterfeit), ia (marriage), ie (sieve), o (women), u (busy), ui (build), ai (mountain), u_e (minute)*.

## Words for Instruction

| | | | | | |
|---|---|---|---|---|---|
| bib | dish | him | milk | sill | tick |
| bid | disk | hip | mill | sink | tip |
| big | drink | his | miss | sip | trick |
| bill | drip | hiss | mitt | sit | trim |
| bit | fib | hit | mix | six | trip |
| blimp | fig | in | nip | skin | twig |
| blink | fill | ink | pick | skip | which |
| brick | fin | inn | pig | skit | whip |
| chick | fish | is | pill | slick | wick |
| chill | fist | it | pin | slid | wig |
| chin | fit | kick | pink | slim | will |
| click | fix | kin | pit | slip | win |
| clip | flick | kiss | rib | splint | wink |
| crib | flip | lick | rich | sprint | wish |
| crisp | gift | lid | rid | stick | wit |
| did | gig | lift | rig | stink | zip |
| dig | gill | link | rim | swim | |
| dill | glint | lip | rip | thin | |
| dim | hid | list | shift | think | |
| dip | hill | lit | ship | this | |

# /o/ as in *lock*

**How formed:** The /o/ sound is referred to as the short-*o* sound. To make the /o/ sound, the central part of the tongue is low in the mouth. The lips are rounded.

**Spellings:** The most common spelling of the /o/ sound is *o (lock)*.

Other spellings of the /o/ sound include: *a (watch), o_e (gone), ach (yacht), au (astronaut), eau (bureaucracy), ou (cough), ho (honor), oh (John), ow (knowledge)*.

## Words for Instruction

| | | | | | |
|---|---|---|---|---|---|
| blob | dock | hog | mom | pop | slot |
| block | doll | hop | mop | pot | sob |
| blot | dot | hot | nod | prop | sock |
| bop | drop | job | not | rob | sod |
| box | flock | jog | on | rock | spot |
| chop | flop | knob | ox | rod | stop |
| clock | fog | knock | plod | rot | tock |
| cob | fox | knot | plop | shock | top |
| cod | frog | lock | plot | shot | trot |
| cot | gob | log | pod | shop | |
| crop | got | lot | pond | slop | |

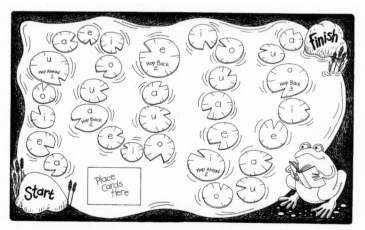

c _ p

d _ sk

fr _ g

h _ n

s _ n

v _ n

Games and learning center activities are a fun way to practice and reinforce skills after initial instruction.

# 35 THE 44 SOUNDS OF ENGLISH — /u/ as in *duck*

**How formed:** The /u/ sound is referred to as the short-*u* sound. To make the /u/ sound, the central part of the tongue is midheight in the mouth. The lips are unrounded and the facial muscles are lax.

**Spellings:** The most common spelling of the /u/ sound is *u (duck)*.

Other spellings of the /u/ sound include: *o (son), o_e (some), ou (double), oe (does), oo (blood), u_e (judge)*.

## Words for Instruction

| | | | | | |
|---|---|---|---|---|---|
| bluff | clump | fun | lug | pup | struck |
| blunt | clunk | fuss | lump | putt | strum |
| blush | clutch | fuzz | much | rub | stub |
| brush | crust | glum | muck | ruff | stuck |
| buck | cub | grub | mud | rug | stump |
| bud | cuff | gruff | mug | run | sub |
| buff | cup | gum | mush | runt | such |
| bug | cut | gust | musk | rush | suds |
| bum | drug | hug | must | rust | sum |
| bump | drum | hum | mutt | rut | sun |
| bun | duck | hunt | nut | shun | truck |
| bunch | dug | hush | pluck | shrub | trunk |
| bunt | dull | husk | plug | shut | tub |
| bus | dump | hut | plum | skunk | tuck |
| but | dunk | jug | plus | slug | tug |
| buzz | dusk | jump | puff | slump | tusk |
| chunk | dust | just | pump | snub | up |
| club | fluff | luck | punt | snug | us |

## 36 THE 44 SOUNDS OF ENGLISH /ə/ as in *alarm*

**How formed:** The /ə/ sound is referred to as the schwa sound or murmur sound. It is graphically represented by an upside-down *e*. Some linguists don't consider it a sound, rather a phonetic variant or allophone. To make the /ə/ sound, the central part of the tongue is midheight in the mouth. The lips are unrounded and the facial muscles are relatively tense.

**Spellings:** The /ə/ sound can be spelled with any vowel—*a (alone), e (happen), i (direct), o (gallop), u (circus)*. Several multisyllabic words beginning with *a* as their first unaccented syllable contain this sound. Below is a list of these words. The schwa sound appears in most multisyllabic words and is the most common sound in English.

### Words for Instruction

| | | | | | |
|---|---|---|---|---|---|
| about | afraid | alarm | anew | ashamed | awake |
| above | again | alas | annoy | ashore | aware |
| account | ago | alone | another | aside | away |
| adult | agree | along | apart | asleep | awhile |
| afloat | ahead | America | appear | avoid | awoke |
| afoot | ajar | among | applause | await | |

## 37 THE 44 SOUNDS OF ENGLISH /â/ as in *chair*

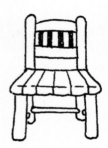

**How formed:** The /â/ sound is an *r*-controlled vowel sound. The diacritical mark above the *a* is known as a circumflex.

**Spellings:** The most common spellings of the /â/ sound include *air (chair), are (bare),* and *ear (wear).*

Other spellings of the /â/ sound include: *eir (their), ere (where), ayer (prayer), aire (doctrinaire), eer (Myneer), ey're (they're).*

### Words for Instruction

| | | | | | |
|---|---|---|---|---|---|
| air. | pair | dare | mare | spare | swear |
| chair | stair | fare | pare | square | wear |
| fair | bare | flare | rare | stare | |
| flair | blare | glare | scare | bear | |
| hair | care | hare | share | pear | |

## 38 THE 44 SOUNDS OF ENGLISH — /û/ as in *bird*

**How formed:** The /û/ sound is an *r*-controlled vowel sound. The diacritical mark above the *u* is known as a circumflex.

**Spellings:** The most common spellings of the /û/ sound include *ur (burn)*, *er (verb)*, and *ir (bird)*.

Other spellings of the /û/ sound include: *ear (learn)*, *err (err)*, *eur (poseur)*, *or (work)*, *our (scourge)*, *urr (purr)*, *yr (myrtle)*.

### Words for Instruction

| | | | | | | | |
|---|---|---|---|---|---|---|---|
| blur | hurt | turtle | fir | squirt | clerk | nerve | swerve |
| burn | nurse | urge | firm | stir | ever | other | term |
| burst | purple | bird | first | swirl | fern | over | under |
| church | purr | birth | flirt | third | germ | perch | verb |
| churn | purse | birthday | girl | thirst | her | perk | verge |
| curb | spur | chirp | quirk | twirl | herd | person | verse |
| curl | surf | circle | shirt | whirl | jerk | river | water |
| curse | Thursday | circus | sir | after | letter | serve | winter |
| curve | turkey | dirt | skirt | better | merge | sister | |
| fur | turn | dirty | squirm | certain | mother | stern | |

## 39 THE 44 SOUNDS OF ENGLISH — /ä/ as in *car*

**How formed:** The /ä/ sound is often an *r*-controlled vowel sound. The diacritical mark above the *a* is known as a dieresis.

**Spellings:** The most common spelling of the /ä/ sound is *a (car, father)*.

Other spellings of the /ä/ sound include: *à (à la mode)*, *aa (bazaar)*, *ah (hurrah)*, *al (calm)*, *as (faux pas)*, *at (éclat)*, *ea (hearth)*, *oi (reservoir)*, *ua (guard)*, *e (sergeant)*.

### Words for Instruction

| | | | | | | | |
|---|---|---|---|---|---|---|---|
| arch | bar | charge | farm | jar | mart | shark | starch |
| Arctic | bark | charm | garden | lard | park | sharp | tar |
| ark | barn | chart | guard | large | part | smart | tart |
| arm | car | dark | hard | march | party | spark | yard |
| art | card | dart | harm | mark | scar | star | yarn |
| artist | cart | far | harp | marsh | scarf | start | |

**/ô/ as in *ball***

**How formed:** The /ô/ sound is referred to as the broad *o* sound. The diacritical mark above the *o* is known as a circumflex. To make the /ô/ sound, the back part of the tongue is midheight in the mouth.

**Spellings:** The most common spellings of the /ô/ sound include *o[r] (for)*, *a[l] (walk)*, *a[ll] (tall)*, *au (haul)*, and *aw (hawk)*.

Other spellings of the /ô/ sound include: *ou (cough)*, *oa (broad)*, *o (toss)*, *ah (Utah)*, *as (Arkansas)*, *augh (caught)*, *ough (sought)*.

## Words for Instruction

| | | | | | |
|---|---|---|---|---|---|
| bore | north | sworn | halt | sauce | paw |
| born | or | thorn | malt | sausage | pawn |
| chore | porch | torch | salt | taught | raw |
| chord | pore | tore | audience | vault | saw |
| cord | pork | torn | August | awful | shawl |
| core | port | wore | author | bawl | slaw |
| cork | scorch | worn | autumn | brawl | sprawl |
| corn | score | chalk | because | caw | squawk |
| door | scorn | stalk | caught | claw | straw |
| dorm | shore | talk | cause | crawl | strawberry |
| for | short | walk | clause | dawn | thaw |
| force | snore | all | daughter | draw | yawn |
| fork | sore | ball | dinosaur | drawn | |
| form | sort | call | fault | fawn | |
| fort | sport | fall | fraud | flaw | |
| forth | store | hall | haul | gnaw | |
| horn | stork | mall | haunt | hawk | |
| horse | storm | small | launch | jaw | |
| more | sword | stall | laundry | law | |
| morning | swore | tall | Paul | lawn | |
| | | wall | pause | lawyer | |

## 41 THE 44 SOUNDS OF ENGLISH — /oi/ as in *boy*

**How formed:** The /oi/ sound is a diphthong.

**Spellings:** The most common spellings of the /oi/ sound include *oi (boil)* and *oy (toy)*.

Other spellings of the /oi/ sound include: *eu (Freud), ois (Iroquois), uoy (buoy)*.

### Words for Instruction

| | | | | | |
|---|---|---|---|---|---|
| avoid | hoist | point | annoy | enjoy | soy |
| boil | join | poison | boy | joy | toy |
| broil | joint | rejoice | cowboy | joyful | voyage |
| choice | moist | soil | coy | loyal | |
| coil | moisture | spoil | decoy | ploy | |
| coin | noise | toil | destroy | Roy | |
| foil | oil | voice | employ | royal | |

## 42 THE 44 SOUNDS OF ENGLISH — /ou/ as in *house*

**How formed:** The /ou/ sound is a diphthong.

**Spellings:** The most common spellings of the /ou/ sound include *ou (shout)* and *ow (town)*.

Other spellings of the /ou/ sound include: *au (landau), ough (bough), hou (hour)*.

### Words for Instruction

| | | | | | |
|---|---|---|---|---|---|
| about | grouch | pouch | spout | crown | plow |
| bounce | ground | pound | sprout | down | powder |
| bound | hound | pout | trout | drown | power |
| cloud | house | proud | allow | fowl | prowl |
| couch | loud | round | bow | frown | sow |
| count | mound | scout | brow | gown | towel |
| crouch | mouse | shout | brown | growl | tower |
| doubt | mouth | snout | chow | how | town |
| flour | noun | sound | clown | howl | vow |
| foul | ouch | sour | cow | now | wow |
| found | out | south | crowd | owl | |

# 43 THE 44 SOUNDS OF ENGLISH  /oo̅/ as in *moon*

**How formed:** The /oo̅/ sound is referred to as the long sound of *oo*. To make the /oo̅/ sound, the back part of the tongue is high in the mouth. The lips are rounded and the facial muscles are tense.

**Spellings:** The most common spellings of the /oo̅/ sound include *oo* (moon), *u* (ruby), *ue* (true), *ew* (chew), and *u_e* (tune).

Other spellings of the /oo̅/ sound include: *o* (do), *ou* (soup), *ui* (suit), *o_e* (move), *eu* (maneuver), *ieu* (lieu), *oe* (canoe), *ou* (route), *ug* (impugn), *ooh* (pooh), *ough* (through), *oup* (coup), *ous* (rendezvous).

## Words for Instruction

| | | | | | | | |
|---|---|---|---|---|---|---|---|
| balloon | goose | moon | shoo | tooth | crew | flute | truth |
| bloom | groom | moose | shoot | troop | dew | June | tuna |
| boo | hoof | noon | sloop | zoo | drew | prune | |
| boom | hoop | ooze | smooth | zoom | flew | reduce | |
| boot | hoot | pool | snoop | blue | grew | rude | |
| broom | igloo | proof | soon | clue | knew | rule | |
| coo | kangaroo | roof | spook | due | new | tube | |
| cool | loom | room | spool | glue | news | tune | |
| coop | loop | root | spoon | sue | screw | duty | |
| doom | loose | school | stool | true | shrew | July | |
| food | loot | scoop | too | blew | stew | junior | |
| fool | moo | scoot | tool | brew | threw | numeral | |
| gloom | mood | shampoo | toot | chew | crude | solution | |

---

## CLASSROOM SPOTLIGHT

### Two oos

The letters *oo* can stand for two sounds about the same percentage of time. Therefore, I often advise children to try both sounds when confronted with an unfamiliar word that contains this spelling. If the word is in their speaking or listening vocabularies, then the approximation resulting from trying one of the sounds will help the students figure out the word. On the Word Wall, I write the /oo̅/ words on moon shapes and the /o͝o/ words on book shapes as visual reminders of the sound the letters *oo* stand for in each word listed.

## 44 THE 44 SOUNDS OF ENGLISH
# /o͝o/ as in *book*

**How formed:** The /o͝o/ sound is referred to as the short sound of *oo*. To make the /o͝o/ sound, the back part of the tongue is high in the mouth. The lips are rounded and the facial muscles are lax.

**Spellings:** The most common spellings of the /o͝o/ sound include *oo (book)* and *u (pull, put, push)*.

Other spellings of the /o͝o/ sound include: *oul (could), o (wolf), oui (bouillon)*.

## Words for Instruction

| | | | |
|---|---|---|---|
| afoot | good | rook | woof |
| book | good-bye | rookie | wool |
| brook | hood | shook | |
| cook | hoof | soot | |
| cookie | hook | stood | |
| crook | look | took | |
| foot | nook | wood | |
| football | notebook | wooden | |

## TRY IT OUT

- Use the word lists to create speed drills or individualized student practice sheets.
- Create phonics games and activities for learning centers using the word lists.
- Connect the word lists to your phonics instruction. Use the word lists for blending practice prior to reading stories or to create sentences and passages for reading practice.

# Creating Lessons for Success

"*The question as to whether phonics should, or should not, be taught has been bandied about a good deal for several years.*"

—Mary Dougherty from 1923

**M**any years ago, Flintstones lunch box in hand, I entered a small, rural classroom in a school building I had occasionally passed by and frequently wondered about. The large, brick building was old and run-down, but memories of the brightly illustrated books and seemingly fun activities my older sister brought home piqued my interest. On my first day of grade one, my teacher (Mrs. Wershaw) distributed to each of us eager, neatly dressed six-year-olds a basal reader and introduced us to three characters we would grow to love—Dick, Jane, and Sally. In addition, she gave us a phonics workbook whose plaid cover had the same design as the girls' skirts at the Catholic school in a neighboring town. Mrs. Wershaw's combined approach to teaching us how to read (sight-word and phonics methods) was the key that unlocked the mysteries of print for me. And, even though some argue about the lack of engaging text in these early readers, I was enthralled by the ability to take those strange-looking lines and squiggles on the page and turn them into something that made sense. This early success was my motivation!

My strongest memory of the impact of these stories came one Friday afternoon. Mrs. Wershaw had a strict rule that we could not read ahead in our basals. So on Friday, when Sally fell headfirst into a clothes hamper and I couldn't turn the page to discover the outcome, I had a weekend of tremendous anxiety. On Monday I raced into school to see if Sally was okay. She was! It was my first taste of suspense in books, and I was forever hooked.

But many wonder (and argue about) how children are being taught to read today. Are teachers using a sight-word method? Are they using a phonics method? Or, as I believe, are they using some combined approach? And what role does phonics play in that instruction? In this chapter I focus on the ways phonics can be taught, provide recommendations for phonics instruction, and give you sample lessons and word lists to help you plan your phonics instruction.

Repeated readings of familiar stories help children to develop fluency and increase reading rate.

## How Phonics Is Taught

When the topic of phonics instruction is raised, I am always reminded of stories I heard, while living in the Appalachian Mountains of West Virginia, about two feuding families—the Hatfields and the McCoys. The two families were so engulfed in their bitter dispute that they had forgotten why they were even fighting. It seems the fight, and declaring a side to support, was more important than dealing with the cause of the disagreement. For a brief period, when Johnson ("Johnse") Hatfield fell in love with Rose Anna McCoy, the common bond between the two groups became apparent. They weren't as different as they had supposed. This romance, however, was eventually stopped so that the battle could rage on. When educators discuss phonics they frequently seem adamant about being either a Hatfield ("phonics will save the world") or a McCoy ("phonics will destroy the world"). Yet it has been my experience that many classroom teachers are neither; rather, they are a mix of the two—a McField, if you like.

Unfortunately, some teachers are forbidden to use phonics materials, and when no one is looking, they sneak them out of the closets and drawers in which they hide. So how is phonics generally taught in classrooms across this country, and what are the best approaches to teaching it?

There are two major approaches to phonics instruction—synthetic and analytic.

The **synthetic approach** is also known as **direct** or **explicit phonics**. This method follows a bottom-up model of learning to read. That is, children begin by learning to recognize letters, then blend words, and finally read connected text. Instruction roughly follows this sequence:

1. The letter names are taught.
2. The sound that each letter stands for is taught and reviewed. Some rules or generalizations might be discussed.
3. The principle of blending sounds to form words is taught.
4. Opportunities to blend unknown words in context are provided.

The following model lesson illustrates how to introduce the /s/ sound using the synthetic approach.

**Model:** Write the letter *s* on the board. Explain to children that the letter *s* stands for the /s/ sound, such as the first sound heard in the word *sat*. Write the word *sat* on the board and have a volunteer circle the letter *s*. Slowly blend the word as you run your finger under each letter. Then ask children for other words that begin with the /s/ sound. List these words on the board. Have volunteers circle the letter *s* in each word. Continue by providing children with simple words containing the /s/ sound to blend. Make sure these words can be decoded based on the sound-spelling relationships previously taught.

The **analytic approach**, also known as **indirect** or **implicit phonics**, is sometimes referred to as the "discovery method." With this approach, children begin with words and are asked to deduce the sound-spelling relationship that is the focus of the current lesson. Instruction in this method roughly follows this sequence:

1. A list of words with a common phonic element is shown. For example, the words *sat, send,* and *sun* might be written on the board.
2. Children are asked to examine the words and discover what they have in common, focusing on finding a similar sound.
3. When the common sound is discovered, the spelling that stands for the sound might be discussed.
4. Children are asked to verbalize a generalization about the sound and spelling, such as, "The letter *s* stands for the /s/ sound."

The analytic approach gained popularity with teachers who believed that if children discovered these principles for themselves, they'd internalize them better. However, one of the drawbacks of this method is that it relies on a child's ability to orally segment words. It isn't effective for children who can't break off the first sound in a given word or who don't understand what is meant by the term *sound*. These children lack the phonemic-awareness skills they need for the analytic approach to have meaning. And the method has proved least effective with students at risk for reading disorders.

In addition to these two methods, some teachers use the Tactile-Kinesthetic approach. In this method, based on the learning styles research of Carbo (1988) and others, children are asked to examine words using a variety of learning modalities, such as visual, auditory, kinesthetic, and tactile. *Tactile* refers to touch. Tactile learners might be asked to make letters out of clay and trace them with their fingers. *Kinesthetic* refers to hand or body movements. Kinesthetic learners might be asked to form letters with their bodies, jump when they hear a particular sound, or use letter cards to build words.

Current research supports a combined approach to teaching phonics, with a heavy emphasis on synthetic (explicit) instruction (Anderson et al., 1985; Adams, 1990). Before I share other recommendations for phonics instruction, it will be helpful to take a brief look at how children's decoding abilities develop. This will help to form the big picture, within which you can make instructional decisions.

During the primary grades, most children are at a stage of reading development referred to as the Initial Reading, or Decoding, Stage (Chall, 1983). It is at this stage that children are taught sound-spelling relationships and how to blend sounds to form words. (For more information on reading development stages, see pages 24–26.) Within each stage of reading development, children progress in roughly predictable ways. Several researchers (Biemiller, 1970; Juel, 1991) have looked at how children progress through the Initial Reading Stage. Juel has outlined three stages, or levels of progression, within the Initial Reading Stage. She calls these the Stages of Decoding.

## The Stages of Decoding

### Stage 1: Selective-Cue Stage

Readers learn about print and its purposes. Activities to help children gain this insight include labeling classroom objects, reading aloud Big Books, group writing exercises such as shared and experience writing, and reading patterned/predictable books. To read words, children rely on three possible cues: (1) *random cues*, which include almost any visual clue that will help the child to remember the word. It can be something as abstract as a thumbprint or smudge next to the word (Gough, 1991); (2) *environmental cues*, which include where the word

Sound-Spelling Cards should be on constant display.

is located on the page; and (3) *distinctive letters*, such as the *y* in *pony* or the two *ll*'s in *yellow*.

### Stage 2: Spelling-Sound Stage

Readers focus on graphophonic cues to learn sound-spelling relationships and the importance of attending to each letter in a word. They learn how to blend words and make full use of their growing knowledge of sound-spelling relationships. Phonics instruction plays a crucial role at this stage.

### Stage 3: Automatic Stage

Readers use both contextual (meaning) and graphophonic (phonics) cues. It's at this point that readers develop fluency (accuracy and speed in decoding). Fluency is critical and comes with "overlearning" (automaticity results, which is an outcome of constant review and repetition using sound-spelling knowledge to blend words in context). This acquired automaticity enables readers to focus on the meaning of increasingly complex passages instead of on the mechanics of reading.

When you think about these stages, it's important to ask yourself, "What do my children need instructionally in order to progress effectively through each of these stages?" Each stage has instructional implications, and an emphasis on any one stage without consideration of the others can cause problems. Well-designed instruction is the key to moving children through these stages efficiently and effectively. For example, one of the instructional problems I see frequently is the failure to connect the sound-spelling relationships children have been taught and the text they are given to practice using these relationships to decode words. That is, few words in the stories contain the same sound-spelling relationships children have been taught during phonics lessons or are decodable based on the sound-spellings learned. Therefore, when children encounter words in the stories, they have few opportunities to use their growing knowledge of sound-spelling relationships. If this happens, children are likely to undervalue the importance of the phonics they're learning. Why should they pay attention during phonics lessons when they rarely use what they learn? As a result, these children don't gain fluency, are forced to rely on meaning cues such as context and pictures, and lose out on important blending practice. Many researchers have found that most poor readers over-rely on meaning cues. They're likely stuck in an earlier stage of decoding, unable to progress because of flawed instruction (Stanovich, 1980).

# Characteristics of Strong Phonics Instruction

Active. Social. Reflective. These three words best express the phonics instruction to strive for in your classroom. Look to design a program that makes children aware of what they're doing, why they're doing it, and how they're progressing. This type of phonics instruction can be described as "metaphonics"—phonics combined with metacognition. As you develop a phonics program, never lose sight of your goal to give children a basic understanding of the alphabetic principle and how to use this insight to read for pleasure and information. "The purpose of phonics instruction is not that children learn to sound out words. The purpose is that they learn to recognize words, quickly and automatically, so that they can turn their attention to comprehension of text" (Stahl, 1992).

Based on my work with teachers, school districts, and publishers, I've determined seven characteristics that all strong phonics programs or systems must have in place. Absence or weakness in any one or more of these characteristics can have negative effects on student learning gains (Blevins, 2016).

1 **Readiness Skills** The two best predictors of early reading success are phonemic awareness and alphabet recognition. Phonemic awareness is the understanding that words are made up of discrete sounds. A range of subskills is taught to develop phonemic awareness, with oral blending and oral segmentation having the most positive impact on reading and writing development. I refer to these skills as the power skills. Alphabet recognition involves learning the names, shapes,

and sounds of the letters of the alphabet with fluency. Phonemic awareness and alphabet recognition are focused on primarily in kindergarten and Grade 1.

**2 Scope and Sequence** A strong scope and sequence that builds from the simple to the complex in a way that works best for student learning is critical to student achievement at all stages of learning. While there is no one "right" scope and sequence, programs that strive to connect concepts and move through a series of skills in a small stair-step way offer the best chance at student success.

**3 Blending** This is the main strategy for teaching students how to sound out words and must be frequently modeled and applied. It is the focus of early phonics instruction, but still plays a role when transitioning students from reading one-syllable words to multisyllabic words.

**4 Dictation** To best transition students' growing reading skills to writing, dictation (guided spelling) is critical and should begin as early as kindergarten. While not a spelling test, this activity can accelerate students' spelling abilities and understanding of common English spelling patterns.

**5 Word Awareness** While the introduction to phonics skills is best when explicit and systematic, students need opportunities to play with words and experiment with how word parts combine to solidify and consolidate their understanding of how English words work. Word sorts and word building are two key activities to increase students' word awareness.

**6 High-Frequency Words** Those high-utility words that are irregular based on common sound-spelling patterns or need to be taught before students have all the phonics skills to access them through sounding out must be addressed instructionally in a different way. Typically the top 200–300 words are taught in Grades K–2. Past Grade 2, when the majority of the key high-frequency words have been introduced, students need to be continually assessed on their mastery of these words, as a lack of fluency can impede comprehension.

**7 Reading Connected Text** The type of text we use in early reading instruction has a powerful effect on the word-reading strategies students develop (Juel & Roper-Schneider, 1985) and can affect student motivation to read (Blevins, 2000). Controlled, decodable text at the beginning level of reading instruction helps students develop a sense of comfort in and control over their reading growth and should be a key learning tool in early phonics instruction.

**PLUS You, the Teacher:** The power and impact of the above characteristics depend on them being implemented by a skilled, informed teacher. Teachers with stronger backgrounds in linguistics and research-based phonics instructional routines are better equipped at noticing and addressing student errors, have improved language of instruction, and can more easily differentiate their teaching to meet student needs. Differentiated professional development can assist schools and districts in building teacher capacity when it comes to phonics instruction.

You can use the checklist on page 140 to evaluate your phonics instruction. It's based on guidelines established by research and practice over the past several decades (Stahl, 1992; Chall, 1996; Vacca, 1995; Beck & McCaslin, 1978).

## Warnings

Some phonics instructional programs fail because (Chall, 1996; Beck & McCaslin, 1978):

- instruction is hit-or-miss, instead of systematic.
- instruction is too abstract.
- children are not taught how to blend words.
- instruction is not connected to actual reading.
- there is not enough review and application.
- too many rules and sound-spelling relationships are taught.
- the pace of instruction is too fast.
- phonics is taught as the only way to figure out unfamiliar words.
- too much time is spent on tasks that have little relationship to reading; for example, children are asked to identify pictures of objects whose names contain a target sound, instead of looking at the letter and responding with its corresponding sound (Bateman, 1979).

## About Scope and Sequence

One of the most difficult decisions to make when developing any phonics program is the order, or *sequence*, in which the sound-spelling relationships are taught. Educators have considerable debates about this issue. One of the key areas of dissent is the teaching of vowel sounds. Some argue that long-vowel sounds should be taught first since these sounds are easier to discriminate auditorily than short-vowel sounds. In addition, the long vowels "say their names." One drawback to this approach is that there are many long-vowel spellings, and introducing children to such complexities before they have gained key insights into how the "system" works might create serious problems. Others argue that short-vowel sounds and their one key spelling should be taught first because many simple CVC (consonant-vowel-consonant) words (such as *cat, sun, hit*) can be generated. Many of these words appear in early reading materials (high utility), and the ease with which the "system" can be taught is increased.

I recommend the following regarding sequence:

- **Teach short-vowel sounds before long-vowel sounds.** Efficiency and ease of learning are critical. The simplicity of using short-vowel spellings and CVC words is beneficial to struggling readers.
- **Teach consonants and short vowels in combination so that words can be generated as early as possible.** Phonics is useless if it can't be applied, and what is not applied is not learned. By teaching short vowels and consonants in combination, you can create decodable, connected text so that children can apply their knowledge of learned sound-spelling relationships.

## Evaluation Checklist

**Your Phonics Instruction . . .**

- ❏ doesn't last too long. *Becoming a Nation of Readers* (Anderson et al., 1985) recommends that formal phonics instruction be completed by the end of second grade. Note that this refers to basic phonics skills. Students in Grades 3 and up will continue to require instruction in multisyllabic words.
- ❏ builds on a foundation of phonemic awareness and knowledge of how language works.
- ❏ is clear, direct, and explicit.
- ❏ contains instruction in blending.
- ❏ is integrated into a total reading program. Reading instruction must include these goals: decoding accuracy and fluency, increased word knowledge, experience with various linguistic structures, knowledge of the world, and experience in thinking about texts. Phonics is one important element.
- ❏ focuses on reading words and connected text, not learning rules.
- ❏ may include invented spelling practice.
- ❏ develops independent word-recognition strategies, focusing attention on the internal structure of words.
- ❏ develops automatic word-recognition skills (fluency) so that students can devote their attention to comprehension.
- ❏ contains repeated opportunities to apply learned sound-spelling relationships to reading and writing.

- **Be sure that the majority of the consonants taught early on are continuous consonants,** such as *f, l, m, n, r,* and *s.* Because these consonant sounds can be sustained without distortion, it's easier to model blending.
- **Use a sequence in which the most words can be generated.** For example, many words can be generated using the letter *t*; however, few can be generated using the letter *x.* Therefore, higher-frequency sound-spelling relationships should precede less-frequent ones.
- **Progress from simple to more complex sound-spellings.** For example, consonant sounds should be taught before digraphs *(sh, ch, th, wh, ph, gh, ng)* and blends *(br, cl, st, and so on).* Likewise, short-vowel sound-spellings should be taught before long-vowel sound-spellings, variant vowels, and diphthongs. Here is a suggested sequence:
  - short vowels and consonants in combination
  - blends (*r*-blends, *s*-blends, *l*-blends)
  - digraphs *(ch, sh, th, wh)*
  - final *e (a_e, e_e, i_e, o_e, u_e)*
  - long vowels (multiple spellings)
  - variant vowels *(oo, au, aw)* and diphthongs *(ou, ow, oi, oy)*
  - silent letters, inflectional endings *(-ed, -s, -ing)*

Following are the Grade 1 phonics skill sequences used in two current basal reading programs known for their strong phonics instruction. Note the similarities. Also note how the sound-spellings taught are highly generative (many words can be formed from them) in the early part of the year.

## Program A

m, a, -ad, l, t, s, o, -ot, -op, h, i, -id, p, -og, f, n, c, b, -ill, w, j, -ab, z, d, r, -op, e, -en, -et, g, x, k, ck, -ap, -ick, u, -un, th, /z/s, -in, y, v, -ut, q, sh, -ob, a_e, -ace, -ake, i_e, o_e, u_e, long e (e, ea, ee), -eat, r-blends, l-blends, s-blends, ch, wh, long a (ai, ay), -ain, /ô/ (all, aw, au), -ed, long o (o, ow), long e (ey, y), long o (oa), /o͝o/, /o͞o/, /ou/ (ou, ow), -ink, -ing, -ank, -unk, long i (igh, y), -ild, -ind

## Program B

m, a, t, h, p, n, c, d, s, i, b, r, f, g, o, x, ar, ck, u, z, l, e, ea, y, w, wh, r-controlled vowels (er, ir, ur), sh, th, ch, tch, k, long a (a, a_e), j, dge, ge, gi, long i (i, i_e), ce, ci, long o (o, o_e), /z/s, v, long u (u, u_e), long e (e, e_e, ea, ee), q, long vowels plus r, long e (y, ie), long a (ai, ay), long i (igh, y, ie), ng, long o (oe, ow, oa), long u (ew, ue), /ou/ (ou, ow), /ô/ (aw, au), /o͝o/ (oo, ue, u_e, u, ew), /o͞o/, kn, /oi/ (oi, oy), wr, ph

Another primary decision is the *scope* of instruction: deciding which sound-spelling relationships are important enough to warrant instruction and which, because of their lower frequency in words, can be learned on an as-needed basis. The chart below shows the most frequent spellings of the 44 sounds covered in this book. These are the sounds and spellings covered in most basal reading programs.

The percentages provided in parentheses are based on the number of times each sound-spelling appeared in the 17,000 most frequently used words (Hanna et al., 1966). These included multisyllabic words.

## The Most Frequent Spellings of the 44 Sounds of English

| Sound | Common Spellings | Sound | Common Spellings |
|---|---|---|---|
| 1. /b/ | b (97%), bb | 18. /z/ | z (23%), zz, s (64%) |
| 2. /d/ | d (98%), dd, ed | 19. /ch/ | ch (55%), t (31%) |
| 3. /f/ | f (78%), ff, ph, lf | 20. /sh/ | sh (26%), ti (53%), ssi, s, si sci |
| 4. /g/ | g (88%), gg, gh | 21. /zh/ | si (49%), s (33%), ss, z |
| 5. /h/ | h (98%), wh | 22. /th/ | th (100%) |
| 6. /j/ | g (66%), j (22%), dg | 23. /tͪ/ | th (100%) |
| 7. /k/ | c (73%), cc, k (13%), ck, lk, q | 24. /hw/ | wh (100%) |
| 8. /l/ | l (91%), ll | 25. /ng/ | n (41%), ng (59%) |
| 9. /m/ | m (94%), mm | 26. /ā/ | a (45%), a_e (35%), ai, ay, ea |
| 10. /n/ | n (97%), nn, kn, gn | 27. /ē/ | e (70%), y, ea (10%), ee (10%), ie, e_e, ey, i, ei |
| 11. /p/ | p (96%), pp | 28. /ī/ | i_e (37%), i (37%), igh, y (14%), ie, y_e |
| 12. /r/ | r (97%), rr, wr | 29. /ō/ | o (73%), o_e (14%), ow, oa, oe |
| 13. /s/ | s (73%), c (17%), ss | 30. /yo͞o/ | u (69%), u_e (22%), ew, ue |
| 14. /t/ | t (97%), tt, ed | 31. /a/ | a (96%) |
| 15. /v/ | v (99.5%), f (of) | 32. /e/ | e (91%), ea, e_e (5%) |
| 16. /w/ | w (92%) | 33. /i/ | i (66%), y (23%) |
| 17. /y/ | y (44%), i (55%) | 34. /o/ | o (79%) |

| Sound | Common Spellings | Sound | Common Spellings |
|---|---|---|---|
| **35.** /u/ | u (86%), o, ou | **40.** /ô/ | o, a, au, aw, ough, augh |
| **36.** /ə/ | a (24%), e (13%), i (22%), o (27%), u | **41.** /oi/ | oi (62%), oy (32%) |
| **37.** /â/ | a (29%), are (23%), air (21%) | **42.** /ou/ | ou (56%), ow (29%) |
| **38.** /û/ | er (40%), ir (13%), ur (26%) | **43.** /ōō/ | oo (38%), u (21%), o, ou, u_e, ew, ue |
| **39.** /ä/ | a (89%) | **44.** /o͝o/ | oo (31%), u (54%), ou, o (8%), ould |

In addition to sound-spelling relationships, other aspects of phonics knowledge, such as word analysis and syllabication, must be covered. You'll find a recommended scope of skills for each grade below (Chall, 1996; Blevins, 1997).

## Scope of Skills

### Kindergarten
- concepts of print
- alphabet recognition
- phonemic awareness
- blending (CVC pattern)
- sense of story
- building world knowledge

### Grade 1
- phonemic awareness
- blending and word building
- short vowels (*a, e, i, o, u*—CVC pattern)
- consonants
- final *e* (*a_e, e_e, i_e, o_e, u_e*—CVCe pattern)
- long-vowel digraphs (*ai, ay, ea, ee, oa, ow*, etc.)
- consonant clusters (*br, cl, st*, etc.)
- digraphs (*sh, ch, th, wh*, etc.)
- some other vowels such as *oo, ou, ow, oi, oy*
- early structural analysis: verb endings (*-ing, -ed*), plurals, contractions, compound words
- connected text reading
- vocabulary development/world knowledge

### Grades 2–3
- Grade 1 skills review
- more complex vowel spellings
- more structural analysis (compound words, affixes, etc.)
- multisyllabic words
- syllabication strategies
- connected text reading
- vocabulary development/world knowledge

After decisions about scope and sequence are made, my last recommendation is that the instruction be systematic. What do I mean by this? **Systematic instruction** follows a sequence that progresses from easy to more difficult. Systematic instruction includes constant review and repetition of sound-spelling relationships, application to reading and writing, and focus on developing fluency through work with reading rate and decoding accuracy. Just because a program has a scope and sequence doesn't mean it is systematic. The instruction must be cumulative. The cumulative nature of children's growing knowledge of sound-spellings should be reflected in the types of literature they are given to practice using these sound-spellings to decode words. In addition, the instruction should help children understand how words "work." That is, how to use knowledge of sound-spellings to blend the sounds in words. In essence, the system should not only be in the reading program, it should be in the children. The type of instruction you give them should enable them to internalize how the "system" works.

# Meeting Rigorous Standards

Current state and national literacy standards provide strong guidelines for what phonics and word study skills need to be taught and at which grade level. Following are the relevant Common Core State Standards for Grades K–3. Standards associated with phonics are grouped in the Foundational Skills section of the standards. However, word study, which begins as early as kindergarten and is taught in tandem with phonics skills, extends beyond the scope of the foundational skills. In most standards documents, word-study skills, such as using affixes, can be found in the Language section (specifically the Vocabulary Acquisition and Use section in the Common Core State Standards). NOTE: There is great consistency in foundational skill standards across the United States and published reading curriculum reflects this. The states that have not adopted the Common Core State Standards have either used the CCSS Foundational Skills in their entirety or closely based their state standards on these well-established ones.

# Reading Standards Foundational Skills

## Kindergarten students

### Print Concepts
1. Demonstrate understanding of the organization and basic features of print.
   - **a.** Follow words from left to right, top to bottom, and page by page.
   - **b.** Recognize that spoken words are represented in written language by specific sequences of letters.
   - **c.** Understand that words are separated by spaces in print.
   - **d.** Recognize and name all upper- and lowercase letters of the alphabet.

### Phonological Awareness
2. Demonstrate understanding of spoken words, syllables, and sounds (phonemes).
   - **a.** Recognize and produce rhyming words.
   - **b.** Count, pronounce, blend, and segment syllables in spoken words.
   - **c.** Blend and segment onsets and rimes of single-syllable spoken words.
   - **d.** Isolate and pronounce the initial, medial vowel, and final sounds (phonemes) in three-phoneme (consonant-vowel-consonant, or CVC) words. (This does not include CVCs ending with /l/, /r/, or /x/.)
   - **e.** Add or substitute individual sounds (phonemes) in simple, one-syllable words to make new words.

### Phonics and Word Recognition
3. Know and apply grade-level phonics and word analysis skills in decoding words.
   - **a.** Demonstrate basic knowledge of one-to-one letter-sound correspondences by producing the primary sound or many of the most frequent sounds for each consonant.
   - **b.** Associate the long and short sounds with common spellings (graphemes) for the five major vowels.*
   - **c.** Read common high-frequency words by sight (e.g., *the, of, to, you, she, my, is, are, do, does*).
   - **d.** Distinguish between similarly spelled words by identifying the sounds of the letters that differ.

## Grade 1 students

### Print Concepts
1. Demonstrate understanding of the organization and basic features of print.
   - **a.** Recognize the distinguishing features of a sentence (e.g., first word, capitalization, ending punctuation).

### Phonological Awareness
2. Demonstrate understanding of spoken words, syllables, and sounds (phonemes).
   - **a.** Distinguish long from short vowel sounds in spoken single-syllable words.
   - **b.** Orally produce single-syllable words by blending sounds (phonemes), including consonant blends.
   - **c.** Isolate and pronounce initial, medial vowel, and final sounds (phonemes) in spoken single-syllable words.
   - **d.** Segment spoken single-syllable words into their complete sequence of individual sounds (phonemes).

### Phonics and Word Recognition
3. Know and apply grade-level phonics and word analysis skills in decoding words.
   - **a.** Know the spelling-sound correspondences for common consonant digraphs.
   - **b.** Decode regularly spelled one-syllable words.
   - **c.** Know final -*e* and common vowel team conventions for representing long vowel sounds.
   - **d.** Use knowledge that every syllable must have a vowel sound to determine the number of syllables in a printed word.
   - **e.** Decode two-syllable words following basic patterns by breaking the words into syllables.
   - **f.** Read words with inflectional endings.
   - **g.** Recognize and read grade-appropriate irregularly spelled words.

| Kindergarten students | Grade 1 students |
|---|---|
| **Fluency**<br>**4.** Read emergent-reader texts with purpose and understanding. | **Fluency**<br>**4.** Read with sufficient accuracy and fluency to support comprehension.<br><br>    **a.** Read grade-level text with purpose and understanding.<br><br>    **b.** Read grade-level text orally with accuracy, appropriate rate, and expression on successive readings.<br><br>    **c.** Use context to confirm or self-correct word recognition and understanding, rereading as necessary. |

**Common Core State Standards, Foundational Skills for Kindergarten (standard K.3.B) states: "Associate the long and short sounds with common spellings (graphemes) for the five major vowels." In Grade 1 (standard 1.3.c) CCSS states: "Know final-*e* and common vowel team conventions for representing long vowel sounds." So, mastery of long vowel spellings is expected in Grade 1. I strongly believe that students in kindergarten should be focused on mastering the reading of CVC short-vowel words only. The inclusion of long-vowel spellings in kindergarten is not appropriate, unless students are above level.

Note that the California Department of Education, when adopting the CCSS, added the caveat that in kindergarten students are expected to know that vowels have two major sounds—long and short, but are only required to learn the spellings for the short-vowel sounds. I think this is a sensible solution and we should not push down the phonics curriculum any more into kindergarten. Give our students time to build a strong foundation without rushing it.

| Grade 2 students | Grade 3 students |
|---|---|
| **Phonics and Word Recognition**<br>**3.** Know and apply grade-level phonics and word analysis skills in decoding words.<br><br>    **a.** Distinguish long and short vowels when reading regularly spelled one-syllable words.<br><br>    **b.** Know spelling-sound correspondences for additional common vowel teams.<br><br>    **c.** Decode regularly spelled two-syllable words with long vowels.<br><br>    **d.** Decode words with common prefixes and suffixes.<br><br>    **e.** Identify words with inconsistent but common spelling-sound correspondences.<br><br>    **f.** Recognize and read grade-appropriate irregularly spelled words. | **Phonics and Word Recognition**<br>**3.** Know and apply grade-level phonics and word analysis skills in decoding words.<br><br>    **a.** Identify and know the meaning of the most common prefixes and derivational suffixes.<br><br>    **b.** Decode words with common Latin suffixes.<br><br>    **c.** Decode multisyllable words.<br><br>    **d.** Read grade-appropriate irregularly spelled words. |

| Grade 2 students | Grade 3 students |
|---|---|
| **Fluency** | **Fluency** |
| **4.** Read with sufficient accuracy and fluency to support comprehension. | **4.** Read with sufficient accuracy and fluency to support comprehension. |
|     **a.** Read grade-level text with purpose and understanding. |     **a.** Read grade-level text with purpose and understanding. |
|     **b.** Read grade-level text orally with accuracy, appropriate rate, and expression on successive readings. |     **b.** Read grade-level prose and poetry orally with accuracy, appropriate rate, and expression on successive readings |
|     **c.** Use context to confirm or self-correct word recognition and understanding, rereading as necessary |     **c.** Use context to confirm or self-correct word recognition and understanding, rereading as necessary. |

# Language Skills

| Kindergarten students | Grade 1 students |
|---|---|
| **Vocabulary Acquisition and Use** | **Vocabulary Acquisition and Use** |
| **4. b.** Use the most frequently occurring inflections and affixes (e.g., *-ed, -s, re-, un-, pre-, -ful, -less*) as a clue to the meaning of an unknown word. | **4. b.** Use frequently occurring affixes as a clue to the meaning of a word. |
| |     **c.** Identify frequently occurring root words (e.g., *look*) and their inflectional forms (e.g., *looks, looked, looking*). |

| Grade 2 students | Grade 3 students |
|---|---|
| **Vocabulary Acquisition and Use** | **Vocabulary Acquisition and Use** |
| **4. b.** Determine the meaning of the new word formed when a known prefix is added to a known word (e.g., *happy/unhappy, tell/retell*). | **4. b.** Determine the meaning of the new word formed when a known affix is added to a known word (e.g., *agreeable/disagreeable, comfortable/uncomfortable, care/careless, heat/preheat*). |
|     **c.** Use a known root word as a clue to the meaning of an unknown word with the same root (e.g., *addition, additional*). |     **c.** Use a known root word as a clue to the meaning of an unknown word with the same root (e.g., *company, companion*). |
|     **d.** Use knowledge of the meaning of individual words to predict the meaning of compound words (e.g., *birdhouse, lighthouse, housefly; bookshelf, notebook, bookmark*). | |

# What Does a Good Phonics Lesson Look Like?

As I've visited classrooms across the country, I've seen a wide range of activities and instructional methods used to teach phonics. Many of these activities and methods have fallen under the umbrella of "explicit" phonics instruction. I've chosen those that are the most effective to help you develop your own guidelines for writing phonics lessons. Here are a few general dos and don'ts of phonics instruction (Groff, 1977; Blevins, 1997).

## Phonics Lesson Dos

- **Use a logical sequence.** Begin with phonemic awareness, then teach sound-spelling relationships. Progress to guided blending practice and conclude with reading and writing opportunities.
- **Be explicit in your introduction of sound-spelling relationships.** Some educators fear that explicit phonics instruction detracts from making meaning from text. They point to students' reading errors to support this notion—nonsense errors that reveal a strong focus on sound-spelling knowledge but less attention to meaning. Research suggests that making these nonsense errors is a stage that children will pass through as they become more accurate and faster decoders and learn how to use other cues to figure out unfamiliar words (Biemiller, 1970).
- **Provide frequent, daily lessons.**
- **Keep the lessons relatively brief and fast-paced.**
- **Keep the lessons focused.** Cover only a small segment at a time.
- **Begin lessons with what children know.**
- **Create a classroom environment in which children become active word watchers or word detectives.** Encourage a curiosity about words.
- **Provide a built-in review** of previously taught sound-spellings in each lesson. Use blending exercises, repeated readings, and so on.
- **Adjust the pace or scope of learning according to children's needs.** Don't set absolute deadlines for how much should be covered in a given time.
- **Regroup children according to their needs.**
- **Link phonics instruction to spelling** using dictation and freewriting activities.

- **Make learning public** by creating word walls, making letter charts, and sharing student writing.
- **Provide instruction that is reflective.** Gaskins et al. (1997) use the "Talk-To-Yourself Chart" with children to engage them in thinking about words. Here is a completed chart for the word *high*.

1. The word is <u>high</u>.
2. Stretch the word. I hear <u>2</u> sounds.
3. I see <u>4</u> letters because *igh* stands for one sound.
4. The spelling pattern is <u>igh</u>.
5. This is what I know about the vowel: <u>It is the long-i sound—/ī/</u>.
6. Another word on the Word Wall with the same vowel sound is <u>light</u>.

## Phonics Lesson Don'ts

- Avoid having children continually wait for turns. Instead, use small groups and every-pupil response cards.
- Avoid instruction that neglects to tell children directly what you want them to perceive and how you want them to respond.
- Avoid immediately correcting children's errors. Provide feedback only after you give children an opportunity to self-monitor and self-correct.
- Avoid inadequately addressing exceptions to the generalizations children are learning.
- Avoid using incorrect language or terminology. Examples:

1. Instead of saying, "You can hear the *f* sound," say, "You can hear the /f/ sound." *F* is a letter, not a sound.
2. Instead of saying, "What sounds do you see at the end of *mint*?" say, "What sounds do you hear at the end of the word *mint*?" You see letters; you hear sounds.
3. Instead of saying, "The letter *t* makes the /t/ sound," say, "The letter *t* stands for or represents the /t/ sound." Letters are inanimate objects, they do not make sounds.
4. Instead of saying, "The blend *st* stands for the /st/ sound," say, "The letters (cluster) *st* stand for the /st/ sounds." *Cluster* refers to a group of letters; *blend* refers to a group of sounds.
5. Instead of saying, "The letters *oi* are a diphthong," say, "The vowel pair (digraph) *oi* stands for the /oi/ sound." A *diphthong* is a sound; a *vowel pair* or *digraph* is a group of letters.

Based on the above guidelines, a phonics lesson should contain the following components, many of which I discuss in depth later.

- **Repeated readings.** Begin each lesson by having children reread a passage or brief story to develop fluency and reading rate. Repeated readings increase automaticity and improve comprehension (Samuels, 1988).
- **Phonemic awareness exercises.** Phonics instruction won't make much sense to children who haven't discovered the insight that a word is made up of a series of discrete sounds. For them, provide phonemic awareness training. For children who do have this insight, use oral blending and oral segmentation exercises as warm-up activities to reinforce it. (For additional information on phonemic awareness, refer to pages 47–62.)
- **Explicit introduction of sound/spelling relationship.** Directly state the relationship between the sound and the spelling that is the focus of the lesson. To help children remember the relationship, many programs provide some type of memory device, such as a key picture/word or a story. (See page 152 for guidelines on selecting key pictures/words.) In addition, provide a word familiar to children that contains the lesson's sound-spelling relationship. Use the word in a sentence. Then write the word on the board. (You'll find sample lessons on pages 178–206.)
- **Blending opportunities.** Model for children how to blend words using the new sound-spelling and provide lists of decodable words for children to practice blending. (See pages 153–156 for additional information on blending.)

In your writing center, provide word lists and prompts that focus on specific phonics skills.

- **Word-building opportunities.** Children need opportunities to play with sounds and spellings. Provide each child with a set of letter cards he or she can use for word building throughout the year. Following each lesson, distribute four to eight cards containing spellings previously taught to each child and allow children time to make as many words as possible. Circulate around the room and help children blend the sound that each spelling stands for to form a word.
- **Controlled text reading opportunities.** Many types of text are necessary in an elementary reading program. One of these is connected text, in which a high proportion of the words are decodable based on the sound-spelling relationships previously taught. Provide repeated reading opportunities of this text. This strategy honors what children are learning by providing a direct connection between the skills taught and actual reading (Adams, 1990; Taylor & Nosbush, 1983).
- **Dictation.** In order to make the reading-writing connection, children need guided opportunities to use the sound-spelling relationships in writing. In addition to this structured writing exercise, provide children with freewriting opportunities. (Additional information on dictation is provided in the sample lessons on pages 178–206.)

## A DAILY SCHEDULE

In addition to your daily 10–15 minute formal phonics lesson, you can embed sound-spelling relationship instruction in many of the activities you do throughout the day. Here's a sample daily schedule from a second-grade classroom. I've **boldfaced** the time periods in which the teacher embedded phonics instruction.

|  |  |
|------|----------|
| 8:45–9:00 | Attendance, Calendar, Lunch Count, **Daily Oral Language** |
| 9:00–10:30 | **Reading/Language Arts Block** |
| 10:30–10:45 | Recess |
| 10:45–11:00 | Phonics |
| 11:00–11:15 | **Spelling** and Handwriting |
| 11:15–11:30 | **Read Aloud Big Book or Trade Book** |
| 11:30–12:00 | Lunch |
| 12:00–1:00 | Math |
| 1:00–2:00 | **Science/Social Studies** |
| 2:00–2:40 | Specials (Physical Education, Music, Art) |
| 2:40–3:00 | Silent Reading |
| 3:00–3:20 | **Extra Language Arts**, *Scholastic News*, Daily Wrap-Up |

# Memory Devices: Choosing the Best

Many reading programs provide key pictures and words for each sound-spelling relationship to help children. Careful selection of the key picture/word is important because some of the most commonly used key pictures/words can cause confusion for children. The vowel sounds are particularly problematic. For example, *egg* is often used for the short-vowel sound /e/. However, many dialects pronounce the *e* in *egg* more like an /ā/ sound than an /e/ sound. Another short-*e* word, *elephant*, is also problematic. Many children perceive the first sound in the word *elephant* as "l." Other key words are simply too long, and children have difficulty focusing on the target sound. I recommend the following in choosing key pictures/words:

- Use simple, short words.
- For consonants, avoid words that begin with blends (for example, use *fish* instead of *frog*).
- For vowels, choose CVC or CVCe words because it is difficult to find picturable words in which the vowel sound is the first sound.

In addition, Moats (1995) suggests that the following words be avoided:

| Vowel | Words to Avoid |
|-------|----------------|
| /a/ | ant, bag, air |
| /e/ | egg, elephant |
| /i/ | igloo, Indian, ink |
| /o/ | on, off |
| /u/ | umbrella, uncle |

See the "Learning About Sounds and Letters" section of this book for key words and pictures for each sound.

Some reading programs embed memory devices in an introductory story by associating actions or characters with the target sounds or spellings. An example of one such story (the first and last sections only) used in a basal reading series (*Collections for Young Scholars*, Open Court Publishing, 1995) follows. Note that the sound is a key component of the story. In fact, at the end of the story, children are asked to produce the sound. They are then shown a card with a picture of the story's character (the gopher) and the spellings for the target sound (/g/). This picture card can be prominently displayed in the classroom for easy reference.

**Sample**

Gary's a gopher.
He loves to gulp down food.
/g/ /g/ /g/ /g/ /g/, gulps the gopher.
Gary the Gopher gobbles in the garden
Until everything is gone.
What sound does Gary the Gopher make?
*(Ask children to join in)* /g/ /g/ /g/ /g/ /g/

# Blending: Teaching Children How Words Work

**Blending** is the primary strategy we teach students to decode, or sound out, words (Resnick and Beck, 1976). It is simply the stringing together of letter-sounds to read a word. For example, if a student sees the word *sat*, he would say the sound for each letter/spelling (/s/ /a/ /t/) and string, or sing together, the sounds (/sat/). This *phonic blending* (visual blending) is different from *oral blending* (auditory blending). Oral blending is a phonemic-awareness skill and doesn't involve print, whereas phonic blending involves the printed word. Oral blending exercises help children understand how sounds can be blended to form words, and these exercises make nice warm-up activities for phonics instruction.

Some children seem to develop the ability to blend sounds in words naturally (Whaley & Kirby, 1980), whereas other children need to be taught this skill explicitly. As a result, blending is a strategy that must be frequently modeled and applied in phonics instruction to have the maximum benefit for students and is critical to enabling children to generalize sound-spelling relationships to new words (Golinkoff, 1978). Research shows that teachers who spend larger than average amounts of time on blending—modeling blending and providing loads of practice blending words in isolation and in context (e.g., daily in early reading instruction and practice)—achieve greater student gains (Rosenshine & Stevens, 1984; Haddock, 1978).

When beginning to teach students how to blend words it is best to use words that start with continuous sounds. These are sounds that can be stretched without distortion. These sounds include the vowel sounds and several of the consonant sounds (/f/, /l/, /m/, /n/, /r/, /s/, /v/, /z/). In this way you can more easily model how to move from one sound to the next, blending them to form a word, as in /sssaaat/ to make /sat/. As a result, words like *am, sad,* and *fan* are great words for beginning blending models. If, for example, you chose the word *bat* instead to introduce how to blend words, there is a great likelihood you would add a vocalization to the end of the /b/ sound since it is a stop sound and very difficult to pronounce purely in isolation. What would result would sound like /buh/ to your students. Now imagine you ask students to string together the sounds in *bat* that you just pronounced individually (/buh/ /a/ /t/). The resulting word would be /buh-at/, instead of /bat/. Once students understand the principle of blending you don't need to worry about this as much. And, when sounding out words beginning with stop sounds like /b/, /k/, and /d/ you can move quickly from the first to the second sound in the word with no pause or a minimal one between them to avoid the vocalized "uh."

Two types of blending are common: *final blending* and *successive blending*. Each has its place in phonics instruction.

### Final Blending

In final blending, you blend one sound at a time as you work through the word. It looks like this for the word *sat*.

- The teacher writes the letter *s* (or displays a letter card), points to it, and says the sound /s/.
- The teacher writes the letter *a* (or displays a letter card), points to it, and says /a/.
- Then the teacher slowly slides her finger under the two letters as she blends the sounds to form /sssaaa/.
- The teacher repeats, but this time slides her finger under the letters and blends more quickly, /sa/.
- The teacher writes the letter *t* (or displays a letter card), points to it, and says /t/.
- The teacher slowly slides her finger under all three letters in the word, stringing together the sounds, to form /sssaaat/.
- The teacher then repeats at a faster pace and says, "The word is *sat*."

This is the type of blending I recommend when first introducing the principle of blending to your students. It allows you to slowly work through the process of sounding out a word while reinforcing each letter sound. However, this is not the most efficient form of blending, and I wouldn't continue it past the first few weeks—after students understand the principle behind blending and have had some practice doing it on their own.

## Extending the Use of Final Blending
## for Struggling Readers

The only time I recommend going back to final blending is when working with struggling readers during small-group differentiation time. Why? If you notice that some of your students are struggling with blending words, it is helpful to work through the word sound by sound to identify if a specific sound-spelling (e.g., the vowel letter-sound) is standing in the way. That is, are there specific letters and sounds that the student hasn't mastered or is confusing with other letter-sounds? This information will assist you in meeting that student's specific phonics needs. As a result, you might need to reteach certain skills and provide extended practice with them. If your student does know each letter and sound in the word, but cannot blend the word, then the issue might be related to phonemic awareness. That is, the student might struggle with oral blending or retaining the sounds long enough in working memory to blend them together.

## Successive Blending

Successive blending is a more efficient form of blending that you will use for the bulk of your phonics instruction. In successive blending, you run your fingers under the letters in a word and string them together. It looks like this for the word *sat*.

- Write the word on the board (or display it using letter cards).
- Put your finger at the beginning of the word. Slowly run your finger under the letters in order as you string together the sounds, /sssaaat/. Do not pause between sounds. Each sound must "melt" into the next sound.
- Slowly compress the word. Therefore, go from /sssaaat/ at a slow pace to /ssaat/ a bit faster to /sat/ at a normal speed. Tell students that the word is *sat*.

Both blending procedures are best introduced in phonics lessons using simple CVC words. These lessons should be the first lessons children are provided. It is the principle of stringing together sounds that is so critical and that students must master. Therefore, teach and model it in the most efficient manner. Some reading programs have children blend only initial consonants onto phonograms (word parts). For example, children might be asked to blend *s* and *at, m* and *at,* and *b* and *at*. The phonogram is treated as a unit to be memorized, and little attention is given to the actual sound-spelling relationship between the letter *a* and the /a/ sound, and the letter *t* and the

/t/ sound. This type of blending isn't as effective as the final and successive blending procedures.

## Controlled Text: What Is It?

"The goal of teaching phonics is to develop students' ability to read connected text independently" (Adams, 1990). Classrooms are filled with a variety of books ranging from wordless picture books to chapter books. Three types of text that should be included in an early reading program are:

1.  **Decodable (controlled) text:** The vocabulary is controlled based on knowledge of sound-spelling relationships.
2.  **Predictable/patterned text:** The vocabulary is predictable based on such factors as repeated text patterns; familiar concepts; match of text with illustrations; rhyme, repetition, and alliteration; cumulative pattern; and familiar story, or sequence. A sample of predictable text follows:

    [Page 1] I see a black car.
    [Page 2] I see a black hat.
    [Page 3] I see a black bird.
    [Page 4] I see a black bat.

3.  **Trade books:** Trade books come in a wide range of genres and formats. To build children's vocabularies and sense of story, read these to children or have children read them independently. I recommend that you read a nonfiction selection aloud to children on at least two out of every five days in order to increase their vocabularies and world knowledge. This increase yields tremendous payoffs in later years when children use the knowledge as background information to read more sophisticated texts.

Some say that variety is the spice of life. Variety is not only the spice of life, it is the spice of early reading instruction and a necessity because one text type cannot meet all your instructional goals. Select each text you use based on what you want it to accomplish. For example, if you have just completed a phonics lesson and want children to practice using their newly taught phonics skill, decodable text is the appropriate choice. If you want to develop children's awareness of syntax and help them to rely on their semantic knowledge, then predictable text is a better choice. Predictable texts are less useful for practicing phonics skills.

Juel and Roper-Schneider (1985) explain why text selection is so critical:

> The selection of text used very early in first grade may, at least in part, determine the strategies and cues children learn to use, and persist in using, in subsequent word identification.... In particular, emphasis on a phonics method seems to make little sense if children are given initial texts to read where the words do not follow regular letter-sound correspondence generalizations.... [T]he types of words which appear in beginning reading texts may well exert a more powerful influence in shaping children's word identification strategies than the method of reading instruction.

This is a powerful statement. If we provide children with an award-winning phonics lesson, then give them text that contains few decodable words to apply the phonics skills, our efforts have been in vain. Why? Let's assume you've just taught students that the letter *s* stands for the /s/ sound. It is early in the year, and you've taught only a handful of other sound-spelling relationships. If you then give children a story in which there are a lot of words that begin with *s*, such as *sand, sister, sandwich*, and *silly*, yet none of these words are decodable based on the sound-spelling relationships you've previously taught, how will children read these words? Well, they'll use context clues and picture clues—not their phonics knowledge—to try and figure out the words. Over time, because they aren't using their phonics skills, children will undervalue their knowledge of sound-spelling relationships and over-rely on context and pictures. Most poor readers over-rely on these types of clues, which quickly become less efficient as the text demands increase and the picture clues decrease (Stanovich, 1989).

Thus, a direct connection between phonics instruction and reading is essential. "Like arithmetic without application, phonics without connected reading amounts to useless mechanics. And like the arithmetic that we never did understand well enough to do the word problems, it is easily forgotten altogether" (Adams, 1990).

Unfortunately, much of the text children are given to read in today's reading programs has little connection to the phonics skills they are learning. This has been an issue for decades (Beck, 1981). One of the reasons publishers have been so hesitant to create this type of text is the great criticism it often receives. Many educators feel that the decodable text of the past was stilted and incomprehensible. And it's true that much of this text bore little resemblance to children's oral language. Therefore, even though children might have been able to decode the words in these stories, they struggled with making sense of the text—assuming that it made sense.

In 1985, the government document *Becoming a Nation of Readers* (Anderson et al.) provided a set of criteria for creating controlled/decodable text. Three mandates required that the text be:

- **Comprehensible.** Vocabulary must be understandable and natural sounding. Words must be derived from children's speaking and listening vocabularies. Sentences must follow natural English sentence structures and patterns.
- **Instructive.** The majority of the words must be decodable based on the sound-spellings previously taught. A strong connection between instruction and text must exist.
- **Interesting.** Connected texts must be engaging enough for students to want to read them again and again. Children need to revisit this text to develop fluency and increase reading rate.

These criteria came with the following warning:

The important point is that a high proportion of the words in the earliest selections children read should conform to the phonics they have already been taught. Otherwise, they will not have enough opportunity to practice, extend, and refine their knowledge of letter-sound relationships. However, a rigid criterion is a poor idea. Requiring that, say, 90% of the words used in a primer must conform would destroy the flexibility needed to write interesting, meaningful stories.

# Another Warning

I want to add to the *Becoming a Nation of Readers* warning. Currently, there is a tendency to measure a text's quality for phonics instruction by the percentage of decodable words it includes. Relying solely on numbers to determine text quality and appropriateness is dangerous. For example, Story A could be written so that on each page the word *run* appears. And on each page, the art would show a different animal running. Let's assume that the word *run* is decodable. Therefore, this text would receive a decodable score of 100%. Story B could be written so that it read something like this: "The cat can run. The dog can run. The rat can run. The man can run." Let's assume that every word in these sentences—except the high-frequency word *the*, which is considered "irregular"—is decodable based on the sound-spellings previously taught. This text would receive a decodable score of 75% because one out of every four words is not decodable. But which story would provide children with the most decoding practice? Story B, of course. Still, Story A might be selected if decodable percentages are the only selection criteria.

So what type of text best meets the criteria established in *Becoming a Nation of Readers*? The answer is a new type of *hybrid text* that contains a large proportion of decodable words as well as some high-frequency words to ensure that the text is natural sounding. When all the words in the text have been controlled (either for sound-spelling pattern or direct teaching of high-frequency words included), children can be held accountable for it because it reflects exactly what they have learned.

**Hybrid texts**

Scholastic

Open Court Publishing

# What If Your Decodable Texts Are Bad?

Unfortunately far too many of the decodable texts available for early readers are of questionable quality and, as a result, teachers avoid using these critical early learning tools. The most common issues in these texts include:

a. The use of low-utility words to try to squeeze in more words with the target skill (e.g., *I can lug the cat with the rug. Let Lin dab a lip. Put it in the vat.*)

b. The use of non-standard English sentence structures (e.g., *Ron did hit it. The pup did run at Kit.*)

**c.** The use of nonsensical sentences or tongue twisters (e.g., *Slim Stan did spin, splat, stop. Fun Fran flips, flaps, flops.*)

**d.** The use of too many referents or pronouns (because they are easier words) instead of specific concrete words, making the meaning difficult to figure out (e.g., *She did not see it, but she did put it in.*)

**e.** Using too simple language to explain scientific concepts due to phonics constraints (e.g., *The sun will make plants rise.*)

**f.** Using odd names to get more decodable words in the story (e.g., *Ben had Mem. Tam had the pup.*)

**g.** Avoiding using the word *the*, the most common word in the English language. Because *the* is NOT counted as decodable until students are taught the digraph *th* and the long-*e* sound spelled *e* (as in *we, he, be*—since it can also be pronounced this way), most writers of decodable text avoid using *the* or replace it with the word *a*. This often results in stilted sentences. Also, the words *the* and *a* have different uses in English. For example, *I see a cat* can refer to any cat. *I see the cat* refers to a specific cat. Therefore, interchanging the two words can also affect understanding. Unfortunately, in most scope and sequences, the word *the* doesn't become decodable until around mid-Grade 1. That's a long time to avoid or use sparingly the most common word in English!

So when choosing, purchasing, or creating decodable texts, keep these criteria in mind:

- Sentences in decodable texts should use high-utility English words (e.g., words students will commonly and regularly encounter when reading books or use when writing) and not be tongue twisters filled with lots of words with the target phonics skill, but lacking in "sense."
- Sentences in decodable texts should ALL follow normal English language speech and writing patterns. This is especially critical for our English learners.
- If your decodable texts break any of the above rules, purchase new texts or find replacements in your curriculum or online.
- If new texts are not available or feasible, rewrite the most problematic sentences in the decodable texts (e.g., tape over replacement sentences).

# Decodable Text—Does It Really Matter?

In 2000, I conducted a study to examine the effectiveness of decodable text in promoting word identification skills, phonics and spelling abilities, as well as positive reading attitudes in early readers. Previous research on the influence of basal readers had indicated that the types of words that appear in beginning reading texts exert a powerful influence in shaping children's word identification strategies (Juel & Roper-Schneider, 1985). However, there had been no research on the direct effects of decodable texts on early reading growth. In my study, I hypothesized that students receiving reading practice with decodable (controlled) text would achieve greater mastery in early reading skills than students who continued reading with standard classroom trade literature as follow-up reading to phonics instruction. I defined decodable text as text in which the vocabulary is controlled based on knowledge of previously taught sound-spelling relationships. Trade literature refers to books with a variety of genres and formats designed for children to build their vocabularies and read independently. These trade books are not controlled for phonic elements.

## Research Questions

My research questions included:

- Does practice with decodable text in conjunction with a systematic phonics program accelerate word identification skills for first-grade students?
- Do first graders who use decodable text demonstrate significantly greater gains in word identification skills than a comparison group of students who use trade literature?

## Sample

Two New York City public schools participated in my study from September of 1999 to February of 2000. There were two first-grade classrooms selected at each school—one experimental classroom using decodable text and one control classroom using trade literature. A total of 101 children in first grade participated in this research. The selected schools were in the lowest third of the district, based on achievement scores. Ninety percent of the students in this district qualify for free or reduced lunch. Sixty-two percent of the students were classified as below grade level, and 80% of the students in the district were identified as Latino. Both schools used the same systematic and explicit phonics instruction covering the identical phonics scope and sequence. The only difference between the experimental and control classrooms was the type of text used for reading practice: the decodable text or the standard trade literature series.

## Program Background

The decodable texts used in the study were written to directly address the requirements outlined in *Becoming a Nation of Readers* (see page 158).

Students in both groups read a major piece of literature for the week and received phonics lessons follow-up practice five days a week. First graders in the experimental group practiced reading with decodable (controlled) text for their phonics lessons follow-up. The controlled texts were 100% controlled for phonics and sight words (for example: *Sam sat. Sam sat in the sand. Sam sat and sat.*). The major reading text was 80% controlled for phonics and sight words, as well as being specially written and illustrated.

In comparison, the control group's phonics lessons follow-up included patterned and predictable text (for example: *Sam sees a sandwich. Sam sees a snake. Sam sees a sailor. Sam sees a lot!*). For its major reading text, the control group used popular first-grade books written by well-known authors. Many of these texts were approximately 35% decodable.

Controlled text percentages were determined through a decodability analysis I did based on a clear scope and sequence of phonics skills. In addition, a review of Marcy Stein's pivotal study "Analyzing Beginning Reading Programs: The Relationship Between Decoding Instruction and Text" (Stein, Johnson, & Gutlohn, 1999) confirmed controlled text percentages for both the experimental and control groups of students.

## Professional Development

I conducted an initial training session with the experimental-group teachers on how to incorporate the decodable text into their comprehensive reading program. Each participating classroom was visited and observed four days per week—two days by me and two days by my research assistant. This method ensured that all teachers stayed on pace, taught the phonics lessons as intended, and read the required books. Detailed anecdotal notes of these sessions were kept. In addition, each classroom was formally observed for two weeks to develop classroom profiles.

## Assessment Measures

This study included four assessment measures:

- **The Woodcock Reading Mastery Test (WRMT)—Word Identification Sub-Test:** Required children to look at printed words and read them aloud.
- **The Blevins Phonics-Phonemic Awareness Quick Assessment:** A simple, five-word spelling test administered at the start of school. Students fall into three categories—below level, on level, and above level. This test quickly identifies students in need of intervention and provides information about students' phonemic awareness and phonics proficiency.
- **Decoding Assessment:** A phonics mastery assessment developed specifically for the study. It consisted of 20 words, all decodable based on the phonics scope and sequence. Ten of the words presented on the assessment appeared multiple times (four or more) in the reading selections read by both groups of students. The other ten words never appeared in the stories read by both groups, or they appeared only once. Ability to decode 75% of the words or more was necessary to receive a "passing" score.
- **Reading Attitudes Survey:** An informal interview-style assessment, which evaluates how children feel about learning to read, as well as how they perceive themselves as readers.

This study included a pre- and posttest design for the WRMT, the Blevins Phonics-Phonemic Awareness Quick Assessment, and the Reading Attitudes Survey. Pretesting was conducted in September 1999, and posttesting was conducted in February 2000. The Decoding Assessment was administered only at the end of the study, in February 2000.

## Data Analysis

### WRMT—Word Identification Sub-Test Results

Results revealed that students in the experimental group significantly outperformed students in the control group on the WRMT. Analysis determined that W-score differences were statistically significant at F (1.69)=12.954, p<.001. The effect size was determined to be ES=.16. See the graph below.

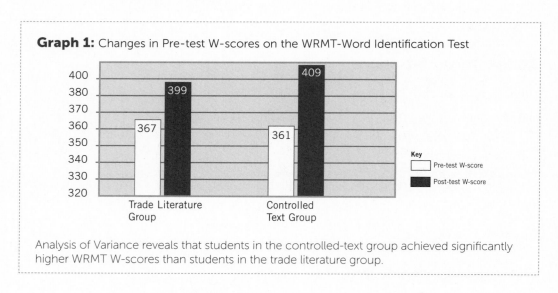

**Graph 1:** Changes in Pre-test W-scores on the WRMT-Word Identification Test

Key
Pre-test W-score
Post-test W-score

Analysis of Variance reveals that students in the controlled-text group achieved significantly higher WRMT W-scores than students in the trade literature group.

Furthermore, results revealed that a significantly greater number of students using the decodable text for their reading practice achieved on-level WRMT mastery: 72% decodable-text students vs. 54% trade-literature students. The controlled-text group made a significant leap from 28% on-level mastery at the beginning of the year to 72% mastery in February. In contrast, the trade-literature group only increased WRMT on-level mastery from 40% in September to 54% in February. Some students in the controlled-text group achieved as much as two years' growth in one half year. The average student growth for this group was one year of growth during one half year of school.

## Phonics-Phonemic Awareness Quick Assessment Results

Findings revealed that a significantly greater number of decodable-text students vs. trade-literature students achieved mastery on the Phonics-Phonemic Awareness Quick Assessment: 92% decodable-text students vs. 66% trade-literature students. Ninety-two percent of controlled-text students were able to spell all five words correctly.

## Decoding (Phonics Mastery) Assessment Results

Results revealed that 87% of the students using the decodable text achieved mastery (75% or higher score) on the Decoding Assessment, as compared with only 54% of the students in the trade-literature group.

## Reading Attitudes Assessment Results

Findings showed that significantly fewer students reading decodable text vs. trade literature reported a dislike of reading or identified themselves as poor readers. Only 3% of decodable-text students reported that they didn't enjoy reading vs. 11% of trade-literature students. The percentage of students in the controlled-text group who reported a dislike of reading decreased during the study, from 14% in September to only 3% in February. I attribute this to their growing sense of confidence and control in their reading. In comparison, the percentage of students in the trade-literature group who reported a dislike of reading actually increased during the study, from 6% in September to 11% in February.

## Classroom Observation Results

Classroom observations indicated that working with controlled/ decodable text carried over to other important areas of teaching, such as read-aloud modeling and writing activities. In general, teachers were observed over time to pay more attention to words and specifically how words work.

As further evidence of the power of controlled text, classroom observations also revealed that children in the controlled-text group were more confident in tackling difficult books for their at-home reading choices. It was observed that children in the experimental group would examine the words in books before selecting a story to take home. Conversely, children in the control group were observed to have difficulty choosing books with appropriate text for their reading level.

## Discussion

Overall, students in the controlled-text group were more prepared to transfer their phonics skills to new words presented to them in formal assessments. In addition, these results reinforce what previous research by motivation experts has shown: reading success breeds reading self-confidence and enjoyment of reading. This study also reinforces that the type of text for beginning readers does matter. Students who use decodable/controlled text in their early reading instruction get off to a stronger start in their reading development.

# Word-Awareness Activities

While the initial introduction of phonics skills is best using an explicit approach, that does not mean there shouldn't be a time during the instructional cycle in which students play with and explore letter-sounds. In fact, I think this exploration is *critical* for students to consolidate and solidify their learning of how words work. Yes, the initial introduction begins this learning efficiently, but it takes time and loads of experiences reading and writing words for that knowledge to be mastered. These types of exploratory activities provide essential thinking time for students as they incorporate new learning into already established learning. When phonics instruction fails, it often does so because it is rote, unthinking, and not applied to real reading and writing experiences.

## Word Building and Word Sorts

The two best types of exploration exercises that increase a student's word awareness are word building and word sorts. Both should be an important part of the phonics instructional cycle for each skill introduced.

In **word building**, students are given a set of letter cards and asked to create a series of words in a specified sequence. This can occur during both whole- and small-group lessons. Generally each new word varies by only one sound-spelling from the previous word there (can be more variance as students progress in skills). For example, students might be asked to build, or make with letter cards, these words in sequence: *sat, mat, map, mop*. Notice how each word varies from the preceding word by only one sound-spelling. As students move up the grades, word building should continue with students using syllables instead of individual letters to build increasingly more complex words.

There are two types of word building, each with a clearly defined instructional purpose.

1.  **Word Building: Blending Focus** In this type of word building, students are asked to make a word, such as *sat*. They are then told to change the letter *s* to the letter *m* and read the new word formed. Thus, the primary goal is for them to blend, or sound out, the new word formed. This is the type of blending you might want to start out with at the beginning of an instructional cycle. It allows students time to decode many words with the new target phonics skills, while also reviewing previously taught skills.

2. **Word Building: Word Awareness Focus** In this type of building, students are asked to make a word, such as *sat*. They are then told to change *sat* to *mat*. This is cognitively more demanding than the blending-focused word building. Why? Students have to consider how the words *sat* and *mat* vary (i.e., which sound is different), which letter must be removed from *sat*, which added to form *mat*, and in which position in the word. That's a lot of thinking about how words work! This is why word building is so beneficial. Students gain flexibility in how to use sound-spellings in words. This type of word building is one you can do later in the week after students have had more exposure to the skill. And, by repeating the word-building sequences multiple times throughout the week with different instructional focuses, you only need to create one set of words and one set of letter cards—saving you valuable planning time.

**Word sorts** also allow students time to think about how words work by drawing their attention to important and common spelling patterns. Generally, in word sorts students are given a set of words that have something in common (e.g., all contain the same vowel sound, but with different spellings, as in *-at* and *-an* words for short *a*). Students are asked to sort the words by their common feature.

There are many types of word sorts, each with a distinct instructional purpose. Below are three of the most common types.

1. **Open Sorts** In these sorts, students are not told how to sort the words. That is, students are given a set of words and allowed to sort them in any way they want. This is a good first sort with a set of words because it tells you a lot about how students are thinking about words and what aspects of words they notice. So, for example, if you gave students these words—*boat, road, throw, grow, soap, show*—and they sorted them by first letter-sound, that would indicate the students are noticing very simplistic aspects of words (initial letter-sounds) and not noticing what is truly common among these words (they all contain the long-*o* sound spelled *oa* or *ow*).

2. **Closed Sorts** In these sorts, students are told how to sort the words. So for the long-*o* sort above, students are told to sort the words into two piles, each representing a different spelling for the long-*o* sound (*oa* or *ow*). These are fairly simple and direct sorts, since students are visually scanning each word for a specified spelling pattern. The value in this type of sort

is the conversation you have with students *following* the sort. For example, you should ask students questions like: *What do you notice about these words? What do you notice about these spellings for long-o? Do you know other words with these spellings?* Then you guide students (if they don't notice on their own) that the *oa* spelling for long *o* never appears at the end of the word. This is really valuable information about how words work that will have positive benefits on students' future reading and writing. That is, when a student encounters a new word when writing (e.g., the word *snow*), what does the student do? He or she thinks about each sound and the associated spelling. Upon reaching the long-*o* sound at the end of the word *snow*, that student knows there are two options—*oa* or *ow*. Which is a better option? Well, if you've had the discussion during the sort, the student will know that the *ow* spelling is the only option since *oa* cannot appear at the end of a word. This is the kind of thinking and knowledge building we want to have happen as a result of word sorts. Word sorts are far more than a quick, visual, sorting task.

3. **Timed Sorts** In these sorts, students are told how to sort a set of words but are given a limited amount of time to do so. This is an ideal type of sort to do with a set of words students have been working with all week (having already completed open and closed sorts). Adding the element of time creates a game-like feel to the task students enjoy. Beyond that, it provides an important benefit. Getting students to readily notice larger word chunks in words, such as these common spelling patterns, is essential to reading longer, multisyllabic words. As students progress up the grades, the words they encounter will increase in length. Instead of reading new words like *cat, soap*, and *barn*, they begin to encounter words like *unexpected, predetermined*, and *unhappily*. It becomes inefficient for students to attack these words letter by letter. Instead, larger chunks of these words need to visually "pop out" so the reader has fewer word parts to tackle, making the reading easier. Doing timed sorts helps to train the eye to quickly see these larger word chunks in new, unfamiliar words. Plus, it's a great way to extend the practice with the word card sets you have created for the week—giving you more bang for your time in creating and organizing the materials for these sorts. You can also set up these timed sorts on a whiteboard

using simple word cards and a timer for students to practice during independent work time alone or with a partner.

Other common sorts include sound sorts, pattern sorts, meaning sorts, buddy sorts, blind sorts, and writing sorts. For more information about these other types of sorts, I recommend *Words Their Way* (Bear et al, 2016).

## Word-Sort and Word-Building Routines

Word building and word sorts should be a key component of each instructional cycle for every new phonics skill. Below are instructional routines for each. You know word building and word sorts are having a positive effect on students' word awareness when you see an increase in students' ability to comment on how words work and evidence that they are fully analyzing similar words and thereby avoiding common reading issues that result when only portions of a word are looked at in order to read it (e.g., using the beginning and perhaps ending letters, then guessing from those clues and the picture). Also, as students have regular weekly practice analyzing words in this way, you will start to see them noticing common spelling patterns and other aspects of words before you teach them. For example, I've had students point out sound-spellings that we will study in upcoming weeks before I formally teach them because they have seen several words with this sound-spelling in books we read together or I read aloud (e.g., the digraph *sh* in *she, should*, and *fish*).

These types of word-awareness activities create students who become *word detectives*—curious about words and always on the lookout for what is common among words. This improved word awareness has generative effects as students progress through the grades and encounter words with prefixes, suffixes, spelling changes, and Greek and Latin roots.

### Word-Sort Routine

**Step 1: Introduce** Name the task and explain its purpose. Distribute the word cards and read each with students to make sure they know all the words. If you are doing a closed sort, introduce the categories in which students will be sorting the words.

**Step 2: Sort** Have students sort the words. If doing a closed sort, model sorting one or two of the words. Then have students sort the remaining words. Circulate and ask students questions about why they are putting specific words into each category.

**Step 3: Check and Discuss** Review the words in each sort category. Ask students what they learned about these words from doing the sort. Guide students to the word-awareness aspect of each sort that will assist them in reading and writing. Have students store the word cards for future sorts (e.g., a timed sort using these words).

Too often word sorts are treated as a simple task of rearranging word cards, and the follow-up discussion to better understand how words work never occurs. Every word sort should end with a question such as, **"What did you notice about these words?"** or **"What did you learn about these spelling patterns?"** Students need to verbalize their thinking about words. Use follow-up questions to guide students if they don't readily recognize important features of the spellings and patterns. For example, "Where does this spelling appear in all the words? How is it different from the other spellings for this sound?" You might include a couple of "outlier" words in a sort to highlight a concept. For example, if you are sorting words with final *e*, like *hope, rope, home, joke*, and *note*, you might want to add the words *come* and *some* and point out common words that break the rule or pattern.

### Word-Building Routine

**Step 1: Introduce** Name the task and explain its purpose to students. Say: *Today we will be building, or making, words using the letters and spellings we have learned.*

**Step 2: Model** Place letter cards in a pocket chart (or use letter cards on a whiteboard) to form the first word you are building. Model sounding out the word. Remember to (a) build words using the new target sound-spelling, (b) add words with review sound-spellings as appropriate to extend the review and application of these skills to achieve mastery, and (c) use minimal contrasts to require students to fully analyze words and notice their unique differences (e.g., *sat/mat, pan/pen, rip/trip, hat/hate, cot/coat*). Say: *Look at the word I've made. It is spelled* s-a-t. *Let's blend the sounds together to read the word*: /sssaaat/, sat. *The word is* sat.

**Step 3: Guided Practice/Practice** Continue by changing one (or more) letters in the word. Have students chorally blend the new word formed. Do a set of eight to ten words. Say: *Change* *the letter* s *in* sat *to* m. *What is the new word?* Or, if students are more advanced in their understanding, say: *Change the first sound in* sat *to* /m/.

If the focus on the word building is word awareness (instead of blending, like the previous example), then tell students what the next word in the sequence is and give them time to form the new word. Circulate and provide assistance and corrective feedback (e.g., model your thinking process, model how to blend the word, etc). Then build the new word in the pocket chart (or on the whiteboard), modeling aloud your thinking.

Upgrade your work with word building by creating an additional activity each week called Word Ladders (created by Dr. Timothy Rasinski). What distinguishes word ladders from the typical word-building exercise is the added element of vocabulary. Instead of asking students to build a word like *top*, then change it to make the word *mop*, you ask students to change "one letter in the word *top* to name something you use to clean a wet floor." This is a fun activity to do at the end of the week, when students have had multiple exposures to the words and know their meanings. Students love figuring out the clues, then determining how to make the new word.

Here is an example of a word ladder I helped create with teachers from a large, urban school district. It was simple and fun to create. Published versions of word ladders also exist, most notably those created by Timothy Rasinski (e.g., *Daily Word Ladders*, Scholastic, 2005). I love his work, and these books are a great resource. I've also included a blank template (Resource 4.1) online for your use. (See page 320 for details on how to access.)

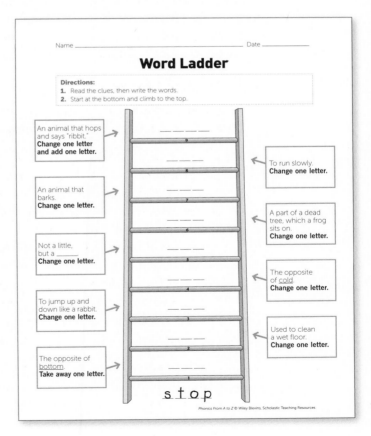

Name _____     Date _____

## Word Ladder

**Directions:**
1. Read the clues, then write the words.
2. Start at the bottom and climb to the top.

An animal that hops and says "ribbit."
**Change one letter and add one letter.**

To run slowly.
**Change one letter.**

An animal that barks.
**Change one letter.**

A part of a dead tree, which a frog sits on.
**Change one letter.**

Not a little, but a _____
**Change one letter.**

The opposite of cold.
**Change one letter.**

To jump up and down like a rabbit.
**Change one letter.**

Used to clean a wet floor.
**Change one letter.**

The opposite of bottom.
**Take away one letter.**

s t o p

Phonics From A to Z © Wiley Blevins, Scholastic Teaching Resources

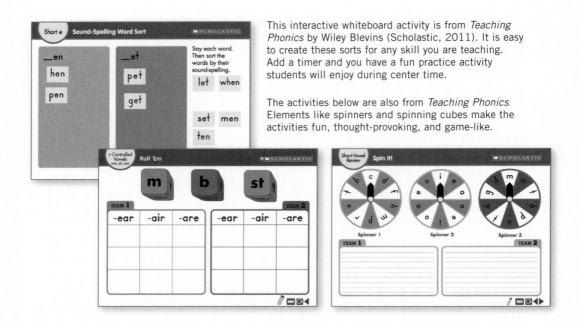

This interactive whiteboard activity is from *Teaching Phonics* by Wiley Blevins (Scholastic, 2011). It is easy to create these sorts for any skill you are teaching. Add a timer and you have a fun practice activity students will enjoy during center time.

The activities below are also from *Teaching Phonics*. Elements like spinners and spinning cubes make the activities fun, thought-provoking, and game-like.

Many apps and interactive whiteboard games exist for word building and word sorts. A few are shown above. These are arguably the easiest to create yourself as they require few elements—word cards, letter cards, sorting space. Adding a timer to the word sorts makes the activity fun and purposeful for review.

# High-Frequency Words

Since high-frequency words play an important role in the new hybrid controlled texts, it's important to define what they are and to examine how to teach them. Of the approximately 600,000-plus words in English, a relatively small number appear frequently in print. Only 13 words *(a, and, for, he, is, in, it, of, that, the, to, was, you)* account for more than 25% of the words in print (Johns, 1980), and 100 words account for approximately 50% (Fry, Fountoukidis, & Polk, 1985; Adams, 1990; Carroll, Davies, & Richman, 1971). About 20% of the 250 most frequently used words by children are function words, such as *a, the,* and *and*. These 250 words make up 70–75% of all the words children use in their writing (Rinsland, 1945).

Although high-frequency word lists disagree on the rank order of words, and many lists contain different words, there is general agreement on the majority of those that are used most frequently. Many of the word lists are based on textbooks used in Grades 1–8

(Harris & Jacobson, 1972). The Dolch Basic Sight Vocabulary contains 220 words (no nouns). Although this list was generated more than 40 years ago, these words account for a large proportion of the words found in textbooks today. The *American Heritage Word Frequency Book*, which lists the 150 most frequent words in printed school English, is also a valuable resource.

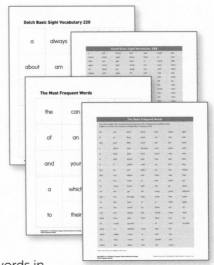

Knowledge of high-frequency words is necessary for fluent reading. Although many high-frequency words carry little meaning, they affect the flow and coherence of text. Many of these words are considered "irregular" because they stray from the commonly taught sound-spelling relationships. Research shows that readers store these "irregular" words in their lexical memory in the same way as they store so-called regular words (Gough & Walsh, 1991; Treiman & Baron, 1981; Lovett, 1987). That is, readers have to pay attention to each letter and the pattern of letters in a word and associate these with the sounds that they represent (Ehri, 1992). Therefore, instruction should focus attention on each letter and/or letter pattern.

The Dolch Basic Sight Vocabulary and the 150 Most Frequent Words lists and word cards can be found online as Resources 4.2 and 4.3; see page 320 for details on how to access.

However, children don't learn "irregular" words as easily or quickly as they do "regular" words. Early readers commonly confuse the high-frequency words *of, for,* and *from*; the reversible words *on/no* and *was/saw*; and words with *th* and *w*, such as *there, them*; *what, were*; *their, then*; *what, where*; *this, these*; *went, will*; *that, this*; and *when, with* (Cunningham, 1995). Therefore, children need to be taught "irregular" high-frequency words with explicit instruction.

The best instructional practices related to high-frequency words are those that accelerate learning and focus on mastery. More recent brain research has further confirmed this understanding.

According to brain research, three parts of the brain must be activated in order for us to learn a word. These parts include where the sounds are stored, where the word's meaning is stored, and where the word's spelling is stored.

Now think about that for a minute and what it means for your instruction. Are you teaching high-frequency words in a way that activates all three parts of the brain necessary to learn a word in your

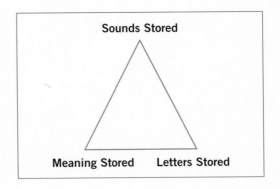

initial introduction of that word? I once heard Isabel Beck describe this process as leaving a deep, dark imprint on the brain when students first learn a new word, instead of a soft, gray imprint that could easily fade away. To do this during initial instruction, I use the following Read-Spell-Write-Extend routine.

## Read-Spell-Write-Extend Routine

**Read:** Write the word in a context sentence and underline the word. Read aloud the sentence, then point to the target underlined word and read it aloud. Have students say the word.

Say: *I see a cat.* [Point to the word *see*.] *This is the word* see. *What is the word?*

**Spell:** Spell the word aloud and have students repeat it. Briefly point out any letter-sounds or spellings students might already know or that are the same as other words students have learned.

Say: *The word* see *is spelled* s-e-e. *Spell it with me:* s-e-e. *What is the first sound in the word* see? *What letter do we write for the* /s/ *sound? Does the word* see *begin with the letter* s?

**Write:** Ask students to write the word multiple times as they spell it aloud. This can be done in the air, on dry-erase boards, or on paper.

Say: *Watch as I write the word. I will say each letter as I write it.* [Model this.] *Now it's your turn. Write the word three times. Say each letter as you write it.*

**Extend:** Connect the word to other words students have learned. For example, if you have a Word Wall, work with students to place the word in the correct spot on the wall. Then ask students to generate oral sentences using the word. Have them work with a partner; provide sentence frames as support, if needed. Then have students write their oral sentence. Build on these sentences as appropriate. These extension activities can be done on the days following the initial instruction when you have additional time to extend in this way.

Say: *Turn to a partner and finish this sentence:* I see a _____. [Provide time for partners to share.] *Now, write on your paper the sentence you just said.* [Wait for students to finish.] *Let's expand our sentences. Tell your partner something about what you see. For example, if your sentence was, "I see a book," you can build on it to say something like, "I see a big book" or "I see a book about dinosaurs." Tell your partner your expanded sentence.* [Provide time for partners to share.] *Now write your new sentence.*

This routine offers a valuable tool for engaging all parts of the brain needed to learn a word, accelerates that learning, and aids in helping irregular words "stick." When you say the word, that "sound" part of the brain is activated. When you read the context sentence and discuss it, the "meaning" part of the brain is activated. And, when you spell the word, the "letters" part of the brain is activated. You know this routine is working when students quickly and automatically identify high-frequency words when reading connected text and easily distinguish visually similar words (e.g., *when* and *then*). To misread one of these words can have a serious impact on understanding.

For children having trouble with high-frequency words, use associative learning by associating the target word with a picture. For example, display a picture of a box of cereal. Write underneath the picture the label "box of cereal" and underline the target word *of*. Then have children create their own picture card and label, writing the target word in the label in red or some other distinguishing color. You might also have these children create word banks that they can refer to when reading or writing.

## Other Popular Techniques for Developing High-Frequency Word Knowledge

### Flash Cards With a Purpose

Flash cards have been used for decades, with mixed results. The hope is that students will transfer their knowledge of isolated sight words to reading words in connected text. However, this is not always the case. To accelerate students' sight-word recognition and ensure the transfer to connected text, write the word on one side of an index card. Then work with students to create and write a meaningful phrase or sentence using the word on the other side of the card. Students, therefore, practice reading the words in isolation and in context.

### Cumulative Sentences

Each week, have students write a meaningful sentence in the back of their writing notebooks for the high-frequency words taught that week. You might work with students to create them. During independent work time, have students reread their sentences from the beginning of the year to a partner. Do this at least twice a week. This cumulative review will increase students' knowledge of these all-important words.

## Top 248 High-Frequency Words in English

Below is a list of the top 248 words in English. These words are collected from the three most frequently used word lists in the United States (*Fry Words: The First Hundred, Dolch Basic Sight Vocabulary 220*, and *American Heritage Word Frequency Book Top 150)*. The words that are irregular and must be memorized are in **bold**. It might take children two or more years to learn all these words.

High-frequency word cards can be used as individual flash cards, or placed on a Word Wall for periodic review.

| Top 248 High-Frequency Words in English | | | | | | |
|---|---|---|---|---|---|---|
| a | any | **been** | **buy** | cut | each | fly |
| about | **are** | before | by | day | eat | for |
| after | around | best | call | did | **eight** | found |
| **again** | as | better | called | different | even | **four** |
| all | ask | big | came | **do** | every | **from** |
| also | at | black | can | **does** | fall | full |
| always | ate | blue | **carry** | **don't** | far | funny |
| am | away | **both** | clean | **done** | fast | gave |
| an | back | bring | cold | down | find | get |
| and | be | brown | **come** | draw | first | **give** |
| another | because | but | **could** | drink | five | go |

| | | | | | | |
|---|---|---|---|---|---|---|
| goes | its | myself | play | small | **through** | **were** |
| going | jump | never | please | so | time | **what** |
| good | just | new | **pretty** | **some** | **to** | when |
| got | keep | no | pull | soon | **today** | **where** |
| green | kind | not | **put** | start | **together** | which |
| grow | know | now | ran | stop | too | white |
| had | **laugh** | number | read | such | try | **who** |
| has | let | **of** | red | take | **two** | why |
| **have** | light | off | ride | tell | under | will |
| he | like | old | right | ten | up | wish |
| help | little | on | round | than | upon | with |
| her | **live** | **once** | run | thank | us | **word** |
| here | long | **one** | **said** | that | use | **words** |
| him | look | only | same | **the** | used | **work** |
| his | made | open | saw | **their** | **very** | **would** |
| hold | make | or | say | them | walk | write |
| hot | man | **other** | see | then | **want** | years |
| how | **many** | our | seven | **there** | **warm** | yellow |
| hurt | may | out | **shall** | these | **was** | yes |
| I | me | over | she | **they** | **wash** | **you** |
| if | more | own | show | things | **water** | **your** |
| in | **most** | part | sing | think | way | |
| into | much | **people** | sit | this | we | |
| is | must | pick | six | those | well | |
| it | my | place | sleep | three | went | |

# Sample Lessons

The following sample lessons are set up as templates for you to use when writing your phonics lessons. They follow a simple five-step procedure:

**Step 1:** Repeated reading and warm-up
**Step 2:** Explicit instruction of sound-spelling relationship
**Step 3:** Blending and word-building exercises
**Step 4:** Reading connected text
**Step 5:** Dictation and writing

Some components of the lessons, such as the warm-up exercises and connected-text reading, will be determined by the materials you have available.

## Consonants

### Guidelines:

- Teach only the most common spelling or spellings for each consonant sound.
- Separate the teaching of visually confusing letters *(b/d)* or auditorily confusing sounds (/g/, /k/).
- Use simple CVC (consonant-vowel-consonant) words in the lessons before teaching words with consonant clusters, consonant digraphs, or multisyllabic words. (Word lists for instruction can be found on pages 93–110.)
- Begin instruction with continuous consonants *(f, l, m, n, r, s, v, z)*, those whose sounds can be sustained without distortion.
  This makes it easier to model blending.

The following lists the rank order of consonants based on their utility in terms of word frequency and ease of teaching blending (Groff, 1972; Dolby & Resnikoff, 1963; Hanna et al., 1966; Blevins, 1997).

| 1. s | 4. f | 7. l | 10. p | 13. d | 16. k | 19. x |
|------|------|------|-------|-------|-------|-------|
| 2. t | 5. r | 8. c | 11. w | 14. g | 17. v | 20. y |
| 3. m | 6. b | 9. h | 12. n | 15. j | 18. z | 21. q |

# Consonants

**Phonic Principle:** The letter *s* stands for the /s/ sound.

**Step 1: Reread** Begin by having children reread a story or passage containing previously taught sound-spelling relationships. Then provide phonemic-awareness exercises (such as oral blending) for children needing this support.

**Step 2: Introduce Sound-Spelling**
Explain to children that the letter *s* stands for the /s/ sound, as in the word *sock*. Write the word *sock* on the board as you display a picture of a sock. Make sure the picture is labeled. Then blend the word *sock* aloud as you run your finger under each letter. Have a volunteer underline the letter *s*. Point to the letter *s* and ask students to state the sound that the letter stands for. Continue by having children generate a list of words containing the /s/ sound. List these words on the board.

**Step 3: Blend Words** Write the following words and sentences on the board. Note that all the words are decodable based on the sound-spelling relationships previously taught. The first line focuses on words with the new sound-spelling. The second line reviews previously taught sound-spellings. The sentences contain some high-frequency words previously taught.

- *sat      sad      sock*
- *mad      mat      rock*
- *Sam is sad.*
- *I sat on the rock.*

Now distribute the following letter-card set to each child: *a, o, i, s, t, m*. Have children build as many words as possible. Ask them to write the words on a sheet of paper. Circulate around the room and model blending when necessary.

**Step 4: Apply to Text** Provide students with connected reading practice. Choose a book in which many of the words are decodable based on the sound-spelling relationships previously taught.

**Step 5: Dictate and Write** Dictate the following words and sentence. Have children write the words and sentence on a sheet of paper. For students who are having difficulty segmenting the sounds in each word, extend the word. You might wish to clap on each sound to provide another clue. Then write the words and sentence on the board. Have the children self-correct their papers. Do not grade this dictation practice. It's designed to help children segment words and associate sounds with spellings.

- *sat      sock*
- *I am sad.*

**Provide freewriting opportunities.**
For example, have children select an object's name that begins with the /s/ sound. Then have them write a sentence about that object. Or have children generate a list of words that begin with the letter *s*. Record the words on chart paper. Then use the words to create a class story. Begin with a title, such as "The Silly Snake."

## Consonant Digraphs

### Guidelines:

- Consonant digraphs are two consonants that appear together in a word and stand for one sound. The consonant digraphs are *sh, ch, th, wh, ph, gh,* and *ng*.
- Teach the consonant digraphs after children have learned the single consonants. Help students become aware of these unique letter pairs by challenging them to be on the lookout for digraphs in words.

## Consonant Clusters

### Guidelines:

- Consonant clusters are two consonants that appear together in a word, with each retaining its sound when blended. The sound that each cluster stands for is called a blend. Therefore, the term *cluster* refers to the written form, and the term *blend* refers to the spoken form.
- The clusters are highly reliable; that is, when we see these letter combinations in words, they almost always stand for the blended sounds of each consonant. The one major exception is *sc*. It can stand for the /sk/ sounds, as in *scare*, or the *c* can be silent, as in *science*. In addition, the consonant cluster *ck* stands for one sound, the /k/ sound.

Sometimes I pair students for the rereading portion of the lesson. In addition, I often have students read to children in lower grades. Many struggling readers enjoy this because it provides them with an opportunity to be the "expert."

- There are three major categories of consonant clusters—
  r-blends *(br, cr, dr, fr, gr, pr, tr)*, s-blends *(sc, sk, sl, sm, sn, sp,
  st, sw)*, and *l*-blends *(bl, cl, fl, gl, pl)*. In addition, a few other
  consonant clusters, such as *tw* and *qu*, can be formed. There
  are also three-letter consonant clusters, such as *str, spr, thr, chr,
  phr*, and *shr*. The clusters *thr, chr, phr*, and *shr* are made up of a
  digraph and a consonant. The cluster *ngth*, as in *strength*, is made
  up of two digraphs—*ng* and *th*.
- Teach the consonant clusters after children have learned the
  single consonant sound-spellings.

## Being in Touch With Families

Communicate with parents frequently and openly. Let them know the skills you are teaching and send home books and activities for them to enjoy with their children. Keep in mind the following guidelines for communication with parents (Shalaway, 1989):

- Recognize that schools and homes have shared goals.

- Respect parents and communicate that respect.

- Acknowledge the changes in the American family. Use the word *families* instead of *parents*. Many children today do not live with both parents; some don't live with either parent.

- Understand the different types of school-family communication and the advantages and limitations of each. Decide which type is best to accomplish your goal (newsletter, phone call, activity, family booklet, website, etc.).

- Tailor communications to your audience.

- Be sure to check written material for spelling, grammar, and punctuation. Nothing is as upsetting to families as errors in materials you create. It decays trust in your abilities.

- Get expert help if you need it. If you are facing a specific issue in your classroom, consult experts at the district level or at a local college or university.

- Communication is a two-way street. Invite responses when communicating with families. Provide opportunities for families to get involved. I always leave a response space on my family newsletters for children to return to me.

# Consonant Digraphs

**Phonic Principle:** The digraph *sh* stands for the /sh/ sound.

**Step 1: Reread** Begin the lesson by having children reread a story or passage containing previously taught sound-spelling relationships. Then provide phonemic-awareness exercises (such as oral blending) for children needing this support.

**Step 2: Introduce Sound-Spelling** Explain to children that when we see the letters *s* and *h* together in words, they often stand for a new sound. Point out that the letters *sh* stand for the /sh/ sound, as in the words *ship* and *dish*. Write the words *ship* and *dish* on the board as you display a picture of each. Make sure the pictures are labeled. Then blend each word aloud as you run your finger under each letter. Have a volunteer underline the letters *sh*. Point to the letters *sh* and ask students to chorally state the sound that the letters stand for. Continue by having children generate a list of words containing the /sh/ sound in the initial and final position. List these words on the board in separate columns.

**Step 3: Blend Words** Write the following words and sentences on the board. Note that all the words are decodable based on the sound-spelling relationships previously taught. The first line focuses on words with the /sh/ sound in the initial position. The contrast provided focuses children's attention on the importance of each letter in a word. The second line focuses on words with the /sh/ sound in the final position.

The sentences contain some high-frequency words previously taught.

- *sack*      *shack*      *hop*      *shop*
- *dish*      *fish*      *mash*      *rush*
- *The ship is big.*
- *I wish I had a red dish.*

Next distribute the following letter-card set to each child: *a, i, o, sh, m, f, w, p*. Have children build as many words as possible. Ask them to write the words on a sheet of paper. Circulate around the room and model blending when necessary.

**Step 4: Apply to Text** Provide students with connected reading practice. Choose a book in which many of the words are decodable based on the sound-spelling relationships previously taught.

**Step 5: Dictate and Write** Have children write the following words and sentence on a sheet of paper as you dictate them. For students who are having difficulty segmenting the sounds in each word, extend the word. You might want to clap on each sound to provide another clue. Then write the words and sentence on the board. Have children self-correct their papers. Don't grade this dictation practice. It is designed to help children segment words and associate sounds with spellings.

- *shot*      *sack*      *fish*
- *We like to shop.*

**Provide freewriting opportunities.** You might have children write a group story, or you might display a picture of an object whose name contains the target sound (such as a fish) and have children write about it.

# Consonant Clusters

**Phonic Principle:** *s*-blends

**Step 1: Reread** Begin the lesson by having children reread a story or passage containing previously taught sound-spelling relationships. Then provide phonemic-awareness exercises (such as oral blending) for children needing this support.

**Step 2: Introduce Sound-Spelling**
Write the words *snake, stone,* and *spot* on the board. Underline the letters *sn, st,* and *sp* in each word. Explain to children that these letters stand for the /sn/, /st/, and /sp/ sounds, respectively. Point out that often when *s* and another consonant appear together in a word, the sounds that both letters stand for are blended together. Blend each word aloud as you run your finger under each letter. Point to each of these clusters and ask students to chorally state the sounds that the letters stand for. Continue by having children generate a list of words containing these sounds. List these words on the board.

**Step 3: Blend Words** Write the following words and sentences on the board. Note that all the words are decodable based on the sound-spelling relationships previously taught. The first line contains contrasts to focus children's attention on the importance of each letter in a word. The sentences contain some high-frequency words previously taught.

- *sell      spell      sack      stack*
- *sneak     speak      stop      spot*
- *Will you spell it?*
- *I need a stamp.*

Next distribute the following letter-card set to each child: *a, o, e, s, m, p, t, sh.* Have children build as many words as possible. Ask them to write the words on a sheet of paper. Circulate around the room and model blending when necessary.

**Step 4: Apply to Text** Provide students with connected reading practice. Choose a book in which many of the words are decodable based on the sound-spelling relationships previously taught.

**Step 5: Dictate and Write** Have children write the following words and sentence on a sheet of paper as you dictate them. For students having difficulty segmenting the sounds in each word, extend the word. You might want to clap on each sound to provide another clue. Then write the words and sentence on the board. Have children self-correct their papers. Do not grade this dictation practice. It's designed to help children segment words and associate sounds with spellings.

- *snack      top      stop*
- *I can smell the cake.*

**Provide freewriting opportunities.**
For example, have children write a different ending for a story they just read.

# r-blends

**br**
brace
Brad
braid
brain
braise
brake
bran
branch
brand
brass
brat
brave
brawl
bray
bread
break
breath
breathe
breeze
brew
brick
bride
bridge
bright
brim
bring
brisk
broad
broil
broke
bronco
bronze
brood
brook
broom
broth
brother
brought
brown
browse
bruise
brush

**cr**
crab
crack
cradle
craft
crane
crash
crawl
crayon
crazy
creek
creep
crib
cricket
cried
croak
crook
crop
cross
crow
crowd
crown
crumb
crunch
crust
cry

**dr**
drab
draft
drag
dragon
drain
drake
drank
drape
draw
dread
dream
dress
drew
drift

drill
drink
drip
drive
droop
drop
drove
drug
drum
dry

**fr**
frail
frame
frank
freak
freckles
free
freeze
freight
fresh
Friday
friend
fright
frill
fringe
frizz
frog
from
front
frost
frozen
fruit
fry
frying

**gr**
grab
grace
grade
graft
grain
gram

grand
grandfather
grandmother
grant
grape
grapes
graph
grasp
grass
grasshopper
grate
grave
gravity
gravy
gray
graze
grease
great
greed
green
greet
grew
grid
grill
grim
grime
grin
grind
grip
grit
groan
groceries
groom
grouch
ground
group
grow
growl
grown
grub
grudge
gruff
grump

**pr**
practice
praise
prance
pray
prayer
precious
prepare
present
president
press
pretty
pretzel
price
pride
priest
prince
princess
principal
print
prison
prisoner
prize
probably
probe
problem
prod
produce
product
professor
program
project
promise
pronoun
pronounce
proof
prop
propeller
protect
proud
prove

prowl
prune
pry

**tr**
trace
track
trade
trail
train
tramp
trap
trash
tray
tread
treat
tree
trek
tribe
trick
trim
trip
troll
tromp
troop
trot
trouble
trough
trout
truck
true
truly
trumpet
trunk
trust
truth
try

## l-blends

**bl**
blab
black
blackboard
blade
blame
blank
blanket
blast
blaze
bleach
bleat
bleed
bleep
blend
bless
blew
blind
blink
blip
blizzard
blob
block
blonde
blood
bloom
blossom
blot
blouse

blow
blue
bluff
blunt
blush

**cl**
clack
clad
claim
clam
clamp
clan
clang
clap
clash
clasp
class
claw
clay
clean
clear
cleat
clerk
click
cliff
climate
climb
cling
clink

clip
cloak
clock
clod
clog
clomp
close
closet
cloth
clothes
clothing
cloud
clove
clown
club
cluck
clue
clump
clutch

**fl**
flag
flake
flame
flap
flare
flash
flashlight
flat
flaw

flea
fleck
fleet
flesh
flew
flex
flick
flight
fling
flint
flip
float
flock
flood
floor
flop
floss
flour
flow
flower
flu
fluff
fluid
fluke
flunk
flush
flute
fly

**gl**
glad
glance
glare
glass
gleam
glee
glide
glitch
gloat
glob
globe
gloom
gloss
glove
glow
glue

**pl**
place
plaid
plain
plan
plane
planet
plank
plant
plate
play
player

plead
pleasant
please
pleat
pledge
plenty
plink
plod
plot
plow
plug
plum
plump

**sl**
slab
slack
slam
slant
slap
slate
sled
sleek
sleep
sleepy
sleet
sleeve
slept
slice
slick

slid
slide
slight
slim
slime
sling
slip
slipper
slit
slope
slot
slow
slowly
slug
slump
slush
sly

## Other Consonant Clusters

**tw**
tweed
tweet
tweezers
twelve
twenty
twice
twig

twin
twine
twinkle
twirl
twist

**thr**
thrash
thread

thrill
throat
throb
throne
through
thrush

**qu**
quack
quail
quake
quality
quarrel
quart
quarter

quartz
queen
quench
quest
question
quick
quiet
quill

quilt
quirk
quit
quiz
quote

# s-blends

## sc
scab
scald
scale
scallion
scallop
scalp
scamp
scan
scar
scarce
scare
scarf
scat
scold
scoop
scoot
scooter
scope
scorch
score
scour
scout
scuba
scuff

## sk
skate
sketch
ski
skid
skill
skillet
skin
skip
skirt
skit
skull
skunk
sky

## sm
smack
small
smart
smash
smear
smell
smile
smock
smog
smoke
smooth
smudge

## sn
snack
snag
snail
snake
snap
snare
snarl
snatch
sneak
sneeze
sniff
snip
snob
snoop
snore
snout
snow
snug
snuggle

## sp
space
span
spare
spark

spat
speak
spear
speck
speech
speed
spell
spend
spent
spike
spill
spin
spine
spire
spirit
spoil
spoke
sponge
spoon
sport
spot
spout
spur
spy

## st
stable
stack
stadium
staff
stage
stain
stair
stake
stale
stalk
stall
stamp
stand
staple

stapler
star
starch
stare
starfish
start
starve
state
station
stationery
statue
stay
steady
steak
steal
steam
steel
steep
steer
stem
step
stereo
stew
stick
sticky
stiff
still
stilt
sting
stingy
stink
stir
stirrup
stitch
stock
stocking
stomach
stone
stool

stoop
stop
store
storm
story
stove
style

## sw
swallow
swam
swamp
swan
swap
swarm
swat
swatch
sway
sweat
sweater
sweep
sweet
sweeten
swell
swept
swerve
swift
swim
swine
swing
swish
switch
swollen
swoop

## scr
scram
scramble
scrap
scrape
scraper
scratch

scrawl
scream
screech
screen
screw
scribble
script
scroll
scrub

## squ
square
squash
squat
squeak
squeal
squeeze
squid
squint
squirm
squirrel
squirt
squish

## str
straight
strain
strainer
strand
strange
stranger
strap
straw
strawberry
stray
streak
stream
street
strength
stretch
stretcher
strict

stride
strike
string
strip
stripe
stroke
stroll
strong
stronger
struck
struggle
strum

## spr
sprain
sprang
sprawl
spray
spread
sprig
spring
springboard
sprinkle
sprinkler
sprint
sprout
spruce

## spl
splash
splendid
splint
splinter
split

# Ending Consonant Clusters

**ct**
act
duct
fact
pact

**ft**
cleft
craft
draft
drift
gift
graft
left
lift
loft
raft
rift
shaft
shift
sift
soft
swift
thrift
tuft

**ld**
bald
bold
build
child
cold
field
fold
gold
held
hold
mild
mold
old
scald
scold
shield
sold
told

weld
wild

**lp**
help
gulp
scalp
yelp

**lt**
belt
bolt
built
colt
dealt
fault
felt
guilt
halt
jolt
kilt
knelt
melt
pelt
quilt
salt
tilt
welt

**mp**
blimp
bump
camp
champ
chimp
chomp
clamp
clump
cramp
crimp
damp
dump
grump
hump
jump

lamp
limp
lump
plump
pump
ramp
romp
shrimp
skimp
slump
stamp
stomp
stump
swamp
thump
tramp
tromp
trump

**nd**
and
band
bend
bind
bland
blend
blind
blond
bond
bound
brand
end
find
found
friend
grand
grind
ground
hand
hind
hound
kind
land
lend

mend
mind
mound
pound
round
sand
send
sound
spend
stand
strand
tend
trend
wand
wind
wound

**nk**
bank
blank
blink
bunk
chunk
drank
drink
dunk
frank
honk
hunk
ink
junk
link
mink
pink
plank
plunk
rank
rink
sank
sink
skunk
stink
stunk
sunk

tank
think
trunk
wink

**nt**
ant
bent
bunt
cent
dent
faint
front
grant
hint
hunt
lent
lint
meant
mint
paint
pint
plant
print
rent
runt
scent
sent
spent
splint
tent
tint
want
went

**pt**
apt
kept
slept
wept

**rd**
bird
board
cord

guard
hard
heard
herd
lard
sword
toward
word
yard

**rk**
ark
bark
clerk
dark
fork
hark
jerk
lark
mark
park
perk
stork
work

**sk**
ask
desk
disk
dusk
mask
risk
task

**sp**
crisp
gasp
wasp

**st**
best
blast
boast
bust
cast
chest

coast
cost
crust
dust
east
fast
fist
ghost
gust
jest
just
last
least
list
lost
mast
mist
most
must
nest
past
pest
post
quest
rest
roast
rust
test
toast
trust
twist
west
wrist

# Silent Letters

Most of the letters in our alphabet are silent in words at one time or another. Frequently, consonants are silent because the pronunciation of a particular word has changed over time, but the spelling has remained constant. Silent consonants also occur in words borrowed from other languages. Our inner speech seems to ignore silent letters when we read.

## Guidelines:

The following list, based on Hanna's 17,000 most frequent words (Burmeister, 1971), shows the 15 most frequent silent-letter spellings and their corresponding sounds.

| | | | | | | | | |
|---|---|---|---|---|---|---|---|---|
| **1.** | tch | /ch/ | (hatch) | | **9.** | lm | /m/ | (calm) |
| **2.** | dg | /j/ | (lodge) | | **10.** | rh | /r/ | (rhino) |
| **3.** | wr | /r/ | (write) | | **11.** | dj | /j/ | (adjust) |
| **4.** | kn | /n/ | (know) | | **12.** | wh | /h/ | (who) |
| **5.** | gn | /n/ | (gnaw, sign) | | **13.** | bt | /t/ | (debt) |
| **6.** | mb | /m/ | (lamb) | | **14.** | gh | /g/ | (ghost) |
| **7.** | ps | /s/ | (psychology) | | **15.** | mn | /m/ | (hymn) |
| **8.** | lk | /k/ | (talk) | | | | | |

The chart below shows the conditions under which each letter is silent and provides some sample words for instruction.

| Letter(s) | Condition | Sample Words |
|---|---|---|
| **b** | • silent before *t* and after *m* unless this letter and the *b* are in separate syllables (*timber*) | *debt, doubt, subtle, lamb, climb, comb, crumb, dumb, tomb, thumb, plumb, numb* |
| **c** | • silent in the cluster *ck* <br> • silent occasionally after *s* <br> • silent in a few other words | *back, pick, sack, lick* <br> *science, scene* <br> *Connecticut, indict* |
| **ch** | • rarely silent | *yacht* |
| **d** | • rarely silent (sometimes a result of lazy pronunciation) | *Wednesday, grandmother, handkerchief* |
| **g** | • silent when it comes before *n* or *m* | *gnat, gnaw, gnarl, gnu, sign, design, assign, resign, phlegm* |

| Letter(s) | Condition | Sample Words |
|---|---|---|
| h | • silent when it follows *r* or *k*<br>• sometimes silent when it follows *x*<br>• often silent between a consonant and the unstressed vowel<br>• silent after vowels at the end of a word<br>• sometimes silent at the beginning of a word | *rhyme, khaki*<br>*exhaust*<br>*shepherd*<br><br>*oh, hurrah*<br>*honor, hour, heir* |
| k | • silent before *n* at the beginning of a word or syllable | *know, knife, knee, knob, kneel, knew, knapsack, knack, knight, knit, knock, knot, knowledge* |
| l | • silent usually before *f*, *k*, *m*, or *v*<br>• silent in the *-ould* spelling pattern | *calf, talk, calm, salve*<br>*would, could, should* |
| m | • rarely silent | *mnemonic* |
| n | • silent after *m* (considered morphophonemic; the *n* is maintained in all derivatives of the word and pronounced in many other forms of the word, such as *hymnal*) | *autumn, hymn* |
| p | • silent before *n*, *s*, or *t* | *pneumonia, psychology, ptomaine* |
| s | • silent sometimes when it follows *i*<br>• silent in the word *Arkansas* | *island, debris, aisle* |
| t | • silent in words with *-sten* and *-stle*<br>• silent in words borrowed from French that end in *-et*, *-ot*, or *-ut* | *fasten, listen, castle, whistle*<br>*bouquet, ballet, depot, debut* |
| th | • rarely silent | *asthma, isthmus* |
| u | • silent sometimes when it follows *g* or *q* | *guard, opaque* |
| w | • silent before *r* at the beginning of a word or syllable<br>• silent in words beginning with *who-*<br>• silent in a few other words | *wrong, write*<br><br>*who, whose, whole*<br>*two, answer, sword* |
| x | • rarely silent | *Sioux* |
| z | • rarely silent | *rendezvous* |

# Silent Letters

**Phonic Principle:** silent letter spelling *wr*

**Step 1: Reread** Begin the lesson by having children reread a story or passage containing previously taught sound-spelling relationships. Then provide phonemic-awareness exercises (such as oral blending) for children needing this support.

**Step 2: Introduce Sound-Spelling**
Explain to children that sometimes a letter stands for no sound in a word; it is silent. Point out that when the letters *wr* appear together at the beginning of a word, such as *write*, the letter *w* is silent. Write the word *write* on the board. Then blend the word *write* aloud as you run your finger under each letter. Have a volunteer underline the letters *wr*. Point to the letters *wr* and ask students to chorally state the sound that the letters stand for. Continue by having children suggest words that begin with *wr*. Encourage them to become "word explorers" and search through classroom books for words. List these words on the board.

**Step 3: Blend Words** Write the following words and sentences on the board. Note that all the words are decodable based on the sound-spelling relationships previously taught. The sentences contain some high-frequency words previously taught.

- *rap       wrap       wing       wring*
- *wreck     wrong      wrist      wrinkle*
- *He will wrap the gift.*
- *I like to write letters.*

Next distribute the following letter-card set to each child: *wr, a, e, i, s, t, p, ck.* Have children build as many words as possible. Ask them to write the words on a sheet of paper. Circulate around the room and model blending when necessary.

**Step 4: Apply to Text** Provide students with connected reading practice. Choose a book in which many of the words are decodable based on the sound-spelling relationships previously taught.

**Step 5: Dictate and Write** Have children write the following words and sentence on a sheet of paper as you dictate them. For students having difficulty segmenting the sounds in each word, extend the word. You might want to clap on each sound to provide another clue. Then write the words and sentence on the board. Have children self-correct their papers. Do not grade this dictation practice. It's designed to help children segment words and associate sounds with spellings.

- *write       read       wreck*
- *Did you wrap that up?*

**Provide freewriting opportunities.**
Have children generate a list of words with the target sound-spelling. List these words on the board. Then, in small groups, have children create a story using as many of the words as possible.

# Short Vowels

**Guidelines:**

- Teach the short vowels using simple CVC (consonant-vowel-consonant) words, such as *cat, sun*, and *big*. Word lists for instruction follow.
- Separate the teaching of the auditorily confusing sounds /e/ and /i/. I suggest this sequence for introducing short vowels: *a, i, o, e, u* or *a, o, i, u, e*.

## CVC Words for Instruction

| short *a* | | short *e* | short *i* | short *o* | short *u* |
|---|---|---|---|---|---|
| bad | pad | bed | bib | box | bud |
| bag | pal | bet | big | cob | bug |
| bat | pan | fed | bit | cot | bun |
| cab | pat | get | did | dot | bus |
| can | rag | hen | dig | fog | but |
| cap | ram | jet | dip | fox | cub |
| cat | ran | led | fin | got | cup |
| dad | rap | leg | fit | hog | cut |
| fan | rat | let | hid | hop | dug |
| fat | sad | men | him | hot | fun |
| gas | sat | met | hip | job | gum |
| had | tag | net | hit | jog | hug |
| ham | tan | pen | kid | log | hut |
| hat | tap | pet | kit | lot | jug |
| jam | van | red | lid | mom | mud |
| lap | wag | set | lip | mop | mug |
| mad | | ten | lit | not | nut |
| man | | vet | pig | pod | pup |
| map | | web | pin | pop | rub |
| mat | | wet | pit | pot | rug |
| nap | | yes | rib | rod | run |
| | | yet | rid | sob | sub |
| | | | rip | top | sum |
| | | | sit | | sun |
| | | | six | | tub |
| | | | tip | | tug |
| | | | wig | | |
| | | | win | | |
| | | | zip | | |

## Books Featuring Short Vowels

The following lists are ideal for independent and instructional reading. In addition to these books, I also recommend decodable book series that come with your basal reading program or other commercially available series.

### Short *a*

*Addie Meets Max* by Joan Robins (Harper & Row)

*Alex and the Cat* by Helen Griffith (Greenwillow)

*Amanda and April* by Bonnie Pryor (Morrow)

*Angus and the Cat* by Marjorie Flack (Doubleday)

*A Birthday Basket for Tia* by Pat Mora (Macmillan)

*Caps for Sale* by Esphyr Slobodkina (Addison-Wesley)

*The Cat in the Hat* by Dr. Seuss (Random House)

*The Fat Cat* by Jack Kent (Scholastic)

*The Gingerbread Man* by Karen Schmidt (Scholastic)

*I Can* by Susan Winter (Dorling Kindersley)

*Jack and Jake* by Aliki (Greenwillow)

*The Little Mouse, the Red Ripe Strawberry, and the Big Hungry Bear* by Don Wood (Child's Play)

*Millions of Cats* by Wanda Gag (Putnam)

*My Friends* by Taro Gomi (Chronicle Books)

*There's an Ant in Anthony* by Bernard Most (Morrow)

*Who Took the Farmer's Hat* by Joan Nodset (Harper & Row)

### Short *e*

*Elephant in a Well* by Marie Hall Ets (Viking)

*Emma's Pet* by David McPhail (Dutton)

*An Extraordinary Egg* by Leo Lionni (Knopf)

*Get Set to Wreck!* by Robert Rector Krupp (Macmillan)

*Hester the Jester* by Ben Shecter (Harper & Row)

*I Don't Believe in Elves* by Jane Thayer (Morrow)

*The Little Red Hen* by Paul Galdone (Scholastic)

*Shoes from Grandpa* by Mem Fox (Orchard Books)

*Ten Pennies for Candy* by Henry Ritchet Wing (Holt)

*Yeck Eck* by Evaline Ness (Dutton)

### Short *i*

*Bit by Bit* by Steve Sanfield (Putnam)

*Call for Mr. Sniff* by Thomas P. Lewis (Harper & Row)

*The Doorbell Rang* by Pat Hutchins (Greenwillow)

*Fix-it* by David McPhail (Dutton)

*Gilberto and the Wind* by Marie Hall Ets (Viking)

*Inch by Inch* by Leo Lionni (Astor-Honor)

*Is It Dark? Is It Light?* by Mary D. Lankford (Knopf)

*My Brother, Will* by Joan Robins (Greenwillow)

*Small Pig* by Arnold Lobel (Harper & Row)

*This Is . . .* by Gloria Patrick (Carolrhoda)

*Titch* by Pat Hutchins (Macmillan)

*Two Crazy Pigs* by Karen Nagel (Scholastic)

*Whistle for Willie* by Ezra Jack Keats (Viking)

*Willy the Wimp* by Anthony Browne (Knopf)

## Short *o*

*All About You* by Catherine Anholt and Laurence Anholt (Viking)

*Animal Tracks* by Arthur Dorros (Scholastic)

*Big Frogs, Little Frogs* by Patricia Miller and Ira Seligman (Holt)

*Drummer Hoff* by Barbara Emberley (Prentice-Hall)

*Flossie & the Fox* by Patricia McKissack (Dial)

*Fox in Socks* by Dr. Seuss (Random House)

*I Need a Lunch Box* by Jeannette Caines (HarperCollins)

*Mogwogs on the March!* by Olivier Dunrea (Holiday House)

*Mop Top* by Don Freeman (Viking)

*Oscar Otter* by Nathaniel Benchley (Harper & Row)

*School Bus* by Donald Crews (Morrow)

## Short *u*

*Big Gus and Little Gus* by Lee Lorenz (Prentice-Hall)

*The Cut-Ups* by James Marshall (Viking)

*Donald Says Thumbs Down* by Nancy E. Cooney (Putnam)

*Fun/No Fun* by James Stevenson (Greenwillow)

*Hunches and Bunches* by Dr. Seuss (Random House)

*Scrawny, the Classroom Duck* by Susan Clymer (Scholastic)

*Seven Little Ducks* by Margaret Friskey (Children's Press)

*Thump and Plunk* by Janice May Udry (Harper & Row)

*The Ugly Duckling* retold by Lillian Moore (Scholastic)

*Umbrella* by Taro Yashima (Viking)

*Where's the Bunny?* by Ruth Carroll (Henry Z. Walck)

# Short Vowels

**Phonic Principle:** The letter *a* stands for the /a/ sound.

**Step 1: Reread** Begin the lesson by having children reread a story or passage containing previously taught sound-spelling relationships. Then provide phonemic-awareness exercises (such as oral blending) for children needing this support.

**Step 2: Introduce Sound-Spelling**
Explain to children that the letter *a* stands for the /a/ sound, as in the word *cat*. Write the word *cat* on the board as you display a picture of a cat. Make sure the picture is labeled. Then blend the word *cat* aloud as you run your finger under each letter. Have a volunteer underline the letter *a*. Point to the letter *a* and ask students to chorally state the sound that the letter stands for. Continue by having children generate a list of words containing the /a/ sound. List these words on the board.

**Step 3: Blend Words** Write the following words and sentences on the board. Note that all the words are decodable based on the sound-spelling relationships previously taught. The sentences contain some high-frequency words previously taught.

- *at      sat      mat      cat*
- *am      mad      lap      sad*
- *Sam is sad.*
- *The cat sat on my lap.*

Next distribute the following letter-card set to each child: *a, s, t, m, c, d, p*. Have children build as many words as possible. Ask them to write the words on a sheet of paper. Circulate around the room and model blending when necessary.

**Step 4: Apply to Text** Provide students with connected reading practice. Choose a book in which many of the words are decodable based on the sound-spelling relationships previously taught. Lists of books containing short-vowel sounds are available in many basal reading series.

**Step 5: Dictate and Write** Have children write the following words and sentence on a sheet of paper as you dictate them. For students having difficulty segmenting the sounds in each word, extend the word. You might want to clap on each sound to provide another clue. Then write the words and sentence on the board. Have children self-correct their papers. Do not grade this dictation practice. It's designed to help children segment words and associate sounds with spellings.

- *sat      am*
- *I am sad.*

**Provide freewriting opportunities.**
For example, display pictures of objects or animals whose names contain the target short-vowel sound. Have children write a sentence describing each picture.

# Long Vowels

## Guidelines:

- Begin instruction with simple, one-syllable words. Start with CVCe (consonant-vowel-consonant-e) words since this pattern is an extremely useful and unencumbered long-vowel pattern. (Word lists are provided on pages 196–197.) The silent *e* (also known as final *e* or the *e*-marker) acts as a diacritical mark, alerting the reader that the preceding vowel probably stands for a long-vowel sound. There are four basic one-syllable patterns in the English language, including the CVCe pattern (Eldredge, 1995). Two additional patterns commonly taught in reading programs are *r*-controlled vowel syllables and consonant + *le* syllables (or final stable syllables).

    1. The **closed syllable pattern** is the most common. There's one vowel in the syllable, and the syllable ends with a consonant. Most of the words using this pattern contain short-vowel sounds. There are 13 variations: CVCC *(hand)*, CVC *(cup)*, CCVCC *(fresh)*, CCVC *(trip)*, CVCCC *(match)*, CVCCe *(judge)*, CCVCCC *(crutch)*, CCVCCe *(grudge)*, CCCVCC *(script)*, VCC *(add)*, VC *(in)*, CCCVC *(scrap)*, VCCC *(inch)*.

    2. The **vowel team (vowel digraph) pattern** is the second most common. There are 12 variations: CVVC *(heat)*, CCVVC *(treat)*, CVVCC *(reach)*, CVV *(pay)*, CCVV *(play)*, CVVCe *(leave)*, CCVVCC *(bleach)*, CCVVCe *(freeze)*, CCCVVC *(sprain)*, VVC *(oat)*, VVCC *(each)*, CCCVV *(three)*.

    3. The **vowel-consonant-silent e pattern** is the third most common. There are four variations: CVCe *(race)*, CCVCe *(shave)*, CCCVCe *(strike)*, VCe *(ate)*.

    4. The **open syllable pattern** is the fourth most common. There's only one vowel in the syllable, and the syllable ends with the vowel's sound. There are two variations: CCV *(she)*, CV *(we)*.

- Use contrasts in instruction *(rat/rate; hat/hate)* so that children can see how one letter can make all the difference in a word's vowel sound. Following is a list of contrasts for CVC and CVCe words. You can also make contrasts for words with vowel digraphs *(pan/pain, cot/coat, red/read)*.

---

### A Note About Silent *e*

The silent *e* is important in English spelling (Moats, 1995). For example, the silent *e* helps to keep some words from looking like plurals (*please*, not *pleas*; and *house*, not *hous*). Since the letter *v* doesn't appear at the end of words, the silent *e* in words such as *dove, love, shove,* and *above* gives them orthographic regularity. Although this silent *e* doesn't indicate that the preceding *o* stands for the long-*o* sound, it does indicate that the preceding *o* is not a short-*o* sound. In essence, the silent *e* helps to create a spelling pattern that is consistent and far from random. The final *e* also indicates when the letter *g* or *c* stands for its "soft" sound (*page, race*).

## Contrasts

| | | | | |
|---|---|---|---|---|
| bit/bite | fin/fine | mat/mate | rid/ride | spin/spine |
| can/cane | glob/globe | not/note | rip/ripe | strip/stripe |
| cap/cape | grad/grade | pal/pale | rob/robe | tap/tape |
| cod/code | hat/hate | pan/pane | rod/rode | twin/twine |
| cub/cube | hid/hide | past/paste | scrap/scrape | us/use |
| cut/cute | hop/hope | pin/pine | shin/shine | van/vane |
| dim/dime | kit/kite | plan/plane | slid/slide | wag/wage |
| fad/fade | mad/made | rag/rage | slim/slime | |
| fat/fate | man/mane | rat/rate | slop/slope | |

# VCe Words for Instruction

## a_e (long a)

| | | | | | | | |
|---|---|---|---|---|---|---|---|
| ace | cape | flame | haze | page | safe | snake | vane |
| age | case | frame | jade | pale | sake | space | vase |
| bake | cave | game | lace | pane | sale | spade | wade |
| base | chase | gate | lake | paste | same | stage | wage |
| blade | crane | gave | lame | pave | save | stake | wake |
| blame | crate | gaze | lane | place | scale | stale | wave |
| blaze | date | glaze | late | plane | scrape | state | waste |
| brace | daze | grace | made | plate | shade | take | whale |
| brake | drape | grade | make | quake | shake | tale | |
| brave | face | grape | male | race | shame | tame | |
| cage | fade | grate | mane | rage | shape | tape | |
| cake | fake | grave | mate | rake | shave | taste | |
| came | fame | haste | name | rate | skate | trace | |
| cane | flake | hate | pace | rave | slate | trade | |

EXCEPTIONS: advantage, are, average, breakage, cabbage, climate, courage, delicate, furnace, have, manage, message, palace, passage, private, purchase, senate, separate, surface, village

## i_e (long *i*)

| | | | | | | | |
|---|---|---|---|---|---|---|---|
| bike | dive | hive | mice | price | slice | strike | vine |
| bite | drive | kite | mile | pride | slide | stripe | while |
| bride | file | lice | mine | rice | slime | swine | white |
| chime | fine | life | nice | ride | smile | tide | wide |
| crime | five | like | nine | ripe | spice | tile | wife |
| dice | glide | lime | pile | rise | spike | time | wipe |
| dime | hide | line | pine | shine | spine | twice | wise |
| dine | hike | live | pipe | side | stride | twine | write |

EXCEPTIONS: active, aggressive, automobile, determine, engine, examine, expressive, favorite, figurine, give, justice, live, machine, magazine, massive, native, notice, office, opposite, police, practice, promise, representative, routine, service

## o_e (long *o*)

| | | | | | | | |
|---|---|---|---|---|---|---|---|
| bone | code | hole | lone | pole | slope | stove | whole |
| broke | cone | home | mole | robe | smoke | stroke | woke |
| choke | dome | hope | nose | rode | spoke | those | zone |
| chose | drove | hose | note | rope | stole | tone | |
| close | globe | joke | poke | rose | stone | vote | |

EXCEPTIONS: above, become, come, done, glove, gone, improve, lose, love, lovely, move, movement, none, purpose, remove, shove, some, something, welcome, whose

## u_e (long *u*)

| | | | | |
|---|---|---|---|---|
| cube | cute | fuse | mule | use |

EXCEPTIONS: assure, conclude, crude, duke, dune, flute, include, June, measure, pleasure, prune, rude, rule, sure, treasure, tube, tune

- In addition to silent *e*, many vowel spellings are formed by **vowel digraphs**, also known as **vowel pairs** or **vowel teams**. These include *ea, ee, oa, ai, ay*, and others. The following chart shows the predictability of various vowel digraphs, many of which are long-vowel digraphs (Burmeister, 1968).

## The Predictability of Common Vowel Digraphs

| Vowel Digraph | Predictability | Vowel Digraph | Predictability |
|---|---|---|---|
| **ai** | /ā/ *(pain)* 74%, air *(chair)* 15% | **ou** | /ə/ *(trouble)* 41%, /ou/ *(house)* 35% |
| **ay** | /ā/ *(say)* 96% | **au** | /ô/ *(haul)* 94% |
| **ea** | /ē/ *(seat)* 51%, /e/ *(head)* 26% | **aw** | /ô/ *(hawk)* 100% |
| **ee** | /ē/ *(feet)* 86%, eer *(steer)* 12% | **oo** | /o͞o/ *(food)* 59%, /o͝o/ *(foot)* 36% |
| **ey** | /ē/ *(key)* 58%, /ā/ *(convey)* 20%, /ī/ *(geyser)* 12% | **ei** | /ā/ *(reign)* 40%, /ē/ *(deceit)* 26%, /i/ *(foreign)* 13%, /ī/ *(seismic)* 11% |
| **oa** | /ō/ *(boat)* 94% | **ie** | /ē/ *(chief)* 51%, /ī/ *(lie)* 17%, /ə/ *(patient)* 15% |
| **ow** | /ō/ *(snow)* 50%, /ou/ *(how)* 48% | **ew** | /yo͞o/ *(few)* 95% |
| **oi** | /oi/ *(soil)* 98% | **ui** | /o͞o/ *(fruit)* 53%, /i/ *(build)* 47% |
| **oy** | /oi/ *(boy)* 98% | | |

## Books Featuring Long Vowels

### Long *a*

*Bringing the Rain to Kapiti Plain* by Verna Aardema (Dial)

*The Lace Snail* by Betsy Byars (Viking)

*Moira's Birthday* by Robert Munsch (Firefly)

*Owl at Home* by Arnold Lobel (HarperCollins)

*The Pain and the Great One* by Judy Blume (Bradbury)

*The Paper Crane* by Molly Bang (Greenwillow)

*Sheila Rae, the Brave* by Kevin Henkes (Greenwillow)

*Taste the Raindrops* by Anna G. Hines (Greenwillow)

### Long *e*

*Arthur's Funny Money* by Lillian Hoban (HarperCollins)

*Brown Bear, Brown Bear, What Do You See?* by Bill Martin, Jr. (Holt)

*Clifford's Puppy Days* by Norman Bridwell (Scholastic)

*Have You Seen Trees?* by Joanne Oppenheim (Young Scott Books)

*Jenny's Journey* by Sheila White Samton (Puffin Books)

*Little Bo Peep* by Paul Galdone (Clarion/Ticknor & Fields)

*Miss Nelson Has a Field Day* by Harry Allard (Houghton Mifflin)

*Never Tease a Weasel* by Jean Soule (Parents Magazine Press)

*Pierre: A Cautionary Tale* by Maurice Sendak (HarperCollins)

*The Screaming Mean Machine* by Joy Cowley (Scholastic)

*"Stand Back," Said the Elephant, "I'm Going to Sneeze!"* by Patricia Thomas (Lothrop, Lee & Shepard)

*Ten Sleepy Sheep* by Holly Keller (Greenwillow)

*We Scream for Ice Cream* by Bernice Chardiet and Grace Maccarone (Scholastic)

### Long *i*

*The Bike Lesson* by Stan and Jan Berenstain (Random House)

*If Mice Could Fly* by John Cameron (Atheneum)

*Jamaica's Find* by Juanita Havill (Houghton Mifflin)

*Night Sounds, Morning Colors* by Rosemary Wells (Dial)

*No Fighting, No Biting!* by Else E. Minarik (HarperCollins)

*Tight Times* by Barbara Hazen (Viking)

*When the Tide Is Low* by Sheila Cole (Lothrop, Lee & Shepard)

*Why Can't I Fly?* by Rita Gelman (Scholastic)

*Wild Wild Sunflower Child Anna* by Nancy White Carlstrom (Macmillan)

*Winter Coats* by Margo Mason (Bantam)

## Long o

*The Adventures of Mole and Troll* by Tony Johnston (Putnam)

*Bob the Snowman* by Sylvia Loretan (Viking)

*The Giant's Toe* by Brock Cole (Farrar, Straus & Giroux)

*Going Home* by Margaret Wild (Scholastic)

*Lost!* by David McPhail (Little, Brown)

*A New Coat for Anna* by Harry Ziefert (Knopf)

*New Shoes for Sylvia* by Johanna Hurwitz (Morrow)

*Night Noises and Other Mole and Troll Stories* by Tony Johnston (Putnam)

*One Monday Morning* by Uri Shulevitz (Scribner)

*Osa's Pride* by Ann Grifalconi (Little, Brown)

*Roll Over!* by Mordicai Gerstein (Crown)

*Snowsong Whistling* by Karen Lotz (Dutton)

*Toad on the Road* by Jon Buller and Susan Schade (Random House)

*When I Am Old With You* by Angela Johnson (Orchard Books)

*White Snow, Bright Snow* by Alvin Tresselt (Lothrop, Lee & Shepard)

## Long u

*"Excuse Me—Certainly!"* by Louis Slobodkin (Vanguard Press)

*Tell Me a Trudy* by Lore Segal (Farrar, Straus & Giroux)

*The Troll Music* by Anita Lobel (Harper & Row)

# Long Vowels

**Phonic Principle:** The letters *ea* and *ee* stand for the /ē/ sound.

**Step 1: Reread** Begin the lesson by having children reread a story or passage containing previously taught sound-spelling relationships. Then provide phonemic-awareness exercises (such as oral blending) for children needing this support.

**Step 2: Introduce Sound-Spelling** Explain to children that the letters *ee* and *ea* can stand for the /ē/ sound, as in *feet* and *seat*. Write the words *feet* and *seat* on the board. Then blend the words aloud as you run your finger under each letter. Have a volunteer underline the letters *ee* or *ea*. Point to the letters and ask students to chorally state the sound that the letters stand for. Continue by having children generate a list of words containing the /ē/ sound. List these words on the board. Have volunteers circle the letters *ee* or *ea* in all the words containing these spellings for the /ē/ sound.

**Step 3: Blend Words** Write the following words and sentences on the board. Note that all the words are decodable based on the sound-spelling relationships previously taught. The first line focuses on short-vowel/long-vowel contrasts. The sentences contain some high-frequency words previously taught.

- *bet        beat        fed        feed*
- *leaf        need        bean        deep*
- *My team will win!*
- *Keep the seeds in the bag.*

Next distribute the following letter-card set to each child: *ee, ea, s, d, t, p, k, l*. Have children build as many words as possible. Ask them to write the words on a sheet of paper. Circulate around the room and model blending when necessary.

**Step 4: Apply to Text** Provide students with connected reading practice. Choose a book in which many of the words are decodable based on the sound-spelling relationships previously taught. Lists of books containing long-vowel sounds are available in many basal reading series.

**Step 5: Dictate and Write** Have children write the following words and sentence on a sheet of paper as you dictate them. For students having difficulty segmenting the sounds in each word, extend the word. You might want to clap on each sound to provide another clue. Then write the words and sentence on the board. Have children self-correct their papers. Do not grade this dictation practice. It's designed to help children segment words and associate sounds with spellings.

- *fed        feed        heat*
- *We need to eat.*

**Provide freewriting opportunities.**
For example, have children write a dramatic version of a story they've just read. Children will enjoy performing these plays for the class.

# Other Vowel Sounds

### Guidelines:

Some vowel digraphs stand for sounds that are not commonly classified as long or short vowels. These include the following, which I've classified according to the way they are grouped in most basal reading programs.

### Variant Vowels

/o͞o/ (f**oo**d), /o͝o/ (f**oo**t), /ô/ (b**a**ll, c**au**se, cl**aw**, f**o**r)

Note that the *o* in *for* can also be classified as an *r*-controlled vowel (see below). The vowel digraph *oo* has a long and a short sound assigned to it. The long sound is more frequent in words than the short sound. Therefore, when children encounter this vowel digraph in a word, they should try the long sound first. The only way for children to know which sound is correct is to try both sounds and see which forms a word that is in their speaking or listening vocabularies (assuming they have heard the word before).

### Diphthongs

/oi/ (b**oi**l, b**oy**), /ou/ (h**ou**se, c**ow**)

Diphthongs are vowel sounds formed by a gliding action in the mouth. That is, unlike other vowel sounds, the tongue and lip positions often change as the sound is formed. For example, say and extend the /a/ sound. Notice the position of the lips and tongue. Do they change while forming the sound? No. Now say the /oi/ sound. Notice how the lips are thrust forward and close together as the sound begins but quickly retract and open slightly as the sound is concluded. This gliding action is characteristic of diphthongs. Many linguists also consider the long-*i* and long-*u* sounds diphthongs.

### *r*-controlled vowels

/âr/ (ch**air**), /ûr/ (f**er**n, b**ir**d, h**ur**t), /är/ (p**ar**k), /ôr/ (h**or**n)

The letter *r* affects the sound of the vowel that precedes it in many ways. The following is a suggested sequence for teaching *r*-controlled vowels based on frequency and predictability of spellings (Groff, 1977; Blevins, 1997): **1.** /ûr/ *(ir, er, ur)* **2.** /ôr/ *(or, ore, oar)* **3.** /är/ *(ar)* **4.** /âr/ *(are, air, eir, ear)*. In addition to the letter *r*, the letters *l* and *w* have effects on the vowels that precede or follow them (e.g., *water, fall, talk*). Instead of trying to explain to children the intricacies of how the vowel sound is affected by these consonants, it's best to teach the sounds as spelling patterns, such as *ar, er, ir, or, ur, air, ear, are, all, alk*, and *wa*.

## Schwa

### /ə/ (alone, happen, direct, gallop, circus)

Some linguists don't consider this a separate sound, but rather an allophone—a variant of a particular sound caused by a reduction in stress on that sound in a word. The schwa is also known as a murmur or neutral sound. Up to 22 different spellings of the schwa sound have been identified (Hanna et al., 1966). It's difficult to teach children rules for identifying this sound in words. Some educators suggest telling children to try the short sound of a questionable vowel when decoding multisyllabic words (Chall & Popp, 1996); others suggest telling children to say "uh" for every vowel sound in a word they are unsure of. They believe that this approximation will be close enough for the child to identify the word if it is in his or her speaking or listening vocabulary.

### Books Featuring Other Vowels

*Everybody Cooks Rice* by Norah Dooley (Carolrhoda)

*Good News* by Barbara Brenner (Bantam)

*Michael Bird-Boy* by Tomie dePaola (Simon & Schuster)

*A Place for Grace* by Jean Davies Okimoto (Sasquatch)

*Sally's Room* by M. K. Brown (Scholastic)

*Song and Dance Man* by Karen Ackerman (Knopf)

*This Is Baseball* by Margaret Blackstone (Henry Holt)

*Too Many Babas* by Carolyn Croll (HarperCollins)

### r-Controlled Vowels

*The Berenstain Bears and the Sitter* by Dan and Jan Berenstain (Random House)

*A House for Hermit Crab* by Eric Carle (Picture Books Studio)

*Ox-Cart Man* by Donald Hall (Puffin)

*Sheep Dreams* by Arthur A. Levine (Dial)

### Diphthongs /ou/ and /oi/

*Baseball Ballerina* by Kathryn Cristaldi (Random Books for Young Readers)

*The Boy of the Three-Year Nap* by Dianne Snyder (Houghton Mifflin)

*The Boy Who Didn't Believe in Spring* by Lucille Clifton (Viking)

*Counting Cows* by Woody Jackson (Harcourt Brace)

*The Cow Who Wouldn't Come Down* by Paul Brett Johnson (Orchard Books)

*Fox on Wheels* by Edward Marshall (Puffin)

*The Leaving Morning* by Angela Johnson (Orchard Books)

*She'll Be Comin' Round the Mountain* adapted by Tom and Debbie Holsclaw Birdseye (Holiday)

*Too Much Noise* by Ann McGovern (Houghton Mifflin)

*The Wheels on the Bus* by Paul Zelinsky (Dutton)

In addition to these books, Scholastic offers several early reader series that are ideal for alphabet and phonics instruction. These include the following:

## Alpha Tales Box Set

**Who is it for?** Each of the 26 books in this series (one for each letter of the alphabet) provides a story for you to read aloud to children. There is also an activity page, alphabet cheer, and lots of vocabulary-building opportunities. The books are for children learning the alphabet and basic letter-sounds.

**What can it do?** This series offers children a fun way to engage with new letters and sounds. It provides a quick way to learn a set of words for each letter of the alphabet that can be used in reading, speaking, and writing.

**How can you use it?** This series is ideal for introducing and reinforcing alphabet letters and sounds. Children will enjoy hearing the stories many times and interacting with the text and pictures through the activities provided. You can page through the book with children, point to each letter, and have children say the letter's name. Point to pictures on the page and help children learn the words that begin with that letter and sound. Keep doing this until children begin to recognize many of the letters and words quickly. This could take weeks. Finally, page through the book, point to the letter, and have children say the letter's sound.

## Nonfiction Alphabet Readers Parent Pack

**Who is it for?** This series has one book for each letter of the alphabet and can also be read aloud to children. Each book includes a large set of new vocabulary words.

**What can it do?** This series is ideal for building vocabulary around specific nonfiction topics. The new words are grouped by beginning letter-sound (e.g., *bear, big, baby, beautiful, best, bee, bug*).

**How can you use it?** The books in this series serve as great informational read-alouds to build knowledge and English vocabulary around topics such as animals, seasons, weather, and transportation. They can also be used as independent reading for older children who have learned most of the basic phonics skills. An activity book provides practice with writing letters.

## Scholastic Decodable Readers Box Set (Levels A–D)

**Who is it for?** The 80 books in this series (20 per level) cover the full range of phonics skills—from short vowels (Level A), to short vowels with blends and digraphs (Level B), to long vowels and diphthongs (Level C), to complex vowels and multisyllabic words (Level D). The series is for all levels of students learning basic reading skills.

**What can it do?** These books provide controlled sentences that use only the letters and sight words children have learned. The books offer a complete course in beginning phonics. Repeated readings of these texts can help children master all the basic phonics skills. They are also ideal for older children who are struggling with reading in English and need more phonics practice.

**How can you use it?** Children can read these books on their own, or with a little help from a more skilled English speaker. Since the books are carefully sequenced, the phonics skills are built-on and reviewed from book to book throughout the sets. Children read at a pace that best meets their learning goals and reading ability.

## Scholastic Phonics Booster Books (Levels 1–6)

**Who is it for?** The 36 books in this series (6 per level) cover the full range of phonics skills—short vowels (Levels 1–2), long vowels (Levels 3–4), and complex vowels (Levels 5–6). The series is for all levels of children learning basic phonics skills. The order in which the phonics skills are taught in this series is the same as the order used in the Scholastic Decodable Readers. However, since there are fewer books, the pace at which children practice these words is faster.

**What can it do?** These books provide controlled sentences that use only the letters and sight words children have learned. The books offer a complete course in beginning phonics. Repeated readings of these stories can help children master all the basic phonics skills. Since there are fewer books than in the Scholastic Decodable Readers, they can also be used as a great review of phonics skills for older readers who need the practice or are able to advance more rapidly in their phonics learning.

**How can you use it?** Children can read these books on their own, or with a little help from a more skilled English speaker. Since the books are carefully sequenced, the phonics skills are built-on and reviewed from book to book throughout the sets.

# Other Vowel Sounds

**Phonic Principle:** The letters *oi* and *oy* stand for the /oi/ sound.

**Step 1: Reread** Begin the lesson by having children reread a story or passage containing previously taught sound-spelling relationships. Then provide phonemic-awareness exercises (such as oral blending) for children needing this support.

**Step 2: Introduce Sound-Spelling**
Explain to children that the letters *oi* and *oy* stand for the /oi/ sound, as in *boil* and *boy*. Write the words *boil* and *boy* on the board. Then blend the words aloud as you run your finger under each letter. Have a volunteer underline the letters *oi* or *oy*. Point to the letters and ask students to chorally state the sound that the letters stand for. Continue by having children generate a list of words containing the /oi/ sound. List these words on the board.

**Step 3: Blend Words** Write the following words and sentences on the board. Note that all the words are decodable based on the sound-spelling relationships previously taught. Contrasts are given in the first line. The sentences contain some high-frequency words previously taught.

- *box      boy      pint      point*
- *coin      joy      toys      noise*
- *The boy will enjoy the game.*
- *I found five coins.*

Next distribute the following letter-card set to each child: *oi, oy, b, l, c, n, j.* Have children build as many words as possible. Ask them to write the words on a sheet of paper. Circulate around the room and model blending when necessary.

**Step 4: Apply to Text** Provide children with connected reading practice. Choose a book in which many of the words are decodable based on the sound-spelling relationships previously taught.

**Step 5: Dictate and Write** Have children write the following words and sentence on a sheet of paper as you dictate them. Then write the words and sentence on the board. Have children self-correct their papers. Do not grade this dictation practice. It's designed to help children segment words and associate sounds with spellings.

- *boy      point      coil*
- *Do you like your new toy?*

**Provide freewriting opportunities.**
For example, have children write a poem using as many words with the target sound as possible.

# Phonograms

Throughout the past two decades, increased attention has been paid to phonograms and their use in early reading instruction. In the classrooms I visit, I see more and more Word Walls containing word lists primarily organized around phonograms. A **phonogram** is a letter (or series of letters) that stands for a sound, syllable, or series of sounds without reference to meaning. For example, the phonogram -*ay* contains two letters and stands for the long-*a* sound. It can be found in words such as *say, may,* and *replay*. The phonogram -*ack* contains three letters, stands for two sounds (/a/ /k/), and can be found in words such as *pack, black,* and *attack*. Phonograms are often referred to as **word families**. The words *face, space,* and *replace* belong to the same word family because they all contain the ending -*ace*. The ending -*ace* is a phonogram.

A linguistic term sometimes substituted for phonogram is **rime**. Rime is generally used in combination with the term **onset**. Onset and rime refer to the two parts of a syllable. In a syllable, a rime is the vowel and everything after it. For example, in the one-syllable word *sat*, the rime is -*at*. The onset is the consonant, consonant blend, or digraph that comes before the rime in a syllable. In the words *sat, brat,* and *chat,* the onsets are *s, br,* and *ch,* respectively. A two-syllable word, such as *pancake*, has two onsets and two rimes. What are the onsets in the word *pancake*? *(p, c)* What are the rimes? *(-an, -ake)* Some words, such as *at, out,* and *up,* contain no onset.

## Phonograms Provide Early Reading Boosts

Phonograms have been used in early reading and spelling instruction dating as far back as the *New England Primer* and *Webster's Blue Back Spelling Books* of the 1600s, 1700s, and 1800s. Phonograms have been used for spelling instruction because word patterns are the most effective vehicle for teaching spelling. Phonograms can also provide a boost to early reading instruction. Many children enter first grade with a fair grasp of consonants and the sounds they represent. By learning a phonogram such as -*at*, they can generate a number of primary-level words, such as *bat, cat, fat, hat, mat, pat, rat,* and *sat*. Students can then use these words in early independent writing and to read connected text. And children will encounter these words in many primary-level stories. Teaching children that words contain recognizable chunks and teaching them to search for these word parts or patterns is an important step to developing reading fluency.

Provide frequent review of challenging sound-spelling relationships for children needing additional support.

As children encounter more and more multisyllabic words, they gain an understanding that words may contain recognizable parts (phonograms, suffixes, prefixes, smaller words). This insight is critical for decoding the words quickly and efficiently.

Another value of phonograms is that they are reliable and generalizable. Of the 286 phonograms that appeared in the primary-level texts reviewed in one classic study, 272 (95%) were pronounced the same in every word in which they were found (Durrell, 1963). In addition, these 272 reliable phonograms can be found in 1,437 of the words common to the speaking vocabularies of primary-age children (Murphy, 1957).

Many educators have noted the utility of phonograms in early reading instruction. In fact, a relatively small number of phonograms can be used to generate a large number of words. According to Wylie and Durrell (1970), nearly 500 primary-grade words can be derived from only 37 phonograms:

| ack | ame | at | ell | ight | ink | oke | uck |
|-----|-----|-----|-----|------|-----|-----|-----|
| ail | an | ate | est | ill | ip | op | ug |
| ain | ank | aw | ice | in | it | ore | ump |
| ake | ap | ay | ick | ine | ock | ot | unk |
| ale | ash | eat | ide | ing | | | |

Wylie and Durrell also discovered some important instructional considerations about phonograms:

- Long-vowel phonograms (*-eat, -oat*) were as easy to learn as short-vowel phonograms (*-ed, -op*).
- Long-vowel phonograms with final *e* (*-ake, -ide, -ope*) were as easy to learn as other long-vowel phonograms.

- Phonograms containing variant vowels *(-ood, -ook)*, *r*-controlled vowels *(-ear, -are)*, and diphthongs *(-out, -oint)* were almost as easy to learn as long- and short-vowel phonograms.
- Phonograms ending in a single consonant *(-at, -ot)* were easier to learn than phonograms ending in consonant clusters *(-ast, -imp)*.

## Teaching With Phonograms

Decoding by analogy is one instructional method that uses phonograms (Cunningham 1975–76; Wagstaff, 1994; Fox, 1996). When decoding by analogy, children look for recognizable chunks within a word to help them figure it out. Cunningham (1995) contends that the brain works as a "pattern detector." As we develop as readers and our knowledge of English orthography increases, we detect more and more of these spelling patterns. Teaching children to decode by analogy helps make them aware of the patterns in our written language. The box below shows how a teacher might model the use of analogies to decode the word *stick*.

**Model:** When I look at this word, I see two parts that remind me of other words I know. First I see the letters *st*, as in the word *stop*. These two letters stand for the /st/ sounds. I also see the word part *-ick* as in the word *pick*. If I blend together these two word parts, I get the word *stick*.

Using phonograms in phonics instruction can also help children gain access to more complex phonics concepts, such as *r*-controlled vowels (Wagstaff, 1994). To explain to children how the *r* in the word *far* affects the sound that the *a* stands for is difficult. However, teaching children the phonogram *-ar* and providing them practice reading words such as *bar, car, far, jar*, and *star* is simpler and arguably more efficient.

## Phonogram Cautions

Although phonograms can provide a boost to early reading instruction, I offer a **strong word of caution**. Phonograms should never be the sole focus of early reading instruction because they provide the developing reader only limited independence in word analysis. Some educators refer to the use of phonograms in phonics instruction as "rudimentary phonics" (Roswell & Natchez, 1971). They found that beginning readers who rely primarily on phonograms to decode by analogy are less skilled at word identification than beginning readers who analyze words fully

(Bruck & Treiman, 1990). Why is this so? Because beginning readers are taught to remember phonograms by sight. Little attention is paid to the actual sound-spelling relationship of the vowel, and almost no attention is paid to the ending consonant sound-spelling relationship. This places fewer phonemic awareness and phonics demands on the reader. When readers use phonograms, they need to focus on only the initial consonant, consonant blend, or digraph. Therefore, when teachers use phonograms to teach vowel sounds, children get little practice in learning vowel sound-spelling relationships. What they are actually practicing are the consonant sound-spelling relationships. But fully analyzing words focuses children's attention on all of the word's sound-spelling relationships.

As you can see, analyzing words in their entirety is essential. Much of what children learn about English orthography (spelling patterns) comes from the constant analysis of words and exposure to an abundance of print. Eventually, multiple exposures to words enable the reader to recognize words by sight and recognize common spelling patterns in unfamiliar words—an important goal in developing reading fluency. The best explanation of how this happens can be gleaned from the work of Ehri (1995). She provides us with a clear model of the **phases children go through in making every word a sight word**. This model includes four phases:

1 **Pre-Alphabetic Phase (Logographic)** Children recognize symbols, such as the "golden arches" of McDonald's, and attach a word or meaning to them. Or they recognize a special feature of a word. For example, a child might remember the word *yellow* because it contains two "sticks" in the middle.

2 **Partial Alphabetic Phase** Children are beginning to learn sound-spelling relationships, yet they are using only some phonics cues to figure out words. For example, a child guesses the word *kitten* based on his knowledge of the sounds associated with the letters *k* and *n*, and his use of picture clues. However, this same child would probably not be able to distinguish the word *kitten* from the word *kitchen* because the word is not being analyzed fully.

3 **Full Alphabetic Phase** Children are using their knowledge of sound-spelling relationships and analyzing words in their entirety. Much practice decoding and multiple exposures to print help children to begin to develop an awareness of spelling patterns.

**4** **Consolidated Alphabetic Phase (Orthographic)** Children's awareness of spelling patterns is stronger, and they're beginning to use this knowledge to quickly and accurately decode unknown words. For example, a child sees the word *stack*. Instead of analyzing the word sound by sound, she almost instantly recognizes the familiar *st* combination from words such as *step* and *stop*, and the word part *-ack*. The efficiency with which this child decodes words is greater than in the previous phase and occurs as a result of many opportunities to fully analyze words, decode many words, and pay attention to word parts within words.

As children repeatedly encounter words, they learn many as sight words. This is the ultimate goal of fast, efficient decoding. Some children require as few as four or five exposures to new words to learn them by sight. For struggling readers, the number of exposures that are needed jumps to 50–100 (Honig, 1996). Learning words by sight requires analyzing many words in their entirety and wide reading. Beginning readers who are taught to look only for phonograms or other word chunks are being treated as skilled readers instead of the developing readers they are. In addition, no reading program can teach the vast number of phonograms children will encounter in words. Therefore, although the use of phonograms to decode by analogy is useful, it is not sufficient. Children must be able to use a variety of decoding strategies including decoding by analogy, blending, recognizing sight words, and using context clues, to figure out the complete range of words in the English language.

Another caution associated with phonograms is the over-reliance on them to create reading materials for phonics practice. Text with a high proportion of phonograms should be avoided (Perfetti & McCutcheon, 1982). This type of text, once common in the so-called linguistic readers of decades ago, is illustrated by the following example:

> *Fat cat. Fat cat sat.*
> *Fat cat sat on bat.*
> *Pat fat cat.*

This type of text—with its minimal contrasts and repetition of phonograms—reads more like a tongue twister than the connected text that enables a child to gain meaning. Though it was designed to help early readers, it often caused serious confusion and lack of comprehension. It's important that early reading text be closer to children's oral language than that used in the "linguistic" readers.

However, by including high-frequency words and words with other patterns, this type of text can be restructured to be more natural sounding.

## How to Use Phonogram Lists

You can use the phonogram lists on pages 213–225 to develop word lists for phonics and spelling instruction. These lists are based on the work of researchers (Fry et al., 1993), textbook publishers, and my tireless searching through children's dictionaries. The lists contain one-syllable words and are organized by vowel sound. Within each list, the words are listed in alphabetical order beginning with single consonant words, then proceeding to words beginning with consonant clusters or digraphs.

Use the lists with care. They can provide a valuable source of words for activities such as word sorts and word building. However, some of the words on the lists may not be appropriate for your instructional needs. For example, if you're working with first and second graders, a few of the words, such as *vat, span,* and *plot,* may not be in your students' speaking or listening vocabulary. Avoid using these words, particularly when you're developing sentences, stories, or any other types of connected text. I have tried to weed out most of the words not common to young children's books or vocabulary. And remember to introduce words beginning and ending with single consonants before words with consonant clusters or digraphs.

# Long-*a* Phonograms

**-ace**
face
lace
mace
pace
race
brace
grace
place
space
trace

**-ade**
fade
jade
made
wade
blade
glade
grade
shade
spade
trade

**-age**
age
cage
gage
page
rage
sage
wage
stage

**-aid**
laid
maid
paid
raid
braid

**-ail**
bail
fail

Gail
hail
jail
mail
nail
pail
quail
rail
sail
tail
wail
flail
frail
snail
trail

**-ain**
main
pain
rain
vain
brain
chain
drain
grain
plain
slain
Spain
sprain
stain
strain
train

**-aint**
faint
paint
saint
taint
quaint

**-aise**
raise
praise

**-ait**
bait
gait
wait
strait
trait

**-ake**
bake
cake
fake
Jake
lake
make
quake
rake
sake
take
wake
brake
drake
flake
shake
snake
stake

**-ale**
bale
Dale
gale
male
pale
sale
tale
scale
stale
whale

**-ame**
came
dame
fame
game
lame

name
same
tame
blame
flame
frame
shame

**-ane**
cane
Jane
lane
mane
pane
sane
vane
wane
crane
plane

**-ange**
range
change
grange
strange

**-ape**
cape
gape
nape
tape
drape
grape
scrape
shape

**-ase**
base
case
vase
chase

**-aste**
baste
haste

paste
taste
waste

**-ate**
date
fate
gate
hate
Kate
late
mate
rate
crate
grate
plate
skate
state

**-ave**
cave
Dave
gave
pave
rave
save
wave
brave
crave
grave
shave
slave

**-ay**
bay
day
gay
hay
jay
lay
may
nay
pay
ray

say
way
clay
fray
gray
play
pray
slay
spray
stay
stray
sway
tray

**-aze**
daze
faze
gaze
haze
maze
raze
blaze
craze
glaze
graze

**-eak**
break
steak

**-eigh**
neigh
weigh
sleigh

**-ey**
hey
grey
prey
they
whey

# Long-*e* Phonograms

**-e**
be
he
me
we
she

**-ea**
pea
sea
tea
flea
plea

**-each**
beach
leach
peach
reach
teach
bleach
breach
preach

**-ead**
bead
lead
read
knead
plead

**-eak**
beak
leak
peak
weak
bleak
creak
freak
sneak
speak
squeak
streak
tweak

**-eal**
deal
heal
meal
peal
real
seal
teal
veal
zeal
squeal
steal

**-eam**
beam
ream
seam
team
cream
dream
gleam
scream
steam
stream

**-ean**
bean
dean
Jean
lean
mean
wean
clean
glean

**-eap**
heap
leap
reap
cheap

**-ear**
dear
fear
gear
hear
near
rear
tear
year
clear
shear
smear
spear

**-ease**
cease
lease
crease
grease

**-east**
beast
feast
least
yeast

**-eat**
beat
feat
heat
meat
neat
peat
seat
bleat
cheat
cleat
pleat
treat
wheat

**-eath**
heath
sheath
wreath

**-eave**
heave
leave
weave
cleave
sheave

**-ee**
bee
fee
knee
Lee
see
tee
wee
flee
free
glee
spree
three
tree

**-eech**
beech
leech
breech
screech
speech

**-eed**
deed
feed
heed
need
reed
seed
weed
bleed
breed
creed
freed
greed
speed
tweed

**-eek**
leek
meek
peek
reek
seek
week

cheek
creek
Greek
sleek

**-eel**
feel
heel
kneel
peel
reel
steel
wheel

**-eem**
deem
seem
teem

**-een**
keen
queen
seen
teen
green
screen

**-eep**
beep
deep
jeep
keep
peep
seep
weep
cheep
creep
sheep
sleep
steep
sweep

**-eer**
deer
jeer
peer
queer

sneer
steer

**-eet**
beet
feet
meet
fleet
greet
sheet
skeet
sleet
street
sweet
tweet

**-eeze**
breeze
freeze
sneeze
squeeze
tweeze
wheeze

**-iece**
niece
piece

**-ief**
brief
chief
grief
thief

**-ield**
field
yield
shield

# Long-*i* Phonograms

**-ibe**
bribe
scribe
tribe

**-ice**
dice
lice
mice
nice
rice
vice
price
slice
splice
thrice
twice

**-ide**
hide
ride
side
tide
wide
bride
glide
pride
slide
snide
stride

**-ie**
die
lie
pie
tie
vie

**-ied**
died
lied
cried
dried
fried
spied
tried

**-ier**
brier
crier
drier
flier

**-ies**
dies
lies
pies
ties
cries
dries
flies
skies
spies
tries

**-ife**
fife
knife
life
rife
wife
strife

**-igh**
high
nigh
sigh
thigh

**-ight**
fight
knight
light
might
night
right
sight
tight
blight
bright
flight
fright
plight
slight

**-ike**
bike
dike
hike
like
Mike
pike
spike
strike

**-ild**
mild
wild
child

**-ile**
file
mile
Nile
pile
tile
vile
smile
while

**-ime**
dime
lime
mime
time
chime
crime
grime
prime
slime

**-ind**
bind
find
hind
kind
mind
rind
wind
blind
grind

**-ine**
dine
fine
line
mine
nine
pine
vine
shine
shrine
spine
swine
whine

**-ipe**
pipe
ripe
wipe
gripe
snipe
stripe
swipe

**-ire**
fire
hire
tire
wire
spire

**-ise**
guise
rise
wise

**-ite**
bite
kite
mite
quite
rite
site
white
write
sprite

**-ive**
dive
five
hive
jive
live
chive
drive
strive
thrive

**-uy**
buy
guy

**-y**
by
my
cry
dry
fly
fry
ply
pry
shy
sky
sly
spy
try
why

**-ye**
bye
dye
eye
lye
rye

# Long-*o* Phonograms

| **-o** | **-oat** | choke | **-olt** | **-ose** | blow |
|---|---|---|---|---|---|
| go | oat | smoke | bolt | hose | crow |
| no | boat | spoke | colt | nose | flow |
| so | coat | stoke | jolt | pose | glow |
| pro | goat | stroke | molt | rose | grow |
| | moat | | volt | chose | show |
| **-oach** | bloat | **-old** | | close | slow |
| coach | float | old | **-ome** | prose | snow |
| poach | gloat | bold | dome | those | stow |
| roach | throat | cold | home | | |
| broach | | fold | Nome | **-ost** | **-own** |
| | **-obe** | gold | Rome | host | known |
| **-oad** | lobe | hold | chrome | most | mown |
| load | robe | mold | gnome | post | sown |
| road | globe | sold | | ghost | blown |
| toad | probe | told | **-one** | | flown |
| | | scold | bone | **-ote** | grown |
| **-oak** | **-ode** | | cone | note | shown |
| soak | code | **-ole** | hone | quote | thrown |
| cloak | lode | dole | lone | rote | |
| croak | mode | hole | tone | vote | |
| | node | mole | zone | wrote | |
| **-oal** | rode | pole | clone | | |
| coal | strode | role | drone | **-ove** | |
| foal | | stole | phone | cove | |
| goal | **-oe** | whole | prone | wove | |
| | doe | | shone | clove | |
| **-oam** | foe | **-oll** | stone | drove | |
| foam | hoe | poll | | grove | |
| loam | Joe | roll | **-ope** | stove | |
| roam | toe | toll | cope | trove | |
| | woe | droll | dope | | |
| **-oan** | | knoll | hope | **-ow** | |
| Joan | **-oke** | scroll | mope | bow | |
| loan | coke | stroll | nope | know | |
| moan | joke | troll | pope | low | |
| groan | poke | | rope | mow | |
| | woke | | scope | row | |
| **-oast** | yoke | | slope | sow | |
| boast | broke | | | tow | |
| coast | | | | | |
| roast | | | | | |
| toast | | | | | |

# Short-*a* Phonograms

| **-ab** | **-ad** | jam | **-ance** | yank | gash | **-at** |
|---|---|---|---|---|---|---|
| cab | bad | Pam | dance | blank | hash | bat |
| dab | dad | ram | lance | clank | lash | cat |
| gab | fad | Sam | chance | crank | mash | fat |
| jab | had | tam | France | drank | rash | gnat |
| lab | lad | yam | glance | flank | sash | hat |
| nab | mad | clam | prance | Frank | brash | mat |
| tab | pad | cram | stance | plank | clash | pat |
| blab | sad | gram | trance | prank | flash | rat |
| crab | tad | scam | | spank | slash | sat |
| drab | Brad | scram | **-anch** | thank | smash | vat |
| flab | Chad | sham | ranch | | stash | brat |
| grab | clad | slam | blanch | **-ant** | thrash | chat |
| scab | glad | swam | branch | pant | trash | flat |
| slab | | | | rant | | scat |
| stab | **-aft** | **-amp** | **-and** | chant | **-ask** | slat |
| | daft | camp | band | grant | ask | spat |
| **-ack** | raft | damp | hand | plant | cask | that |
| back | waft | lamp | land | scant | mask | |
| hack | craft | ramp | sand | slant | task | **-atch** |
| Jack | draft | vamp | bland | | flask | batch |
| knack | graft | champ | brand | **-ap** | | catch |
| lack | shaft | clamp | gland | cap | **-asm** | hatch |
| Mack | | cramp | stand | gap | chasm | latch |
| pack | **-ag** | scamp | strand | lap | plasm | match |
| quack | bag | stamp | | map | spasm | patch |
| rack | gag | tramp | **-ang** | nap | | scratch |
| sack | jag | | bang | rap | **-asp** | snatch |
| tack | lag | **-an** | fang | sap | gasp | thatch |
| black | nag | ban | gang | tap | hasp | |
| clack | rag | can | hang | yap | rasp | **-ath** |
| crack | sag | Dan | pang | chap | clasp | bath |
| shack | tag | fan | rang | clap | grasp | math |
| slack | wag | man | sang | flap | | path |
| smack | brag | pan | clang | scrap | **-ast** | wrath |
| snack | crag | ran | slang | slap | cast | |
| stack | drag | tan | sprang | snap | fast | **-ax** |
| track | flag | van | twang | strap | last | lax |
| whack | shag | bran | | trap | mast | Max |
| | snag | clan | **-ank** | wrap | past | tax |
| **-act** | stag | plan | bank | | vast | wax |
| fact | | scan | Hank | **-ash** | blast | flax |
| pact | **-am** | span | lank | bash | | |
| tact | dam | than | rank | cash | | |
| tract | ham | | sank | dash | | |
| | | | tank | | | |

# Short-*e* Phonograms

**-ead**
dead
head
lead
read
bread
dread
spread
thread
tread

**-ealth**
health
wealth
stealth

**-eath**
death
breath

**-eck**
deck
heck
neck
peck
check
fleck
speck
wreck

**-ed**
bed
fed
led
Ned
red
Ted
wed
bled
bred
fled
Fred
shed
shred

sled
sped

**-edge**
hedge
ledge
wedge
dredge
pledge
sledge

**-eft**
left
cleft
theft

**-eg**
beg
keg
leg
Meg
peg

**-eld**
held
meld
weld

**-elf**
self
shelf

**-ell**
bell
cell
dell
fell
jell
Nell
sell
tell
well
yell
dwell
shell

smell
spell
swell

**-elp**
help
kelp
yelp

**-elt**
belt
felt
knelt
melt
pelt
welt
dwelt

**-em**
gem
hem
stem
them

**-en**
Ben
den
hen
Ken
men
pen
ten
yen
Glen
then
when
wren

**-ence**
fence
hence
pence
whence

**-ench**
bench
clench
drench
French
quench
stench
trench
wrench

**-end**
end
bend
fend
lend
mend
send
tend
vend
blend
spend
trend

**-ength**
length
strength

**-ense**
dense
sense
tense

**-ent**
bent
cent
dent
gent
Kent
lent
rent
sent
tent
vent
went

scent
spent

**-ep**
pep
rep
prep
step

**-ept**
kept
wept
crept
slept
swept

**-esh**
mesh
flesh
fresh

**-ess**
Bess
guess
less
mess
bless
chess
dress
press
stress

**-est**
best
jest
lest
nest
pest
rest
test
vest
west
zest
blest
chest

crest
quest
wrest

**-et**
bet
get
jet
let
met
net
pet
set
wet
yet
Chet
fret

**-etch**
fetch
sketch
wretch

**-ext**
next
text

# Short-i Phonograms

**-ib**
bib
fib
rib
crib
glib

**-ick**
Dick
kick
lick
Nick
pick
quick
Rick
sick
tick
wick
brick
chick
click
flick
slick
stick
thick
trick

**-id**
bid
did
hid
kid
lid
mid
rid
grid
skid
slid
squid

**-iff**
cliff
sniff

stiff
whiff

**-ift**
gift
lift
rift
sift
drift
shift
swift
thrift

**-ig**
big
dig
fig
gig
jig
pig
rig
wig
brig
sprig
swig
twig

**-ilk**
milk
silk

**-ill**
ill
bill
dill
fill
gill
hill
Jill
kill
mill
pill
quill
sill
till

will
chill
drill
frill
grill
skill
spill
still
thrill
trill
twill

**-ilt**
kilt
tilt
wilt
quilt
stilt

**-im**
dim
him
Jim
Kim
rim
Tim
brim
grim
prim
slim
swim
trim
whim

**-imp**
limp
blimp
chimp
crimp
primp
skimp

**-in**
bin
fin

kin
pin
tin
win
chin
grin
shin
skin
spin
thin
twin

**-ince**
mince
since
prince

**-inch**
inch
cinch
finch
pinch
clinch
flinch

**-ing**
bing
ding
king
ping
ring
sing
wing
zing
bring
cling
fling
sling
spring
sting
string
swing
thing
wring

**-inge**
binge
hinge
singe
tinge
cringe
fringe

**-ink**
kink
link
mink
pink
rink
sink
wink
blink
brink
clink
drink
shrink
slink
stink
think

**-int**
hint
lint
mint
tint
glint
print
splint
sprint
squint
stint

**-ip**
dip
hip
lip
nip
quip
rip

sip
tip
zip
blip
chip
clip
drip
flip
grip
ship
skip
slip
snip
strip
trip
whip

**-is**
is
his

**-ish**
dish
fish
wish
swish

**-isk**
disk
risk
brisk
frisk
whisk

**-isp**
lisp
wisp
crisp

**-iss**
hiss
kiss
miss
bliss
Swiss

**-ist**
fist
list
mist
wrist
twist

**-it**
bit
fit
hit
kit
knit
lit
pit
quit
sit
wit
flit
grit
skit
slit
spit
split

**-itch**
ditch
hitch
pitch
witch
switch

**-ive**
give
live

**-ix**
fix
mix
six

# Short-o Phonograms

| -ob | sock | -oft | -ond | -ot | -otch |
|-----|------|------|------|-----|-------|
| Bob | tock | loft | bond | cot | botch |
| cob | block | soft | fond | dot | notch |
| gob | clock | | pond | got | blotch |
| job | crock | **-og** | blond | hot | |
| knob | flock | bog | | jot | **-ough** |
| lob | frock | cog | **-op** | knot | cough |
| mob | shock | dog | bop | lot | trough |
| rob | smock | fog | cop | not | |
| sob | stock | hog | hop | pot | **-ox** |
| blob | | jog | mop | rot | ox |
| glob | **-od** | log | pop | tot | box |
| slob | cod | clog | sop | blot | fox |
| snob | mod | flog | top | clot | lox |
| throb | nod | frog | chop | plot | pox |
| | pod | smog | crop | shot | |
| **-ock** | rod | | drop | slot | |
| dock | sod | **-omp** | flop | spot | |
| hock | clod | pomp | plop | trot | |
| knock | plod | romp | prop | | |
| lock | prod | chomp | shop | | |
| mock | trod | stomp | slop | | |
| rock | | | stop | | |

Many popular rhymes and songs feature phonograms.

**Little Bo-Peep**

Little Bo-Peep
has lost her sheep
and doesn't know where
to find them.

Leave them alone,
and they'll come home,
wagging their tails
behind them.

**Hickory, Dickory, Dock**

Hickory, dickory, dock,
the mouse ran up the clock.

The clock struck one.
The mouse ran down.

Hickory, dickory, dock.

## Short-*u* Phonograms

**-ome**
come
some

**-on**
son
ton
won

**-ough**
rough
tough
slough

**-ove**
dove
love
glove
shove
above

**-ub**
cub
dub
hub
nub
rub
sub
tub
club
flub
grub
scrub
shrub
snub
stub

**-uch**
much
such

**-uck**
buck
duck
luck
muck
puck
suck

tuck
Chuck
cluck
pluck
stuck
struck
truck

**-ud**
bud
cud
dud
mud
crud
spud
stud
thud

**-udge**
budge
fudge
judge
nudge
drudge
grudge
sludge
smudge
trudge

**-uff**
buff
cuff
huff
puff
ruff
bluff
fluff
gruff
scuff
sluff
snuff
stuff

**-ug**
bug
dug
hug

jug
lug
mug
pug
rug
tug
chug
drug
plug
shrug
slug
smug
snug
thug

**-ulk**
bulk
hulk
sulk

**-ull**
cull
dull
gull
hull
lull
mull
skull

**-um**
bum
gum
hum
mum
sum
chum
drum
glum
plum
scum
slum
strum
swum

**-umb**
dumb
numb

crumb
plumb
thumb

**-ump**
bump
dump
hump
jump
lump
pump
rump
chump
clump
frump
grump
plump
slump
stump
thump
trump

**-un**
bun
fun
gun
pun
run
sun
shun
spun
stun

**-unch**
bunch
hunch
lunch
munch
punch
brunch
crunch
scrunch

**-ung**
hung
lung
rung

sung
clung
flung
sprung
stung
strung
swung
wrung

**-unk**
bunk
dunk
hunk
junk
sunk
chunk
drunk
flunk
plunk
shrunk
skunk
slunk
spunk
stunk
trunk

**-unt**
bunt
hunt
punt
runt
blunt
grunt
stunt

**-up**
cup
pup
sup

**-us**
bus
plus
thus

**-ush**
gush

hush
lush
mush
rush
blush
brush
crush
flush
plush
slush
thrush

**-ust**
bust
dust
gust
just
must
rust
crust
thrust
trust

**-ut**
but
cut
gut
hut
jut
nut
rut
glut
shut
strut

**-utch**
Dutch
hutch
clutch
crutch

**-utt**
butt
mutt
putt

## Variant Vowel /âr/ Phonograms

| **-air** | chair | dare | ware | snare | **-ear** |
|---|---|---|---|---|---|
| air | flair | fare | blare | spare | bear |
| fair | stair | hare | flare | square | pear |
| hair | | mare | glare | stare | wear |
| lair | **-are** | pare | scare | | swear |
| pair | bare | rare | share | | |
| | care | | | | |

## Variant Vowel /ûr/ Phonograms

| **-earn** | **-erm** | **-ird** | **-irt** | **-urb** | **-urk** |
|---|---|---|---|---|---|
| earn | germ | bird | dirt | curb | lurk |
| learn | term | third | flirt | blurb | murk |
| yearn | | | shirt | | |
| | **-ern** | **-irk** | skirt | **-urge** | **-urse** |
| **-erb** | fern | quirk | squirt | urge | curse |
| herb | stern | shirk | | purge | nurse |
| verb | | smirk | **-irth** | | purse |
| | **-erve** | | birth | **-url** | |
| **-erge** | nerve | **-irl** | girth | curl | **-urt** |
| merge | serve | girl | | furl | curt |
| serge | swerve | swirl | **-ur** | hurl | hurt |
| verge | | twirl | fur | | blurt |
| | **-ir** | whirl | blur | **-urn** | spurt |
| **-erk** | fir | | slur | burn | |
| jerk | sir | **-irst** | spur | turn | |
| clerk | stir | first | | churn | |
| | whir | thirst | | spurn | |

## Variant Vowel /är/ Phonograms

| **-ar** | spar | **-arge** | park | **-arn** | **-art** |
|---|---|---|---|---|---|
| bar | star | barge | Clark | barn | cart |
| car | | large | shark | darn | dart |
| far | **-ard** | charge | spark | yarn | mart |
| jar | card | | stark | | part |
| mar | guard | **-ark** | | **-arp** | tart |
| par | hard | bark | **-arm** | carp | chart |
| tar | lard | dark | arm | harp | smart |
| char | yard | hark | farm | tarp | start |
| scar | | lark | harm | sharp | |
| | | mark | charm | | |

# Variant Vowel /ô/ Phonograms

| **-all** | **-alt** | taunt | **-awl** | **-ong** | **-ost** |
|---|---|---|---|---|---|
| all | halt | flaunt | bawl | bong | cost |
| ball | malt | **-ault** | brawl | dong | lost |
| call | salt | fault | crawl | gong | frost |
| fall | **-aught** | vault | drawl | long | **-oth** |
| hall | caught | **-aw** | scrawl | song | moth |
| mall | naught | caw | shawl | tong | broth |
| tall | taught | gnaw | **-awn** | prong | cloth |
| wall | fraught | jaw | dawn | strong | froth |
| small | **-aunch** | law | fawn | wrong | sloth |
| squall | haunch | paw | lawn | **-oss** | **-ought** |
| stall | launch | raw | pawn | boss | ought |
| **-alk** | paunch | saw | yawn | loss | bought |
| balk | staunch | claw | brawn | moss | fought |
| talk | **-aunt** | draw | drawn | toss | sought |
| walk | daunt | flaw | prawn | cross | brought |
| chalk | gaunt | slaw | | floss | thought |
| stalk | haunt | squaw | | gloss | |
| | jaunt | straw | | | |

# (/ô/ With *r*)

| **-oar** | **-ord** | pore | **-ork** | **-orn** | **-ort** |
|---|---|---|---|---|---|
| boar | cord | sore | cork | born | fort |
| roar | ford | tore | fork | corn | port |
| soar | lord | wore | pork | horn | sort |
| **-oor** | chord | chore | York | morn | short |
| door | sword | score | stork | torn | snort |
| floor | **-ore** | shore | **-orm** | worn | sport |
| **-orch** | bore | snore | dorm | scorn | **-our** |
| porch | core | spore | form | sworn | four |
| torch | fore | store | norm | thorn | pour |
| scorch | gore | swore | storm | | |
| | more | | | | |

## Diphthong /oi/ Phonograms

| **-oil** | | **-oint** | **-oist** | **-oy** | toy |
|---|---|---|---|---|---|
| oil | broil | joint | foist | boy | ploy |
| boil | spoil | point | hoist | coy | |
| coil | | | moist | joy | |
| foil | **-oin** | **-oise** | | Roy | |
| soil | coin | noise | | soy | |
| toil | join | poise | | | |
| | loin | | | | |
| | groin | | | | |

## Diphthong /ou/ Phonograms

| **-ouch** | **-ounce** | wound | **-out** | **-outh** | **-owl** |
|---|---|---|---|---|---|
| couch | ounce | ground | out | mouth | fowl |
| pouch | bounce | | bout | south | howl |
| vouch | pounce | **-our** | (about) | | growl |
| crouch | trounce | our | gout | **-ow** | prowl |
| grouch | | hour | pout | bow | scowl |
| slouch | **-ount** | sour | rout | cow | |
| | count | flour | tout | how | **-own** |
| **-oud** | mount | scour | clout | now | down |
| loud | | | scout | sow | gown |
| cloud | **-ound** | **-ouse** | shout | vow | town |
| proud | bound | house | snout | brow | brown |
| | found | louse | spout | chow | clown |
| | hound | mouse | sprout | plow | crown |
| | mound | blouse | stout | | drown |
| | pound | spouse | trout | | frown |
| | round | | | | |
| | sound | | | | |

Many trade books feature words with phonograms. These books can be used for independent reading.

# Variant Vowel /oo̅/ Phonograms

*These words contain the long-u sound, /yoo̅/.

| **-ew** | **-ood** | **-oon** | **-oot** | **-ude** | **-une** |
|---|---|---|---|---|---|
| dew | food | boon | boot | dude | dune |
| few* | mood | loon | hoot | rude | June |
| knew | brood | moon | loot | crude | tune |
| new | | noon | moot | prude | prune |
| pew* | **-oof** | soon | root | | |
| blew | goof | croon | toot | **-ue** | **-ure** |
| brew | roof | spoon | scoot | cue* | cure* |
| chew | proof | swoon | shoot | due | lure |
| crew | spoof | | | hue* | pure* |
| flew | | **-oop** | **-ooth** | Sue | sure |
| grew | **-ool** | coop | booth | blue | |
| screw | cool | hoop | tooth | clue | **-use** |
| threw | fool | loop | | glue | use* |
| | pool | droop | **-ooze** | true | fuse* |
| **-o** | tool | scoop | ooze | | muse* |
| do | drool | sloop | snooze | **-uke** | ruse |
| to | school | snoop | | duke | |
| who | spool | stoop | **-oup** | puke* | **-ute** |
| | stool | swoop | soup | fluke | cute* |
| **-oo** | | swoop | croup | | jute |
| boo | **-oom** | troop | group | **-ule** | lute |
| coo | boom | | | mule* | mute* |
| goo | doom | **-oose** | **-ube** | rule | brute |
| moo | loom | goose | cube* | Yule | chute |
| too | room | loose | lube | | flute |
| woo | zoom | moose | tube | **-ume** | |
| zoo | bloom | noose | | fume* | **-uth** |
| shoo | broom | | **-uce** | plume | Ruth |
| | gloom | | spruce | | truth |
| | groom | | truce | | |

# Variant Vowel /oŏ/ Phonograms

| **-ood** | **-ook** | | **-ould** | **-ull** | **-ush** |
|---|---|---|---|---|---|
| good | book | brook | could | bull | bush |
| hood | cook | crook | would | full | push |
| wood | hook | shook | should | pull | |
| stood | look | | | | |
| | nook | **-oot** | | | |
| | took | foot | | | |
| | | soot | | | |

# What About Rules?

Use *i* before *e* except after *c*. When two vowels go walking, the first does the talking. Don't stand on that table! Sit up straight, Wiley! These and other rules swim around in my head when I think about my early school days. Although I do sit up straight today and avoid standing on tables, when it comes to reading I often wonder how many rules I actually recall and use as a skilled reader and writer. This list is probably quite small. So how useful are these rules, and should we spend much instructional time teaching them?

"Effective decoders see words not in terms of phonics rules, but in terms of patterns of letters that are used to aid in identification" (Stahl, 1992). **Through phonics instruction that focuses children's attention on each letter in a word, teaches blending, and highlights common spelling patterns, children will begin to internalize rules, or generalizations, about words.** For example, when children encounter words in which the letter *c* stands for either the /s/ sound or the /k/ sound, we want them to be able to generalize the conditions under which each is likely to occur. Rules can be used to help children attend to this specific spelling pattern or organize their thinking about it. As time progresses and children are provided more opportunities to review and apply this rule, they will internalize it.

In addition, teachers of reading need to be aware of rules so that they can verbalize them for children who would benefit from this instruction (Durkin, 1993). However, since few rules are 100% reliable, they should never be taught as absolutes. That is one reason why I prefer the term *generalization* rather than *rule*.

## Guidelines for Using Rules/Generalizations

- **Don't make rules/generalizations the emphasis of phonics instruction.** Instead, use them as one tool to help children focus on important spelling patterns and recognize unfamiliar words.
- **Teach only those rules/generalizations with the most utility.** For example, teaching children that the spelling pattern *-ough* can stand for up to six sounds is wasteful. In addition, avoid generalizations that are wordy or full of technical language.
- **Emphasize applying the rules/generalizations** rather than verbalizing them. Remember that once children can apply the generalizations, there is no need to spend instructional time on them.

- **Don't teach the rules/generalizations too soon or too late.**
  Teach them at a point when children can best understand
  and apply them.
- **Never teach rules as absolutes.** Since children tend to think
  of rules as absolutes, it's better to use the term *generalization*.
  And be sure to make the children aware of important exceptions
  to generalizations.

The classic study on generalizations and their utility was conducted
in 1963 (Clymer). Clymer examined 45 generalizations (rules) taught by
basal reading programs. He found that many of these generalizations
were of limited value. In fact, less than half of the rules worked as much
as 75% of the time. The following chart shows the generalizations he
examined. I've updated the wording of some of the generalizations so
that they're consistent with the language used in today's basals.

## Utility of Phonics Generalizations

| Generalizations | | Example | Exception | % Utility |
|---|---|---|---|---|
| **CONSONANT GENERALIZATIONS** | | | | |
| 1. | When two of the same consonants appear side by side in a word, only one is heard. | *berry* | *suggest* | 99 |
| 2. | When the letter *c* is followed by the letter *o* or *a*, the *c* stands for the /k/ sound. | *cat* | | 100 |
| 3. | The digraph *ch* is usually pronounced /ch/ as in *watch* and *chair*, not /sh/. | *batch* | *machine* | 95 |
| 4. | When the letters *c* and *h* appear next to each other in a word, they stand for only one sound. | *rich* | | 100 |
| 5. | The letter *g* often has a sound similar to that of the letter *j* in *jump* when it comes before the letter *i* or *e*. | *ginger* | *give* | 64 |
| 6. | When the letter *c* is followed by the letter *e* or *i*, the /s/ sound is likely to be heard. | *cent* | *ocean* | 96 |
| 7. | When a word ends in the letters *ck*, it has the /k/ sound, as in *book*. | *sick* | | 100 |
| 8. | When the letters *ght* appear together in a word, the letters *gh* are silent. | *fight* | | 100 |
| 9. | When a word begins with the letters *kn*, the letter *k* is silent. | *know* | | 100 |
| 10. | When a word begins with the letters *wr*, the letter *w* is silent. | *write* | | 100 |

| Generalizations | Example | Exception | % Utility |
|---|---|---|---|
| **VOWEL GENERALIZATIONS** | | | |
| **11.** If there is one vowel letter in an accented syllable, it has a short sound. | *city* | *lady* | 61 |
| **12.** When a word has only one vowel letter, the vowel sound is likely to be short. | *lid* | *mind* | 57 |
| **13.** When two vowels appear together in a word, the long sound of the first one is heard and the second is usually silent.* | *seat* | *chief* | 45 |
| **14.** When a vowel is in the middle of a one-syllable word, the vowel is short. | *best* | *gold* | 62 |
| **15.** The letter *r* gives the preceding vowel a sound that is neither long nor short. | *torn* | *fire* | 78 |
| **16.** When there are two vowels, one of which is final *e*, the first vowel is long and the *e* is silent. | *hope* | *come* | 63 |
| **17.** The first vowel is usually long and the second silent in the digraphs *ai, ea, oa,* and *ui.* | *nail/said* 64%<br>*bead/head* 66%<br>*boat/cupboard* 97%<br>*suit/build* 6% | | 66 |
| **18.** When words end with silent *e*, the preceding *a* or *i* is long. | *bake* | *have* | 60 |
| **19.** When the letter *y* is the final letter in a word, it usually has a vowel sound. | *dry* | *tray* | 84 |
| **20.** When the letter *y* is used as a vowel in words, it sometimes has the sound of long *i*. | *fly* | *funny* | 15 |
| **21.** When *y* or *ey* appears in the last syllable that is not accented, the long-*e* sound is heard. | *baby* | | 0 |
| **22.** The letter *a* has the same sound as /ô/ when followed by *l, w,* and *u*. | *fall* | *canal* | 48 |
| **23.** The letter *w* is sometimes a vowel and follows the vowel digraph rule. | *snow* | *few* | 40 |
| **24.** When there is one *e* in a word that ends in a consonant, the *e* usually has a short sound. | *pet* | *flew* | 76 |
| **25.** In many two- and three-syllable words, the final *e* lengthens the vowel in the last syllable. | *invite* | *gasoline* | 46 |
| **26.** Words having double *e* usually have the long-*e* sound. | *feet* | *been* | 98 |
| **27.** The letters *ow* stand for the long *o* sound. | *own* | *town* | 59 |
| **28.** When the letter *a* follows the letter *w* in a word, it usually has the sound that *a* stands for as in *was*. | *watch* | *swam* | 32 |
| **29.** In the vowel spelling *ie*, the letter *i* is silent and the letter *e* has the long vowel sound. | *field* | *friend* | 17 |

*This is the old "When two vowels go walking, the first does the talking" rule.

| Generalizations | Example | Exception | % Utility |
|---|---|---|---|
| **30.** In *ay*, the *y* is silent and gives *a* its long sound. | *play* | *always* | 78 |
| **31.** If the only vowel letter is at the end of a word, the letter usually stands for a long sound. | *me* | *do* | 74 |
| **32.** When the letter *e* is followed by the letter *w*, the vowel sound is the same as represented by *oo* (/$\overline{oo}$/). | *blew* | *sew* | 35 |
| **33.** When the letter *a* is followed by the letter *r* and final *e*, we expect to hear the sound heard in *care*. | *dare* | *are* | 90 |
| **34.** When the letter *i* is followed by the letters *gh*, the letter *i* usually stands for its long sound and the *gh* is silent. | *high* | *neighbor* | 71 |
| **SYLLABLE GENERALIZATIONS** | | | |
| **35.** If the first vowel sound in a word is followed by two consonants, the first syllable usually ends with the first of the two consonants. | *bullet* | *singer* | 72 |
| **36.** If the first vowel sound in a word is followed by a single consonant, that consonant usually begins the second syllable. | *over* | *oven* | 44 |
| **37.** In a word of more than one syllable, the letter *v* usually goes with the preceding vowel to form a syllable. | *cover* | *clover* | 73 |
| **38.** If the last syllable of a word ends in *le*, the consonant preceding the *le* usually begins the last syllable. | *tumble* | *buckle* | 97 |
| **39.** When the first vowel in a word is followed by *th, ch,* or *sh*, these symbols are not broken when the word is divided into syllables, and they may go with either the first or second syllable. | *dishes* | | 100 |
| **40.** In most two-syllable words, the first syllable is accented. | *famous* | *polite* | 85 |
| **41.** When the last syllable is the sound /r/, it is unaccented. | *butter* | *appear* | 95 |
| **42.** In most two-syllable words that end in a consonant followed by *y*, the first syllable is accented and the last is unaccented. | *baby* | *supply* | 96 |
| **43.** If *a, in, re, ex, de,* or *be* is the first syllable in a word, it is usually unaccented. | *above* | *insect* | 87 |
| **44.** When *tion* is the final syllable in a word, it is unaccented. | *nation* | | 100 |
| **45.** When *ture* is the final syllable in a word, it is unaccented. | *picture* | | 100 |

# Structural Analysis: Using Word Parts

When they begin reading increasingly complex texts, children encounter growing numbers of multisyllabic words. Teaching word analysis provides strategies to help them tackle these longer, more difficult words. These lessons can begin as early as first grade and should continue throughout the elementary grades. The following section provides guidelines and word lists for introducing the following word-analysis skills in the primary grades:

1. Compound words
2. Prefixes
3. Suffixes (including plurals and inflectional endings)
4. Homophones
5. Syllabication

Children in fourth grade and above should also receive instruction in Latin and Greek roots and how to use them to read and spell words. For more information, see *Teaching Phonics and Word Study in the Intermediate Grades* (Blevins, 2017).

## Compound Words

### Guidelines:

- A **compound word** is a word made up of two smaller words. Often the meaning of a compound word can be derived from the meaning of the two smaller words. For example, a *doghouse* is a "house for a dog." However, there are notable exceptions, such as *butterfly*.
- There are three types of compound words: open *(fire drill)*, closed *(doghouse)*, and hyphenated *(send-off)*.
- Encourage children to look for smaller words in larger words to help them pronounce—and sometimes figure out the meanings of—the larger words. Compound-word instruction introduces this concept. However, guide children to look for words with more than two or three letters in a larger word. Identifying a two-letter word isn't always helpful. For example, finding the word *to* in *town* or *tornado* is useless for determining either pronunciation or meaning.
- Point out to children that when a compound word is divided, each remaining smaller word must be able to stand on its own.

# Compound Words

| | | | | |
|---|---|---|---|---|
| afternoon | backstop | birdhouse | coal mine | eardrum |
| aftershave | backstroke | birdseed | collarbone | earthquake |
| air bag | backyard | birthday | cookbook | electric guitar |
| air mattress | bagpipe | blackbird | cornbread | everybody |
| airhole | bandleader | blackboard | corncob | everyday |
| airmail | barnyard | blindfold | cornfield | everyone |
| airplane | baseball | blueberry | countdown | everything |
| airsick | basketball | bluebird | cowboy | everywhere |
| airtight | bath mat | blueprint | crossword | eyeball |
| anteater | bathrobe | boathouse | cupcake | eyeglasses |
| anthill | bathroom | book bag | daydream | eyelid |
| anybody | bathtub | bookcase | daylight | eyesight |
| anyhow | bathwater | bookmark | diving board | faraway |
| anyone | beanbag | broomstick | doghouse | farmhouse |
| anything | beanpod | bulldog | dollhouse | father-in-law |
| anytime | beanpole | bullfrog | doorbell | finger bowl |
| anywhere | bed rest | butterfly | doorknob | finger hole |
| applesauce | bedroll | buttermilk | doormat | fingernail |
| armchair | bedroom | buttonhole | doorstep | finger-paint |
| armrest | bedside | bypass | doorway | fingerprint |
| back room | bedspread | campfire | doubleheader | fingertip |
| backboard | bedspring | campground | downhill | fire drill |
| backbone | bedtime | candlelight | downstairs | fire engine |
| backdoor | beehive | candlestick | downtown | fire escape |
| backfield | beeline | cardboard | dragonfly | fire station |
| background | bird dog | cheerleader | dressmaker | fire truck |
| backpack | birdbath | classroom | driveway | fire-eater |
| backseat | birdcage | clothespin | drumstick | fireboat |
| backstage | birdcall | clubhouse | dugout | firefighter |

| | | | | |
|---|---|---|---|---|
| firefly | handbook | hot dog | nightgown | roadside |
| firehouse | handmade | houseboat | notebook | roof garden |
| firelight | handpick | ice cream | outdoors | rooftop |
| fireplace | handsaw | ice skate | outfield | rosebud |
| firewood | handshake | iceberg | outside | rosebush |
| fireworks | handstand | inchworm | overlook | rowboat |
| flowerpot | handwrite | inside | overnight | sailboat |
| football | headache | jellyfish | overtake | sandbox |
| footbridge | headband | keyboard | pancake | sandpaper |
| footpath | headphone | keyhole | passer-by | saucepan |
| footprint | headstand | lawn mower | peanut | sawdust |
| footrest | henhouse | lifetime | pillowcase | scarecrow |
| footstep | high chair | lighthouse | pinecone | scrapbook |
| footstool | high jump | living room | pinwheel | sea breeze |
| give-and-take | high noon | lookout | playground | sea captain |
| goldfish | high school | loudspeaker | playhouse | seagull |
| grapevine | high-rise | lunchroom | playpen | sea horse |
| grasshopper | hilltop | mailbox | pocketbook | seacoast |
| greenhouse | home plate | masterpiece | poison ivy | seafood |
| grown-up | home run | merry-go-round | polar bear | seaport |
| hairbrush | homegrown | milkshake | popcorn | seashell |
| haircut | homemade | moonbeam | postcard | seashore |
| hairnet | homeroom | moonlight | railroad | seaside |
| hairpiece | homesick | mother-in-law | rain forest | seat belt |
| hairpin | hometown | motorboat | rainbow | seaweed |
| hairstyle | homework | motorcycle | raincoat | send-off |
| hand-feed | horseback | mousetrap | raindrop | shopkeeper |
| handbag | horsefly | music box | rainfall | shoreline |
| handball | horseshoe | newspaper | ringmaster | sidewalk |

| | | | | |
|---|---|---|---|---|
| sideways | somehow | sunflower | toeshoe | waterfall |
| skyline | someone | sunlight | toolbox | whatever |
| skyscraper | something | sunrise | toothache | wheelchair |
| smokestack | spaceship | sunset | toothbrush | whiteboard |
| snapshot | spacesuit | sunshine | toothpaste | windmill |
| snowball | springtime | supermarket | townspeople | windpipe |
| snowfall | starfish | swimming pool | tree house | windshield |
| snowflake | starlight | tablespoon | treetop | wintertime |
| snowman | starship | teacup | tugboat | wishbone |
| snowplow | steamboat | teaspoon | underground | within |
| snowshoe | stepladder | tennis court | underwater | without |
| snowstorm | storehouse | thunderstorm | upstairs | workbench |
| snowsuit | storeroom | tightrope | wallpaper | workday |
| somebody | storyteller | toadstool | washcloth | worktable |
| someday | sunburn | toenail | watchdog | wristwatch |

# Prefixes

## Guidelines:

- A **prefix** is a group of letters that appears at the front of a word. A prefix affects the meaning of the root or base word to which it is attached. To determine whether a group of letters is a prefix, remove them from the word. If a known word remains, you have a prefix. For example, remove the letters *un* from the following words: *unhappy, untie, uncle, uninterested*. In which word are the letters *un* not a prefix? *(uncle)*

- Make students aware of the following warnings about prefixes.

   1. **Most prefixes have more than one meaning.** For example, the prefix *un* can mean "not," as in *unhappy*, or "do the opposite of," as in *untie*. Teach the multiple meanings of the most common prefixes and use careful language during lessons, such as, "the prefix *un* sometimes means 'not.'"

2. **Be careful of letter clusters that look like prefixes but aren't.** For example, when the letters *un* are removed from *uncle*, no recognizable root or base word is left. And when the letters *in* are removed from *invented*, the word that remains is not related to the whole word. The prefixes that are most troublesome are *re, in,* and *dis.*

3. **Don't rely solely on word-part clues.** Students should use context clues as well as examine prefixes to verify a word's meaning. For example, a student might think the word *unassuming* means "not assuming/not supposing" instead of its actual meaning, "modest." It is estimated that about 15–20% of the prefixed words students encounter share this complexity (White et al., 1989).

- Teach only the most common prefixes. The chart below shows the most common prefixes, based on a count of prefixed words appearing in the *Word Frequency Book* (Carroll, Davies, & Richman, 1971). The prefix *un* alone accounts for almost one-third of the total. The top three account for more than half. In first through third grades, only the prefixes *un* and *re* need to be formally taught since these have the highest utility and are the most likely to appear in primary-level materials.

| Rank | Prefix (meaning) | % |
|------|-----------------|---|
| 1. | un (not, opposite of) | 26 |
| 2. | re (again) | 14 |
| 3. | in, im, ir, il (not) | 11 |
| 4. | dis (not, opposite of) | 7 |
| 5. | en, em (cause to) | 4 |
| 6. | non (not) | 4 |
| 7. | in, im (in or into) | 4 |
| 8. | over (too much) | 3 |
| 9. | mis (wrongly) | 3 |
| 10. | sub (under) | 3 |

| Rank | Prefix (meaning) | % |
|------|-----------------|---|
| 11. | pre (before) | 3 |
| 12. | inter (between, among) | 3 |
| 13. | fore (before) | 3 |
| 14. | de (opposite of) | 2 |
| 15. | trans (across) | 2 |
| 16. | super (above) | 1 |
| 17. | semi (half) | 1 |
| 18. | anti (against) | 1 |
| 19. | mid (middle) | 1 |
| 20. | under (too little) | 1 |

All other prefixes (about 100) account for only 3% of the words.

# Suffixes

## Guidelines:

- A **suffix** is a letter or group of letters that is added to the end of a root or base word. Common suffixes include *s, ed, ing, ly*, and *tion*. A suffix changes the meaning of the root or base word and, often, the part of speech. Therefore, children need to understand the meaning of a suffix and how it affects the word it's attached to. By helping children quickly identify a suffix and visually remove it to identify the base word, you'll help them figure out the meaning of the whole word.

- Adding a suffix sometimes changes the spelling of a base word. It's important to teach those suffixes that cause spelling changes directly. The three most common spelling changes caused by adding suffixes are:

  1. **consonant doubling** *(runner, running)*: The consonant is doubled so that the first syllable will form a CVC pattern. Most CVC words contain a short-vowel sound. Therefore, the second consonant—acting as a diacritical mark—ensures that the short-vowel sound of the base word is maintained.

  2. **changing y to i** *(flies, happiest, loneliness)*: The letter *y* at the beginning of a word or syllable acts as a consonant and stands for the /y/ sound. However, the letter *y* at the end of a word either stands for a vowel sound *(fly)* or is part of a vowel digraph *(play)*. The change from *y* to *i* ensures that the vowel sound the *y* stands for in the word is maintained.

  3. **deleting the silent e** *(making)*: When a word ends in silent *e*, the letter is usually removed before the suffix (except *s*) is added because most common suffixes begin with vowels and a double vowel would create a vowel digraph and cause confusion.

- Teach only the most commonly used suffixes. The following chart shows the 20 most frequent suffixes, based on a count that appears in the *Word Frequency Book* (Carroll, Davies, & Richman, 1971). The suffixes *s, es, ed,* and *ing* account for almost two-thirds of the words. The suffixes *s* and *es* are used to form the plurals of most nouns. The suffixes *ed* and *ing* are inflectional endings added to verbs to change their tense. These four suffixes are generally introduced to children in first grade.

| Rank | Suffix (meaning) | % | Rank | Suffix (meaning) | % |
|---|---|---|---|---|---|
| 1. | s, es (plurals) | 31 | 11. | ity, ty (state of) | 1 |
| 2. | ed (/d/), ed (/ed/), ed (/t/) (past-tense verbs) | 20 | 12. | ment (action or process) | 1 |
| 3. | ing (verb form/present participle) | 14 | 13. | ic (having characteristics of) | 1 |
| 4. | ly (characteristic of) | 7 | 14. | ous, eous, ious (possessing the qualities of) | 1 |
| 5. | er, or (person connected with) | 4 | 15. | en (made of) | 1 |
| 6. | ion, tion (act, process) | 4 | 16. | er (comparative) | 1 |
| 7. | able, ible (can be done) | 2 | 17. | ive, ative, itive (adjective form of a noun) | 1 |
| 8. | al, ial (having characteristics of) | 1 | 18. | ful (full of) | 1 |
| 9. | y (characterized by) | 1 | 19. | less (without) | 1 |
| 10. | ness (state of, condition of) | 1 | 20. | est (comparative) | 1 |

All other suffixes (about 160) account for only 7% of the words.

## Homophones

### Guidelines:

- **Homophones** are words that sound the same but have different meanings and spellings. Each homophone contains the same number of phonemes but different graphemes. The spellings of homophones are critical because they provide clues to the word's meaning.

- Homophones can be taught as early as first grade. Some of the simplest homophones students will encounter are listed here. It is helpful to have children write and read these words in multiple contexts.

## Homophones for Instruction

| | | | | |
|---|---|---|---|---|
| aloud/allowed | heal/heel | not/knot | sail/sale | two/to/too |
| ate/eight | heard/herd | oh/owe | see/sea | waist/waste |
| bear/bare | here/hear | one/won | seem/seam | way/weigh |
| beat/beet | horse/hoarse | peace/piece | seen/scene | weak/week |
| blew/blue | hour/our | peak/peek | so/sew | wear/where |
| brake/break | I/eye | pear/pair | some/sum | weight/wait |
| by/buy | knew/new | plain/plane | son/sun | which/witch |
| cent/sent | know/no | read/reed | stare/stair | whole/hole |
| deer/dear | knows/nose | real/reel | steal/steel | wood/would |
| do/due/dew | made/maid | red/read | tale/tail | wrap/rap |
| fare/fair | mail/male | right/write | there/their/they're | |
| flour/flower | main/mane | road/rode | through/threw | |
| for/four | meet/meat | roll/role | tied/tide | |
| hair/hare | night/knight | rose/rows | toe/tow | |

# Syllabication

### Guidelines:

- A **syllable** is a unit of pronunciation. Each syllable contains only one vowel sound. Finding the vowels in a word is an important starting point for breaking it apart by syllables. However, each syllable may have more than one vowel letter. For example, the word *boat* contains one vowel sound, therefore one syllable. However, the vowel sound is represented by the vowel digraph *oa*.

- Whether a group of letters forms a syllable depends on the letters that surround it (Adams, 1990). For example, the letters *par* form a syllable in the word *partial* but not in the word *parade*.

- One syllable in a multisyllabic word receives more emphasis or stress. The vowel sound in this syllable is heard most clearly. Stress is indicated in dictionary pronunciation keys by accent marks. In addition to one primary accent, some words have one or more secondary accents. Vowels in unstressed syllables become schwas (/ə/). Generally, in words with prefixes and suffixes, the prefix or suffix forms a separate syllable and the accent falls on the root or base word. In compound words, the accent generally falls on or within the first word. The accent in most two-syllable words falls on the first syllable.

- To decode multisyllabic words, children must be able to divide words into recognizable chunks. Some readers develop a sense of syllabication breaks independently through their exposures to print, while others have great difficulty and need instruction (Just & Carpenter, 1987). For some children, their phonics skills break down when confronted by multisyllabic words because they cannot readily identify syllable boundaries (Eldredge, 1995).

- Children need training in dividing words according to syllables. They must first understand how to figure out the vowel sound in one-syllable words. (Teach them common one-syllable spelling patterns, such as CVC and CVCe.) Then they must understand that a syllable has only one vowel sound, but that vowel sound may be spelled using more than one vowel.

### There are six basic syllable spelling patterns in English that children should be taught (Moats, 1995):

1. **closed:** These syllables end in a consonant. The vowel sound is generally short (examples: _rab bit_, _nap kin_).

2. **open:** These syllables end in a vowel. The vowel sound is generally long (examples: _tiger_, _pilot_).

3. _r_-**controlled:** When a vowel is followed by _r_, the letter _r_ affects the sound of the vowel. The vowel and the _r_ appear in the same syllable (examples: _bird_, _turtle_).

4. **vowel team:** Many vowel sounds are spelled with vowel digraphs, such as _ai, ay, ea, ee, oa, ow, oo, oi, oy, ou, ie_, and _ei_. The vowel digraphs appear in the same syllable (examples: _boat_, _explain_).

5. **vowel—silent e:** These syllables generally represent long-vowel sounds (examples: _compete_, _decide_).

6. **consonant + _le_:** Usually when _le_ appears at the end of a word and is preceded by a consonant, the consonant + _le_ form the final syllable (examples: _table_, _little_). The following chart shows consonant + _le_ words that can be used for instruction.

## Consonant + -*le* Words

| | | | | | |
|---|---|---|---|---|---|
| bubble | uncle | saddle | jungle | steeple | settle |
| double | vehicle | ankle | shingle | temple | title |
| fable | bridle | crinkle | single | battle | dazzle |
| marble | bundle | sparkle | struggle | bottle | fizzle |
| noble | fiddle | sprinkle | wiggle | cattle | muzzle |
| pebble | handle | wrinkle | apple | gentle | puzzle |
| rumble | kindle | angle | maple | kettle | |
| stubble | middle | bugle | purple | little | |
| tumble | needle | eagle | sample | mantle | |
| circle | puddle | giggle | simple | rattle | |

- Children can use syllabication strategies to approximate a word's pronunciation. This approximation is generally close enough for the reader to recognize the word if it is in the reader's speaking or listening vocabularies. This is another reason why developing children's speaking and listening vocabularies and combining the development of background knowledge with vocabulary instruction are so critical.

- Some words can be divided in more than one way. For example: *treat-y, trea-ty, tr-ea-ty*. However, the fewer the chunks, the easier it is to decode the word.

- Traditional syllabication strategies can be ineffective. For example, clapping syllables doesn't work because the child has to already know the word in order to clap the syllables (Johnson & Bauman, 1984). Likewise, memorizing countless syllabication rules has little effect on a child's ability to decode multisyllabic words. (Note: *syllabication* and *syllabification* are synonymous terms.)

- Few syllabication generalizations are very useful to children, but some are worth pointing out. These include the following (Chall & Popp, 1996). State them in simple, clear terms; focus on their application, not their recitation.

1. If the word is a compound word, divide it between the two smaller words. If either or both of the smaller words have more than one syllable, follow the syllabication generalizations below.

2. Inflectional endings such as *ing, er, est,* and *ed* often form separate syllables. The remaining portion of the word is the root or base word. Looking for these and other meaning units in words is known as morphemic analysis. A **morpheme** is a meaning unit. There are *free morphemes*—whole words that can stand alone and cannot be divided into other meaning units (base words). And there are *bound morphemes*—word parts that cannot stand alone and must be combined with a free morpheme (suffixes and prefixes). Bound morphemes alter the meaning of the free morphemes to which they are attached (example: *un + happy = unhappy*).

3. When two or more consonants appear in the middle of a word, divide the word between them (CVC•CVC) (example: *basket*). Then try the short sound for the vowel in the first syllable. This generalization does not apply if the two consonants form a digraph such as *ch, tch, ph, sh,* or *th*. These digraphs cannot be separated across syllable boundaries.

4. When only one consonant appears between two vowels, divide the word before the consonant. Then try the long sound of the first vowel (examples: *tiger, pilot*). This works about 55% of the time. If a recognizable word is not formed using the long sound, divide the word after the consonant and try the short sound for the first syllable (examples: *exit, second*). This works about 45% of the time.

5. When a two-syllable word ends in a consonant plus *le*, the consonant and *le* form the last syllable. If the preceding syllable ends in a consonant, try the short sound of the vowel (examples: *wiggle, sample*). If the preceding syllable ends with a vowel, try the long sound of the vowel (examples: *table, bridle*).

6. When a two-syllable word ends in a consonant plus *re*, the consonant and *re* form the last syllable. If the preceding syllable ends with a vowel, try the long sound of that vowel (example: *acre*).

7. Never break apart vowel digraphs or diphthongs across syllable boundaries.

- Begin syllabication instruction in first grade by pointing out compound words, words with double consonants, and words with common prefixes and suffixes such as *un-, re-, -s, -es, -ing,* and *-ed.* In later grades, focus instruction on additional prefixes and suffixes, as well as common base words. Having children practice recognizing common syllabic units is beneficial.

- Teach syllabication strategies using known words, then provide ample opportunities for students to apply each strategy in context.

- Most dictionaries divide words according to how the word should be hyphenated when it's breaking across lines. This sometimes has little to do with the division of the word into its syllables for pronunciation. Therefore, use dictionaries with caution.

## Transitioning to Multisyllabic Words: The Issue

Most curriculum focuses on one-syllable words for a large portion of Grade 2, yet the stories students read at that grade are filled with more challenging, multisyllabic words. This mismatch between instruction and text poses challenges to many students who don't have the tools to effectively transition to reading these longer, more complex words. As a result, more emphasis needs to be given to transitioning to longer words at this grade (e.g., going from known to new words like *can/ candle* and teaching the six major syllable patterns).

In Grade 2 there is often some multisyllabic work, but too much occurs at or near the end of the year. Our second graders need to transition to multisyllabic words at a much faster rate than is provided in most curriculum because they will encounter these words in increasing numbers in the books and stories they read. So, for example, if you are reviewing short vowel CVC words at the <u>beginning</u> of the year, then add challenge words for <u>all</u> students that focus on a multisyllabic skill, such as "consonant + le." As a result, students would read words like *can, candle, bat, battle, rat, rattle.* This easy transition using known words to build to new words is a simple and scaffolded first step to reading longer words without students becoming overwhelmed. I recommend beginning this transition to longer words (and adding blending lines for all students) in late Grade 1. Add this "transition to longer words" work to your weekly lessons from the beginning of the year onward in Grade 2.

Start by modifying your blending instruction to incorporate multisyllabic words. Following is an example of blending work for Grade 2 that does this. This lesson is taught the first week of school when students are reviewing short vowels. Notice that Column 1 goes from known words to multisyllabic words using the known word. Column 2 goes from closed syllables (one syllable) to multisyllabic words. Column 3 goes from open syllables (one syllable) to multisyllabic words. This lesson builds from the simple to the complex and gives the teacher an opportunity to review or introduce several syllable types (closed, open, consonant + le).

| Column 1 | | Column 2 | | Column 3 | |
|---|---|---|---|---|---|
| can | candle | drib | dribble | ta | table |
| bat | battle | peb | pebble | bu | bugle |
| scram | scramble | puz | puzzle | bri | bridle |
| jig | jiggle | un | uncle | fa | fable |
| bun | bundle | stum | stumble | ma | maple |
| sad | saddle | jun | jungle | ti | title |
| rid | riddle | ped | peddle | a | able |
| pick | pickle | tum | tumble | bi | bible |

Directly teach the six syllable patterns in English to students in late-Grade 1 and up. You might wish to introduce only a couple of syllable types in Grade 1, then cover all of them beginning in Grade 2. Closed and open syllables are the most common and should be taught first.

## What About High-Utility Syllables?

When I travel to elementary classrooms across the country, I notice the countless hours teachers spend helping students master the alphabet (the ABCs and their associated sounds) as well as the various spellings for the 44 sounds in English (e.g., the letters oa stand for the long-o sound). These high-utility sound-spellings aid students in becoming efficient decoders of one-syllable words. However, I rarely see any time spent on teaching and reviewing high-utility syllables—the building blocks for multisyllabic words. For some reason, we stop. Let's not! On the following pages, you will find a list of the 322 most common syllables in the 5,000 most frequent English words (Sakiey, Fry, Goss, & Loigman, 1980). Research has shown that 92% of the syllables found in primary grade readers have no more than two pronunciations, and 66% have only one pronunciation (Sakiey et al., 1980). This makes them highly reliable to teach. Numerous weekly activities can be created around these syllables (Blevins, 2011). By focusing on these syllables, we can give our students a leg up in their decoding of longer, more complex words. Over time, students will begin to automatically recognize these common syllables in words and use that knowledge to aid in their decoding.

## 322 Most Common Syllables in the 5,000 Most Frequent English Words

| | | | | | | | |
|---|---|---|---|---|---|---|---|
| 1. ing | 24. ry | 47. ca | 70. ful | 93. can |
| 2. er | 25. u | 48. cal | 71. ger | 94. dy |
| 3. a | 26. ti | 49. man | 72. low | 95. et |
| 4. ly | 27. ri | 50. ap | 73. ni | 96. it |
| 5. ed | 28. be | 51. po | 74. par | 97. mu |
| 6. i | 29. per | 52. sion | 75. son | 98. no |
| 7. es | 30. to | 53. vi | 76. tle | 99. ple |
| 8. re | 31. prow | 54. el | 77. day | 100. cu |
| 9. tion | 32. ac | 55. est | 78. ny | 101. fac |
| 10. in | 33. ad | 56. la | 79. pen | 102. fer |
| 11. e | 34. ar | 57. lar | 80. pre | 103. gen |
| 12. con | 35. ers | 58. pa | 81. tive | 104. ic |
| 13. y | 36. ment | 59. ture | 82. car | 105. land |
| 14. ter | 37. or | 60. for | 83. ci | 106. light |
| 15. ex | 38. tions | 61. is | 84. mo | 107. ob |
| 16. al | 39. ble | 62. mer | 85. on | 108. of |
| 17. de | 40. der | 63. pe | 86. ous | 109. pos |
| 18. com | 41. ma | 64. ra | 87. pi | 110. tain |
| 19. o | 42. na | 65. so | 88. se | 111. den |
| 20. di | 43. si | 66. ta | 89. ten | 112. ings |
| 21. en | 44. un | 67. as | 90. tor | 113. mag |
| 22. an | 45. at | 68. col | 91. ver | 114. ments |
| 23. ty | 46. dis | 69. fi | 92. ber | 115. set |

| | | | | |
|---|---|---|---|---|
| **116.** some | **143.** but | **170.** ted | **197.** su | **224.** har |
| **117.** sub | **144.** cit | **171.** tem | **198.** tend | **225.** ish |
| **118.** sur | **145.** cle | **172.** tin | **199.** ther | **226.** lands |
| **119.** ters | **146.** co | **173.** tri | **200.** ton | **227.** let |
| **120.** tu | **147.** cov | **174.** tro | **201.** try | **228.** long |
| **121.** af | **148.** da | **175.** up | **202.** um | **229.** mat |
| **122.** au | **149.** dif | **176.** va | **203.** uer | **230.** meas |
| **123.** cy | **150.** ence | **177.** ven | **204.** way | **231.** mem |
| **124.** fa | **151.** ern | **178.** vis | **205.** ate | **232.** mul |
| **125.** im | **152.** eve | **179.** am | **206.** bet | **233.** ner |
| **126.** li | **153.** hap | **180.** bor | **207.** bles | **234.** play |
| **127.** lo | **154.** ies | **181.** by | **208.** bod | **235.** ples |
| **128.** men | **155.** ket | **182.** cat | **209.** cap | **236.** ply |
| **129.** min | **156.** lec | **183.** cent | **210.** cial | **237.** port |
| **130.** mon | **157.** main | **184.** ev | **211.** cir | **238.** press |
| **131.** op | **158.** mar | **185.** gan | **212.** cor | **239.** sat |
| **132.** out | **159.** mis | **186.** gle | **213.** coun | **240.** sec |
| **133.** rec | **160.** my | **187.** head | **214.** cus | **241.** ser |
| **134.** ro | **161.** nal | **188.** high | **215.** dan | **242.** south |
| **135.** sen | **162.** ness | **189.** il | **216.** dle | **243.** sun |
| **136.** side | **163.** ning | **190.** lu | **217.** ef | **244.** the |
| **137.** tal | **164.** n't | **191.** me | **218.** end | **245.** ting |
| **138.** tic | **165.** nu | **192.** nore | **219.** ent | **246.** tra |
| **139.** ties | **166.** oc | **193.** part | **220.** ered | **247.** tures |
| **140.** ward | **167.** pres | **194.** por | **221.** fin | **248.** val |
| **141.** age | **168.** sup | **195.** read | **222.** form | **249.** var |
| **142.** ba | **169.** te | **196.** rep | **223.** go | **250.** vid |

| | | | | |
|---|---|---|---|---|
| **251.** wil | **267.** east | **283.** lent | **299.** ried | **315.** tors |
| **252.** win | **268.** fect | **284.** less | **300.** round | **316.** tract |
| **253.** won | **269.** fish | **285.** lin | **301.** row | **317.** tray |
| **254.** work | **270.** fix | **286.** mal | **302.** sa | **318.** us |
| **255.** act | **271.** gi | **287.** mi | **303.** sand | **319.** vel |
| **256.** ag | **272.** grand | **288.** mil | **304.** self | **320.** west |
| **257.** air | **273.** great | **289.** moth | **305.** sent | **321.** where |
| **258.** als | **274.** heav | **290.** near | **306.** ship | **322.** writ |
| **259.** bat | **275.** ho | **291.** nel | **307.** sim | |
| **260.** bi | **276.** hunt | **292.** net | **308.** sions | |
| **261.** cate | **277.** ion | **293.** new | **309.** sis | |
| **262.** cen | **278.** its | **294.** one | **310.** sons | |
| **263.** char | **279.** jo | **295.** point | **311.** stand | |
| **264.** come | **280.** lat | **296.** prac | **312.** sug | |
| **265.** cul | **281.** lead | **297.** ral | **313.** tel | |
| **266.** ders | **282.** lect | **298.** rect | **314.** tom | |

# 35 Quick and Easy Phonics and Word Analysis Games

Many wonderful educational games and activities providing phonics practice are available from educational supply companies. But you can prepare countless simple and engaging activities yourself. Here are some of the easiest and best activities I have used or collected over the years.

**1** **Sound Bingo** Make copies of a 5-by-5-square bingo game board. Use the letters that follow to fill in the cards: Game 1: *b, c, d, f, g, h, l, m, n, p, s, t;* Game 2: *l, t, s, k, n, g, sh, f, p.* Use each letter at least twice per game board (see right). Put the letters in a different order for each card. Also place picture cards in a bag. The picture names must contain the sounds that the letters represent.

Sound Bingo is played just like regular bingo. Before the game begins, give each player a game board and ample space markers. The caller (teacher) draws one picture card from the bag and displays it. If a player's game board contains the letter that begins the picture's name, he or she places a marker over the space. The first player to get five markers in a row, either vertically, horizontally, or diagonally, yells, "Sound Bingo!" The player then states aloud the letter and sound it stands for as the caller checks it against the picture cards drawn from the bag. If these match, the player wins. Players then clear their boards, the picture cards go back in the bag, and a new game begins. (Game 2 is played in the same way but focuses on ending sounds.)

**2** **Living Words** On large note cards, write letters or spellings you want to review. Distribute one card to each student. Then have three students stand in front of the class. Ask them to stand in a sequence that forms a word. Each group must determine its word. For example, you might call on the

students with the *s, u,* and *n* cards. When the students have formed the word *sun*, ask a volunteer to read aloud the word. Show children how to blend the word. Continue by forming a new word or substituting letters in the existing word (for example, have the student with the *b* card replace the student with the *s* card and blend the new word formed).

**3 Change-a-Letter** Write an incomplete sentence on the board, such as, "I like to pet my \_\_\_\_." Then write a word that is one letter away from being the correct answer, such as *cab*. Ask a volunteer to change one letter in the word to form a word that will complete the sentence. Have the student write the word on the blank *(cat)*. Continue with other incomplete sentences and change-a-letter words.

**4 Spin It!** Cut out three spinners and dials (see right). On the outside edge of the first spinner write the letters *t, b, c, d, f, h, m, p, r,* and *s*. On the outside edge of the second spinner, write the letters *a, e, i, o,* and *u* two times. On the outside edge of the third spinner, write the letters *m, n, t, b, p, d,* and

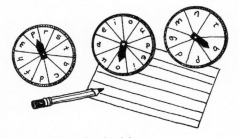

*g*. Paste the spinners in sequence on a piece of tagboard or the inside of a folder. Using brass fasteners, attach the dials to the spinners. Then have each student spin all three spinners. If a word can be formed, the student writes the word on a sheet of paper. Each word is worth one point. Students can continue until they've formed five words, or they can challenge each other to see who can form the most words. As the year progresses, replace the short-vowel spellings with long-vowel spellings, and the consonants with clusters and digraphs.

**5 Phonogram Families** Distribute letter cards to each student. On each letter card write a consonant, cluster, or digraph. Then display a phonogram card. Students come to the front of the classroom if they're holding a card that when combined with the phonogram card can form a word. These are members of this phonogram's "family." Invite each student to place his or her card in front of the phonogram card and blend aloud the word formed.

**6 Build It** Draw a picture of a house or pyramid on a sheet of paper. Divide the house or pyramid into smaller segments, such as squares or rectangles (see right). Make enough copies of the page for each student to have one. Then make several sets of word-building cards. On each card, write a consonant, cluster, digraph, vowel, or phonogram, depending on the phonics skills you are reviewing. Make enough cards for each so that many words can be formed. Divide the class into small groups, distribute a pyramid page to each child, and place a set of cards facedown on the table or floor in front of each group. One at a time, each student in the group draws a set of five cards and builds as many words as possible. The student writes each word in one segment of the house or pyramid, or colors in one segment for each word. The student who builds (completes) the house or pyramid first wins.

**7 Sound Checkers** Write a word on each square of an old checkerboard. Each word should contain a spelling that you want children to review. The game is played just like checkers, except each player must read the word written on each space he or she lands on. If a player cannot read the word, he or she returns to the original space.

**8 Sound Hunt** Assign each student a letter or spelling that you want to review. (You might want to have students work with partners or in small groups.) Then have children search for objects in the classroom whose names contain the sound represented by the letter or spelling. Provide time for students to share their findings. **Variation:** Have students also search through books, magazines, and newspapers for words that contain the letter or spelling.

**9 Environmental Print Boards** As you teach each sound and spelling, challenge children to find examples of the sound-spelling relationship in words on signs, cereal boxes, advertisements, junk mail, and other environmental print items. Have children bring these items to class (suggest they take a photo or draw a picture if it's a large sign) and attach them to an environmental-print bulletin board to refer to throughout the week.

**10 Letter Tic-Tac-Toe** Make copies of tic-tac-toe game boards. On each game board write incomplete words. For example, you might write each word, leaving a blank for the first letter. Then place the game boards in a folder. Have pairs of children each select a game board. The game is similar to a standard game of tic-tac-toe. Each player chooses to be X or O. In turn, each player marks an X or O on one square of the grid. But in order to mark an X or O on a square, the player must complete the square's word by writing the missing letter and reading aloud the completed word. The winner is the first player to get three X's or three O's in a row horizontally, vertically, or diagonally.

**11 Graph It** Have children create graphs to combine language arts with math concepts. For example, students might search a passage for all the words with short *a, i,* and *u* and list them. Then, using their word list, they can create a bar graph showing the number of words found. **Variation:** Have students examine the length of words (start with the length of their names) to create a graph. For example, how many students' names contain four letters? Five letters? Display the graphs throughout the room.

**12 Word Baseball** This game can be played much like the original game. Divide the class into two teams. One at a time, each player is up at bat. Show the child a word card. If the player reads the word card, he or she goes to first base. If the player is unable to read the word, the team receives an out. The team at bat continues until it receives three outs. The winning team is the one with the most points after nine innings. (You might want to limit the game to fewer innings.) **Variation:** To make the game more exciting, make some word cards worth a base hit, others worth a double or triple, and a few worth the treasured home run. You might also ask the player at bat to read the word, then state a word that rhymes with it or that contains the same vowel sound.

**13 Word Toss** Tape several plastic foam or paper cups to the floor close together. This should resemble the setup commonly seen at carnivals with the goldfish bowls and Ping-Pong balls. Inside each cup, write a letter or spelling. Have each child toss a button into the mass of cups. When his or her button lands in a cup, the child states a word that contains the sound that the letter or spelling in the cup stands for. Continue until each child has had multiple turns.

**14 Sound Hopscotch** Using chalk, create several large hopscotch grids on a paved area of your playground (or use masking tape on the floor of your classroom). In each section of the boards, write a sound-spelling (example: *ay*) you want to review. Then read aloud a word or call out a sound. Students hop to the space on the hopscotch board that contains the spelling called out. If you are calling out a word, designate the position (initial, medial, final) in which the sound occurs in the word.

**15 Concentration** This classic game can be played by two or three students to review almost any skill. Make a set of 12 to 20 playing cards. On each card write a word. For example, if you are reviewing compound words, you will write words that, when combined, can form compound words. Place the cards facedown on the table or floor. Each player chooses two cards. If the cards form a compound word, the player keeps them. The player with the most cards at the end of the game wins. When reviewing vowel sounds, make a set of cards in which rhyming word pairs can be found.

**16** **Word Wall** As each sound-spelling is introduced, place a large card showing it on the wall and add words to the card that contain the sound-spelling. These words can be revisited throughout the week by having the class chorally read them, and they can be referred to by students while reading or writing. In addition to grouping words by common sound-spellings, add cards to the Word Wall containing high-frequency words.

**17** **High-Frequency Box** Place a set of high-frequency word cards in a shoebox. Throughout the day, ask volunteers to select a card, spell aloud the word, read it, and use it in a sentence. The rest of the class must write the word on a sheet of paper as they say each letter aloud. Then display it in a pocket chart. At the end of the day, collect the students' papers and have the class read the word cards in the pocket chart chorally. By the end of the week, this small set of words will have been reviewed many times.

**18** **Fish for It** Make word cards using decodable words or high-frequency words you want to review. Glue a small bar magnet on the back of each card, or attach a paper clip. Then make a fishing pole, with a paper clip or magnet for a hook. Divide the class into teams. Place the word cards in a bag. One student from each team must "fish" for a word card. When the card is drawn, the student spells the word aloud, then blends it. The rest of the class determines whether the word is correct. If it is correct, the team earns one point. Play until one team earns ten points.

**19** **Pin It** String a long clothesline across one section of your classroom. Place clothespins along the clothesline at various

intervals. On each clothespin write the beginning part of a word, such as a consonant, cluster, or digraph. On note cards, write the ending part of a word (phonogram). Have children form words by pinning each note card to a clothespin.

**20** **Sound Play** Throughout the year, help children create letter cards. For each sound-spelling relationship you teach, distribute an index card to each student. Have students write the spelling on the card and add the card to their growing set. Several times a week, provide time for students to play with the cards by combining them to form words. Circulate around the room and help children blend the words they have formed.

**21** **What Am I?** Select a classroom object and provide clues to help children guess its identity. For example, you might say, "The name of this object begins with /ch/." Then write students' guesses on the board. Continue with other clues. After you give each new clue, allow the students to modify their guesses. When the class agrees on the item, confirm its identity.

**22** **Password** Provide a set of word cards, each containing a decodable word. One student of a pair selects a card, then provides clues for his or her partner to figure out the word. For example, if a student draws the word card "sun," he or she might say, "My word begins with the letter *s*. It has three letters and describes something very bright." The student provides clues until the partner figures out the word. Then partners change roles.

**23** **Word Ladders** Draw a ladder on the board. On the first step, write a word. Then ask a volunteer to change one letter in the word to form a new word. Write the new word on the second step. Continue until the ladder is completed.

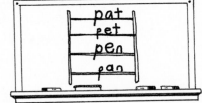

**24** **What's Missing?** Display a picture of an animal or object and, leaving out one letter, write its name on the board. For example, display a picture of a cat and write "c_t" on the board. Then have a volunteer fill in the missing letter. Continue with other pictures representing spellings you want to review.

**25** **Word Sort** Provide students with sets of word cards. Have them sort the word cards first in any way they choose, such as by common sounds or word length. Then suggest a way for the students to sort the words. Be sure that the words you provide can be sorted in more than one way. For example, use words containing the long-*a* sound spelled *a_e*, *ai*, and *ay*. To make the word sorts more engaging, have the children sort cleverly shaped word cards into appropriate containers. For example, have them sort egg-shaped word cards into egg cartons labeled according to specific spellings.

**26** **Bowling for Words** Make a bowling score sheet for each student (see sample). Then make a set of large tagboard or construction paper bowling pins. On each pin, write a word and a number from 1 to 10. Make the words with the highest numbers the most difficult. Divide the class into small teams. Place the bowling pins in a bag or box so that students can't see them. One player from each team reaches in and selects a pin. If the player can correctly read the word, he records the score

| BOWLING FOR WORDS | | | | | | | | | | TOTAL |
|---|---|---|---|---|---|---|---|---|---|---|
| Max | 6 | o | 7 | 8 | 1 | 0 | 3 | 9 | 0 2 | 36 |

on his or her score sheet. If the player can't read the word, he or she receives a "gutter ball," or a score of 0. The game ends when all ten frames of the bowling game have been played and the scores tallied. You might want to have teams use calculators to tally their scores.

**27** **Missing Words** Write a brief story or paragraph on a chart. Place sticky notes over every fifth or tenth word. Or select words with target sounds you want to review and cover those up. Another option is to write the story or paragraph, leaving blanks for each word you want students to figure out. When you get to a missing word, have students guess it. Before telling children whether they are correct, write the correct spelling for the first sound in the word and let children modify their guesses. (For example, you would write "sh" for the first sound in the word *shop*.) Continue this way until the whole word is spelled.

**28** **Syllable Race** Create a game board such as the one shown at right. Then make word cards, each containing a one-, two-, or three-syllable word. Each player draws one card and reads aloud the word. If the player reads the word correctly, he or she moves the

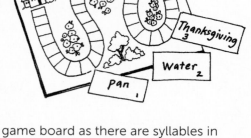

same number of spaces on the game board as there are syllables in the word. You might want to write this number under the word on each card for students to refer to. The game continues until one player reaches the end.

**29** **Silent Riddles** Write a set of words, each containing a silent letter, on the board. Then read a clue, such as, "I am something you use to fix your hair. What am I?" Have a volunteer circle the word on the board that answers the riddle *(comb)*. Then have another volunteer draw a line through the silent letter. Continue until all the words have been used.

**30 Make a Match** Write word parts on note cards. Make enough cards so that each student can receive one, and be sure that every card can be combined with at least one other to form a word. Distribute one card to each student. Play music while students search for their match—the student with another word part that can be combined with their card to form a word. When all students find their match, provide time for them to share their words with the class. Continue with other word-part cards, or challenge students to find another match.

**31 Unscramble It** Divide the class into teams of three or four. Provide each team with a list of ten scrambled words. Allow each team five minutes to unscramble as many words as possible. You can vary this activity by providing each team with scrambled sentences.

**32 Word Card File** At the beginning of the year, have each student bring in a card file box and blank index cards. Every week, provide time for students to write a word they are having trouble reading or spelling on one of the index cards. Suggest that they add a sentence or picture clue to the card to help them remember the word. Have them keep their cards in alphabetical order and periodically review them. Point out opportunities for them to use their file cards.

**33 Book Chat** Divide the class into groups of four or five. Have each student tell the group a little—just a few sentences—about a book he or she has recently read. Students might also enjoy reading aloud a favorite paragraph or page. Remind children not to give away the ending if the book is fiction. Encourage students in each group to read one of the books they heard about from their classmates. These book chats honor students' accomplishments and remind them of the purpose of learning sound-spelling relationships: to read great books.

**34 Time It** Make enough sets of word cards for each of several small teams. The cards in each set should contain the same mix of base words, prefixes, and suffixes. Distribute a set to each group. Timed by a three-minute egg timer, each team uses its cards to form words. One player records the words on a sheet of paper. Teams earn one point for each word. At the end of the game, each team reads aloud the words they formed.

**35** **Other Children's Games** Many popular children's games are excellent for developing students' awareness of sound-spelling relationships. These include Scrabble, hangman, crossword puzzles, and search-and-finds. Stock your learning centers with these and other games.

# Workbooks

Worksheets are viewed by many as a dirty word in phonics instruction. Generally, "seatwork is associated with lower levels of engagement and achievement" (Rosenshine & Stevens, 1984). However, you can use well-designed workbook pages to provide a quick paper-and-pencil assessment of a child's growing knowledge of phonics. A well-designed workbook page goes beyond having children circle and color by providing connected text for children to read and respond to. Nevertheless, workbook pages should not be the instructional emphasis of any phonics program and should not be used as busy work to keep children occupied. There is no better way for children to apply their growing phonics skills than to read. So if you choose to use workbook pages as part of your phonics instruction, evaluate them carefully and provide a reading assignment as a follow-up to each page. For example, after completing a workbook page, have the child reread a passage from a previously read story or article and respond to it in writing on the back of the workbook page. Or have the child read something new and respond to it in writing. Children need to have successful reading opportunities every day in order to develop into skilled, fluent, and enthusiastic readers. Statistics show that the average first grader reads approximately 1,900 words a week. The typical poor first-grade reader reads only 16

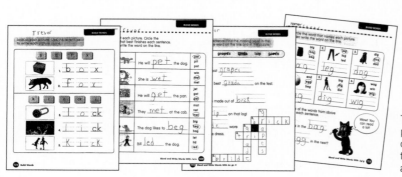

These activity pages provide multiple opportunities for children to read words in context and to write. (© Scholastic)

words a week (Allington, 1984). Daily reading opportunities, including the rereading of stories and articles, are critical. Spending too much time on workbook pages is wasteful.

The following is a list of picturable items that can be used to develop quality workbook pages or to make instructional picture cards. (Remember that picture cards can provide excellent visual clues for students learning English as a second language.)

## 500 Picture Words

| | | | | | |
|---|---|---|---|---|---|
| ant | big | bush | circus | dance | fifty |
| apple | bike | button | city | deer | fin |
| ax | bird | cab | clap | desk | finger |
| baby | black | cage | clay | dice | fire |
| backpack | block | cake | cliff | dig | fish |
| bag | blow | camel | clock | dinosaur | five |
| ball | blue | camera | cloud | dive | flag |
| balloon | boat | can | clown | dog | flashlight |
| banana | boil | candle | coat | doll | float |
| band | bone | cane | coins | door | floor |
| bank | book | cap | cold | dot | flower |
| barn | boot | car | comb | draw | flute |
| baseball | bow | carrot | cone | dress | fly |
| basket | bowl | cat | cook | drip | fold |
| bat | box | cave | corn | drum | foot |
| bath | boy | ceiling | cot | duck | football |
| beach | bread | chain | cow | eat | fork |
| beak | brick | chair | crab | egg | forty |
| bean | bride | chalk | crawl | elbow | four |
| bear | bridge | check | crib | elephant | fox |
| bed | broom | cheese | crown | envelope | frame |
| bee | brown | cherry | crutches | face | fright |
| beg | brush | chest | cry | fall | frog |
| bell | bug | chimney | cub | fan | frown |
| belt | building | chin | cube | feather | fruit |
| bench | bun | chop | cup | feet | fry |
| bib | bus | circle | cut | fence | game |

| | | | | | |
|---|---|---|---|---|---|
| garden | hole | ladder | moon | pet | quilt |
| gate | hood | lake | mop | phone | quiz |
| gift | hop | lamp | mouse | photograph | rabbit |
| giraffe | horn | lap | mouth | piano | rag |
| girl | horse | leaf | mule | pie | rain |
| glass | hose | leash | mushroom | pig | rainbow |
| globe | hot | leg | music | pillow | rake |
| glue | house | lemon | nail | pin | rat |
| goat | hug | letter | neck | pink | read |
| gold | hump | lid | necklace | plane | red |
| goose | hut | light | needle | plant | right |
| grapes | ice | line | nest | plate | ring |
| graph | inch | lion | net | plow | rip |
| grass | ink | lips | night | plug | road |
| grasshopper | itch | list | nine | plus | robe |
| green | jacks | lock | nose | point | robot |
| grill | jam | log | nurse | pole | rock |
| groom | jar | lunch | nut | pond | roof |
| guitar | jet | mail | octopus | pony | roots |
| gym | jug | mailbox | oil | pool | rope |
| ham | juggle | man | ox | pop | rose |
| hammer | jump | map | page | popcorn | row |
| hand | kangaroo | mask | pail | porch | rug |
| hat | key | mat | paint | pot | ruler |
| hawk | kick | match | pan | pretzel | run |
| hay | king | meat | paw | prize | sand |
| heart | kiss | men | pay | pumpkin | sandwich |
| heel | kit | mice | peach | purse | saw |
| hen | kitchen | milk | pear | puzzle | scale |
| hide | kite | mirror | peas | quack | scarf |
| hill | knee | mitt | peel | queen | school |
| hippo | knife | mitten | pen | question | seal |
| hit | knock | mix | pencil | quick | seed |
| hive | knot | monkey | penguin | quiet | seven |

| | | | | | |
|---|---|---|---|---|---|
| shadow | smile | street | tie | vacuum | white |
| shark | smoke | stump | tiger | valentine | wig |
| shave | snail | suit | tire | van | window |
| sheep | snake | sun | toad | vase | wing |
| shelf | snow | sweep | toast | vegetable | worm |
| shell | soap | swim | toe | vest | wrist |
| ship | sock | swing | tooth | vine | write |
| shirt | spider | table | top | violin | yard |
| shoe | spill | tack | toys | volcano | yarn |
| shoelace | spin | tail | train | wagon | yawn |
| shorts | spoon | tape | tray | wallet | yell |
| shout | spray | team | tree | wash | yellow |
| shovel | spring | teeth | triangle | watch | yo-yo |
| sink | square | ten | truck | watermelon | yolk |
| sit | squeeze | tent | trunk | wave | zebra |
| six | squirrel | thermometer | tub | wax | zero |
| skate | stamp | thirteen | turkey | web | zigzag |
| skirt | star | thirty | turtle | well | zipper |
| skunk | steam | thorn | twenty | wet | zoo |
| sled | steps | three | two | whale | |
| sleep | stir | throne | umbrella | wheel | |
| slide | stop | throw | under | wheelchair | |
| smell | strawberry | thumb | up | whistle | |

# Assessments

The following standardized diagnostic test batteries with tests or subtests measuring word recognition have good reliability and validity:

- Durrell Analysis of Reading Difficulty (3rd Edition) Pearson
- Gates-McKillop-Horowitz Reading Diagnostic Tests (2nd Edition)
- Stanford Diagnostic Reading Test (4th Edition)
- Woodcock Reading Mastery Test, Revised (3rd Edition)

In addition, you can use the following three quick assessments, which are available at www.scholastic.com/phonicsfromatoz. (See page 320 for details on how to access these assessments.)

# Nonsense Word Test

The Nonsense Word Test (Blevins, 1997) assesses children's decoding abilities without allowing their sight-word knowledge to interfere. Administer this text no earlier than the spring of Grade 1. Another good test to use if you are uncomfortable with nonsense-word assessments is the Names Test (Cunningham, 1990), which is available online as Resource 4.4 (see page 320 for details on how to access).

### Preparing the Test

Print two copies of the Nonsense Word Test for each student you plan to assess—one for the student and one for you to use for recording the student's responses.

### Administering the Test

Administer the test to one student at a time.

1. Explain to the student that he or she is to read each word. Point out that the words are nonsense, or made-up, words.
2. Have the student read the entire list.
3. Write a check mark on the answer sheet for each word read correctly.

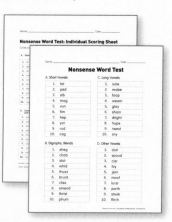

The Nonsense Word Test can be found online as Resource 4.5; see page 320 for details on how to access.

### Scoring the Test

1. Count a word correct if the pronunciation is correct according to common sound-spelling relationships.
2. Total the number of words the student read correctly. Analyze the mispronounced words, looking for patterns that might give you information about the student's decoding strengths and weaknesses.
3. Focus future instruction on those sound-spelling relationship categories (short vowels, long vowels, and so on) in which the student made three or more errors.

# San Diego Quick Assessment

The San Diego Quick Assessment (LaPray & Ross, 1969) contains words common to children's reading materials at a number of grade levels. I've included only the portion of the test pertaining to the elementary grades.

### Preparing the Test

1. To prepare word list cards, print the San Diego Quick Assessment. Cut apart the word lists and glue each to a note card. Write

the grade level on the back of each card for your reference.

2. Print out a copy of the assessment for each student you plan to assess to use for recording his or her responses.

The San Diego Quick Assessment can be found online as Resource 4.6; see page 320 for details on how to access.

## Administering the Test
Administer the test to one student at a time.

1. Start with a card that is at least two years below the student's grade level. Have the student read aloud the words on the list. If he or she misreads any words, go to an easier list until the student makes no errors. This indicates the base reading level.

2. Then have the student read each subsequent card in sequence, and record all incorrect responses. Encourage the student to read all the words so that you can determine the strategies he or she uses to decode.

3. Continue the assessment until the student misses at least three words on one of the lists.

## Scoring the Test
Use the assessment results to identify the student's independent, instructional, and frustration levels. You can provide instructional and independent reading materials for each child based on the results of this assessment.

- Independent level = no more than one error on a list
- Instructional level = two errors on a list
- Frustration level = three or more errors on a list

# Comprehensive Phonics Survey (for use with students in Grades 2–3)

This assessment consists of 50 nonsense words to confirm students' decoding skills. Some students do well on real-word tests of phonics due to their wide sight-word knowledge, yet struggle when applying those same decoding skills to new words. The nonsense-word test accounts for this and assesses true decoding application. Administer this test as a follow-up to the real-word tests (cumulative phonics assessments), especially for students who do okay on these assessments, but seem to struggle decoding while reading.

The Comprehensive Phonics Survey can be found online as Resource 4.7; see page 320 for details on how to access.

### Preparing the Test

Print out a class supply of the Comprehensive Phonics Survey: Nonsense Word Reading and Comprehensive Phonics Survey: Individual Scoring Sheet. Also print a copy of the Comprehensive Phonics Survey: Class Record Sheet.

### Administering the Test

Administer the assessment to each child in the class three times a year—at the beginning, middle, and end.

1. Show the student the Comprehensive Phonics Survey: Nonsense Word Reading page.
2. Have the student point to each word and read it aloud. Circle each correct response. Record the student's errors to use for error analysis (for example, *send* for *smend*). Record the number correct and note the speed in the boxes on the Comprehensive Phonics Survey: Individual Scoring Sheet.

### Scoring the Test

1. Total the number of words the student read correctly. Analyze the mispronounced words, looking for patterns that might give you information about the student's decoding strengths and weaknesses.
2. Focus future instruction on those sound-spelling relationship categories (short vowels, long vowels, etc.) in which the student made three or more errors.
3. Use the Comprehensive Phonics Survey: Class Record Sheet to gather and record all students' scores for each testing period to determine small-group differentiated instructional needs.

## TRY IT OUT

- Select one activity from the "35 Quick and Easy Phonics and Word Analysis Games" to try out with your students.
- Write this week's phonics lesson using the models provided as a guide.
- Evaluate your prefix and suffix instruction based on the frequency charts provided.
- Match classroom trade books to specific phonics skills. Determine where in your phonics scope and sequence the majority of the words in each book is decodable. Sequence the books accordingly.
- Assess your students using the Nonsense Word Assessment. Form small groups based on the results.

# Meeting Individual Needs

*❝Do I have to read that now, Mr. B.? Can't I just help you clean out the hamster cage or somethin'?❞*

—Billy, age nine, struggling reader

What do Thomas Edison, Albert Einstein, Woodrow Wilson, Nelson Rockefeller, Hans Christian Andersen, George Patton, Galileo, Leonardo da Vinci, Michelangelo, Winston Churchill, and Tom Cruise have in common? These notable individuals were all dyslexic. Each struggled in his own way to master the art of reading.

One of the most difficult aspects of teaching is watching a child struggle with learning to read. Early in my teaching career, I was given a class of 30 second- and third-grade struggling readers. My class was designated a Chapter 1 classroom, and most students had serious reading difficulties. A few students were getting extra help from the Resource Room teacher, but most of them received all their instruction from me and my teaching partner, a highly skilled veteran teacher. The range of abilities in the class was broad. Matthew was a nonalphabetic reader with almost no sight-word knowledge; Bradley had severe motor-coordination problems that hampered his ability to form letters; Christon couldn't recall the alphabet; Brian and Ryan had serious behavioral problems; Billy's learned helplessness and lack of motivation were constant issues; Darlene could read on grade level but had trouble organizing thoughts and ideas in a logical manner; Jason had accurate but labored decoding skills; and the list went on.

This same situation exists in many classrooms across the country but with only one full-time teacher in the room. Certainly, meeting the individual needs of each student in your class is perhaps the greatest challenge you will face.

Many sobering statistics regarding the state of reading instruction in this country circulate in the media each year. According to the 2015 National Assessment of Educational Progress (NAEP), 36% of fourth-graders read at or above the proficient level. This is only slightly higher than 20 years ago when the 1994 NAEP reported 60% of students at or above the basic level. What was even more sobering back in 1994 (and little has changed) was that only 5% to 6% of these children can be classified as having severe learning disorders (Lyon, 1996). "The others are likely to be suffering the consequences of inappropriate teaching, low standards, and/or disadvantageous environmental circumstances for learning to read" (Moats, 2000). In addition, Miller (1993) cited the following:

- Approximately 60 million U.S. citizens read below the eighth-grade reading level.
- About 85% of the juveniles appearing in juvenile court are functionally illiterate.
- Approximately 50–60% of U.S. prison inmates are functionally illiterate.
- About 75% of unemployed adults are illiterate.

As you can see, learning to read goes well beyond an educational issue; it is an extremely serious and important social issue. In a country with such tremendous wealth and resources, there's no excuse for the high numbers of children who leave our schools each year unable to meet the most basic reading demands of adult life. We must do all we can to reverse these troubling statistics. Solutions often cited include improved teacher training, adequate instructional materials, smaller class sizes, family and community support, early preventive measures, and strong intervention programs.

All these solutions can and will help. But you still may be teaching in an overcrowded classroom with insufficient materials and little parental support. So what can you do, given the resources available?

In this chapter I briefly examine why some children have difficulties learning to read, focusing on children who struggle learning phonics. I also offer some tried-and-true practical suggestions to help you plan appropriate and purposeful instruction for these children.

We read to obtain information. We also read for pleasure. For some children, however, reading is neither easy nor enjoyable. While some children seem to learn to read with relative ease, others experience great difficulties. Children with learning disabilities (e.g., dyslexia) have normal or high intelligence and have few problems with vocabulary or understanding English syntax. However, they do struggle with sounds and print. Estimates show that 10–20% of all students are dyslexic. Some estimates put the percentage even higher.

Children with reading difficulties can be hindered by a wide range of language deficits. They might have problems with phonemic awareness, phonics, comprehension, or processing verbal information. And they might lack the auditory and visual skills needed for reading. Often memory and concentration are a problem. The causes are many, including educational, psychological, physiological, and social. Educational factors cited as causes of reading difficulties include instruction that is inconsiderate of a child's unique needs, inappropriately paced instruction, and large class sizes. A child's emotional reaction to these difficulties might compound them. Because they aren't succeeding, many of these children think they're incapable of learning to read. This "learned helplessness" may cause them to stop trying. "Part of teaching children with reading problems is convincing them that they can learn to read, despite their experience to the contrary" (Stahl, 1997).

# Types of Readers

The following groupings classify four types of students with reading problems.

**Nonalphabetic** These children have difficulties during the first stage of reading development. They don't grasp the alphabetic principle, need much phonological awareness training, and benefit most from explicit instruction in alphabet recognition and sound-spelling relationships. They have extremely poor word-recognition skills and grasp at any visual clue they can find to read a word, such as its shape, length, or position on the page.

**Compensatory** These children have a limited grasp of the alphabetic principle and weak phonemic-awareness skills. Therefore, they have trouble using a knowledge of sound-spelling relationships to decode words. They compensate by relying on their sight-word knowledge and on context and picture clues. These children do okay with easy material, but they have serious difficulties when the reading demands increase.

**Nonautomatic** These readers can accurately sound out words but with great effort. Since their word-recognition skills are not automatic, decoding requires much of their mental energy. Therefore, comprehension suffers, and they may have motivational problems. These children need practice and repetition to build fluency.

**Delayed** These readers have automatic word-recognition skills but acquired them much later than their peers. Therefore, they weren't ready when reading comprehension demands increased. The instruction designed to help children comprehend text had had little effect, since decoding was still an issue. Thus, these children are less skilled at using comprehension strategies and need a great deal of instruction in that area. They might also benefit from further instruction in phonics and spelling.

All four types of readers generally suffer from low motivation, low levels of practice, and low expectations. It's important to address these problems as well as the skill deficits. The following checklist of behaviors are characteristic of these and other children who might benefit from intervention. However, these characteristics may not apply to all children and should not be viewed as the causes of the reading problems.

To help children with reading problems, it's important to assess what they can and cannot do and then plan an intervention program to meet their unique instructional needs. They may not need a different reading program or instructional method but rather adjustments to their existing program, including more time, instructional support, and practice reading connected text.

----

**▌▌Phonics must not be made to carry the whole burden of reading instruction, especially if students have difficulty with it. Although research and experience have demonstrated again and again that phonic knowledge and skill are essential for learning to read, and that they speed up learning to read, there is also considerable evidence that reading development depends on wide reading of connected text, the development of fluency, and the growth of vocabulary, knowledge and reasoning. Thus, it is wise for all students, even those having extreme difficulty with phonics, to read books they find interesting, learn the meanings of ever more difficult words, and continue to acquire knowledge. ▌▌** (Chall & Popp, 1996)

----

# Checklist: Possible Characteristics of Student With Reading Problems

❏ reads slowly and with great effort, as if seeing the words for the first time

❏ frequently pauses while reading

❏ has difficulty remembering high-frequency words

❏ reads in a choppy, word-by-word fashion with improper stress and intonation

❏ has difficulty learning letter sounds

❏ has difficulty blending sounds in words

❏ uses only the first, or first and last, letters of a word to decode it

❏ reverses letter order when blending or has difficulty remembering letter order when spelling

❏ fails to use context clues to figure out new words

❏ substitutes a word that is close in meaning while reading, such as *small* for *little*

❏ has difficulty remembering an entire sentence during dictation exercises

❏ has difficulty remembering names, events in sequence, or directions

❏ reads too fast, making multiple errors

❏ cannot copy accurately

❏ often loses place or skips lines while reading

❏ shows reading improvement with larger print or fewer distractions on the page

❏ has illegible handwriting

❏ writing shows letters colliding and no space between word boundaries

❏ has mirror writing (hold the paper up to the mirror and you can read it)

❏ makes the same error again and again

❏ is visually or auditorily distractible

❏ has a short attention span

❏ is withdrawn

❏ is anxious, tense, or fearful

❏ has difficulty with auditory discrimination

❏ may do better with word identification in isolation than in sentence context

❏ has difficulty responding to higher-level comprehension questions

❏ cannot think in an orderly, logical manner

# How to Help: Effective Intervention Strategies

Effective interventions for students having trouble learning to read are generally characterized by the following:

- They are applied as early as possible (as soon as a problem is diagnosed).
- They involve well-trained, highly skilled teachers and specialists.
- They are intensive.
- They close the reading gap for poor readers.
- They are short-lived, lasting only as long as needed.
- They help children overcome "learned helplessness."

Kindergarten retention does not appear to be a generally effective form of intervention (Mantzicopoulos & Morrison, 1992; Adams, 1990).

## Ten Techniques That Support Intervention Instruction

1 **Prompting** While a child reads a passage, provide prompts that help him or her focus attention on reading strategies. For example, when a child encounters an unfamiliar word, use prompts such as, "What letter sounds do you know in the word?" or, "Are there any word parts you know in the word?" You can also create and display strategy picture cards for children to refer to when they read independently. These cards provide written and illustrated cues to help children deal with reading stumbling blocks. For example, one card might remind children to reread a confusing sentence or passage.

2 **Assisted Reading** Have a child read with you or an audiobook. Gradually lessen the assistance so that eventually the child is reading independently. Assisted reading sessions are particularly helpful for text that is at a child's frustration level. I always use this technique with social studies and science textbooks and my below-level readers.

3 **Supported Contextual Reading** This technique was developed by Stahl (1997) and is designed to help children use their phonics knowledge. The assumption behind the technique is that many children with reading difficulties have phonics knowledge but can't use it effectively. The technique requires using material one or two years above the child's instructional level. First, read the text aloud

to the child and ask comprehension questions to make sure he or she understands the passage. This takes advantage of the child's oral listening skills and promotes concept development. Then, conduct an echo reading (see number 5, below) of the text. Next, send the text home for the child to practice reading. Support the family in helping their child with home reading by providing a checklist of tips and prompts for them to use. Back at school, have the child read that same text again and again to master it.

**4** **Repeated Readings** This popular technique was developed by Samuels (1988). Time the child as he or she reads a passage at his or her instructional level. Give the child feedback on word-recognition errors and the number of words read accurately per minute, and record the data on a graph (see Repeated Reading Chart, right). Then have the child practice reading the text independently or with a partner. (Have children use the Partner Fluency Feedback Chart online to evaluate their partner's reading.) During the time the child is practicing, periodically conduct timed readings and plot progress on the graph. This continues until the child masters that passage. These multiple repetitions of words help children build large sight-word vocabularies.

The Repeated-Reading Chart and Partner Fluency Feedback Chart can be found online as Resource 5.1; see page 320 for details on how to access.

**5** **Echo Reading** Read a phrase or sentence in the text and have the student repeat it. Continue this throughout the text. Alternatively, you can record the text, leaving pauses so that the child can echo the reading as he or she follows along in the text.

**6** **Cloze Passages** Write on a chart a passage that the child has previously read or had read to him or her. Leave out every fifth or tenth word (using a blank line) or cover words with sticky notes. Then ask the child to fill in the missing words by using his or her background knowledge and understanding of English syntax. I like to provide the first letter or cluster of letters in each word to help the child use phonics cues, too.

**7** **Oral Reading by the Teacher** Being read to is critical for developing children's listening/speaking vocabularies and world knowledge—especially for children with reading difficulties. Since their knowledge of vocabulary and concepts is not being developed through their reading, they must be read to a lot.

When giving tests in content areas, such as science or social studies, read aloud the tests to your struggling readers. This way, you can more accurately assess their content knowledge rather than their ability to read the test.

**8 Constructing Word Families** Building words belonging to the same word family can help children's reading and spelling by focusing their attention on common word parts. Use letter cards and pocket charts, magnetic letters, or any other type of manipulative available. You might use the word families to create lists for a Word Wall in your classroom.

**9 Elkonin Boxes** This technique is described in Section 2 (see page 60) and is particularly effective for helping children orally segment words. You can use it during spelling practice in which you have children use the Elkonin boxes and counters to orally segment words. Children then replace each counter with the letter or letters that stand for each sound.

**10 Language Experience** Using a prompt, such as a field trip or a displayed object, have children create a passage. Record the passage on a chart as children state aloud each sentence. This technique is motivational and honors children's experiences and oral language patterns. Later revisit that text for rereadings, focusing on words with target sounds or on proofreading and revising.

# Removing Reading Roadblocks— Principles of Intervention Instruction

In my years of teaching and in the mountain of reading research that exists on intervention, I've seen the emergence of many ideas and techniques for meeting the individual needs of students. I've narrowed these down to four basic principles:

1. **Begin intervention at the level children need it most.**
   Treat the cause, not just the symptoms of reading difficulties. This requires looking at deficits in prerequisite skills.

2. **Assess, assess, assess.** Effective diagnosis and ongoing assessment are critical.
3. **Select the appropriate literature for instructional and independent use.** Be sure that the literature you select for students is not at their frustration level.
4. **Maintain consistency.** Often multiple methods serve only to confuse children. Instead of one clearly designed method of instruction, children are asked to learn a multitude of methods and techniques that may be at odds with one another.

## PRINCIPLE 1: Begin intervention at the level children need it most.

The tendency is to treat the symptoms of reading difficulties, rather than the causes. For example, I recently met with a teacher who was spending a lot of time reteaching sound-spelling relationships to one of her students. She commented that this didn't seem to have much effect. When I asked her if the child had weak phonemic-awareness skills, she didn't know. After doing a phonemic-awareness assessment, we discovered that the child's skills in this area were indeed quite weak. He couldn't orally blend words effectively and had little knowledge of how words "work." I suggested providing the child with phonemic-awareness training. It helped.

This anecdote illustrates the need to find out a child's lowest deficit skill and begin instruction there. Not doing this is like building a house on sand. Without a strong foundation, the house is sure to collapse. Skills necessary for phonics learning include phonemic awareness and strong alphabet recognition. And I should point out that simply treating a lower-deficit skill isn't necessarily enough to correct the reading problem. It will remove a reading "roadblock," but there's more to do. "That is, the lowest level deficit should be identified and repaired, followed by a reevaluation of the reader for additional problems, and by further instructional intervention to repair newly identified problems" (Royer & Sinatra, 1994).

*"Provisions must be made for the student's continued conceptual and informational development while the reading issues are dealt with. If not, the reader will lose out on the knowledge, vocabulary, and concepts needed for further education and also as background information for reading in [later stages] and beyond."* (Chall, 1996)

Although intervention techniques might not differ much from regular classroom instructional methods, I offer the following suggestions:

- Interventions should begin as early as possible.
- Teach only one skill at a time and teach it until it is overlearned.
- Adjust the pace at which you introduce skills. Allow children time to master each skill before moving on.
- Constantly review and reinforce learning.
- Apply the learning to real reading and writing. Reading in context is critical.

Since I don't attempt to cover the entire scope of intervention, I direct you to the following excellent resources for further information on meeting individual needs in your classroom. See the professional organization and periodical listings at the end of this section for additional sources.

*Complete Reading Disabilities Handbook* by W. H. Miller. San Francisco, CA: Jossey-Bass, 1997.

*No Quick Fix: Rethinking Literacy Programs in America's Elementary Schools* by R. L. Allington and S. A. Walmsley. New York, NY: Teachers College Press, 2007.

*Off Track: When Poor Readers Become "Learning Disabled"* by L. Spear-Swerling and R. J. Sternberg. Boulder, CO: Westview Press, 1997.

*Preventing Misguided Reading* by J. M. Burkins and M. Croft. Thousand Oaks, CA: Corwin Press, 2010.

*Reading With the Troubled Readers* by M. Phinney. Portsmouth, NH: Heinemann, 1988.

*Reading Recovery: A Guidebook for Teachers in Training* by M. Clay. Portsmouth, NH: Heinemann, 1993.

In addition to these resources, I encourage you to find out more about some of the most successful intervention programs currently in use. The best include:

**Reading Recovery** (Clay, 1985). This program was originally developed by Marie Clay in New Zealand and imported to the U.S. by professors at Ohio State University. The program consists of daily 30-minute sessions involving a student and a highly trained tutor. The instruction entails the tutor and student rereading familiar books, writing, and reading new text, and the tutor taking running records. The intervention supplements regular classroom instruction and ends in about 12 to 20 weeks for most children.

**Success for All** (Madden et al., 1987). This is a school restructuring program that targets schools with large numbers of economically disadvantaged students. The intervention, which supplements the regular classroom instruction, is administered by trained teachers and consists of daily 20-minute sessions for as long as the child needs it.

**Benchmark School (Word Identification Program)** (Gaskins et al., 2000). The Benchmark School in Media, Pennsylvania, is dedicated to getting struggling readers on track. The program is closely monitored by a team of reading experts and researchers who have published accounts of its success.

**Orton-Gillingham Method** (Orton, 1937). This synthetic, multisensory approach to phonics instruction is geared for children with severe reading difficulties.

**McGraw-Hill *Reading Wonders* Adaptive Learning** (McGraw-Hill, 2013) This program, one of many adaptive phonics programs currently being offered by major educational publishers, offers an individualized learning path for students at all levels of phonics learning.

## A Word About Adaptive Technology

The burden of creating and maintaining a phonics scope and sequence that meets the daily needs of all your students is greatly lessened with the use of an adaptive technology phonics and word study program. Adaptive technology holds the promise of future instruction. Companies are beginning to create phonics adaptive programs that can be used as stand-alone supports for classroom instruction (especially in the area of differentiation with ease) or with digital teaching and learning platforms. Although these programs have yet to meet their full promise, they are improving each year and hopefully will become a mainstay of phonics instruction in classrooms within the next five to ten years. It is an area of instruction in which I have great interest, having designed a couple of adaptive systems for publishers. Why? These programs create an individualized learning pathway for each student based on his or her strengths and weaknesses. Also, the stronger programs provide graduated levels of support based on student responses as they complete the individual activities. Students receive just what they need when they need it—no more and no less. Plus, the better programs have loads of practice activities and built-in review to ensure mastery.

It is a tool that can greatly assist you in providing all your students the differentiated support they need.

## 14 Phonics Problems—and Solutions

Following is a partial list of some phonics-related difficulties students might have and some suggestions for helping them overcome these difficulties. This is not an exhaustive list of the many types of reading difficulties or the multitude of methods used in schools around the country to meet students' needs. Rather, it provides a few suggestions as starting points. Note that the best instructional procedure for a particular child is frequently discovered only after tutoring begins and a few techniques are tried. Many reading specialists suggest trying brief sample lessons using several procedures to find the one each child best responds to (Harris & Sipay, 1990). As your instruction proceeds, continue to assess children's progress and modify instruction as needed.

### PROBLEM 1: My student refuses to try to decode many words while reading.

**Possible Solutions:** A refusal to attempt words probably stems from inadequate word-recognition skills. Children often omit words, saying they don't know the words, and wait for the teacher to provide the word. This generally results from prolonged frustration with reading or characterizes a child who isn't a risk taker when reading. One solution is to stop providing words for the child as soon as he pauses. Allow him time to analyze the word and then provide prompts such as, "What letter sounds do you know in the word?" or "Are there any word parts that you recognize in the word?" Also model how to blend the sounds in the word. These strategies will reassure your student that he can become a successful reader.

### PROBLEM 2: My student has difficulty remembering sound-spelling relationships.

**Possible Solutions:** A student having this difficulty needs a great deal of review and repetition. Often, too much is taught too fast. Assess the child's decoding abilities; then go back and reteach at the appropriate level. Emphasize wordplay. Provide letter cards and a pocket chart, magnetic letters and a pie tin, or foam letters and an overhead for word building. In addition, have the child frequently read simple, decodable text. You may also need to provide other cues such as picture cards for each sound-spelling so the child associates a letter with an image and a key word. Or use a story that dramatizes a sound. For example, you might tell a story about a hissing snake to help the child remember the /s/ sound of the letter *s*, a story about a ticking clock for the /t/ sound of *t*, or a story about the sound we make when we are surprised (long *o*).

## PROBLEM 3: My student still confuses certain letters and words.

**Possible Solutions:** Some children need much attention put on the visual differences between confusing letters and words. Spend time discussing these differences. Use the memory devices highlighted in previous chapters. Provide practice reading word lists containing the confusing letters or words. Use minimal variations to focus your students' attention. For example, when working with the letters *b* and *d*, you might provide sentence completion exercises such as the following:

| | | | |
|---|---|---|---|
| *The dog sits on the* _____. | bad | bed | dad |
| *We have a pet* _____. | bog | dog | dot |

## PROBLEM 4: My student has trouble with multisyllabic words.

**Possible Solutions:** Beginning in second grade, children encounter greater numbers of multisyllabic words and begin having difficulties if their decoding skills are weak—especially if they are not beginning to recognize larger chunks (spellings) in words. These children need lots of practice in analyzing words into usable parts. For example, when they encounter the word *chalkboard*, children should be able to see the two smaller words in the compound word, or readily recognize common spelling patterns such as *ch*, *-alk,* or *-oar*. Have your students search words for common spelling patterns and circle or highlight the pattern. I sometimes provide word lists in which a common spelling pattern is written in a different color. I then help children blend the words. I follow up by giving them a list of words with the same spelling pattern and asking them to find it in the words. We then read together a passage that contains some of these words. I remind children to look for these spelling patterns while they read. Word-search puzzles and timed speed drills are effective and a lot of fun. In second grade and beyond, it's important to provide a lot of instruction on syllabication.

**Consonant + *le* Syllable Speed Drill**

Underline the consonant + le in each word. (The consonant + le appears in the same syllable.) Then practice reading the words until you are ready to be timed.

| | | | | |
|---|---|---|---|---|
| bubble | battle | angle | bridle | apple |
| ankle | double | bottle | bugle | bundle |
| circle | crinkle | fable | cattle | eagle |
| fiddle | maple | dazzle | marble | gentle |
| giggle | handle | purple | fizzle | noble |
| kettle | jungle | kindle | sample | muzzle |
| pebble | little | shingle | middle | simple |
| puzzle | rumble | mantle | single | needle |
| steeple | sparkle | stubble | rattle | struggle |
| puddle | temple | sprinkle | tumble | settle |
| wiggle | puddle | uncle | wrinkle | title |
| saddle | vehicle | bubble | double | battle |
| fable | bottle | angle | title | cattle |
| eagle | circle | fiddle | bundle | handle |
| middle | steeple | marble | apple | gentle |
| rumble | giggle | tumble | maple | kettle |
| sample | rattle | needle | uncle | pebble |
| vehicle | purple | jungle | little | bridle |
| simple | settle | saddle | single | struggle |
| ankle | stubble | puzzle | wrinkle | wiggle |

RESOURCE 5.2 Consonant + le Syllable Speed Drill          Phonics from A to Z, 3rd Edition © Wiley Blevins, Scholastic Inc.

The Consonant + *le* Syllable Speed Drill can be found online as Resource 5.2; see page 320 for details on how to access.

> ❝A large proportion of the ability to decode words effectively is the ability to locate usable elements.❞ (Bond, Tinker, & Wasson, 1994)

## PROBLEM 5: My student seems to overanalyze words.

**Possible Solutions:** Some students develop an over-reliance on one reading strategy. This might be a result of the instructional focus of the classroom teacher, the child's compensating by using the one strategy that seemed to work best early on, or the child's having a weak understanding of the many strategies that can be used to decode words. Children who overanalyze words often sound out words that they should be able to recognize by sight, particularly the words taught as sight words, such as *the* and *of*. These children break these and other words into too many parts. To help your student, use flash cards and timed tests to develop quick sight-word recognition of common words. Also help her focus on larger word parts while reading. For example, point out spellings or word chunks and remind her that some letters together stand for one sound, such as *ch* or *igh*. In addition, stress the flexible use of a small repertoire of strategies and model when each of these can be used while reading. Periodically, ask the child to explain the strategies she's using. If she always says, "I'm sounding it out letter by letter," then point out more efficient ways to decode the word, if appropriate. The following self-monitoring prompts can help children focus on the many ways to figure out unfamiliar words.

### Self-Monitoring Prompts

- What letter do you see at the beginning [end] of the word? What sound does it stand for?
- What word parts do you know?
- What word would make sense there?
- You said the word _____. Does that make sense in the sentence?
- Look at the picture. What clues to the word does it provide?
- Try the word again, thinking about what word would fit in the sentence.
- Try reading ahead for a clue to the word that you don't know.
- How does that sound to your ears?
- Read the sentence again to check on all of the words.
- Do you think the word looks like _____?
- Look at the letters. Could the word be _____ or _____?
- Can you think of a word that makes sense there and starts with those letters?
- If the word were _____, what letter(s) would you expect to see at the beginning? The end?
- Since that word has an *e* at the end, what sound do you think this vowel in the middle stands for?
- What sound does the letter _____ usually stand for?

- The word might be _____, but look at which letters it starts [ends] with.

---

**"** Many children have difficulty in word recognition because they are too dependent on one technique or because they do not use the most efficient ones. . . . The exercises must encourage a diversified and flexible attack on words. They also must emphasize orderly progression through the word from its beginning element to its end. **"**
(Ekwall & Shanker, 1993)

---

In addition to self-monitoring prompts, provide corrective feedback while the child is reading. Much learning occurs during corrective feedback. Give feedback in direct response to your student's reading miscues. The feedback can be immediate or delayed. It can also be terminal (providing the word) or sustaining (providing prompts/clues). To provide children with opportunities to self-monitor their reading, I recommend delayed, sustaining feedback.

### PROBLEM 6: My student has extremely weak language skills, which seems to be affecting his reading.

**Possible Solutions:** Certainly language skills play a crucial role in reading. A child's vocabulary and sense of story structure are important. Engage your students in frequent conversations and in acting out stories. Also, writing exercises can begin as lengthier discussions. In addition, reading larger amounts of nonfiction to expand children's world knowledge is critical. I strongly recommend reading at least two nonfiction books a week to your students.

### PROBLEM 7: My student struggles with the phonemic-awareness exercises.

**Possible Solutions:** For children with weak phonemic-awareness skills, I strongly recommend a phonemic-awareness program such as the ones listed in Section 2 (see page 62). In addition, during the exercises, consider focusing on mouth position and throat vibration while making specific sounds. Or you might limit the number of choices a student has when responding. For example, during an oddity task, provide only two words *(cat, hat)* and ask if they rhyme instead of providing three choices *(cat, hat, run)* and asking the child to pick out the two rhyming words.

### PROBLEM 8: My student cannot blend or segment words.

**Possible Solutions:** Again, I recommend a phonemic-awareness training program. The frequent modeling of blending using an extended method, such as *sssssaaaat*, is beneficial. Add movements when going from one sound to the next to highlight the different sounds. For segmentation, use Elkonin boxes and counters.

## PROBLEM 9: My student doesn't recognize many high-frequency words.

**Possible Solutions:** The quick and automatic recognition of the most common words appearing in text is necessary for fluent reading. Review these words daily in context and in isolation. Use a strategy that includes saying, writing, and reading the word many times. For example, select the word from a set of words, write the word in the air, write the word on paper, discuss interesting features of the word, and look for the word in books and environmental print. The technique for introducing high-frequency words described in Section 4 is quite effective (see page 174). In addition, make word cards with these and other words and build sentences using them. Remember, attention to the spelling patterns of both decodable and "irregular" words is essential. Wide reading and repeated readings are also necessary for developing high-frequency word knowledge. The following list includes other techniques:

- **Dictated stories:** Children dictate a story as you write it on a chart. Reread the story (perhaps chorally) and revisit it on subsequent days. Highlight the high-frequency words and write them on index cards to add to a Word Wall.
- **Predictable books:** Predictable books, such as Eric Carle's *Have You Seen My Cat?* or Bill Martin Jr.'s *Brown Bear, Brown Bear, What Do You See?*, are usually patterned to repeat specific high-frequency words. Reading this type of text ensures multiple exposures to important high-frequency words. Many quality, grade-appropriate predictable books are available.
- **High-frequency word banks:** Use the banks to periodically review the words. Students can also refer to them while they're writing.
- **Multisensory techniques:** These include tracing, copying, writing the words in sand, or forming the words using glue and small objects, such as beans and macaroni.
- **Technology:** Many current computer programs contain a voicing feature that allows the child to click on a word and hear it read aloud. Below are two examples.
  - **Interactive Phonics Readers** (Scholastic): This software combines leveled decodable reading practice with phonemic awareness, phonics, spelling, and fluency games. Students can click on a word and hear it sounded out. Explicit, targeted

corrective feedback is provided when children make errors during the games. Students automatically advance through the program based on phonics mastery.

- **Reading Mentor** (Learning Resources): Children build words using Reading Rods, then place them into the hardware to hear the word sounded out. This electronic tool is ideal for learning centers and for children needing immediate corrective feedback (e.g., special needs children and English-language learners).

## PROBLEM 10: My student frequently mispronounces words either at the beginning, in the middle, or at the end.

**Possible Solutions:** Some students have difficulties visually analyzing words or do not analyze words in their entirety. These children need much practice in learning left-to-right progression and focusing on the word parts they frequently neglect. Errors can occur in the initial, medial, or final position.

- **Initial errors:** Errors at the beginning of words are infrequent and generally involve letter reversals *(b-d)*, confusion of similar words *(when, then)*, or words beginning with single vowels that represent a schwa sound *(again, other)*. Use forced-choice exercises that draw attention to confusing beginning letters, alphabetizing exercises, or calling attention to the schwa sound at the beginning of words. I suggest building a picture dictionary with children, doing multiple alphabetizing exercises, and doing exercises in which answers are visually similar at the end so children will have to focus on other parts of the word. For example:

  *The _____ ran up the tree. mat cat bat*

- **Medial errors:** For these errors, reteach vowel sounds. You might also have children copy or trace words and complete exercises in which the answers vary only in the middle. For example:

  *The _____ ran up the tree. cot cut cat*

- **Ending errors:** These errors are common. Focus children's attention on larger word parts, such as word families or common affixes. In addition, provide exercises in which the word choices vary only at the end. For example:

  *The _____ ran up the tree. cab cat can*

## PROBLEM 11: My student frequently substitutes words.

**Possible Solutions:** Substitutions are the most common type of oral reading error. Frequent substitution of words is often a sign of an over-reliance on context and not enough attention to the sound-spelling relationships in words. Sometimes children substitute an occasional word because their natural speech patterns and vocabulary differ from the language of the text. However, frequent substitutions are a cause for concern. Make sure the text your student is reading is at her instructional level. Reinforce word-attack strategies by using prompts that focus on word parts.

### PROBLEM 12: My student frequently adds or leaves out words.

**Possible Solutions:** Your student may be making frequent additions to try and make the sentence fit his oral language patterns. Or he may be reading too rapidly to pay attention to each word. Ask him questions about the text that require him to read entire sentences or passages in which additions occurred.

Omissions may indicate that the student is editing out words that he doesn't need to make meaning from the text or that don't fit his dialect. At other times, a child may omit words because he has weak decoding skills and can't figure those words out. The letters and syllables children omit most frequently are those at the end of words. They may be paying too little attention to that part of words, reading too quickly, experiencing dialect interference, or having difficulty decoding the phonic elements. Children sometimes omit entire lines of print because they're having trouble keeping their place on the page or with the concept of return sweeps. Use a place marker as long as they need one.

If the number of words your student omits decreases when he's reading an easier passage, he probably has decoding difficulties. If the number of omissions stays the same, he has fluency difficulties. When the child omits a word, point out the word and ask him to pronounce it. If he can't, help him blend the word. You might want to have him preread the passage silently before reading aloud. Having the child point to each word as he reads can also be helpful. But don't continue this technique for a long time. One technique I like is to record children's readings and then have them listen to their recordings and follow along to discover their omissions.

### PROBLEM 13: My student often repeats words while she's reading.

**Possible Solutions:** Repetitions are sometimes caused by slow and labored word recognition. The child sounds out the word, then repeats it at a more natural pace. Or the child may realize that the reading doesn't make sense and "retrace" her steps to try to figure out the text.

This indicates that the child is self-monitoring her comprehension of text but that the text may be too difficult for independent or instructional reading. Call your student's attention to repetitions if they are a recurring problem. Echo readings and repeated readings can be helpful. In addition, record the child reading a passage and have her listen and follow along to recognize when and why repetitions are occurring. Note that some children repeat words during oral reading not because they have difficulties decoding, but rather because they're nervous or lack confidence in their abilities. Encouragement and praise are great remedies, as are opportunities for the child to rehearse the text before reading aloud.

## PROBLEM 14: My student reads word by word in a slow, labored manner.

**Possible Solutions:** "Slow word-recognition can adversely affect fluency and comprehension" (Beck, 1981). This sluggish word-recognition ability is common at the beginning of formal reading instruction. However, if it continues, slow reading may indicate reading problems. There are many reasons why children fail to read fluently. Allington (1983) cites the following:

- **Lack of exposure:** Some children have never been exposed to fluent reading models. These children come from homes in which little or no reading occurs and few opportunities exist to experience books.
- **The good-reader syndrome:** In school, good readers are more likely to receive positive feedback, and more attention is paid to reading with expression and making meaning from text. Poor readers receive less positive feedback, and the focus of instruction is often on figuring out words or attending to word parts.
- **Lack of practice time:** Good readers generally spend more time reading during instructional time and therefore become better readers. Good readers also engage in more silent reading. This additional reading practice leads to positive gains in their reading growth.
- **Frustration:** Good readers have more encounters with text that is at their independent reading level, whereas poor readers frequently encounter text at their frustration level. This generally results in poor readers' giving up because they make so many errors.

- **Missing the "why" of reading:** Good readers tend to view reading as making meaning from text, whereas poor readers tend to view reading as trying to read words accurately.

To find out why your student is reading so slowly, ask him to read a passage from a book at a lower reading level. If he reads the passage slowly, the problem is probably a result of poor fluency. If he can read the text easily, the problem is probably due to decoding or comprehension difficulties. One way to determine whether the child is having decoding or comprehension difficulties is to have him read an on-level passage, then ask a series of questions. If he answers 75% or more of the questions accurately, the problem is one of weak decoding skills. If this is so, have him read from material at a lower level. Make time for repeated reading or echo readings, and use dictated stories for reading instruction and practice.

Another way to determine the child's problem is to give him a running list of the words he'll encounter in the text. If he can't recognize 95% of the words, then decoding may be the problem. If the child does recognize 95% or more of the words, but has difficulty reading, then comprehension or fluency is the problem.

## PRINCIPLE 2: Assess, assess, assess.

A comprehensive diagnosis of each child is necessary because the causes of reading difficulties can be many. I am constantly reminded of the old saying, "An ounce of prevention is worth a pound of cure." And certainly the best way to prevent reading difficulties is through properly designed instruction and early detection of difficulties. Frequently monitor the child's progress to determine the causes of reading difficulties and the success of your teaching strategies. However, even with these safeguards, some children's struggles with learning to decode words persist.

You can assess children in many ways. These include (California Department of Education, 1996):

- **screening assessments** of phonics, phonemic awareness, concepts of print, alphabet recognition, writing
- **checklists** of phonics, phonemic awareness, alphabet recognition, reading and writing attitudes
- **miscue analysis** (running records) for assessing students' reading accuracy, identifying and analyzing consistent reading errors, and determining instructional and independent reading levels

- **individual and group-administered tests** including formal assessments, basal reading program tests, and reading inventories
- **portfolios** containing student work throughout the year

**Formal assessments** for decoding abilities (listed on page 257) are generally administered by specialists and provide greater reliability and validity than other forms of assessment. However, many **informal assessments**, such as observation and miscue analysis, can give you vital information to guide instruction and determine what a child already knows so that you can explicitly reinforce it. It's important to collect diagnostic information daily, weekly, and monthly.

I recommend using a nonsense-word test beginning in Grade 2. This type of assessment relies on a student's decoding abilities to figure out unknown words and eliminates the risk of decoding using sight-word knowledge.

## Observation

Frequent and systematic observations of children's reading abilities will help you modify instruction to meet individual needs. Select a few children each week to observe formally. A miscue analysis is a valuable assessment tool for these observations. Oral reading miscues reveal a child's reading strategies. (For more information on taking a miscue analysis, see the "Running Records" description in *The Early Detection of Reading Difficulties* by M. Clay, 1985.) It's useful to take a miscue analysis about every six weeks for all children. Repeat this more often for children who need intervention.

To begin, establish a system or observation schedule. For example, you might choose one child per school day, keeping the dated record and analysis in each child's file to monitor his or her progress during the year. Select a time when you can hear the child read

A child's miscues can provide valuable insights.

without interruptions, such as when other children are engaged in individual quiet reading.

Use the following steps to complete a miscue analysis:

- **Choose a book for the child to read.** Select a book the child knows but that isn't too familiar. If it's too familiar, the reading may not reveal much information about the child's thinking. Make a photocopy of the story that you'll use to mark the child's miscues while he or she reads. This photocopy, along with your observational marks, will be your miscue analysis.
- **Ask the child to read the whole book aloud.** You might want to record the reading for later review.
- **Listen carefully as the child reads and use your copy of the story to record any miscues.** Examples of some usual marking conventions are shown in the chart on page 283. Miscues are errors that are graphophonic (visual cues), syntactic (structure cues), or semantic (meaning cues) in nature.
- **When the child has finished reading, tally the miscues.** Begin by examining the symbols or marking conventions you used to indicate what the child is doing. Consider the child's successes and reading miscues. Ask yourself why the child makes each error. To determine what cues the child depends on, ask yourself:

  - Does the child use visual cues from letters and words, such as *they* for *them*? *(visual)*
  - Does the child use context clues to construct meaning? Inaccurate reading that makes sense indicates that the child is using knowledge of oral language. *(meaning)*
  - Does the child use knowledge of the grammatical structure of language? The child's own oral language may influence his or her reading of the text. *(structure)*

Figure out as well as you can what cues the child uses, recording by the miscue a *V* for visual cues, an *M* for meaning cues, and an *S* for structure cues. A child may use one or more types of cues for any miscue. By analyzing each miscue in this way you can get an indication of the strategies the child is using, as well as those he or she is not using or is overusing. Also notice instances of self-correction, considering what additional information the child uses to self-correct. Self-correction is an important skill in good reading. Finally, make any notes on the miscue analysis about behaviors during the session. All of this information will assist you in assessing the child.

After you've analyzed the miscues, look for patterns that indicate what the child is paying attention to. Notice the information sources that are used and those that are neglected. As the child rereads the book and reads other texts, help him or her pay attention to the cues that he or she is consistently using as well as those he or she should be using.

You can help children who aren't looking at visual information by increasing their opportunities to write and to read familiar books. Help them form words and learn about words by providing letter cards and magnetic letters.

Sometimes, when children are paying close attention to print, they run the risk of losing the meaning. If that happens, draw their attention to pictures and have conversations about illustrations. Extending stories through art or other activities is another way to help children think about meaning. Also encourage them to talk about the story. Notice whether they use the language of the particular story.

Avoid focusing instruction solely on students' weaknesses. This can become frustrating for them. Continue to highlight those reading strategies children use effectively and provide them with practice using a variety of strategies. Acknowledge their progress and praise their efforts.

## SOME USUAL CONVENTIONS

| | |
|---|---|
| **Accurate Reading** | ✔ ✔ ✔ (checks follow text pattern) |
| **Substitution** | set  (child)<br>sent  (text) |
| **Attempt** | s–se–set<br>sent |
| **Self-Correction** | set<br>sent          SC |
| **Omission** | – (or circle word)<br>sent |
| **Insertion** | is (or use caret)<br>sent |
| **Teacher Told** | – (or underline word)<br>sent  T |
| **Repetition**<br>(of word/sentence) | R2    (number indicates repeats)<br>sent (or use wavy lines) |

## PRINCIPLE 3: Select the appropriate literature for instructional and independent use.

It is critical that you select the appropriate literature for instructional and independent uses. Not only do children need to be reading successfully during formal reading instruction, they also need to have successful independent reading opportunities each day. Children need to be placed with text that gives them a sense of control and comfort. The relationship between silent reading (and out-of-school reading) and reading growth has been well documented (Rosenshine & Stevens, 1984). As Allington (1984) pointed out, good first-grade readers read about 1,900 words a week, whereas their poorer reading counterparts read only about 16 words a week. You can't become a skilled reader if you rarely read. The following guidelines highlight the differences among a child's independent, instructional, and frustration reading levels.

*"*To encourage optimal progress with the use of any of these early reading materials, teachers need to be aware of the difficulty level of the text relative to a child's reading level. Regardless of how well a child already reads, high error rates are negatively correlated with growth; low error rates are positively linked with growth. A text that is too difficult, then, not only serves to undermine a child's confidence and will, but also diminishes learning itself.*"*
(California Department of Education, 1996)

### Levels of Reading

**Independent or Free Reading Level** The level at which a student can read a text without the teacher's assistance. Comprehension should average 90% or better, and word recognition should average 95% or better.

**Instructional Reading Level** The level at which a student should receive reading instruction. The student reads the text with teacher guidance and is challenged enough to stimulate reading growth. Comprehension should average 75% or better, and word recognition should average 90% or better.

**Frustration Reading Level** The level at which a student cannot read a text adequately. At this level, the student often shows signs of discomfort. Comprehension averages 50% or less, and word recognition averages less than 90%.

To determine a child's independent, instructional, and frustration reading levels, use an individual reading inventory. This inventory asks a student to read a passage or series of passages. The reading is generally followed by sight-word tests, graded word lists, or comprehension questions. The following are commercially available reading inventories:

- Scholastic Reading Inventory (Scholastic, 2007)
- Analytical Reading Inventory (Merrill, 10th Edition, 2014)
- Basic Reading Inventory (Kendall/Hunt, 11th Edition, 2012)
- Classroom Reading Inventory (William C. Brown, 2013)
- Ekwall/Shanker Reading Inventory (Allyn and Bacon, 6th Edition, 2013)
- Burns/Roe Informal Reading Inventory (Houghton Mifflin, 2010)
- New Sucher-Allred Reading Placement Inventory (McGraw-Hill, 1986)

You can also create your own informal reading inventories by selecting 100-word passages from books of various levels. Ask a child to read a passage at each level, count the reading errors, and then ask a series of comprehension questions. Use this informal assessment to select the appropriate literature for each child.

Use a readability formula such as the Spache, Dale-Chall, or Fry to determine reading levels. Another popular leveling system is the Lexile system, developed by MetaMetrics Inc. This system is currently being used to level trade books. Each book is assigned a level (for example, 200–400 = Grade 1), and children's scores on a reading inventory are used to help the teacher match a child to an appropriate text. You can use a selection from each level to create your own reading inventory. Of course, matching children to text requires more than a readability formula or test. A child's background knowledge and experiences, as well as his or her interest in a particular topic, can affect the difficulty of a text.

## PRINCIPLE 4: Maintain consistency.

In order for intervention to be successful, consistency must be maintained among the many teachers and reading specialists who are instructing the child. I frequently see that each instructor is providing thorough programs of instruction. But the methods each is using sometimes differ and conflict in terms of emphasis. For example, a child might be receiving explicit phonics instruction with practice reading controlled text in the Resource Room, yet be reading uncontrolled text, in which using knowledge of sight words and context clues is emphasized, in the regular classroom. The result is confusion that stands in the way of the child's learning to read. Make sure to communicate with the other teachers of the children in your classroom. Maintain consistency among the methods or techniques used. For example, if the child receives a lot of instruction in sounding out words in the Resource Room, reinforce this learning while the child is reading in your classroom.

---

**"The paradox of children with reading problems is that they get more phonics instruction than children reading at expected levels, yet they have continued difficulties decoding words. . . . I recommend a two-pronged solution—first, providing a clear and consistent program of phonics instruction, and second, providing copious amounts of reading of connected text."** (Stahl, 1997)

---

# Fluency

**Fluency** is the ability to read smoothly, easily, and readily with freedom from word-recognition problems. Fluency is necessary for good comprehension and enjoyable reading (Nathan & Stanovich, 1991). A lack of fluency is characterized by a slow, halting pace; frequent mistakes; poor phrasing; and inadequate intonation (Samuels, 1979)— all the result of weak word-recognition skills. Fluent reading is a major goal of reading instruction because decoding print accurately and effortlessly enables students to read for meaning. That is, students who decode words effortlessly can focus more of their conscious attention on making meaning from text.

Fluency begins in Stage 2, the "Confirmation, Fluency, and Ungluing from Print" stage (see Chall's Stages of Reading Development, pages 24–26), around Grades 2 to 3 for many students. During this fluency stage, the reader becomes "unglued" from the print; that is, students can recognize many words quickly and accurately by sight and are skilled at sounding out those they don't recognize by sight. A fluent reader can:

- read at a rapid rate (pace—the speed at which oral or silent reading occurs)
- automatically recognize words (smoothness/accuracy—efficient decoding skills)

- phrase correctly (prosody—the ability to read a text orally using appropriate pitch, stress, and phrasing)

Although research has shown that fluency is a critical factor in reading development, many teachers and publishers have failed to recognize its importance to overall reading proficiency. Few teachers teach fluency directly, and elementary reading textbooks give fluency instruction short shrift. Consequently, Allington (1983) has called fluency the "neglected goal" of reading instruction.

> The number of words read correctly per minute is an important indicator of a student's progress in all aspects of reading—decoding, fluency, and comprehension. Twenty years of research by Germann (Edformation, 2001) has shown strong correlations between a student's standardized achievement test scores and the number of words he reads correctly per minute (WCPM).

## Six Ways to Develop Fluency

1 **Model Fluent Reading** Students need many opportunities to hear texts read. This can include daily teacher read-alouds, audiobooks, and books read by peers during book-sharing time. It's particularly critical for poorer readers who've been placed in a low reading group to hear text read correctly because they are likely to repeatedly hear the efforts of other poor readers in their group. They need proficient, fluent models; that is, they need to have a model voice in their heads to refer to as they monitor their own reading. While you read aloud to students, periodically highlight aspects of fluent reading. For example, point out that you read dialogue the way you think the character might have said it or that you speed up your reading when the text becomes more exciting and intense. Talk about fluency—how to achieve it, and why it's important. Continually remind students that, with practice, they can

> **Three Signs of Automaticity**
> A child is reading fluently if he can:
> - read with expression.
> - read aloud and then retell the story or describe the content of the selection (decode and comprehend at the same time).
> - comprehend equally well a similar passage read or listened to.

become fluent readers. Another important benefit of daily read-alouds is that they expose students to a wider range of vocabulary.

**2 Provide Direct Instruction and Feedback** Direct instruction and feedback in fluency includes, but isn't limited to, independent reading practice, fluent reading modeling, and monitoring students' reading rates. The following are ways to include this instruction in your classroom:

- Explicitly teach students the sound-spelling correspondences they struggle with, high-utility decoding and syllabication strategies, and a large core of sight words.
- Time students' reading occasionally and compare their results to grade-level expectations.
- Find alternatives to round-robin reading so that students are reading every story multiple times—both fiction and nonfiction.
- Use speed drills to increase students' automaticity with phonics patterns and sight words.
- Motivate students to read more, using incentives, charting, and rewards.

**3 Provide Reader Support** Readers need to practice reading both orally and silently. There are several ways to support students' oral reading without evoking the fear and humiliation struggling readers often feel when called on to read aloud. Below are the most popular techniques (always use text at the student's instructional level that enables you to model natural language patterns):

- Reading aloud simultaneously with a partner or small group
- Echo reading
- Readers Theater
- Choral reading
- Paired repeated readings
- Audiobooks

**4 Use Repeated Readings of One Text** Repeated reading, a popular technique developed by Samuels (1979), has long been recognized as an excellent way to help students achieve fluency. It has been shown to increase reading rate and accuracy and to transfer to new texts. As a child reads a passage at his or her instructional level, the teacher times the reading. The teacher then gives feedback on word-recognition errors and the number of words per minute the child has read accurately and records this data on a graph. The child then

## Nonfluent Readers

Nonfluent readers read slowly and spend so much time trying to identify unfamiliar words that they have trouble comprehending what they're reading.

Automaticity theory, developed by LaBerge and Samuels (1974), helps explain how reading fluency develops. *Automaticity* refers to knowing how to do something so well you don't have to think about it. As tasks become easier, they require less attention and practice. Think of a child learning to play basketball. As initial attention is focused on how to dribble the ball, it's difficult for the child to think about guarding the ball from opponents, shooting a basket, or even running quickly down the court. However, over time, lots of practice makes dribbling almost second nature. The player is ready to concentrate on higher-level aspects of the game.

For reading, automaticity refers to the ability to accurately and quickly recognize many words as whole units. The advantage of recognizing a word as a whole unit is that words have meaning, and less memory is required for a meaningful word than for a meaningless letter. The average child needs between 4 and 14 exposures to a new word to recognize it automatically. However, children with reading difficulties need 40 or more exposures to a new word. Therefore, it's critical that students get a great deal of practice reading stories at their independent reading level to develop automaticity (Beck & Juel, 1995; Samuels, Schermer, & Reinking, 1992).

To commit words to memory, children need to decode many words sound by sound, and then progress to recognizing the larger word chunks. Now, instead of focusing on sounding out words sound by sound, the reader can read whole words, thereby focusing attention on decoding and comprehension simultaneously. In fact, the hallmark of fluent reading is the ability to decode and comprehend at the same time.

practices reading the same selection independently or with a partner. The process is repeated and the child's progress plotted on the graph until the child masters the passage (see right). This charting is effective because (1) students become focused on their own mastery of the task and competing with their own past performance, and (2) students have concrete evidence that they are making progress. In addition, repeating the words many times helps students build a large sight-word vocabulary.

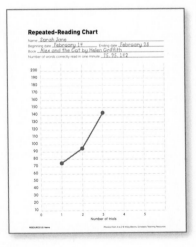

**5** **Cue Phrase Boundaries in Text** One of the characteristics of proficient (fluent) readers is the ability to group words together in meaningful units—syntactically appropriate phrases. "Proficient reading is characterized not only by fast and accurate word recognition, but also by readers' word chunking or phrasing while reading connected discourse" (Rasinski, 1994). Students who are having trouble with comprehension may not be putting words together in meaningful phrases as they read. Their oral reading is characterized by a choppy, word-by-word delivery that impedes comprehension. In addition, some of these students disregard punctuation, committing what I term "punctuation drive-bys." They fly through the punctuation, thereby chunking the text in unnatural ways. These students need instruction in phrasing written text into appropriate segments.

One way to help students learn to recognize and use natural English phrase boundaries—and thus improve their phrasing, fluency, and comprehension—is phrase-cued text practice. *Phrase-cued text* is a short passage marked by a slash (or some other visual) at the end of each phrase break. The longer pause at the end of the sentence is marked by a double slash (//). The student practices reading the passage with the slashes, then without. Here's an example:

*In the summer/ I like to swim/ at the beach.//*

**6** **Provide Students With Easy Reading Materials** Students need an enormous amount of individualized reading practice in decodable materials that are not too difficult. Fluency develops through a great deal of practice in reading stories in which students can use sound-spelling (phonics) strategies (as opposed to contextual strategies—trying to figure out words using one or two letters and sentence or picture clues) to figure out a majority of the unfamiliar words. It is critical that practice reading materials be at a child's instructional or independent reading levels, NOT at a child's frustration level. That is, at least 90% of the words should be known.

## Fluency: The Next Generation

The next wave of researchers are expanding their definition of fluency and exploring the effect of automaticity in areas such as performing phonemic-awareness tasks, recognizing the letters of the alphabet, stating common sound-spellings, and identifying high-utility sight words. What they are discovering is that it is not just a student's accuracy in recognizing letters and words or performing phonemic-awareness tasks, rather it is the speed with which a child can perform these tasks that is critical and telling in terms of the child's reading progress.

If you are teaching the primary grades, you may wish to use the following assessments to check the fluency of your students.

## Phonemic Awareness

Researchers at the University of Oregon are leading the way in developing assessments to test the accuracy and speed with which children can perform phonemic awareness tasks such as sound matching and oral segmentation. For more information on these assessments, see http://dibels.uoregon.edu.

## Alphabet Recognition

Display the Letter-Name Assessment (see online and page 31). Ask the student to say the letter names as quickly as possible. Time the student. Slow, labored identification is common with children who struggle with reading. Much work with recognizing and writing the letters in and out of order will be necessary to help these children catch up. A good follow-up to this test is to have children name the sound that each letter stands for.

## Phonics

Use the Nonsense Word Test (see online and page 258) to assess students' phonics skills. This assessment is NOT recommended for children in Grade 1, since the concept of nonsense words may confuse them. However, nonsense words work well with older children because older children can recognize a word by sight and thus are required to use their knowledge of sound-spellings to decode each word.

## Sight Words

To develop fluency, children must be able to recognize the most common words in written English automatically. The San Diego Quick Assessment (see online and page 258) can be used to assess each child's automaticity with these words. Again, it is not just accuracy, but speed that must be monitored.

If available, use the TOWRE (Test of Word Reading Efficiency) in place of this assessment. The TOWRE is a nationally normed test available from PRO-ED. The address is: PRO-ED, 8700 Shoal Creek Blvd., Austin, TX 78757-6897.

See *Building Fluency* (Scholastic, 2002) by Wiley Blevins for more information. Another great resource for planning and implementing fluency instruction is *Tiered Fluency Instruction: Supporting Diverse Learners in Grades 2–5* by Chase Young and Timothy Rasinski (Capstone Classroom, 2016).

# Phonics and the English-Language Learner: Guiding Principles

With the dramatic increase of English-language learners in our nation's classrooms, most teachers are busy searching for those special techniques and materials to help these students learn the sound-spelling system of English and/or quickly transfer their native language skills to their new language. From 2013–2014, the percentage of English learners in the U.S. reached 9.3%, an increase from previous years. Now, there are nearly 5 million ELLs in the United States. Although more than 70% of these students are native Spanish-speakers, these students have incredibly diverse language needs. Many enter the United States with variant levels of English proficiency and a wide range of reading skills in their native languages. Some speak and read languages that use a Roman alphabetic system like that of English; others do not. All these factors, and others, make teaching English-language learners quite complex.

However, these students do have a few things in common: all these students need explicit instruction in how English works, a focus on vocabulary development, lots of safe opportunities to use language, wide reading of simple English texts, and an opportunity to transfer their existing skills into English.

Below I present my ten guiding principles for you to consider as you plan your phonics instruction for these English newcomers.

## PRINCIPLE 1: Connect phonics and vocabulary instruction.

You can do this by choosing key content words to match the phonics skills you are teaching. For example, when teaching the /b/ sound, use key words (and visuals) that children need to learn in order to communicate effectively in school. These may include *ball, book, boy, black,* and *bathroom*. Below is a sample of how one teacher accomplishes this. She chooses one key phonics-related word each day to focus on.

### Word of the Day

- Tell children that every day of the school year, there will be a special "word of the day." When children hear this word throughout the lesson, they should clap their hands and say the word. They will earn one point for each time they hear, see, or use the word throughout the lesson. You will keep track on the board of the points they earn.

- Introduce the word of the day: *ball*.
- Display the ball picture card. Tape it to the board and write the word *ball* beside it. Point to the ball and say: *ball*. Ask children to repeat.
- Then show a real ball. Pass it around the class. Ask children to bounce it and say "ball."
- Then toss the ball to a student. Tell the student: *Say your name as I toss you the ball. Then toss it to another child.*

If you are using word lists to practice phonics skills, decode the words first, then revisit the list to work on meaning. That is, define the words and help students use them in speaking, reading, and writing.

| Sample /a/a Word List | |
|---|---|
| *cat* (use visual) | *can* (use visual) |
| *bat* (use visual) | *pan* (use visual) |
| *fat* (use visual) | *man* (use visual) |
| *hat* (use visual) | *fan* (use visual) |
| *mat* (use visual) | *ran* (use action) |
| *sat* (use action) | *van* (use visual) |

Note that many English-language learners, especially those who have already learned to read in their native language, can become good "word callers" with limited understanding of what they are reading, unless we focus on meaning during decoding instruction. It is essential that we build oral language while teaching English sound-spellings to our students.

# PRINCIPLE 2: Use kinesthetic activities to connect a sound to an action.

Instruction that activates various modalities of learning not only makes the instruction more engaging, it helps students more easily retain the new information. Below is an example of how I teach the /b/ sound, spelled *Bb*, to my English-language learners. You can connect any sound to an action. I have included the actions I use for each letter-sound in the chart that follows.

**Bounce the Ball (Sample Lesson for /b/b)**

- Display a ball. Say: *This is a ball. What is this?* (Children chorally say "ball.")
- Bounce the ball as children watch. As you bounce the ball, say /b/ /b/ /b/.
- Tell children: *The word ball begins with the /b/ sound.* Say: *Listen as I say the word* ball—/b/. . . all, ball.
- Have a volunteer bounce the ball as he or she says /b/ /b/ /b/. Then have all the children pantomime bouncing a ball as they say /b/ /b/ /b/.
- Then tell children to say /b/ as they write the capital and small letter *Bb* five times on paper or dry-erase boards.

## A–Z Motions

| | | |
|---|---|---|
| **Aa** | apple | /a/ /a/ apple. Bite that apple. |
| **Bb** | bounce ball | /b/ /b/ /b/ Bounce the ball (fast and slow). |
| **Cc** | click camera | /k/ /k/ /k/ Click the camera to take a picture of classroom objects and friends. |
| **Dd** | dance | /d/ /d/ /d/ Dance around the desk (change beat and speed). |
| **Ee** | slowly start engine | /e/ /e/ /e/ Slowly goes the engine up the hill. |
| **Ff** | fan | /f/ . . . /f/ . . . the fan starts, then /f/ /f/ /f/ /fffffffffffff/ Can you feel the fan's breeze? |
| **Gg** | girl gulping grape juice | /g/ /g/ /g/ /g/ /g/ /g/ (quickly) The girl gulps her grape juice—that's good! |
| **Hh** | hot (fan face with hands) | /h/ /h/ /h/ It's so hot in here (fan yourself with your hands). |
| **Ii** | icky insect | /iiiii/ That's an icky insect! |
| **Jj** | jump rope | /j/ /j/ /j/ Swing the jump rope 'round and 'round. |
| **Kk** | kick the ball | /k/ /k/ Kick that ball. |
| **Ll** | lick the lollipop | lllllllllick the lllllollipop (Must stick tongue out to lick the lollipop.) |
| **Mm** | say /mmm/ when tasting yummy food | /mmmmmm/ That mango/melon/(local food) smells/tastes yummy. |
| **Nn** | no-no-no | nnnnnnno (Shake head as you say "no.") |
| **Oo** | say "o" during doctor visit | /oooooo/ Keep your mouth open as the doctor looks inside. |
| **Pp** | popcorn popping | /p/ /p/ /p/ Listen to the popcorn pop in the pot. |

| Qq | timer ticking to quitting time | /kw/ /kw/ /kw/ /kw/ quit. Move hands as if moving around a clock—start at 12, then go to 6 (point out that *qu* appears together and together stands for the /kw/ sounds). |
|---|---|---|
| Rr | racing racecar | /rrrrrrrrrr/ Listen to the racecar race around the track (louder and softer). |
| Ss | hissing snake | /sssss/ Can you hear the snake hissing? |
| Tt | tick-tock like a clock | /t/ . . /t/ . . /t/ . . /t/ The clock ticks and tocks (swing head back and forth slowly). |
| Uu | push open an umbrella | /u/ /u/ Up goes the umbrella. |
| Vv | play the violin | /vvvvvv/ /vvvvvv/ /vvvvv/ /vvvvvv/ /vvvvvv/ /vvvvv/ /vvvvv/ Play the violin (pantomime playing violin while singing /vvvv/ at different tones). |
| Ww | wash the window | /w/ /w/ Wash the window (move hands in a circle as if washing a window). |
| Xx | cut the box open | /ks/ /ks/ /ks/ Cut the box open with your scissors. |
| Yy | spin a yo-yo | /y/ /y/ /y/ See the yo-yo go up and down. |
| Zz | zip a zipper | /zzzzz/ Zip that zipper up and down. |

# PRINCIPLE 3: Work on articulation.

Help students focus on the unique sounds in English and the differences between English and their native language. Take time to model how sounds are formed when you introduce a new sound or when students experience difficulty pronouncing a specific sound. Below are a few examples. I suggest that you use small mirrors during instruction. Have students watch how you make a specific sound, then they can attempt making the sound by paying close attention to the position of their lips, teeth, mouth, and tongue in their mirrors.

**Long e** The long-*e* sound is a "smile sound." Your mouth is in a smiling position when making the sound. The lips are close together, but not closed. Ask students to say the sound with you, noticing your mouth position. Have students place their hand under the chin as they say each of the following sounds in sequence: /ē/, /i/, /ā/, /e/, /a/, /ī/, and /o/. Help them notice that their mouth opens slightly with each sound.

**Short o** The short-*o* sound is a doctor sound. Your mouth is in the shape of a small circle when making the sound, as if the doctor is checking your tonsils and you are saying, "ah." Ask students to say the sound. Point out that the mouth is in the shape of a circle. Draw a circle on the board. Tell children that the letter *o* is also a circle. We write the letter *o* when we make the /o/ sound.

**Consonant /b/** The /b/ sound is a stop sound and, therefore, cannot be stretched. The lips are together when the sound is made. Have students place their hand in front of their mouth as they say the /b/ sound. Ask them whether they feel a puff of air. (They should.) Then have them put their hand on their throat and say /b/. Ask them whether they feel a slight shaking, or vibration. (They should.)

Contrast this with the /p/ sound, in which the lips are also together, a puff of air is felt, but there is no throat vibration.

**Consonant /f/** The /f/ sound is made by placing the top teeth on the bottom lip. Make the sound for students. Stretch the sound to emphasize the way it is formed. Then have students make the sound, using their mirrors to note the position of their teeth and lips. You may wish to contrast the /f/ sound with the /v/ sound. Both sounds are made in the same way. However, the /f/ sound produces no throat vibration; the /v/ sound does.

## PRINCIPLE 4: Learn the confusing sounds for each language your students speak.

Many languages do not have words with consonant blends. Some languages have few words that end in consonants. Other languages may have similar sounds, but students will consistently replace these sounds when speaking. Spanish speakers often replace the /b/ sound when they read words beginning with the letter *v*, or children who speak one of the many Asian languages tend to replace the long-*e* sound with the more familiar /i/ sound. Following is a chart showing the similarities and differences in English and several other languages.

For your Spanish-speaking students, be aware that the following sounds might present pronunciation difficulties:

- Might replace /d/ in *dog* with /th/, saying "thog."
- Might replace /j/ in *jar* with /ch/, saying "char."
- Might replace /r/ in *ran* with a rolled *r*.

- Might replace /v/ in *very* with /b/, saying "bery."
- Might replace /z/ in *zoo* with /s/, saying "soo."
- Might replace /sh/ in *ship* with /ch/, saying "chip."
- Might add an "eh" to the beginning of words with *s*-blends, saying "eschool" for *school*.
- Might drop the final consonant off words that end with blends, saying "car" for *cart*, "sin" for *sing*, or "pos" for *post*.

## Language Chart

| ENGLISH | | SPANISH | | CANTONESE | |
|---|---|---|---|---|---|
| Sound | Spelling | Sound Transfer? | Spelling Match? | Sound Transfer? | Spelling Match? |
| /b/ | b | yes | yes | @ | no |
| /k/ | c | yes | yes | yes | no |
| /d/ | d | @ | yes | @ | no |
| /f/ | f | yes | yes | yes | no |
| /g/ | g | yes | yes | @ | no |
| /h/ | h | yes | no | yes | no |
| /j/ | j | no | no | @ | no |
| /l/ | l | yes | yes | yes | no |
| /m/ | m | yes | yes | yes | no |
| /n/ | n | yes | yes | yes | no |
| /p/ | p | yes | yes | yes | no |
| /kw/ | qu | yes | no | @ | no |
| /r/ | r | @ | @ | no | no |
| /s/ | s | yes | yes | yes | no |
| /t/ | t | yes | yes | yes | no |
| /v/ | v | yes | yes | no | no |
| /w/ | w | yes | yes | yes | no |
| /ks/ | x | yes | yes | no | no |
| /y/ | y | yes | yes | yes | no |
| /z/ | z | no | no | no | no |

Note: @ stands for approximately.

| ENGLISH | | SPANISH | | CANTONESE | |
|---|---|---|---|---|---|
| Sound | Spelling | Sound Transfer? | Spelling Match? | Sound Transfer? | Spelling Match? |
| /ch/ | ch | yes | yes | @ | no |
| /sh/ | sh | no | no | no | no |
| /hw/ | wh | no | no | no | no |
| /th/ | th | @ | no | no | no |
| /ng/ | ng | yes | yes | yes | no |
| /a/ | a | @ | no | no | no |
| /e/ | e | yes | yes | @ | no |
| /i/ | i | @ | no | @ | no |
| /o/ | o | @ | no | @ | no |
| /u/ | u | @ | no | @ | no |
| long a | a_e, ai, ay | yes | no | @ | no |
| long e | ee, ea, y | yes | no | @ | no |
| long i | i_e, igh, y | yes | no | @ | no |
| long o | o_e, oa, ow | yes | no | @ | no |
| long u | u_e, ue | yes | no | @ | no |
| /r/ as in *star* | ar | @ | yes | @ | no |
| /ôr/ | or | @ | yes | @ | no |
| /ûr/ as in *her, bird, hurt* | er, ir, ur | @ | yes (er) no (ir, ur) | @ | no |
| /är/ as in *chair* | air, ear | no | no | no | no |
| /oi/ | oi, oy | yes | yes | @ | no |
| /ou/ | ou, ow | yes | no | @ | no |
| /ô/ as in *ball* | aw, aw, all | @ | no | @ | no |
| /o͞o/ as in *moon* | oo, ew | yes | no | @ | no |
| /o͝o/ as in *book* | oo | no | no | @ | no |

Note: @ stands for approximately.

# Language Chart

| ENGLISH | | VIETNAMESE | | HMONG | |
|---|---|---|---|---|---|
| Sound | Spelling | Sound Transfer? | Spelling Match? | Sound Transfer? | Spelling Match? |
| /b/ | b | @ | yes | @ | no |
| /k/ | c | yes | yes | yes | no |
| /d/ | d | @ | yes | yes | yes |
| /f/ | f | yes | no | yes | yes |
| /g/ | g | yes | yes | @ | no |
| /h/ | h | yes | yes | yes | yes |
| /j/ | j | @ | no | no | no |
| /l/ | l | yes | yes | yes | yes |
| /m/ | m | yes | yes | yes | yes |
| /n/ | n | yes | yes | yes | yes |
| /p/ | p | yes | yes | @ | yes |
| /kw/ | qu | yes | yes | no | no |
| /r/ | r | no | no | no | no |
| /s/ | s | yes | yes | yes | no |
| /t/ | t | @ | yes | @ | yes |
| /v/ | v | yes | yes | yes | yes |
| /w/ | w | no | no | no | no |
| /ks/ | x | no | no | no | no |
| /y/ | y | no | no | yes | yes |
| /z/ | z | yes | no | no | no |
| /ch/ | ch | no | no | yes | no |
| /sh/ | sh | yes | no | yes | no |
| /hw/ | wh | no | no | no | no |
| /th/ | th | @ | yes | no | no |
| /ng/ | ng | yes | yes | yes | no |
| /a/ | a | @ | yes | yes | yes |
| /e/ | e | @ | yes | no | no |
| /i/ | i | no | no | no | no |
| /o/ | o | @ | yes | @ | yes |
| /u/ | u | yes | no | no | no |
| long a | a_e, ai, ay | @ | no | @ | no |

Note: @ stands for approximately.

| ENGLISH | | VIETNAMESE | | HMONG | |
| --- | --- | --- | --- | --- | --- |
| Sound | Spelling | Sound Transfer? | Spelling Match? | Sound Transfer? | Spelling Match? |
| long e | ee, ea, y | yes | no | yes | no |
| long i | i_e, igh, y | yes | no | yes | no |
| long o | o_e, oa, ow | @ | no | no | no |
| long u | u_e, ue | no | no | no | no |
| /r/ as in *star* | ar | no | no | no | no |
| /ôr/ | or | no | no | no | no |
| /ûr/ as in *her, bird, hurt* | er, ir, ur | no | no | no | no |
| /är/ as in *chair* | air, ear | no | no | no | no |
| /oi/ | oi, oy | @ | yes | no | no |
| /ou/ | ou, ow | yes | no | @ | no |
| /ô/ as in *ball* | aw, aw, all | yes | no | @ | no |
| /o͞o/ as in *moon* | oo, ew | @ | no | yes | no |
| /o͞o/ as in *book* | oo | @ | no | no | no |

Note: @ stands for approximately.

## PRINCIPLE 5: Use music, body language, and realia/visuals to teach new words and concepts.

Students can quickly learn the melody of many simple songs that contain repetition. Although they may not know all the words, students become more aware of the sounds of English and begin to attend to common words and phrases. In addition, body language and realia (real objects) or visuals (photos, simple drawings on the board) are the quickest ways to teach concrete concepts and vocabulary. If the student already knows the object or action, then the task involves attaching a new label (an English word) to the object or action. A visual can facilitate this learning. When teaching a new word, write it on the board and highlight the pronunciation and key sound-spellings.

## PRINCIPLE 6: Connect phonics learning to writing and real-life applications.

English-language learners will accelerate their learning of English vocabulary and its sound-spelling system as they attempt to write for real-life purposes, such as creating a list of favorite foods, writing a letter to a friend, or making labels for classroom and home objects. In addition, provide students opportunities to think about and use the words in meaningful situations. For example, to focus on the word *collect* you might ask students, "Would you rather collect bugs or games?" Students are required to consider the meaning of the word, connect it to their personal lives, then respond using their level of English proficiency.

## PRINCIPLE 7: Use technology.

There is no safer or less threatening learning situation than that experienced by one student working on the computer. Publishers are beginning to increase the options for young language learners. The best programs combine vocabulary learning with basic decoding instruction. Below are two exemplary resources.

### *Zip, Zoom English* by Scholastic
This software program, originally developed and tested by the research team at PREL (Pacific Resources for Education and Learning), is divided into levels based on vocabulary learning and phonics skills. The program is accompanied by carefully leveled books developed under the guidance of renowned literacy educator and researcher Elfrieda Hiebert. For more information, see www.scholastic.com.

### *Sesame Street* language learning DVDs
These language DVDs are divided into content categories, such as food and clothing. Each DVD is in two languages: English and the child's native language. These DVDs take advantage of Sesame Street's extensive work across the world and are ideal for at-home language learning. For more information, see www.sesameworkshop.com.

## PRINCIPLE 8: Provide each student with a bilingual dictionary.

Students need easy access to words they don't know. Having a bilingual dictionary at their fingertips is helpful. Even students who are just learning to read can benefit from a simple bilingual picture dictionary. You, a teacher's aide, or your school's language specialist can use this picture dictionary during instruction and one-on-one discussions with each student.

## PRINCIPLE 9: Provide comprehensible input.

This means that you need to adjust your speech during instruction based on the level of students' English proficiency. For example, focus on speaking a bit more slowly and carefully articulating sounds. It is common for native English speakers to trail off at the end of a word. Therefore, you will need to more carefully and clearly enunciate words during instruction. In addition, provide clear, simple explanations of learning tasks. Offer visuals, gestures, hands-on explanations, or body language to fully communicate the task. And, rather than constantly repeating yourself, paraphrase for students.

## PRINCIPLE 10: Modify your response expectations based on each student's level of language proficiency.

See the following chart in order to better understand the types of responses you can reasonably expect from your students as they progress in learning English. You can also use this chart to monitor each student's language development.

| Levels of Language Proficiency | | |
| --- | --- | --- |
| **Beginning** | **Intermediate** | **Advanced** |
| These students respond using one-word answers, pointing, or saying "yes" or "no" to questions posed to them. Some students will even go through a silent phase, in which they are taking in language but still feel too insecure or unsure to attempt to use it. This phase is one that many language learners experience. | These students respond using simple phrases and sentences. Model responses using sentence stems to assist these students. For example, hold an apple as you say, "I like the apple." Hand the apple to a student and ask, "What do you like?" Assist the student in responding by providing the sentence starter, "I like the _____ ." | These students respond using complete sentences, often with more complex sentence structures, yet they still have issues with English grammar and structure. When students respond using incorrect grammar, model by restating their answer using correct grammar, then move on. Instead of pointing out every language error, consistent modeling of correct language usage will be most beneficial. |

# Standard English Learners

## Who Are SELs?

Students come to our classrooms with a wide range of literacy experiences, including great variation in the amount and form of English spoken at home. Standard English Learners (SELs) are native speakers of English who are ethnic minorities and use an ethnic-specific nonstandard dialect of English, such as African American English (AAE) or Chicano English (CE). That is, the home language of these students differs from the language of schools. (White students who live in impoverished communities can also be categorized as Standard English Learners.)

African American English and Chicano English are language systems with well-informed rules for sounds, grammar, and meanings. They show the influence of other languages, such as sounds, words, and sentence patterns in languages from Mexico (Náhuatl) or West Africa. Over years, these dialects have developed into consistent rule-based forms of English common to a particular community. They reflect how the people in these communities hear and "feel" language.

African American English and Chicano English serve as a way for many students to identify with their specific community and are often a source of pride. In schools, it is important to take an additive approach to language learning for all our students. That is, we use the language students come to school with and add on the rules of standard English and the contexts in which both (standard English and AAE or CE) is most appropriately used. Students who can successfully code switch between the two forms of English increase their chances of success in academic and workplace settings. This is the goal of our instruction.

## How Can I Help SELs?

Throughout the year you will help students speaking African American English and Chicano English to learn standard English by focusing on those places where AAE and CE differ from standard English and on those patterns that will have the most immediate impact on the students' reading, writing, and speaking development.

These students will need help in understanding that what is appropriate in one setting is not appropriate in another, so they can shift easily and competently between varieties in different social contexts. Instruction will be more effective if it identifies nonstandard varieties of English as different, rather than inferior. All students should be taught standard English in a way that respects their home language.

The charts on pages 307–310 focus only on phonics and phonemic-awareness differences associated with African American English and Chicano English. These are a small subset of the many differences prevalent in these forms of English, most of which deal with grammatical issues. When focusing on phonics and phonemic awareness, provide students with clear enunciation examples during lessons targeting difficult sounds. Additional practice can be provided during small-group phonics and spelling lessons.

## Instructional Routines and Activities

### Contrastive Analysis Drills

Instructional activities that compare and emphasize the differences in standard English versus African American English and Chicano English in terms of usage and situational appropriateness are the most effective. These include a wide variety of translation drills and discrimination drills.

**Translation Drills** In translation drills, students are given a sentence in African American English or Chicano English and asked to restate it orally or rewrite it in standard English (or vice versa). You can create sentences based on a specific instructional focus for the week or drawn from students' writing and speech. It is helpful for teachers of SELs to keep a notebook where they record these sample sentences throughout the week for use in these drills.

**Discrimination Drills** In discrimination drills, students hear or see two words or sentences and are asked if they are the same or different. For example, the teacher might say "help" and "hep" or "I help my sister" and "I hep my sister." A discussion of the difference (e.g., sounds in a specific word) provides articulation and spelling support. There are many different types of discrimination drills, including word discrimination drills (focusing on pronunciation of specific sounds in words), sentence discrimination drills (focusing on pronunciation of words in context), and home-school discrimination drills (focusing on the difference between home dialect and standard English).

## On-the-Spot Recasting

**Recasting**, or restating the words of a particular student speech to address pronunciation or grammar issues, is best done one-on-one or during small-group lessons in which the focus is on speaking using standard English. We never want to create a classroom environment in which students feel too intimidated to talk for fear of being wrong or constantly criticized. Remember that you are the best model of standard English for your students and should take available opportunities to provide these explicit models.

Since pronunciations can greatly affect students' spelling of words, use oral-segmentation exercises for target sounds. For example, distribute sound boxes to students (see next page). Say a word, such as *sand* (ending in a consonant blend, which breaks the phonological rules of AAE and CE). Clearly state and stretch the sounds. Have students repeat it. Then have them write one letter in each box for each sound they hear. This guided spelling practice (dictation) will assist students in remembering the standard English pronunciation and correct spelling.

**Sample Sound Box**

| | | | |
|---|---|---|---|
| | | | |

**Additional Resources**

The California Department of Education provides additional resources for Standard English Learner professional development.

The California Adoption Framework, Chapter 9, provides background information on Standard English Learners and designing culturally and linguistically responsive teaching. Go to http://www.cde.ca.gov/ci/rl/cf/elaeldfrmwrksbeadopted.asp.

For more information on African American English, go to https://www.sdcity.edu/Portals/0/CollegeServices/StudentServices/LearningCommunities/Af.Amer.CRR.PDF.

For more information on Chicano English, go to http://achieve.lausd.net/cms/lib08/CA01000043/Centricity/Domain/217/MEXICAN%20AMERICAN_TEACHER%20GUIDE.PDF.

# African American English (AAE) Phonics Differences

| English/Language Arts Skill | Linguistic Differences and Instructional Modifications |
|---|---|
| **Digraph *th* as in *bathroom*** | For many speakers of African American English, the initial /th/ sound in function words like *this* and *then* is often produced as a /d/ sound. In some words, such as *thing* and *through*, the /th/ sound is produced as a /t/ sound. At the ends of words and syllables, such as *bathroom*, *teeth*, *mouth*, and *death*, the /th/ sound is replaced by the /f/ sound. In the word *south*, it is replaced by the /t/ sound (sout'). This will affect students' spelling and speaking. Students will need articulation support prior to spelling these words. |
| **Final consonant *r*** | Many speakers of African American English drop the /r/ sound in words. For example, these students will say *sto'* for *store* or *do'* for *door*. They might also replace it with the "uh" sound, as in *sista* for *sister*. Clearly pronounce these words, emphasizing the /r/ sound. Have students repeat several times, exaggerating the sound before spelling these words. |
| ***r*-blends** | Many speakers of African American English drop the /r/ sound in words with *r*-blends. For example, these students will say *th'ow* for *throw*. Clearly pronounce these words in the lesson, emphasizing the sounds of the *r*-blend. Have students repeat several times, exaggerating the sound. |
| **Final consonant *l* and final *l*-blends** | Many speakers of African American English drop the /l/ sound in words, particularly in words with *-ool* and *-oal* spelling patterns, such as *cool* and *coal*, and when the letter *l* precedes the consonants *p*, *t*, or *k*, as in *help*, *belt*, and *milk*. The /l/ sound might also be dropped when it precedes /w/, /j/, /r/ (a'ready/already); /u/, /o/, /aw/ (poo/pool), or in contractions with *will* (he'/he'll). These students will drop the *l* when spelling these words, as well. Provide additional articulation support prior to reading and spelling these words. |
| **Final consonant blends (when both are voiced as in *ld* or voiceless as in *sk*)** | Many speakers of African American English drop the final letter in a consonant blend (e.g., *mp*, *nd*, *nt*, *nk*, *kt*, *pt*, *ld*, *lt*, *lk*, *sk*, *st*, *sp*) or consonant blend sounds formed when adding *-ed* (e.g., /st/ as in *missed* or /pt/ as in *stopped*). For example, they will say *des'* for *desk*. Clearly pronounce the final sounds in these words and have students repeat several times, exaggerating the sound. |
| **Other final consonants** | Many speakers of African American English drop the final consonant in a word when the consonant blend precedes a consonant, as in *bes'kind* for *best kind*. They also drop the final consonant sound in words ending in *-ed*, as in *rub* for *rubbed*. Provide additional articulation support prior to reading and spelling these words. |

## African American English (AAE) Phonics Differences *continued*

| English/Language Arts Skill | Linguistic Differences and Instructional Modifications |
|---|---|
| **Plurals** | When the letter *s* is added to a word ending in a consonant blend, such as *test (tests)*, many speakers of African American English will drop the final sound. This is due to the phonological (pronunciation) rules of AAE that restricts final consonant blends. Therefore they will say *tes'* or *tesses*. These students will need additional articulation support. |
| **Contractions** | Many speakers of African American English drop the /t/ sound when pronouncing the common words *it's*, *that's*, and *what's*. These words will sound more like *i's*, *tha's*, and *wha's*. These students will need additional articulation support in order to pronounce and spell these words. |
| **Short vowels *i* and *e*** | When the /i/ and /e/ sounds appear before the consonants *m* or *n* in words such as *pen/pin* and *him/hem*, many speakers of African American English won't pronounce or hear the difference. Focus on articulation, such as mouth position for each vowel sound, during lessons. |
| **Inflectional ending -*ing*** | Many speakers of African American English will pronounce words with -*ing* as /ang/. For example, they will say *thang* for *thing*. Emphasize the /i/ sound in these words to help students correctly spell and pronounce them. |
| **Stress patterns** | Many speakers of African American English place the stress on the first syllable in two-syllable words instead of the second syllable (more common in standard English). For example, they will say *po'lice* instead of *police*. These students will need additional articulation support in order to pronounce these words. |
| **Homophones** | Due to the phonological rules of AAE, many words that are not homophones in standard English become homophones in African American English. This will affect students' spelling and understanding of these words. Some examples include *find/fine, run/rung, mask/mass, pin/pen, coal/cold, mold/mole*. Focus on articulation, such as mouth position, and differences in meaning for each word pair during lessons. |

# Chicano/a English (CE) Phonics Differences

| English/Language Arts Skill | Linguistic Differences and Instructional Modifications |
|---|---|
| **Final consonants** | Many speakers of Chicano English will drop sounds in words or syllables that end with multiple final consonants, thereby reducing the consonant cluster sound to one consonant sound. For example, they will say *mine* instead of *mind* or *harware* for *hardware*. This occurs when consonant clusters are voiced and unvoiced, as in *prized/price*, *worst/worse*, and *strict/strick*. Other consonant clusters that are problematic include *ft*, *sk*, *sp*, and *pt*. This will affect students' spelling and speaking. Students will need articulation support prior to spelling these words. Clearly pronounce these words. Have students repeat them several times, exaggerating the final consonant sounds before spelling these words. |
| **Digraphs /ch/ and /sh/** | Many speakers of Chicano English will switch (or merge) the /ch/ and /sh/ sounds. This is more common in Tejanos (Chicanos from Texas) than Californianos. Some examples include *teacher/teasher*, *watch/wash*, *chop/shop*, *chair/share*, *shake/chake*, *shy/chy*, *shame/chame*, *shop/chop*, *share/chair*. Provide articulation support. Exaggerate the sound and have students repeat. |
| **Consonants /z/ and /v/** | Many speakers of Chicano English will replace the /z/ sound with /s/ and the /v/ sound with /f/. Examples include *prized/price*, *fuzz/fuss*, *raise/race*, *(When I don't race my hand the teasher makes a fuzz)* and *lives/lifes*, *save/safe (The hero safe many lifes)*. Articulation support connected to word meanings will be beneficial. |
| **Homophones** | Because of the unique phonological rules of Chicano English, many words that are not homophones in standard English will sound like homophones. For example, *fine* will be used for both *fine* and *find*, *tin* will be used for both *tin* and *ten*, and *pen* will be used for both *pen* and *pin*. Clearly pronounce these words and focus on mouth position during articulation. Have students repeat several times, exaggerating the sound before spelling these words. |
| **Stress patterns** | In Chicano English, stress is placed on one-syllable prefixes as well as roots. The stress is also often elongated. For example, speakers of Chicano English will say *tooday* for *today*, *deecide* for *decide*, and *reepeat* for *repeat*. Articulation work will be needed. |
| **Intonation** | Many speakers of Chicano English will exhibit a pattern of intonation that is different from standard English. This pattern, derived from the Náhuatl language, involves a rise and sustain (or rise and fall) at the end of a phrase or sentence. For example, these speakers will say, "Doont be baaad." Provide articulation support. Recast students' sentences to emphasize intonation when working with students one-on-one. |

| Chicano/a English (CE) Phonics Differences *continued* | |
|---|---|
| **English/Language Arts Skill** | **Linguistic Differences and Instructional Modifications** |
| **Consonant /w/** | Many speakers of Chicano English will pronounce the /w/ sound with an added breath so that it sounds more like /wh/. As a result, words like *with* sound like *whith* and *will* like *whill*. This might also affect students' spelling. Contrast words beginning with *w* and *wh* and have students keep lists in their writing notebooks. |
| **Pronouncing "the"** | The word *the* is pronounced in standard English with a schwa sound *(thuh)* before a word beginning with a consonant, and a long-*e* sound *(thee)* before a word beginning with a vowel. Many speakers of Chicano English will use the schwa pronunciation for all words. Point out the distinction and usage of each pronunciation. |

# Professional Development

On a final note, I encourage you to continue your professional development. Below is a list of professional organizations and periodicals that might assist you. In addition, continue to take graduate-level courses and share your expertise with fellow teachers. As I travel around the country, I am struck by the wealth of untapped talent of our nation's school teachers. I constantly remind teachers that their best resources for professional growth are their colleagues. I wish you all much success!

## Professional Organizations

American Library Association (ALA)
50 E. Huron
Chicago, IL 60611

American Speech-Language-Hearing Association (ASLHA)
2200 Research Boulevard
Rockville, MD 20850

Council for Learning Disabilities
11184 Antioch Road
Overland Park, KS 66210

International Dyslexia Association
40 York Road
Baltimore, MD 21204

International Literacy Association (ILA)
P.O. Box 8139
Newark, DE 19714-8139

Learning Disabilities Association of America (LDA)
4156 Library Road
Pittsburgh, PA 15234

National Center for Learning Disabilities
32 Laight Street
New York, NY 10013

ProLiteracy
104 Marcellus Street
Syracuse, NY 13204

Reading Is Fundamental (RIF)
1730 Rhode Island Ave. NW
Suite 1100
Washington, DC 20036

## Professional Periodicals

*Annals of Dyslexia*
International Dyslexia Association
40 York Road
Baltimore, MD 21204

*Educational Research Quarterly*
P.O. Box 571
Grambling, LA 71245

*Educational Technology*
Educational Technology Publications
700 Palisade Avenue
Englewood Cliffs, NJ 07632

*Elementary School Journal*
The University of Chicago Press Journals
1427 East 60th Street
Chicago, IL 60637

*Exceptional Children*
Council for Exceptional Children
2900 Crystal Drive
Suite 1000
Arlington, VA 22202

*Gifted Child Quarterly*
National Association for Gifted Children
1331 H Street NW
Suite 1001
Washington, DC 20005

*Harvard Educational Review*
Harvard University Graduate School of Education
8 Story Street
Cambridge, MA 02138

*Reading Research Quarterly*
International Literacy Association
P.O. Box 8139
Newark, DE 19714-8139

*The Reading Teacher*
International Literacy Association
P.O. Box 8139
Newark, DE 19714-8139

*Scholastic Teacher*
Scholastic Inc.
557 Broadway
New York, NY 10012-3999

# Bibliography

Adams, M. J. (1990). *Beginning to read: Thinking and learning about print*. Cambridge, MA: Massachusetts Institute of Technology.

Adams, M. J., Treiman, R., & Pressley, M. (1996). Reading, writing, and literacy. In I. Sigel & A. Renninger (Eds.), *Handbook of child psychology, 4*. New York: Wiley.

Akmajian, A., Demers, R. A., Farmer, A. K., & Harnish, R. M. (1995). *Linguistics: An introduction to language and communication*. (4th ed.). Cambridge, MA: MIT Press.

Alexander, A., Anderson, H., Heilman, P. C., Voeller, K. S., & Torgesen, J. K. (1991). Phonological awareness training and remediation of analytic decoding deficits in a group of severe dyslexics. *Annals of Dyslexia, 41*.

Allington, R. L. (1983). The reading instruction provided readers of different reading abilities. *Elementary School Journal, 83*

Allington, R. L. (1984). Oral reading. In D. D. Pearson (Ed.), *Handbook of reading research*. New York: Longman.

Allington, R. L., & Walmsley, S. A. (Eds.). (1995). *No quick fix: Rethinking literacy programs in America's elementary schools*. New York: Teachers College Press.

Anderson, R. C., Hiebert, E. H., Scott, J. A., & Wilkinson, I. A. G. (1985). *Becoming a nation of readers: The report of the commission on reading*. Champaign, IL: Center for the Study of Reading and National Academy of Education.

August, D. (2003). Supporting the development of English literacy in English language learners—Key issues and promising practices. Center for Research on the Education of Students Placed At Risk (CRESPAR), Johns Hopkins University.

Avery, P., & Ehrlich, S. (1992). *Teaching American English pronunciation*. New York: Oxford University Press.

Bailey, M. H. (1967). Utility of phonic generalizations in grades one through six. *The Reading Teacher, 20*.

Ball, E. W., & Blachman, B. A. (1991). Does phoneme awareness training in kindergarten make a difference in early word recognition and developmental spelling? *Reading Research Quarterly, 26(1)*.

Baskwill, J., & Whitman, P. (1995). *Learner support program: A framework for classroom-based reading intervention*. New York: Scholastic.

Bateman, B. (1979). Teaching reading to learning disabled and other hard-to-teach children. In L. A. Resnick and P. A. Weaver (Eds.), *Theory and practice of early reading, 1*. Hillsdale, NJ: Erlbaum.

Bear, D. R., Templeton, S., Invernizzi, M., & Johnston, F. (1996). *Words their way: Word study for phonics, vocabulary, and spelling instruction*. Englewood Cliffs, NJ: Merrill/Prentice-Hall.

Bear, D. R., Templeton, S., Invernizzi, M., & Johnston, F. (2016). *Words their way: Word study for phonics, vocabulary, and spelling instruction* (6th ed.). Upper Saddle River, NJ: Pearson.

Beck, I. (1981). Reading problems and instructional practices. In G. E. MacKinnon and T. G. Waller (Eds.), *Reading research: Advances in theory and practice, 2*. New York: Academic Press.

Beck, I., & Juel, C. (1995, Summer). The role of decoding in learning to read. *American Educator*.

Beck, I., & McCaslin, E. (1978). An analysis of dimensions that affect the development of code-breaking ability in eight beginning reading programs. LRDC Report No. 1978/6. Pittsburgh, PA: University of Pittsburgh Learning Research and Development Center.

Berninger, V. W., Thalberg, S. P., De Bruyn, I., & Smith, R. (1987). Preventing reading disabilities by assessing and remediating phonemic skills. *School Psychology Review, 16(4)*.

Biemiller, A. (1970). Relationships between oral reading rates for letters, words, and simple text in the development of reading achievement. *Reading Research Quarterly, 13*.

Biemiller, A. (1970). The development of the use of graphic and contextual information as children learn to read. *Reading Research Quarterly, 6*.

Bishop, A., & Bishop, S. (1996). *Teaching phonics, phonemic awareness, and word recognition*. Westminster, CA: Teacher Created Materials.

Blevins, W. (1996). *Quick-and-easy learning games: Phonics*. New York: Scholastic.

Blevins, W. (1997). *Phonemic awareness activities for early reading success*. New York: Scholastic.

Blevins, W. (2001). *Building fluency: Lessons and strategies for reading success*. New York: Scholastic.

Blevins, W. (2011). *Week-by-week phonics and word study activities for the intermediate grades*. New York: Scholastic.

Blevins, W. (2012). *Teaching phonics: A flexible, systematic approach to building early reading skills*. New York: Scholastic.

Blevins, W. (2016). *A fresh look at phonics: Common causes of failure and 7 ingredients for success*. Thousand Oaks, CA: Corwin.

Bond, G. L., Tinker, M. A., Wasson, B. B., & Wasson, J. B. (1994). *Reading difficulties: Their diagnosis and correction*. Boston: Allyn and Bacon.

Bowen, J. D. (1985). *TESOL techniques and procedures*. Rowley, MA: Newbury House.

Bristow, P. S. (1985). Are poor readers passive readers? Some evidence, possible explanations, and potential solutions. *The Reading Teacher, 39*(3).

Bruck, M. (1992). Persistence of dyslexics' phonological awareness deficits. *Developmental Psychology, 28*(5).

Bruck, M., & Treiman, R. (1990). Phonological awareness and spelling in normal children and dyslexics: The case of initial consonant clusters. *Journal of Experimental Child Psychology, 50.*

Bryant, P., & Bradley, L. (1985). *Children's reading problems: Psychology and education*. New York: Basil Blackwell.

Bryson, B. (1990). *The mother tongue: English and how it got that way*. New York: Avon.

Burmeister, L. E. (1968). Usefulness of phonic generalizations. *The Reading Teacher, 21.*

Burmeister, L. E. (1968). Vowel pairs. *The Reading Teacher, 21.*

Burmeister, L. E. (1969). The effect of syllabic position and accent on the phonemic behavior of single vowel graphemes. In J. A. Figurel (Ed.), *Reading and realism*. Newark, DE: International Reading Association.

Burmeister, L. E. (1971). Content of a phonics program based on particularly useful generalizations. In N. B. Smith (Ed.), *Reading methods and teacher improvement*. Newark, DE: International Reading Association.

Burmeister, L. E. (1975). *Words: From print to meaning*. Reading, MA: Addison-Wesley.

Byrne, B., & Fielding-Barnsley, R. (1991). Evaluation of a program to teach phonemic awareness to young children. *Journal of Educational Psychology, 83*(4).

Byrne, B., & Fielding-Barnsley, R. (1991). *Sound foundations*. Artarmon, New South Wales, Australia: Leyden Educational Publishers.

Cairney, T. & Munsie, L. (1992). *Beyond tokenism: Parents as partners in literacy*. Australian Reading Association.

California Department of Education. (1996, Summer). *Teaching reading: A balanced, comprehensive approach to teaching reading in prekindergarten through grade three*. Sacramento, CA.

Carbo, M. (1988). The evidence supporting reading styles: A response to Stahl. *Phi Delta Kappan, 70.*

Carnine, L., Carnine, D., & Gersten, R. (1984). Analysis of oral reading errors made by economically disadvantaged students taught with a synthetic-phonics approach. *Reading Research Quarterly, 19.*

Caroline, Sister Mary. (1960). *Breaking the sound barrier: A phonics handbook*. New York: Macmillan.

Carroll, J. B. (1990, May). Thoughts on reading and phonics. Paper presented at the National Conference on Research in English, Atlanta, GA.

Carroll, J. B., Davies, P., & Richman, B. (1971). *Word frequency book*. Boston: Houghton Mifflin.

Castiglioni-Spalten, M. L., & Ehri, L. C. (2003). Phonemic awareness instruction: Contribution of articulatory segmentation to novice beginners' reading and spelling. *Scientific Studies of Reading, 7*(1).

Chall, J. S. (1967). *Learning to read: The great debate*. New York: McGraw-Hill.

Chall, J. S. (1983). *Stages of reading development*. New York: McGraw-Hill.

Chall, J. S. (1996). *Stages of reading development*. Orlando, FL: Harcourt.

Chall, J. S., & Popp, H. (1996). *Teaching and assessing phonics: Why, what, when, how*. Cambridge, MA: Educators Publishing Service.

Chaney, J. H. (1993). Alphabet books: Resources for learning. *The Reading Teacher, 47*(2).

Clark, D. B., & Uhry, J. K. (1995). *Dyslexia: Theory and practice of remedial instruction*.

Clay, M. (1979). *The early detection of reading difficulties*. Portsmouth, NH: Heinemann.

Clay, M. (1985). *The early detection of reading difficulties*. (3rd ed.). Portsmouth, NH: Heinemann.

Clay, M. (1991). *Becoming literate: The control of inner control*. Portsmouth, NH: Heinemann.

Clay, M. (1993). *An observation survey of early literacy achievement*. Portsmouth, NH: Heinemann.

Clay, M. (1993). *Reading recovery: A guidebook for teachers in training*. Portsmouth, NH: Heinemann.

Clymer, T. (1963). Utility of phonics generalizations in the primary grades. *The Reading Teacher, 16*.

Criscuolo, N. (1979). Activities that help involve parents in reading. *The Reading Teacher, 32*(4).

Cunningham, J. (1979). On automatic pilot for decoding. *The Reading Teacher, 32*(4).

Cunningham, P. M. (1975–76). Investigating a synthesized theory of mediated word identification. *Reading Research Quarterly, 11*.

Cunningham, P. M. (1978, April). Decoding polysyllabic words: An alternative strategy. *Journal of Reading*.

Cunningham, P. M. (1990). The names test: A quick assessment of decoding ability. *The Reading Teacher, 44*.

Cunningham, P. M. (1995). *Phonics they use: Words for reading and writing*. New York: HarperCollins.

Cunningham, P. M., & Cunningham, J. W. (1992). Making words: Enhancing the invented spelling-decoding connection. *The Reading Teacher, 46*(2).

Diamond, L., & Mandel, S. (1996). Building a powerful reading program: From research to practice. Discussion sponsored by California Education Policy Seminar and California State University Institute for Education Reform.

Diegmueller, K. (1996, May/June). The best of both worlds. *Teacher Magazine*.

Dolby, J. L., & Resnikoff, H. L. (1963). *Prolegomena to a study of written English*. Palo Alto, CA: Lockheed Missiles and Space Company.

Dougherty, M. (1923). *How to teach phonics*. Boston: Houghton Mifflin.

Duffelmeyer, F. A., & Black, J. L. (1996). The names test: A domain-specific validation study. *The Reading Teacher, 50*(2).

Durkin, D. (1978). *Phonics, linguistics, and reading*. New York: Teachers College Press.

Durkin, D. (1993). *Teaching them to read*. Boston: Allyn and Bacon.

Durr, W. K. (Ed.). (1970). *Reading difficulties: Diagnosis, correction, and remediation*. Newark, DE: International Reading Association.

Durrell, D. (1963). *Phonograms in primary grade words*. Boston: Boston University.

Ehri, L. C. (1987). Learning to read and spell words. *Journal of Reading Behavior, 19*.

Ehri, L. C. (1991). Development of the ability to read words. In R. Barr, M. Kamil, P. Mosenthal, & P. D. Pearson (Eds.), *Handbook of Reading Research, 2*. New York: Longman.

Ehri, L. C. (1992). Reconceptualizing the development of sight word reading and its relationship to recoding. In P. Gough, L. Ehri, & R. Treiman (Eds.), *Reading acquisition*. Hillsdale, NJ: Erlbaum.

Ehri, L. C. (1994). Development of the ability to read words: Update. In R. Ruddell, M. Ruddell, & H. Singer (Eds.), *Theoretical models and processes of reading*. Newark, DE: International Reading Association.

Ehri, L. C. (1995). Phases of development in reading words. *Journal of Research in Reading, 18*.

Ehri, L. C. (2005). Learning to read words: Theory, findings, and issues. *Scientific Studies of Reading, 9*(2).

Ehri, L. C., & Robbins, C. (1992). Beginners need some decoding skill to read words by analogy. *Reading Research Quarterly, 27*(1).

Ekwall, E., & Shanker, J. (1988). *Diagnosis and remediation of the disabled reader*. Boston: Allyn and Bacon.

Ekwall, E., & Shanker, J. (1993). *Locating and correcting reading difficulties*. New York: Merrill.

Eldredge, J. L. (1995). *Teaching decoding in holistic classrooms*. Englewood Cliffs, NJ: Merrill.

Elkonin, D. B. (1973). In J. Downing (Ed.), *Comparative reading: Cross national studies of behavior and processes in reading and writing*. New York: Macmillan.

Felton, R. H., & Wood, F. B. (1989). Cognitive deficit in reading disability and attention deficit disorder. *Journal of Learning Disabilities, 22*.

Flesch, R. (1955). *Why Johnny can't read: And what you can do about it*. New York: Harper & Row.

Foorman, B. (1995, October). *School Psychology Review*.

Foorman, B., Jenkins, L., & Francis, D. J. (1993). Links among segmenting, spelling, and reading words in first and second grades. *Reading and Writing: An Interdisciplinary Journal, 5*.

Foorman, B., Novy, D. M., Francis, D. J., & Liberman, D. (1991). How letter-sound instruction mediates progress in first-grade reading and spelling. *Journal of Educational Psychology, 83*(4).

Fox, B. J. (1996). *Strategies for word identification: Phonics from a new perspective*. Englewood Cliffs, NJ: Prentice-Hall.

Fox, B., & Routh, D. (1975). Analyzing spoken language into words, syllables, and phonemes: A developmental study. *Journal of Psycholinguistic Research, 4*.

Freedman, S. W., & Calfee, R. C. (1984). Understanding and comprehending. *Written Communication, 1*.

Fry, E. (1995). *How to teach reading: For teachers and parents.* Laguna Beach, CA: Laguna Beach Educational Books.

Fry, E. B., Fountoukidis, D. L., & Polk, J. K. (1985). *The new reading teacher's book of lists.* Englewood Cliffs, NJ: Prentice-Hall.

Fry, E. B., Kress, E. & Fountoukidis, D. L. (1993). *The new reading teacher's book of lists.* Englewood Cliffs: NJ: Prentice-Hall.

Gaskins, I. (1997). Word identification: Research-based maxims. Paper presented at International Reading Association, Preconvention Institute.

Gaskins, I., Downer, M., Anderson, R. C., Cunningham, P. M., Gaskins, R., Schommer, M., & the Teachers of Benchmark School. (1988). A metacognitive approach to phonics: Using what you know to decode what you don't know. *Remedial and Special Education, 9*(1).

Gaskins, I., Ehri, L., Cress, C., O'Hara, C., & Donnelly, K. (1996–97). Procedures for word learning: Making discoveries about words. *The Reading Teacher, 50*(4).

Gentile, L. M., & McMillan, M. M. (1991). Reading, writing and relationships: The challenge of teaching at risk students. *Reading Research and Instruction, 30*(4).

Gillet, J. W., & Temple, C. (1994). *Understanding reading problems: Assessment and instruction.* New York: HarperCollins.

Golinkoff, R. M. (1978). Phonemic awareness skills and reading achievement. In F. B. Murray & J. H. Pikulski (Eds.), *The acquisition of reading: Cognitive, linguistic, and perceptual prerequisites.* Baltimore, MD: University Park.

Goodman, Y. M. (1987). *Reading miscue inventory.* New York: Richard C. Owen.

Gough, P. B., & Juel, C. (1991). The first stages of word recognition. In L. Rieben & C. A. Perfetti (Eds.), *Learning to read: Basic research and its implications.* Hillsdale, NJ: Erlbaum.

Gough, P. B., & Walsh, M. A. (1991). Chinese, Phoenicians, and the orthographic cipher of English. In S. A. Brady & D. P. Shankweiler (Eds.), *Phonological process in literacy: A tribute to Isabelle Y. Liberman.* Hillsdale, NJ: Erlbaum.

Gough, P. B., Alford, J. A. Jr., & Holley-Wilcox, P. (1981). Words and context. In O. J. L. Tzeng & H. Singer (Eds.), *Perception of print.* Hillsdale, NJ: Erlbaum.

Gough, P. B., Juel, C., & Roper-Schneider, D. (1983). A two-stage model of initial reading acquisition. In J. A. Niles & L. A. Harris (Eds.), *Searches for meaning in reading/language processing and instruction.* Rochester, NY: National Reading Conference.

Griffith, P. L., & Klesius, J. P. (1992). Kindergarten children's developing understanding of the alphabetic principle. Paper presented at the annual meeting of the National Reading Conference, San Antonio, TX.

Griffith, P. L., & Olson, M. W. (1992). Phonemic awareness helps beginning readers break the code. *The Reading Teacher, 45*(7).

Groff, P. (1971–72). Sequences for teaching consonant clusters. *Journal of Reading Behavior, 4.*

Groff, P. (1972). A phonemic analysis of monosyllabic words. *Reading World, 12.*

Groff, P. (1976). Blending: Basic process or beside the point? *Reading World, 15.*

Groff, P. (1977). *Phonics: Why and how.* Morristown, NJ: General Learning Press.

Haddock, M. (1976). Effects of an auditory and an auditory visual method of blending instruction on the ability of prereaders to decode synthetic words. *Journal of Educational Psychology, 68.*

Haddock, M. (1978). Teaching blending in beginning reading instruction is important. *The Reading Teacher, 31.*

Hanna, P. R., Hodges, R. E., Hanna, J. L., & Rudolph, E. H. (1966). *Phoneme-grapheme correspondences as cues to spelling improvement.* Washington, DC: U.S. Office of Education.

Harris, A. J., & Jacobson, M. D. (1972). *Basic elementary reading vocabularies.* New York: Macmillan.

Harris, A. J., & Sipay, E. R. (1990). *How to increase reading ability: A guide to developmental and remedial methods.* White Plains, NY: Longman.

Harris, T., & Hodges, R. (Eds.). (1995). *The literacy dictionary: The vocabulary of reading and writing.* Newark, DE: International Reading Association.

Haskell, D. W., Foorman, B. R., & Swank, P. R. (1992). Effects of three orthographic/ phonological units on first-grade reading. *Remedial and Special Education, 13*(2).

Hattie, J. A. C. (2009). *Visible learning: A synthesis of over 800 meta-analyses relating to achievement.* London, UK: Routledge.

Hattie, J. A. C. (2012). *Visible learning for teachers.* London, UK: Routledge.

Heilman, A. W. (1993). *Phonics in proper perspective* (7th ed.). New York: Merrill.

Henderson, E. (1967). *Phonics in learning to read: A handbook for teachers.* New York: Exposition Press.

Hiebert, E. H., & Sawyer, C. C. (1984). Young children's concurrent abilities in reading and spelling. Paper presented at the annual meeting of the American Educational Research Association, New Orleans, LA.

Hiebert, E., & Taylor, B. (1994). *Getting reading right from the start.* Boston: Allyn and Bacon.

Honig, B. (1995). *How should we teach our children to read?* Center for Systemic School Reform, San Francisco State University.

Honig, B. (1996). *Teaching our children to read: The role of skills in a comprehensive reading program.* Thousand Oaks, CA: Corwin Press.

Hull, M. A. (1994). *Phonics for the teacher of reading* (6th ed.), Upper Saddle River, NJ: Merrill.

Johns, J. L. (1980). First graders' concepts about print. *Reading Research Quarterly, 15.*

Johns, J. L., & Ellis, D. W. (1976). Reading: Children tell it like it is. *Reading World, 16.*

Johnson, D., & Bauman, J. (1984). Word identification. In P. D. Pearson, R. Barr, M. L. Kamil, & P. Mosenthal (Eds.), *Handbook of reading research.* New York: Longman.

Juel, C. (1988). Learning to read and write: A longitudinal study of fifty-four children from first through fourth grades. *Journal of Educational Psychology, 80.*

Juel, C. (1991). Beginning reading. In R. Barr, M. L. Kamil, P. Mosenthal, & P. D. Pearson (Eds.), *Handbook of reading research, 2.* New York: Longman.

Juel, C., & Roper-Schneider, D. (1985). The influence of basal readers on first-grade reading. *Reading Research Quarterly, 20.*

Juel, C., Griffith, P. & Gough, P. (1986). Acquisition of literacy: A longitudinal study of children in first and second grade. *Journal of Educational Psychology, 78.*

Just, M. A., & Carpenter, P. A. (1987). *The psychology of reading and language comprehension.* Boston: Allyn and Bacon.

Kress, J. E. (1993). *The ESL teacher's book of lists.* West Nyack, NY: Center for Applied Research in Education.

LaBerge, D., & Samuels, S. J. (1974). Toward a theory of automatic information processing in reading. *Cognitive Psychology, 6*(2).

LaPray, M., & Ross, R. (1969). The graded word list: Quick gauge of reading ability. *Journal of Reading, 12*(4).

Lesgold, A. M., & Curtis, M. E. (1981). Learning to read words efficiently. In A. M. Lesgold & C. A. Perfetti (Eds.), *Interactive processes in reading.* Hillsdale, NJ: Erlbaum.

Lesgold, A. M., & Resnick, L. B. (1982). How reading disabilities develop: Perspectives from a longitudinal study. In J. P. Das, R. Mulcahy, & A. E. Walls (Eds.), *Theory and research in learning disability.* New York: Plenum.

Lindamood, C. H., & Lindamood, P. C. (1979). *Auditory discrimination in depth.* Hingham, MA: Teaching Resources Corporation.

Lindfors, J. (1987). *Children's language and learning* (2nd ed.). Englewood Cliffs, NJ: Prentice-Hall.

Lovett, M. W. (1987). A developmental approach to reading disability: Accuracy and speed criteria of normal and deficient reading skill. *Child Development, 58.*

Lundberg, I. (1984, August). Learning to read. *School Research Newsletter.* Sweden: National Board of Education.

Lundberg, I., Frost, J., & Petersen, O. P. (1988). Effects of an extensive program for stimulating phonological awareness in preschool children. *Reading Research Quarterly, 23*(3).

Lyon, G. R. (1996). Learning disabilities. *The Future of Children: Special Education for Students With Disabilities, 6*(1).

Maclean, M., Bryant, P., & Bradley, L. (1987). Rhymes, nursery rhymes, and reading in early childhood. *Merrill-Palmer Quarterly, 33.*

Manguel, A. (1996). *A history of reading.* New York: Viking.

Mann, V. A. (1991). Language problems: A key to early reading problems. In B. Y. L. Wong (Ed.), *Learning about learning disabilities.* San Diego, CA: Academic Press.

Mann, V. A., Tobin, P., & Wilson, R. (1987). Measuring phonological awareness through the invented spellings of kindergartners. *Merrill-Palmer Quarterly, 33.*

Mantzicopoulos, P., & Morrison, D. (1992). Kindergarten retention: Academic and behavioral outcomes through the end of second grade. *American Educational Research Journal, 29.*

Manzo, A., & Manzo, U. (1993). *Literacy disorders: Holistic diagnosis and remediation.* New York: Harcourt.

Mathes, P., Simmons, D., & Davis, B. (1992). Assisted reading techniques for developing reading fluency. *Reading Research and Instruction, 31*(4).

Mazurkiewicz, A. (1976). *Teaching about phonics.* New York: St. Martin's Press.

McCarthy, P., Newby, R., & Recht, D. (1995). Results of an early intervention program for first grade children at risk for reading disability. *Reading Research Instruction, 34*(4).

McConkie, G. W., & Zola, D. (1987). Two examples of computer-based research on reading: Eye-movement monitoring and computer-aided reading. In D. Reinking (Ed.), *Reading and computers: Issues for theory and practice*. New York: Teachers College Press.

McMackin, M. C. (1993, Spring). The parents' role in literacy development: Fostering reading strategies at home. *Childhood Education*.

Miller, W. (1993). *Complete reading disabilities handbook*. West Nyack, NY: Center for Applied Research in Education.

Moats, L. C. (1995, Summer). The missing foundation in teacher education. *American Federation of Teacher*.

Moats, L. C. (1995). *Spelling: Development, disabilities, and instruction*. Timonium, MD: York Press.

Moats, L. C. (2000). *Speech to print*. Baltimore, MD: Paul Brookes Publishing Co., Inc.

Morris, D., Ervin, C., & Conrad, K. (1996). A case study of middle school reading disability. *The Reading Teacher, 49*(5).

Murphy, H. A. (1957). The spontaneous speaking vocabulary of children in primary grades. *Journal of Education, 140*.

Nathan, R. G., & Stanovich, K. E. (1991). The causes and consequences of differences in reading fluency. *Theory Into Practice, 30*.

National Center for Education Statistics. (2002). *Schools and staffing survey, 1999–2000*. Retrieved November 14, 2017, from http://nces.ed.gov/pubs2002/2002313.pdf.

National Clearinghouse for English Acquisition. (2002). The growing numbers of limited English proficient students.

National Institute of Child Health and Human Development. (2000). Report of the National Reading Panel. Teaching children to read: An evidence-based assessment of the scientific literature on reading and its implications for reading instruction. (NIH Publication No. 00-4769). Washington, DC: U.S. Government Printing Office.

Nicholson, T. (1992). Historical and current perspectives on reading. In C. J. Gordon, G. D. Lahercano, & W. R. McEacharn (Eds.), *Elementary reading: Process and practice*. Needham, MA: Ginn.

Open Court. (1995). *Collections for young scholars*. Peru, IL: Open Court Publishing.

Orton, S. T. (1937). *Reading, writing, and speech problems in children*. New York: Norton.

Osborn, J., Wilson, P., & Anderson, R. (1985). *Reading education: Foundations for a literate America*. Lexington, MA: D. C. Heath.

Pavlak, S. (1985). *Classroom activities for correcting specific reading problems*. West Nyack, NY: Parker Publishing.

Perfetti, C. A., & McCutcheon, D. (1982). Speech processes in reading. In N. Lass (Ed.), *Speech and language: Advances in basic research and practice, 7*. New York: Academic Press.

Phillips, B. M., Piasta, S. B., Anthony, J. L., Lonigan, C. J., & Francis, D. J. (2012). IRTs of the ABCs: Children's letter name acquisition. *Journal of School Psychology, 50*.

Phinney, M. Y. (1988). *Reading with the troubled reader*. Portsmouth, NH: Heinemann.

Piasta, S. B. (2014). Moving to assessment-guided differentiated instruction to support young children's alphabet knowledge. *The Reading Teacher, 68*.

Pinnell, G. S. (1994). Children's early literacy learning. Scholastic Literacy Research Paper.

Popp, H. M. (1964). Visual discrimination of alphabet letters. *The Reading Teacher, 17*.

Putnam. L. R. (Ed.). (1996). *How to become a better reading teacher: Strategies for assessment and intervention*. Englewood, NJ: Merrill.

Rasinski, T. V. (1994). Developing syntactic sensitivity in reading through phrase-cued texts. *Intervention in School and Clinic, 29*.

Read, C. (1986). *Children's creative spelling*. London: Routledge and Kegan Paul.

Resnick, L., & Beck, I. (1976). Designing instruction in reading: Initial reading. In A. J. Harris & E. R. Sipay (Eds.), *Readings on reading instruction*. New York: Longman.

Reutzel, D. R. (2015). Early literacy research: Findings primary-grade teachers will want to know. *The Reading Teacher, 69*.

Reutzel, D., & Cooper, R. B. (1992). *Teaching children to read: From basals to books*. New York: Merrill.

Rhodes, L. K., & Nathenson-Mejia, S. (1992). Anecdotal records: A powerful tool for ongoing literacy assessment. *The Reading Teacher, 45*(7).

Rinsland, H. D. (1945). *A basic vocabulary of elementary school children*. New York: Macmillan.

Rosenshine, B., & Stevens, R. (1984). Classroom instruction in reading. In P. D. Pearson, R. Barr, M. L. Kamil, & P. Mosenthal (Eds.), *Handbook of reading research*. New York: Longman.

Rosner, J. (1993). *Helping children overcome learning difficulties*. New York: Walker.

Roswell, F., & Natchez, G. (1971). *Reading disability*. New York: Basic Books.

Routh, D. K., & Fox, B. (1984). 'MM . . . is a little bit of may': Phonemes, reading, and spelling. In K. D. Gadow & I. Bialer (Eds.), *Advances in learning and behavioral disabilities, 3*. Greenwich, CT: JAI Press.

Royer, J., & Sinatra, G. (1994). A cognitive theoretical approach to reading diagnostics. *Educational Psychology Review, 6*(2).

Sakiey, E., Fry, E., Goss, A., & Loigman, B. (1980). A syllable frequency count. *Visible Language, 14*(2).

Samuels, J. (1979). The method of repeated readings. *The Reading Teacher, 32*.

Samuels, S. J. (1988). Decoding and automaticity: Helping poor readers become automatic at word recognition. *The Reading Teacher, 41*(8).

Samuels, S. J., Shermer, N., & Reinking, D. (1992). Reading fluency: Techniques for making decoding automatic. In S. J. Samuels & A. E. Farstrup (Eds.), *What research has to say about reading instruction*. Newark, DE: International Reading Association.

Scholastic. (1997). *Scholastic Phonemic Awareness Kit.*

Scholastic. (1998). *Scholastic Spelling.*

Shalaway, L. (1989). *Learning to teach . . . Not just for beginners*. New York: Scholastic.

Shankweiler, D., & Liberman, I. (1989). *Phonology and reading disability: Solving the reading puzzle*. Ann Arbor, MI: University of Michigan Press.

Share, D. L, Jorm, A. F., Maclean, R., & Matthews, R. (1984). Sources of individual differences in reading acquisition. *Journal of Educational Psychology, 76*.

Sittig, L. H. (1982). Involving parents and children in reading for fun. *The Reading Teacher, 36*(2).

Snider, V. E. (1995). A primer on phonemic awareness: What it is, why it's important, and how to teach it. *School Psychology Review, 24*(3).

Snow, C. E., Burns, M. S., & Griffin, P. (Eds.). (1998). *Preventing reading difficulties in young children*. Washington, DC: National Academy Press.

Spafford, C. S., & Grosser, G. S. (1996). *Dyslexia: Research and resource guide*. Boston: Allyn and Bacon.

Spann, M. B. (1996). *Quick-and-easy learning centers: Phonics*. New York: Scholastic.

Spear-Swerling, L., & Sternberg, R. J. (1996). *Off track: When poor readers become "learning disabled."* Boulder, CO: Westview Press.

Stahl, S. (1992). Saying the 'P' word: Nine guidelines for exemplary phonics instruction. *The Reading Teacher, 45*(8).

Stahl, S. (1997). Teaching children with reading problems to recognize words. In L. Putnam (Ed.), *Readings on language & literacy: Essays in honor of Jeanne S. Chall*. Cambridge, MA: Brookline Books.

Stahl, S., & Miller, P. D. (1989). Whole language and language experience approaches for beginning reading: A quantitative research synthesis. *Review of Educational Research, 59*.

Stahl, S., Osborn, J., & Pearson, P. D. (1992). The effects of beginning reading instruction: Six teachers in six classrooms. Unpublished paper. University of Illinois at Urbana-Champaign.

Stanovich, K. E. (1980). Toward an interactive compensatory model of individual differences in the development of reading fluency. *Reading Research Quarterly, 21*.

Stanovich, K. E. (1984). Toward an interactive-compensatory model of reading: A confluence of developmental, experimental, and educational psychology. *Remedial and Special Education, 5*.

Stanovich, K. E. (1986). Matthew effects in reading: Some consequences of individual differences in the acquisition of literacy. *Reading Research Quarterly, 21*.

Stanovich, K. E. (1989). Has the learning disabilities field lost its intelligence? *Journal of Learning Disabilities, 22*.

Stanovich, K. E. (1992). Speculations on the causes and consequences of individual differences in early reading acquisition. In P. B. Gough, L. C. Ehri, & R. Treiman (Eds.), *Reading acquisition*. Hillsdale, NJ: Erlbaum.

Stanovich, K. E. (1993–94). Romance and reality. *The Reading Teacher, 47*(4).

Stanovich, K. E., & West, R. F. (1989). Exposure to print and orthographic processing. *Reading Research Quarterly, 24*.

Stein, M., Johnson, B., & Gutlohn, L. (1999). Analyzing beginning reading programs: The relationship between decoding instruction and text. *Remedial and Special Education, 20*(5).

Sulzby, E. (1985). Children's emergent reading of favorite storybooks: A developmental study. *Reading Research Quarterly, 20*(4).

Tangel, D. M., & Blachman, B. A. (1992). Effect of phoneme awareness instruction on kindergarten children's invented spelling. *Journal of Reading Behavior, 24*.

Tansley, A. E. (1967). *Reading and remedial reading*. New York: Humanities Press.

Taylor, B. M., & Nosbush, L. (1983). Oral reading for meaning: A technique for improving word identification skills. *The Reading Teacher, 37*.

Topping, K. J. (1995). Cued spelling: A powerful technique for parent and peer tutoring. *The Reading Teacher, 48*(5).

Torgesen, J. K., & Bryant, B. (1994). *Phonological awareness training for reading*. Austin, TX: Pro-Ed.

Torgesen, J. K., & Bryant, B. (2004). *Test of phonological awareness—second edition: Plus*. Austin, TX: Pro-Ed.

Torgesen, J. K., & Hecht, S. (1996). Preventing and remediating reading disabilities: Instructional variables that make a difference for special students. In M. Graves, P. van den Broek, & B. Taylor (Eds.), *The first R: Every child's right to read*. New York: Teachers College Press.

Torgesen, J. K., Morgan, S., & Davis, C. (1992). The effects of two types of phonological awareness training on word learning in kindergarten children. *Journal of Educational Psychology, 84*.

Torgeson, J. K., & Mathes, P. G. (2000). *A basic guide to understanding, assessing, and teaching phonological awareness*. Austin, TX: Pro-Ed.

Trachtenburg, P. (1990). Using children's literature to enhance phonics instruction. *The Reading Teacher, 43*(9).

Treiman, R. (1992). The role of intrasyllabic units in learning to read and spell. In P. B. Gough, L. C. Ehri, & R. Treiman (Eds.), *Reading acquisition*. Hillsdale, NJ: Erlbaum.

Treiman, R., & Baron, J. (1981). Segmental analysis ability: Development and relation to reading ability. In G. E. MacKinnon & T. G. Waller (Eds.), *Reading research: Advances in theory and practice, 3*. New York: Academic Press.

U.S. Public Law 10−110. 107th Congress, 1st session, 8 January 2002. No Child Left Behind Act of 2001.

Vacca, J., Vacca, R., & Gove, M. (1995). *Reading and learning to read*. New York: HarperCollins.

Vellutino, F. R., & Scanlon, D. M. (1987). Phonological coding, phonological awareness, and reading ability: Evidence from a longitudinal and experimental study. *Merrill-Palmer Quarterly, 33*.

Vukelich, C. (1984). Parents' role in the reading process: A review of practical suggestions and ways to communicate with parents. *The Reading Teacher, 37*(6).

Wagstaff, J. (1994). *Phonics that work!* New York: Scholastic.

Whaley, W. J., & Kirby, M. W. (1980). Word synthesis and beginning reading achievement. *Journal of Educational Research, 73*.

White, T. G., Sowell, J., & Yanagihara, A. (1989). Teaching elementary students to use word-part clues. *The Reading Teacher, 42*.

Wilde, S. (1997). *What's a schwa sound anyway? A holistic guide to phonetics, phonics, and spelling*. Portsmouth, NH: Heinemann.

Wong, M. (2015, May 29). Brain wave study shows how different teaching methods affect reading development. Retrieved November 14, 2017, from http://medicalxpress.com/news/2015-05-brain-methods-affect.html.

Wood, K., & Algozzine, B. (Eds.). (1994). *Teaching reading to high-risk learners*. Boston: Allyn and Bacon.

Wylie, R., & Durrell, D. (1970). Teaching vowels through phonograms. *Elementary Education, 47*.

Yeh, S. S., & Connell, D. B. (2008). Effects of rhyming, vocabulary and phonemic awareness instruction on phoneme awareness. *Journal of Research in Reading, 31*.

Yoncheva, Y. N., Wise, J., & McCandliss, B. (2015). Hemispheric specialization for visual words is shaped by attention to sublexical units during initial learning. *Brain and Language*.

Yopp, H. K. (1992). Developing phonemic awareness in young children. *The Reading Teacher, 45*(9).

Yopp, H. K. (1995). A test for assessing phonemic awareness in young children. *The Reading Teacher, 49*(1).

Yopp, H. K. (1995). Read-aloud books for developing phonemic awareness: An annotated bibliography. *The Reading Teacher, 48*(6).

Zutell, J. (1996). The directed spelling thinking activity (DSTA): Providing an effective balance in word study instruction. *The Reading Teacher, 50*(2).

# How to Access Downloadable Resources

Go to **www.scholastic.com/phonicsfromatoz** and enter your email address and this code: **SC811349**.

| PAGE | RESOURCE |
|------|----------|
| 31 | RESOURCE 2.1: **Letter-Name Assessment** |
| 31 | RESOURCE 2.2: **Letter-Sound Assessment** |
| 55 | RESOURCE 2.3: **Phonemic Awareness Assessment** |
| 171 | RESOURCE 4.1: **Word Ladder Template** |
| 173 | RESOURCE 4.2: **Dolch Basic Sight Vocabulary 220** |
| 173 | RESOURCE 4.3: **150 Most Frequent Words** *(American Heritage Word Frequency Book)* |
| 258 | RESOURCE 4.4: **The Names Test** |
| 258 | RESOURCE 4.5: **Nonsense Word Test** |
| 258 | RESOURCE 4.6: **The San Diego Quick Assessment** |
| 259 | RESOURCE 4.7: **Comprehensive Phonics Survey** |
| 267 | RESOURCE 5.1: **Repeated Reading Chart and Partner Fluency Feedback Chart** |
| 273 | RESOURCE 5.2: **Consonant + *le* Syllable Speed Drill** |